Elizabeth

RELATED TITLES FROM PALGRAVE MACMILLAN

Pauline Croft, *King James*
Susan Doran and Thomas S. Freeman (eds), *The Myth of Elizabeth*
Carole Levin, *The Reign of Elizabeth I*
A. L. Rowse, *The England of Elizabeth*
A. L. Rowse, *The Expansion of Elizabethan England*
Julia Walker, *Elizabeth I as Icon*

Elizabeth's Wars

War, Government and Society in Tudor England, 1544–1604

Paul E. J. Hammer

First published 2003 by
PALGRAVE MACMILLAN
Houndmills, Basingstoke, Hampshire RG21 6XS and
175 Fifth Avenue, New York, N. Y. 10010
Companies and representatives throughout the world

PALGRAVE MACMILLAN is the global academic imprint of the Palgrave
Macmillan division of St. Martin's Press, LLC and of Palgrave Macmillan Ltd.
Macmillan® is a registered trademark in the United States, United Kingdom
and other countries. Palgrave is a registered trademark in the European
Union and other countries.

ISBN 0–333–91943–2 paperback
ISBN 0–333–91942–4 hardback

This book is printed on paper suitable for recycling and
made from fully managed and sustained forest sources.

A catalogue record for this book is available from the British Library.

Library of Congress Cataloging-in-Publication Data

Hammer, Paul E. J.
   Elizabeth's wars : war, government, and society in Tudor England,
1544–1604 / Paul E. J. Hammer.
      p. cm.
   Includes bibliographical references and index.
   ISBN 0–333–91942–4—ISBN 0–333–91943–2 (pbk.)
   1. Great Britain—History—Elizabeth, 1588–1603. 2. Great
Britain—Politics and goverment—1558–1603. 3. Great Britain—History,
Military—1485–1603. 4. England—Social conditions—16th century.
I. Title

DA355.H26 2003
942.05'5'092–dc21   2003049804

10   9   8   7   6   5   4   3   2   1
12 11 10 09 08 07 06 05 04 03

Typeset by Cambrian Typesetters, Frimley, Surrey
Printed and bound in Great Britain by
Creative Print & Design (Wales), Ebbw Vale

Contents

Maps

Tables

Technical Terms and Conventions

Glossary

arquebus: the main form of firearm used by infantry during the first half of the sixteenth century; lighter and shorter-ranged than the musket; also called a hackbut in England.

arquebusier (or **harquebusier** or **hackbutter**): infantryman armed with an arquebus.

bill: a weapon adapted from pruning hooks; it was about six feet long and designed for slashing; originally common across Europe, its use became increasingly restricted to England.

caliver: an improved version of the arquebus which became the standard infantry firearm in the mid-sixteenth century; it was gradually supplemented, and ultimately replaced, by the musket.

carrack: a very large Portuguese merchant vessel, specifically designed to make the long voyages to and from the East Indies.

company: the basic infantry unit used in all armies; its strength could vary from 100–250 men; a company was commanded by a captain.

cornet: the basic cavalry unit, equivalent to a company; commanded by a captain, its strength could vary from 50–100 men.

corslet: armour worn by a pikeman; technically a 'corslet' was the armour covering the torso, but the term was sometimes used as a synonym for a fully equipped pikeman.

enclosure: the division of previously open land into private allotments with hedges or fences.

flyboat: small Dutch cargo vessel, often used for carrying troops or supplies.

frigate: fast Spanish sailing ship used for carrying messages and (from 1588) silver across the Atlantic.

galleon: a large sail-powered warship which emerged in the mid-sixteenth century and featured a galley-style bow carrying heavy guns; a galleon's keel length was at least three times as great as its width.

galley: warship powered by oars which was rowed by slaves; it carried heavy guns in the bow and a large number of soldiers for boarding or amphibious operations.

hackbut: see arquebus.

Huguenot: French Protestant.

javelin: a light spear for throwing; often called a dart.

landsknecht: (technically the plural is *landsknechte*) German mercenary infantry; originally armed mainly with pikes, they increasingly used firearms in combination with pikes.

light horse: in English usage, a cavalryman wearing armour only on the torso and armed with sword, pistol and a staff; while heavy cavalry (lancers) were intended mainly for direct attacks against the enemy, light horse provided support and performed key roles in scouting and pursuit.

longbow: a single-piece wooden bow, up to six feet in length; it required enormous strength (and practice and good health) to draw properly.

musket: a heavy firearm which usually required a rest or stand for firing, developed from the arquebus; its greater penetration and weight (which encouraged its use by larger soldiers, who also received higher pay) created the connotation of muskets being the weapon of the élite; muskets ultimately displaced calivers as the basic infantry firearm.

pike: a long thrusting spear, ten to 16 feet long.

reiter: a German mercenary horseman, usually armed with pistols and sword.

shot: generic term for soldiers equipped with firearms (as in the phrase 'pike and shot').

Technical Terms and Conventions

subsidy: the main form of direct taxation in England, approved by parliament as one-off grants which might be collected in several instalments over two or three years; traditionally, a subsidy was only sought by the crown during time of war.

tercio: the standard large unit of the Spanish army, containing 10–20 companies and comprising 1,000–5,000 men.

trace italienne: the generic term used for fortifications which were designed to counter the effects of cannon fire; characterised by low and extremely thick ramparts and star-like geometry, which minimised the damage caused by besiegers' cannonballs and maximised the field of fire for the defenders' own guns.

Dates

All dates in this book are Old Style, which reflects the usage of Tudor men and women, except that the New Year is treated as 1 January rather than 25 March. New Style dating, which runs ten days ahead of Old Style, was adopted by Continental countries within a year or so of its promulgation by Pope Gregory XIII in February 1581, but was not adopted by England until 1752. As a result, the naval skirmishes of the Armada campaign in 1588 occurred in the last days of July according to English sources, but at the start of August according to Spanish sources.

Weights and Measures

This book uses the usual English measures of the period. Distances are given in miles (1 mile = 1.6km) and weights in pounds (1lb = 0.37kg). A quarter of grain was 8 bushels or 480lb, while a barrel of butter was 4 firkins or 224lb. Gunpowder was measured by the barrel (100lb) or the last, which was equivalent to 24 barrels (2400lb). Figures cited for ship size reflect contemporary estimates of carrying capacity, not displacement. These figures were calculated by shipbuilders according to the dimensions and shape of each vessel.

England and Wales

Except where specific reference is made to Wales, the term 'England' is used in this book to refer to both England and Wales because the government of the principality of Wales was closely integrated with the kingdom of England by the mid-sixteenth century.

Acknowledgements

I would like to record my gratitude to some of the people and institutions which helped me to write this book. I am indebted to the Australian Research Council for financial support; to Roger Hainsworth and Trevor Wilson for reading and commenting upon draft chapters; to Sabina Flanagan and Wilfrid Prest for allowing me to occupy their house while they were on sabbatical, which gave me unaccustomed space for writing and piling up books and notes; to Ian McLean for helping me to grapple with inflation and deflators; to the staff of the Barr Smith Library at the University of Adelaide, whose extraordinary holdings in early modern British history I commend to the attention of other scholars resident in, or visiting, Australasia; and, more generally, to my (now former) colleagues in the Department of History at the University of Adelaide, for being good friends throughout my time there. It seemed especially encouraging that three of us in our small Department were writing books for Palgrave at the same time – and that I was not the last to finish. Outside Adelaide, I owe particular thanks to Mark Fissel and Peter Cunich, and to Patrick O'Brien for allowing me access to his important calculations on Tudor royal income and the impact of inflation. I also wish to record my special gratitude to David Trim, who allowed me privileged access to his unpublished data on the recruitment of soldiers in Elizabeth's reign and responded freely to my many nit-picking queries about the content and implications of his figures. I salute both his expertise in early modern military affairs and his generous spirit. Citations from the Cecil MSS at Hatfield House, Hertfordshire, are quoted by kind permission of the Marquess of Salisbury. Lastly, Palgrave Macmillan proved remarkably understanding when this book was delayed by several months and arrived somewhat longer than the contracted word-limit. I am most grateful for this flexibility and I hope it has made a better final product.

Introduction

'If the late queen had believed her men of war as she did her scribes, we had in her time beaten that great empire in pieces, and made their kings kings of figs and oranges, as in old times. But her majesty did all by halves, and by petty invasions taught the Spaniard how to defend himself'.[1] So wrote Sir Walter Ralegh, a decade after the death of Elizabeth I, about the great war fought between Elizabethan England and the empire ruled by the kings of Spain, which lasted from 1585 until 1604. Ralegh was never more than a second-rank soldier during Elizabeth's reign and (ironically) only attained true fame after James I imprisoned him for treason in 1603, but his comments accurately convey the frustration which Elizabeth's military men felt about their queen's aversion to heavy expenditure and her habitual unwillingness to commit herself to any course of action without lengthy delay. Ralegh also captures the widespread disappointment – both during the war and afterwards – that Elizabethan England was never able to land a decisive blow which could defeat Spain and shatter its 'great empire in pieces'.

Such sentiments might be dismissed as empty boasting, given that England never came close to shattering Spanish power. Indeed, for most of the war, Spain's chief military effort was directed at other enemies than England. Nevertheless, the very fact that English men and women might express disappointment about failing to defeat Spain reflected a remarkable turn-around from the early years of Elizabeth's reign. When England first came into conflict with Spain in the 1560s, the contest seemed like an utter mismatch – so much so that the queen and her government did everything possible to avoid open war. England was critically weak in the 1560s and early 1570s, both economically and militarily, while Philip II of Spain possessed the most effective army in western Europe and could call upon the resources of an empire which spanned Spain, Italy, Flanders and the New World. This book tells the story of how Elizabethan England not only avoided defeat in its war with Spain, but even performed well enough for individuals like Ralegh to dream of reducing Spain's imperial power to 'figs and oranges'.

In the sixteenth century, war posed particular difficulties for female rulers such as Elizabeth. Ralegh's tone, and especially his comment that 'her majesty did all by halves', hints at the widespread contemporary belief that Elizabeth was unable to lead England to victory because she was a woman. Although countless panegyrics publicly praised Elizabeth as a war-leader, both during her lifetime and after her death, the private opinions of her generals and admirals were rather different. They believed that the queen's gender made her indecisive, unable to persist with a course of action, excessively parsimonious and prone to pacifist sentiments. While Elizabeth was queen, her generals and councillors normally kept such thoughts to themselves, but Robert Devereux, second earl of Essex, was less discreet. Although he built his early career upon her royal favour, Essex repeatedly complained that Elizabeth's female qualities (as he saw them) interfered with her performance as a war-leader. In 1595, he became so frustrated with Elizabeth that he and the Spanish refugee Antonio Perez privately nicknamed her Juno – the classical goddess who sought to thwart the hero Aeneas, and the future greatness of Rome, out of sheer female irrationality. In 1598, Essex bluntly told a French envoy that England's government was hampered by 'two things . . . delay and inconstancy, which proceeded chiefly from the sex of the queen'. More dangerously, the earl increasingly believed that Elizabeth's gender required him to try to force her into actions which he considered necessary for the safety of the realm. This set the scene for a painful 'war' within the Elizabethan regime itself during the late 1590s which might have had disastrous consequences if Essex and his followers had been able to act upon their convictions with greater resolution.[2]

Although this near-disaster during the closing years of her reign represented its most extreme form, Elizabeth battled male prejudice and attempts to dictate her actions throughout her life. Her response was to develop a style of queenship which suppressed any signs of competition for attention by female courtiers and forced her male courtiers to compete for her royal favour as if they meant to woo her. By playing them off against each other in the manner of 'courtly love', Elizabeth ensured that her leading male subjects could not gang up and try to force her to approve policies which they had already agreed among themselves. This form of (literal) man-management required careful handling to avoid creating dangerous divisions at court, but Elizabeth proved as shrewd at sustaining the system as in creating it. A complementary strategy was simply to delay making difficult decisions. Elizabeth postponed hard decisions because she wanted to keep her options open for as long as possible and because she instinctively disliked committing herself to policies which might limit her ability to change her mind in the future. For Elizabeth, preserving the unfettered ability to choose was critical because it encapsulated much of what she believed it meant to be queen. As one of Elizabeth's courtiers famously advised another, the greatest mistake that a suitor for the queen's favour could make was to let her 'imagine that yow goe about to imprison her fancie and to wrappe her grace within your disposition'.[3]

This idiosyncratic style of queenship represented a brilliant piece of political improvisation which transmuted the handicap of her gender into an advantage. However, it did not work so well during wartime. This problem is one of the sub-themes of this book. Once England entered open war against Spain in 1585, military necessity and the need for urgent decisions consistently 'imprisoned' Elizabeth's 'fancie'. The remorseless demand for more and more money to sustain ships and armies also caused her deep distress. It is a truism, recognised since the dawn of recorded history, that money is 'the very sinewes and hartstrings of warre' – which is why this book pays so much attention to the crown's getting and spending of money.[4] Nevertheless, repeated and heavy wartime taxation induced a grumbling among her subjects which made Elizabeth's finely tuned political antennae almost vibrate with pain.

War also foregrounded the question of gender. As a woman, Elizabeth could not lead her army into battle like her father Henry VIII, and was forced to depend upon men to fight and manage the war for her. War was the quintessential male activity and brought out all the prejudices of men who believed that a woman – even one as intelligent as Elizabeth – could not really understand it. An undercurrent to the wars fought during Elizabeth's reign, therefore, was the personal struggle which she had to fight to maintain her royal authority in the face of male demands for policies which conferred greater power upon men. Like the war against Spain itself, this was a multi-faceted struggle in which success primarily meant staving off defeat. Ultimately, Elizabeth proved able to defend her royal authority, but the pressures of wartime government – as exemplified by Essex – reduced her system of man-management to a hollow shell.

If one incident captures the public image of Elizabeth as a war-leader, it is her celebrated visit to the army which gathered at Tilbury to oppose Spain's *Gran Armada* in August 1588. Unable to bear arms herself, she instead wielded words and gestures in defence of her realm. Addressing the troops, perhaps even wearing a stylised form of armour, she famously proclaimed 'I know I have the bodie but of a weake and feeble woman, but I have the heart and stomach of a king.' This episode has long exerted a peculiarly strong hold on the popular imagination because it encapsulates the tensions implicit in Elizabeth's position as a female war-leader and places her at the very centre of one of the most famous events in British history, when England's supposedly out-matched navy was able to defeat Spain's supposedly 'invincible' Armada. This piece of theatre succeeded so well that Elizabeth's defiance and the Armada victory of 1588 subsequently became potent symbols of English heroism and will to resist whenever the realm was threatened with invasion from abroad. Indeed, the myth-making built around Elizabeth's performance at Tilbury was perhaps not supplanted as the key image of defiant English leadership until Churchill's cigar, V-sign and 'we-will-fight-them-on-the-beaches' rhetoric offered an alternative better suited to a democratic age and the new technologies of cinema and radio.[5]

The power of the mythology surrounding the battle against the Spanish Armada of 1588 has been so great that it has not only fostered erroneous ideas about the Armada campaign itself, but has almost completely overshadowed military events during the remainder of Elizabeth's reign. England was openly at war with Spain for almost half the period Elizabeth was queen – 18 years out of 44 – and her government also waged major campaigns in Scotland, France and Ireland before 1585, as well as conniving at 'deniable' forms of war by English 'volunteer' soldiers in France and the Low Countries and by English privateers at sea. War, or the avoidance of war, should therefore be central to our understanding of the reign. However, Elizabeth's wars – both overt and covert – cannot be properly understood unless they are themselves seen in the context of events which occurred before her accession to the throne. England's military and economic weakness when Elizabeth became queen in 1558, which shaped her subsequent diplomacy and military strategy, was a direct result of events during the reigns of her father Henry VIII (1509–47), and her half-siblings Edward VI (1547–53) and Mary I (1553–8).

In many ways, the real starting-point for the problems which made war-fighting so difficult in Elizabeth's reign – and hence the point of departure for this book – is Henry VIII's invasion of France in 1544. Not only was this England's first war against a major European power for almost 20 years, but it marked the first great test of the new 'imperial' style of royal power which Henry had fashioned during the 1530s. 'Imperial' kingship meant that Henry recognised no intervening authority in his kingdom between himself and God – not even the pope – and ultimately resulted in his seizure of control over the English Church, the dissolution of the monasteries, and a vast increase in the wealth and power of the crown. Ironically, this expansion of royal authority was triggered by Elizabeth's own impending birth – and Henry's consequent need to override papal opposition to his marriage to her mother, Anne Boleyn – in 1533. Elizabeth was still only a girl when Henry's invasion of France in 1544 caused the financial underpinning of this new kingship to start unravelling with alarming speed. Subsequent wars under Edward VI and Mary only made things worse and increased the political damage. By the time Elizabeth became queen, she inherited little more than the husk of Henry's 'imperial' crown and a dangerously withered military capacity.

The bitter experiences of the 1540s and 1550s help to explain why Elizabeth saw foreign wars so differently from her father. While Henry regarded the pursuit of military 'glory' as the ultimate sport of kings, Elizabeth harboured far less romantic notions. In addition to being excluded from martial culture by her gender, she saw (and understood) the political consequences of heavy military expenditure in the 1540s and 1550s, and the corrosive effects which endless revenue-raising had upon royal authority. Where Henry sought 'glory' to augment his power, she therefore focused upon the 'cost' of war and feared its potential to undermine her power. For Elizabeth, foreign war was at best a necessary evil – and one that should be avoided if possible.

A comparison of the resources which Elizabeth and her father committed to war shows that she was right to be anxious about the burden which war placed upon her crown. Sir Walter Ralegh spoke more truly than he knew when he complained that 'her majesty did all by halves'. Ralegh presumably knew the largest armies which Elizabeth's government sent overseas – those commanded by the earl of Essex and Lord Mountjoy in Ireland between 1599 and 1603 – were just under half the size of the army which Henry VIII took to France in 1544. More importantly, though, the financial resources available to Elizabeth were considerably smaller than those deployed by her father. Thanks to the disposal of assets and the effects of inflation, the peaks in crown revenues under Elizabeth – at the beginning of her reign and in the final years – were actually less than half the value, in real terms, of Henry's revenues in the mid-1540s.[6] Elizabeth and her government were therefore constrained to wage what was, by Henrician standards, a cut-price version of war. This caused considerable friction between the queen and her military men, who regularly felt themselves short-changed in the struggle for money and resources. However, the budgetary strait-jacket also makes it all the more remarkable that Elizabethan England could sustain war for 18 years, often on multiple fronts and spanning a vastly greater geographic range than the conflicts of the 1540s and 1550s. This represents a major military and political achievement and helps to explain Ralegh's exuberant claims about 'figs and oranges' – if England could sustain such a war for so long and emerge undefeated, almost anything seemed possible if pursued with sufficient determination. In reality, this sort of optimism ran far ahead of England's resources. Although Elizabeth's reign saw significant achievements and developments pregnant with future possibilities, the continuing financial weakness of the crown meant that it ultimately represented a false dawn for English arms.

One way and another, a great deal has already been published about Tudor England's involvement in war and the writing of yet another book on the subject requires some justification. In reality, the quantity of work published on Tudor wars is somewhat illusory. Most work published on sixteenth-century England treats war as a kind of background roar which only occasionally comes into focus. Even when it does so, the discussion of war is usually limited to its political or economic impact on the realm. There is a rich specialist literature on the military history of Tudor England, but it is very heavily weighted towards naval affairs. Thanks to the enduring fame of events in 1588 and the importance which the Royal Navy of the late nineteenth century placed upon 'naval history' as a means of educating its officers, the study of Tudor maritime developments has been particularly well-served by scholarship. Spurred by first-rate historians such as J. K. Laughton, Julian Corbett and Michael Oppenheim, and aided by the superb editions of important sources published by the Navy Records Society and Hakluyt Society, the historiography of the Elizabethan navy, in particular, is both voluminous and of exceptional quality. Although there is occasional criticism of specific events, the general tone of this literature is overwhelmingly positive, emphasising the ways in which Elizabethan seamen pioneered technology and strategies which would later contribute to the development of British naval supremacy.[7]

By contrast, the literature on Tudor armies is small and consistently negative. According to Sir Charles Oman in his influential survey of sixteenth-century warfare, 'the reign of Elizabeth makes a very depressing chapter in the history of the English Art of War'. Subsequent scholars such as Charles Cruickshank, whose study of Elizabethan armies remains the standard work on the subject, have largely endorsed this view. English soldiers are consistently described as incompetent and corrupt. This characterisation is often emphasised by allusion to comic Shakespearean characters such as Falstaff and Pistol and the criticisms of contemporary military reformers – even though Shakespeare was writing for dramatic effect and Elizabethan reformers make unreliable witnesses because they often exaggerated their criticism to justify the adoption of their own theories. The growing body of scholarship on other nations' armies in sixteenth century Europe also suggests that many of the failings of Elizabethan soldiers were shared by their foreign contemporaries. Nevertheless, the abysmal historical reputation of Elizabeth's armies remains strongly entrenched. Even in the mid-1980s, one renowned scholar of early modern Europe repeatedly asserted that 'studying the Elizabethan army is like studying the Swiss navy'.[8]

Perhaps the most striking feature of Tudor military history is that very few works discuss events on land *and* sea. Indeed, with the partial exceptions of R. B. Wernham's multi-volume history of England's foreign relations in the sixteenth century (which includes a lot of military information, although little detail about the fighting) and Bruce Lenman's recent survey of England's 'colonial wars', there is no combined narrative of Tudor land and sea operations. This has had some unfortunate results, which this book seeks to address. As Wernham repeatedly observed, the preponderance of works glorifying the Elizabethan navy has created a false impression of the relative military importance of land and sea operations. Despite its success in 1588 and its precocious efforts to wage oceanic naval warfare, the military performance of Elizabeth's navy in the 1580s and 1590s was actually rather stuttering. The war against Spain after 1585 was substantially a land war fought on the Continent and the real 'heavy lifting' in England's war effort was done by the queen's armies. Elizabeth's wars in Ireland were also essentially land operations. However, as this book emphatically asserts, land and sea operations cannot be properly understood in isolation from each other. Tudor governments repeatedly had to make choices between spending on the navy and the army and the development of each service was strongly influenced by the nature of its counterpart. English forces were also most successful when ships and soldiers operated together and created military synergies. Elizabeth's wars, like those of the 1540s and 1550s, were fought on both land and sea, and our understanding of these events needs to reflect this basic fact.[9]

1 The Glory of War:
operations and developments,
1544–1558

In July 1544, Henry VIII landed in Calais to launch the major offensive of his third and last war against France. The troops accompanying Henry, together with the contingents which had already been shipped across the Channel, totalled over 32,000 men. They were joined by some 6000 German and Dutch auxiliaries provided (and paid for) by the king's ally, the Holy Roman Emperor Charles V, and another 4000 mercenaries whom Henry had hired to boost his army's fighting power still further. Accompanied by a large train of artillery, 20,000 horses, hundreds of carts and a steady stream of supplies shipped from England and Flanders, Henry's force was the largest and most powerful army fielded by the English crown until the time of William III, 150 years later.[1]

The precise reasons for the war in which this massive force would fight remain somewhat obscure. In sharp contrast to Elizabeth's later insistence on waging war only for clearly argued political reasons, Henry's approach to war was decidedly personal, even wilful. Although it is difficult to plumb the king's mind, the ultimate origin of the conflict probably sprang from the approach of his fiftieth birthday in June 1541 and his recognition that he would soon be unable to lead an army into battle, as he believed kings should do. In the early months of 1541, Henry became depressed and shut himself away from his wife and courtiers at Hampton Court. By the time he recovered his equilibrium at Easter, it seems that he had made some kind of decision not to let himself simply become a bitter recluse. Despite – or perhaps because of – his advancing age, the constant pain of suppurating ulcers on his legs and the discomfort of his vast corpulence, he would return to the battlefield one more time. If recent arguments about his dealings with James V of Scotland during the remainder of 1541 are correct, Henry emerged from his brief period of introspection spoiling for a fight. Despite his professed aim of seeking an accommodation with his northern neighbour, he actually sought to goad James into war, hoping to bludgeon Scotland into quiescence and perhaps also to use the 'auld alliance' between Scotland and France to his own advantage by providing himself with an excuse to wage war on France. Much to his chagrin, however, James V refused to take the bait.[2]

War and the role of warrior-king were profoundly important to Henry's public and private sense of self and he had shown a hunger for martial glory from the opening days of his reign in 1509. Insofar as he can be said to have had any role-model, Henry aspired to be a second and greater Henry V, whose victory at Agincourt in 1415 loomed ever larger in English minds as the glory days of the Hundred Years War receded into increasingly distant memory. Even during the long years of peacetime, Henry surrounded himself with the chivalric trappings of war, stockpiled munitions and visited warships, preparing for the next round of conflict. Although modern Western opinion tends to regard war as morally repugnant and a course of extreme last resort, this was not a view shared by the aristocrats of medieval and early modern Europe. They believed it was entirely natural that rulers should wage war on one another. In an age which placed an enormous premium upon martial exploits, wars were in fact a necessary part of political and social life, while prolonged peace (except in the minds of idealistic clerics) represented stagnation, moral decline and the loss of opportunity to display skill and courage – and to win rewards. In the minds of Henry and his land-owning subjects, the aim was not to avoid wars, but to wage them successfully, according to internationally accepted standards of behaviour, and to ensure that those who fought well were rewarded appropriately. If the king were victorious, even the common soldiers, who might die in their thousands, were expected to be grateful for the chance to share in their sovereign's triumph. In this light, Henry's desire for one last hurrah in pursuit of the military glory which would make his name outshine that of Henry V seems entirely understandable. Judging by the alacrity with which they committed themselves to this war – the realm's first Continental war in over 20 years – the king's leading subjects shared his hunger for success.[3]

Although the concept of an impersonal 'state' or 'nation' was beginning to develop in the sixteenth century, this was still overwhelmingly a period in which decisions of the most profound national and international importance were made according to the gut instincts and calculations of individual hereditary rulers. Relations between states were based upon the personal relations – or rivalries – between their respective sovereigns and were conditioned by previous dealings between their respective royal families. Politics and diplomacy were deeply personal. One might wonder, for example, how far Henry VIII's consistent underestimation of the Scots reflected his sense of being the head of a family in which James V (the son of Henry's older and less-favoured sister Margaret) was a subordinate member – although a sovereign in his own right, the Scottish king was also Henry's nephew. However, when important decisions were taken, such emotional considerations were usually balanced, or at least rationalised, by political calculation and advice received from the king's councillors. In the case of the march towards war in the early 1540s, Henry's desires were undoubtedly given added impetus – and made easier for his advisers to accept and act upon – by considerations of diplomatic advantage.

During much of the previous decade, Henry's break from Rome placed England in a distinctly uncomfortable position with western Europe's two superpowers, the France of Francis I and the great network of states ruled by the emperor Charles V. From late 1538 until early 1540, it even seemed that these two inveterate enemies might band together against England, prompting Henry to begin a massive programme of coastal fortification and to step up his diplomatic contacts with German Protestants. It was during this nervous period when invasion seemed possible that Henry's marriage to Anne of Cleves was negotiated – only to be hastily repudiated in June 1540, when the danger had passed and the bride proved insufficiently alluring to the king. By the end of 1540, it was obvious that Charles and Francis were not only not planning to attack England, but were

moving towards another war against one another. This changed
the game completely because an alliance with England would be
useful to both sides. Instead of being something of a pariah in the
eyes of Charles and Francis, England was now actively courted by
them. Although his natural instinct was to make war on France,
Henry was able to play Charles and Francis off against each other,
holding out for the most attractive offer for his support. This
pleased Henry immensely. One of the great ironies of his creation
of a more exalted 'imperial' kingship during the 1530s was that the
circumstances in which it was forged had also cut him off from
normal dealings with the only two sovereigns whom he considered his equals – Charles V and Francis I – and forced him into
close contact with German princelings and Protestant theologians
whom he considered beneath him. Now he was again able to bargain with Charles and Francis as an equal. Although Henry's status
as supreme head of the nationalised Church of England caused
major diplomatic headaches almost to the very day when he committed himself to an alliance with the emperor, the changed international situation of 1541–42 allowed Henry to take the sort of
place in European affairs which he believed was his right as an
'imperial' sovereign. Going to war against France in alliance with
Charles V put a definitive end to any sense of English diplomatic
isolation or inferiority. Moreover, the military success which
Henry confidently expected to score from this alliance would be
the capstone of his newly augmented royal power, the crowning
achievement that would confirm his standing in the pantheon of
English monarchs.[4]

   In a sense, Henry VIII's new, more powerful and exalted kingship
– which had seen him overturn centuries of tradition and become
supreme head of the English Church, absorb the lands and wealth of
the monasteries, benefit from the subordination of local liberties to
royal power, and even proclaim himself king of Ireland in 1541 –
needed to demonstrate its mettle in war. Despite the pious hopes of
those intellectuals who hoped it might be applied to philanthropy,
the dominant mindset of the age meant that such an accumulation
of wealth and power must inevitably be applied to the pursuit of
martial glory – only in war was to be found the ultimate measure of

a king. Henry's new wealth and resources certainly provided much greater means to pursue the military success which had eluded him earlier in his reign. Thanks to his headship of the Church and the dissolution of the monasteries, he now had the power to tax the clergy and controlled a vastly increased crown estate, which provided hefty rents and a much larger pool of tenants who could serve as royal soldiers. The heavy costs associated with the invasion scare of 1538–40 were substantially covered by new taxes and a 'loan' from his richer subjects. Although the king spent very lavishly and money was usually slow to come in, the royal finances were in excellent shape and the king's coffers were positively brimming with cash. In 1543, Henry even felt able to loan Charles V 40,000 ducats (approx. £14,666). Henry's realm was also better prepared militarily than ever before. In 1539, the threat of invasion had prompted a fresh bout of training for the militia, refurbishment of the system of warning beacons and the setting-out of a powerful fleet. By the end of 1540, 24 new fortifications had also been built and manned, with more under construction. This feverish building programme – the most elaborate and expensive system of coastal defences constructed in England since Roman times – meant that the areas of the realm most vulnerable to raids from the Continent were now permanently screened by gun emplacements. Henry also created the Gentlemen Pensioners, a socially élite force intended to act as his bodyguards on the battlefield, which soon grew to 50 members, backed up by a similar number of supernumeraries. Military training in London also benefited from the activities of the new Guild of St George, later known as the Honourable Artillery Company, which received a royal charter in late 1537 to encourage practice with bows and guns. All in all, Henry's regime seemed ideally placed to wage war. Even the increasingly obvious and unbridgeable divide in England between those who still preferred the old religious practices and those who leaned towards the new ideas associated with Protestantism worked in favour of war. If he did not think so before, the bitter court politics of 1543, when the conservatives sought to bring down Archbishop Cranmer, clearly encouraged Henry to appreciate the value of focusing his subjects' energies against a common external foe.[5]

War with Scotland, 1542–44

Henry's negotiators finally sealed a military alliance with Charles V on 11 February 1543. Both sovereigns agreed to invade France within two years, each employing at least 5000 cavalry and 20,000 footmen and campaigning for at least four months. Charles would also provide 2000 German infantry (*landsknechte*) for Henry and ease England's chronic shortage of heavy cavalry by providing 2000 horsemen. However, the treaty was kept secret and Henry's attentions remained heavily focused on his dealings with Scotland. This preoccupation with Scottish affairs would ultimately ensure that Henry's plan to invade France in the summer of 1543 fell by the wayside, much to the alarm of his imperial ally. Although an ultimatum was despatched to Francis I in late May which constituted a formal declaration of war (which came into effect in June), all that England contributed to the joint war effort against France during 1543 was an expeditionary force of 5000 men under Sir John Wallop, which joined Charles V's unsuccessful siege of Landrecies during the late summer and autumn.[6]

Henry was distracted from the war with France for much of 1543 because his efforts to bully Scotland proved all too successful. In late 1542, a Scottish army was routed at the Battle of Solway Moss and James V himself died only a few weeks later. James's unexpected death brought the crown of Scotland to his only child, Mary – better known as Mary Queen of Scots – who was less than a week old at the time of her father's death. The resultant power vacuum meant that the Scottish noblemen captured at Solway Moss now offered Henry a means to control Scotland. By January 1543, ten of the aristocratic prisoners had become his 'assured lords' and returned to Scotland to do his bidding. The accession of Mary also offered Henry an utterly unexpected and unique opportunity to solve England's problems with Scotland permanently by marrying the infant queen to his young son, Edward. This union would ensure that the kingdom of Scotland, while retaining its own identity and laws, would become subordinate to England and that future generations of Tudors would rule both realms as their own. This enormously appealing possibility (at least in English eyes) seemed close to realisation when Scottish commissioners signed the Treaties of Greenwich on 1 July, which ended the conflict between England and Scotland and pledged Mary's hand to Edward. However, Henry's plans fell apart during the remainder of 1543, as the Scottish government (with active encouragement and hefty pensions from Francis I) gradually moved back towards its traditional alignment with France and the 'assured lords' distanced themselves from the English cause. Henry became so infuriated that he again declared open war on Scotland. English policy was now literally to force Mary's marriage to Edward upon the unwilling Scots – a strategy which later became known as the 'Rough Wooing'. In December, the Scottish parliament voided the Treaties of Greenwich and renewed the 'auld alliance' with France. These actions meant that all benefit from the victory at Solway Moss had now been lost to England and that the national pride of the two kingdoms was now engaged in a struggle which made the English objective – royal marriage and a willing union of crowns – utterly impossible to achieve.[7]

Henry's response to the growing intractability of the Scottish situation was to launch a fresh blow against Scotland in the spring of 1544, even though he had committed himself to invading France in the summer. This required an operation which would, by sixteenth-century standards, be a model of military efficiency. Sustaining large armies on the Anglo-Scottish borders for any length of time was very difficult. With few supplies available in the region, everything an army needed had to be transported north by sea, which made the army critically dependent on favourable winds. Once ashore, supplies had to be transported on a limited number of carts over rough roads which the rain often turned into mud and which were vulnerable to raids by hostile borderers. If these logistical bottlenecks were not enough, the topography of the borders restricted large armies to advancing along narrow corridors which could be easily defended. To avoid such problems, Edward Seymour, earl of Hertford, mounted a meticulously planned expedition which combined land and sea power to overwhelm and overawe the Scots. Sailing from Newcastle on 1 May 1544 with 200 ships of all sizes, he arrived off Leith, the port adjacent to Edinburgh, three days later. This move outflanked Scotland's defences and outpaced its mobilisation. Disembarking in only four hours, Hertford's army of 16,000 men quickly routed a Scottish force which had been hastily gathered at Leith by Cardinal Beaton. 'Perceiving our devotion to see his holiness was such as we were ready to wet our feet for that purpose', the Scots fled towards Edinburgh, leaving their cannon behind them. Leith itself was quickly taken and later sacked, as was the town of Edinburgh and the surrounding region. However, Edinburgh Castle held out and Hertford's army was forced to head home, burning its way southwards towards the safety of Berwick. Although the Scots tried to ambush Hertford's force in a narrow defile south of Dunbar, the shock of the English campaign had unnerved the Scots so greatly that they fled at the first exchange of shots, despite the strength of their position. The English army marched into Berwick the next day, where it linked up again with the fleet. In 18 days and with fewer than 40 fatal casualties, Hertford's expedition had re-emphasised English military dominance over Scotland and cleared the way for Henry's invasion of France. Nevertheless, despite its technical virtuosity, this textbook combined arms operation also made a political solution to England's conflict with Scotland even more difficult, fanning the flames of Scottish resentment at English arrogance and their own apparent powerlessness.[8]

The Invasion of France, 1544

Although Hertford's expedition provided little more than temporary relief on England's northern borders, its success ensured that Henry could commit almost his full military capacity to invading France. Imperial and French forces had been locked in combat since July 1542 on the Franco-Spanish border, in northern Italy and along France's north-eastern border with Flanders and Germany. According to a new agreement made on 31 December 1543, Charles and Henry would break this military deadlock by launching coordinated offensives aimed at the heart of France, with imperial forces advancing westwards through the Champagne region and English troops marching south through Picardy from the English territory around Calais. To overwhelm French resistance, both invasions would involve at least 42,000 men. Although the final goal of the two armies was Paris,

Henry and Charles were allowed to tailor their plans 'as strategy, victuals and the enemy shall permit'. This provision was important because Henry had no serious intention of launching an attack deep into France. He had adopted this strategy, against his own better judgement, during his last war with France in 1523 and it had almost proved disastrous. Similarly, in his first war against France in 1513, he had been prevailed upon by his imperial ally to concentrate English efforts against the French towns of Thérouanne and Tournai, even though their capture would benefit the emperor rather than England. Although Henry had stubbornly retained Tournai for several years, it cost far more to defend than it ever produced in revenue and was finally sold back to France in 1519 at a substantial loss. This time around, Henry decided that he would wage war for his own benefit, rather than for that of his ally, and with minimum risk. As he had argued in 1523, it made more sense for England to expand its territory around Calais by seizing a nearby French port like Boulogne than to strike inland in the hope of forcing Francis into a decisive battle, with all the difficulties that entailed. In the weeks before he departed for France, Henry made it very clear to the imperial ambassador in England that he would fight the forthcoming campaign in the light of his bitter experience in 1523: 'it would be better to take two or three frontier places than to have burnt Paris'. Henry was therefore not only well prepared for war in 1544, but determined to apply the lessons learned in his previous campaigns.[9]

Henry's offensive against France began at the end of June, when the duke of Norfolk and Lord Russell marched two-thirds of the English army into Picardy to besiege Montreuil. However, this operation was merely a gesture towards the kind of offensive which Charles had wanted. Even supported by imperial auxiliaries, the army at Montreuil was too small simultaneously to fully blockade the town, contain the garrison and guard its own extended supply lines. Instead of surrounding Montreuil, the army blockaded only one side of the town, allowing it to be freely reinforced by the French, who taunted the allies over the utter ineffectiveness of this half-siege. Supply problems soon made life thoroughly unpleasant for the English soldiers and the futility of the whole operation only compounded their misery. Once it became clear that the real action and priority for supplies rested with the king's other army, the troops at Montreuil became increasingly demoralised and unwilling to risk their lives for a mere sideshow.[10]

The real value of the miserable, half-hearted siege of Montreuil was that it kept French troops well clear of Henry's main operation to capture Boulogne. This effort began on 19 July, when troops commanded by the duke of Suffolk surrounded the port and began to dig trenches and to pound its walls with a huge siege train which ultimately totalled some 250 guns. The arrival of the king – whose bulk and lack of athleticism meant that he could only mount a horse with the aid of a crane – added almost 4000 mercenaries to the army on the 26 July. Once the attackers had seized the weak outer defences of Boulogne, the sheer volume of cannon fire seemed overwhelming. Allegedly, over 100,000 rounds of heavy shot were poured into the town. The projectiles included huge round 'plums' weighing 25kg or more and 'apples' which consisted of newfangled incendiary shells. Henry's plan was not to take the town by undermining its walls or slowly starving it into submission, but to overwhelm the defenders with massed firepower and force them to beg for mercy. In contrast to the precarious supply situation at Montreuil, here 'there was no sparing of powder, iron balls, and stones, and lead, all flying in the fastest and most deadly way that any one could desire.' Nevertheless, the bombardment failed to make Boulogne surrender and a frontal assault on 2 September was a bloody failure. In the end, Boulogne capitulated because the defenders ran short of ammunition and their commander despaired of receiving relief while the main French army was tied up fighting imperial troops in Champagne. On 14 September, the remnants of the garrison marched out of the ruined town, along with 2000 French civilians who were too afraid of the English to stay. The king himself entered four days later – presumably once the more noisome results of the siege had been removed. However, on the very day that Henry went to view his new prize, unbeknown to him, Charles V and Francis I concluded a separate peace between themselves by signing the Treaty of Crépy.[11]

The sudden withdrawal of England's imperial ally put the king and his councillors in a very difficult situation. Instead of confronting France's second-string forces while the main French armies were tied up fighting imperial troops, the English army would now have to take the full brunt of French military power. Moreover, Charles's retreat into neutrality meant that the auxiliary forces which he had provided for Henry were now recalled. This left a large hole in the English army which could only be filled by urgently calling for fresh drafts from home and recruiting extra mercenaries. It also meant the end of the shambolic operation at Montreuil, from where the army beat a hasty retreat towards Boulogne, where the king's engineers were beginning to rebuild the town's defences. Henry himself returned to England on 30 September – ensuring that he took all the credit for the victory, while distancing himself from any defeat which might occur before the campaign season ended. He had spent 79 days in France, 67 of them within sight of the fighting. Inevitably, the king's departure undermined the confidence of the commanders whom he left behind. With their troops in confusion and rumours swirling that the approaching French army was 50,000 strong, Norfolk and Suffolk promptly scampered for the relative safety of Calais, leaving only 3000 men to garrison the shattered port of Boulogne under the command of John Dudley, Viscount Lisle. The confusion among the retreating army was so great – and the weather so appalling – that most of the troops were shut out of Calais and many of the sick were abandoned to the elements. This effectively marked the end of the campaign for the bulk of Henry's army, whose chief concern now became winning a place on a boat home. For the troops at Boulogne, the French counter-offensive still loomed. This reached its peak on 9 October, when French troops launched a surprise night attack and swiftly captured the outer parts of the town, slaughtering the unsuspecting English defenders. However, so preoccupied were the French troops with plundering English supplies and hunting down unarmed survivors that they lost cohesion in the dark, and were taken by surprise when English reinforcements streamed out of Boulogne's upper town. Now the boot was on the other foot and many of the attackers were trapped and cut down by furious English defenders who were bent upon revenge and self-preservation. The French commander, the French king's son and heir, Henri, was so disheartened by the casualties that he declined to renew the assault. Despite having large numbers of fresh reserves, he saw 'that the English had made capons [i.e. neuters] of his gentlemen cocks and that it would be futile to send the chickens in their place'.[12]

After this bloody battle, the war between England and France petered out over the winter. Both sides were eager to make peace, but Henry's adamant refusal to return Boulogne meant the war could not be ended. England would consequently have to face France – and Scotland – alone in 1545. This prospect threatened the very viability of England's basic military strategy. Traditionally, England would only invade France in tandem with a Continental ally, preferably once the French crown had already committed the bulk of its troops to a region distant from the English enclave around Calais. English invasions were also restricted to a few months at a time, which allowed the bulk of the army to return home at the end of the campaign and reduced costs. This opportunistic raiding strategy was well known to the French and helps to explain why they feared England far less than the emperor. The point was made very forcibly to the duke of Norfolk by the commander of Montreuil: 'let it be known to him that I will keep this town as well as I kept the castle of Hesdin against him. Therefore he can take his pleasure in hunting with hawks and hounds about the country while the weather is fine and mild and by winter, according to the old English custom, you will go home to your kinsmen.' The recruitment of Henry's army and the system of financing war by a parliamentary grant reflected this seasonal approach to war. Although able to generate men and resources for a short period of intense campaigning, neither system was intended to wage sustained warfare. Nevertheless, it was precisely a prolonged war effort that England now faced. Worse, it would be a full-scale war on two fronts – and all the more draining because Henry would also have to refortify and defend the shattered wreck of Boulogne. The second season of Henry's wars against France and Scotland therefore drove England into a strategic *terra incognita* and forced the realm to cope with the consequences of its military and administrative structures being pushed to breaking point and beyond.[13]

War on Two Fronts, 1544–46

If the war had been expensive and alarming during 1544, it would now become far more threatening and costly. The difficulties which

Scotland presented to England became obvious when a large English raiding party was ambushed and annihilated at Ancrum Moor in February 1545. Eight hundred of the raiders were killed and another 1000 were taken prisoner. Compounding the blow to England, and the boost to Scottish spirits, was news that French troops would soon be dispatched to reinforce the Scots. In the event, it was not until June that 3500 French soldiers arrived in Scotland and, despite various alarms, no large-scale actions actually occurred in the north. Nevertheless, the prospect of a Franco-Scottish invasion compelled England to ready an army of 27,500 men from its northern counties, stiffened by more than 3000 foreign mercenaries shipped into Newcastle. Month after month, the bored Spanish, Italian, German and Albanian mercenaries waited for action in their various billets, often causing trouble with the local inhabitants. Several hundred more mercenaries spent the summer in camps in Essex and Kent. England's defensive measures against direct attack from France also involved calling up the militia to create three armies of about 30,000 men each to defend the southern coasts, while another 12,000 men served aboard the fleet. There were also 7000 men at Boulogne and at least 15,000 in and around Calais, many of them foreigners. All up, Henry's government had over 150,000 men in arms during the summer of 1545. Even if several thousand of these troops were costly foreign mercenaries, this was an extraordinary degree of mobilisation at a time when the total population of England and Wales was less than three million.[14]

The great French offensive finally began in mid-July, when a fleet variously estimated at 30,000 men and 150 to 300 ships, including 26 oar-powered galleys, sailed from Normandy towards Portsmouth. The English fleet, under the lord admiral, Lord Lisle (who had been recalled from Boulogne at the end of 1544), numbered about 160 ships of all sizes. Although both fleets were built around a hard core of large royal warships, most vessels were armed merchantmen carrying contingents of soldiers who would defend their own ship, or attack an enemy vessel, using bows, handguns, bills and javelins. Most ships carried various forms of cannon, but there were relatively few large guns even aboard the biggest royal warships. The *Mary Rose*, one of the largest English warships, nominally carried 126 guns, but 50 of these were handguns, 20 fired light hailshot and only 12 were heavy bronze cannon. The ship also carried 250 bows, 400 sheaves of arrows and 300 staff weapons. Although the ship carried 185 soldiers and 30 gunners, many of these hand weapons were intended for the sailors, who were expected to fight when necessary. This was essential because naval combat was fought at close quarters. While cannon fire from a few hundred yards might damage an enemy ship and occasionally perhaps even land a crippling blow, the real fighting usually involved showering the enemy with arrows and iron and stone shot from short range, before finally boarding the now-battered enemy hulk and capturing it hand to hand.[15]

Naval warfare was also critically dependent upon fickle winds. In late June, Lisle tried to launch a pre-emptive strike against the French fleet while it still lay in harbour. Unfortunately, the wind failed as the English fleet closed in, leaving it suddenly stranded and open to attack from the French galleys, whose oars enabled them to manoeuvre while the sailing ships were immobilised. Potential disaster for the English was only averted when a fresh breeze sprang up. This forced the galleys to seek shelter because the same wind which filled the sails of the English fleet and restored its mobility also made the sea too rough for galleys to function effectively. However, sixteenth-century sailing ships were very limited in their ability to sail at an angle to the wind and this breeze soon threatened to blow the English fleet into treacherous shallows. Lisle wisely chose to withdraw and return home rather than risk shipwreck.[16]

This frustrating engagement set the pattern for the naval campaign of 1545. When the French fleet finally arrived in the Solent on 19 July, the same light winds which had cost it nine days in crossing the Channel made it very difficult for the English fleet even to get out of Portsmouth. When Lisle's fleet finally put to sea, the *Mary Rose* broached dramatically, drowning almost its whole crew in full view of the king, who was watching from ashore. Although the French claimed that it had been sunk by gunfire from a galley, it seems that the ship was flooded with water when its over-eager commander neglected to have the lower portholes closed before hoisting full sail. Incompetence was not restricted to the English side. The French admiral twice had to transfer his flag even before the voyage had begun because his first flagship caught fire and exploded, while the second ran aground in leaving harbour. Nevertheless, such dramas did not reflect the larger course of events. Frustrated by weeks of fluctuating winds and unwilling to risk precipitate action, neither side could get to grips with the other and force the sort of close-range combat necessary for decisive results. Although a few French troops landed on the Isle of Wight – where they were ambushed by the local militia and forced to withdraw – and 7000 men went ashore to reinforce the French army which was now besieging Boulogne, a full month's manoeuvring off the English coast produced no result and the French fleet was forced to head home. Packed into their ships for weeks on end and suffering from poor victuals and hygiene, the soldiers and sailors of the French fleet had begun to sicken and die. This was the regular fate of fleets in the early modern period and a reminder that staying power was often no less important than firepower. In this instance, neither side was able to strike a telling blow and the English victory ultimately came from outlasting the enemy. The only decisive action came at the beginning of September when Lisle burned the French port of Tréport and destroyed 30 vessels in its harbour. However, disease showed no respect for nationality and the English fleet soon began to suffer the same fate as its French counterpart. By the middle of September, the naval campaign was over and both sides were trying to disinfect and demobilise their ships.[17]

While most of the resources of the realm were engaged in resisting the first of the great armadas which would threaten England during the course of the sixteenth century, the garrison of Boulogne faced a siege by 21,000 French troops, aided by 12,000 pioneers employed to dig the necessary trenches and earthworks. Although 5000 reinforcements were sent across the Channel, more grandiose plans to bolster Boulogne with 30,000 men under the duke of Suffolk collapsed with the latter's sudden death at the end of August. The siege of Boulogne therefore became a feverish competition between English attempts to rebuild and strengthen the town's defences and French efforts to threaten them. The English position often seemed parlous and the constant demand for fresh troops scraped the bottom of the barrel in terms of manpower. Many of the king's troops around Calais were foreign mercenaries who sometimes showed dubious loyalty, while the latest English recruits were described by one veteran captain as 'callow boys' whose officers were 'weak, cheerless and senseless'. At Boulogne itself, the officers allegedly spent their time away from the action gambling and whoring (many prostitutes having relocated there after the recent closure of London's official brothels), while the common soldiers had to survive both French bullets and rotten food: 'it was an abomination to weak bowels to have to eat hard dry bitter bread baked from the powder of grey corn, and old meat which had got spoiled in the air and was fly blown before it was put in salt. Or old butter gone so mouldy and of so many colours that a man had to hold his nose before coming near it, or old hard dry cheese.' Fortunately for the English, the French suffered similar problems and the approach of winter reduced the campaign to spadework and occasional raids.[18]

The failure of the vast and costly French efforts to intimidate England and recover Boulogne finally allowed Henry to turn his attention to Scotland and revenge for the humiliation of Ancrum Moor. Henry's immediate response to the disaster had been to demand massive retaliation against the Scots, but the French threat made this impossible. The operation which was finally launched in the autumn was more modest. In early September, the earl of Hertford simply marched into Scotland with 16,000 men, including 1000 heavily armoured knights and contingents of Albanian light cavalry and Spanish infantry. Although a sharp engagement was required to storm Kelso, Hertford's army met little resistance and spent a fortnight ravaging the Scottish border region before withdrawing. Hertford's dispatches pandered to Henry's thirst for news that the Scots were suffering terribly for their defiance, but the earl was well aware that burning crops and towns was a poor reward for such an expensive operation and brought no lasting strategic benefit, merely reinforcing Scottish hostility towards England.[19]

The appalling financial, material and human cost of the campaigns of 1545 left all of the combatants desperate for peace. By September, with the war reduced to an exhausted stalemate, Henry's privy council were so eager to end the conflict that they urged the king to return Boulogne to France, but he would not even consider the proposition. After the frustrations of his earlier wars against France, Henry was determined to retain this tangible proof of his military success. For his part, Francis I was equally determined not to accept the loss of French soil. Diplomatic contacts made little headway during the winter of 1545–46. However, both sides were now so exhausted and short of money that serious negotiations finally began in the following spring and six weeks of hard bargaining produced agreement. The so-called Treaty of Camp (or Treaty of Ardres, to the French) was signed on 7 June in a tent erected in the no-man's land between French and English territory near Calais. Boulogne was to be returned to France in eight years' time, but only if France paid the enormous sum of two million crowns (£700,000). England would also desist from making war on Scotland, unless the Scots broke the peace, in which case France would supposedly aid England against its former ally. At the outset of the negotiations, Henry had hoped that the treaty with France might even be used to force the Scots into honouring their commitment of 1543 to marry Mary to Prince Edward – which would have represented an extraordinary triumph for England – but French diplomacy and Scottish intransigence ensured that this remained a forlorn hope. Although the Treaty of Camp ended open hostilities between England, France and Scotland, it brought only an uneasy peace. English and French forces still occasionally 'bickered' around the limits of Boulogne, while Scotland was rocked by the assassination of Cardinal Beaton by pro-English Scottish Protestants and the subsequent siege of St Andrew's Castle. Rather than initiating genuine peace, the treaty spawned a kind of cold war wariness (and occasional shooting) between the former combatants.[20]

The Cost of Henry's Wars

Henry VIII entered his war against France in 1544 under conditions which were as favourable as could be imagined for any sixteenth-century war. His treasury was bulging, his realm's defences on land and sea had been freshly overhauled, Scotland was cowed, and he was able to enter the conflict when France was already tired from two years of fighting and faced a simultaneous assault by his ally Charles V. Henry also applied the lessons he had learned during his previous wars against France. Despite promising to march on Paris, his real target – Boulogne – was deliberately modest and its close proximity to the English territory around Calais meant that the operation would involve few risks and offered the prospect of long-term occupation. To minimise the risks still further, Henry deliberately used a sledgehammer to crack a walnut, deploying an army which ultimately peaked at 48,000 men, including more than 10,000 foreign troops, and 250 cannon. The benefits of past campaigns were also evident in elaborate efforts to improve the flow of supplies, including such innovations as mobile ovens for baking bread. Even though the supply system inevitably suffered hiccups (especially at Montreuil) and the oven wagons proved insufficiently robust for French roads, Henry's commissariat performed tolerably well under extreme stress, especially compared with previous efforts.[21]

Yet, despite beginning with a hand full of aces, or at least of picture cards, Henry's wars against France and Scotland rapidly spiralled out of control and brought his realm to the brink of financial and psychological exhaustion within less than two years. By late 1545, the attitude of the privy council towards the war and its endless appetite for more men, money and supplies was epitomised by the despair of the lord chancellor, Sir Thomas Wriothesley: 'God help us; for mine own part, it maketh me weary of my life.'[22] Military commanders like the duke of Norfolk were equally pessimistic and, by the spring of 1546, even Henry himself finally recognised that the realm needed urgent relief from the war.

It is difficult to give hard figures for the human cost of Henry's wars in the 1540s because there are no cumulative casualty figures. Impressionistic evidence suggests that the cost was fairly high, especially given England's small population. When Lisle's fleet returned from its raid on Tréport in early September 1545, 8488 men were present at the final muster, while 3512 (nearly 30 per cent of those who had set out) were missing because they were sick, dead or had already been invalided home. Contemporary opinion held that armies in the field normally lost half their strength within six months, but the attrition rate was sometimes much higher. At Boulogne, 1200 pioneers were working on harbour defences in January 1545. By June, so many had died or become unfit for work that the number was down to 300. By July there were only 100.

Some 2000 replacements arrived in August, but few of them still remained by the following March.[23]

As in every war before the modern era, the vast majority of such casualties sprang from disease rather than enemy action. Bloody battles like the defeat at Ancrum Moor or the French night attack on Boulogne were rare and constituted an exceptional military and political crisis. In the case of the pioneers at Boulogne, the chief killers were not bullets, but plague and 'the bloody flux', which also claimed 300 soldiers of the garrison during the early summer of 1545. The frequent need to forage for supplies, proximity to disembarkation ports and slack discipline – not to mention fear of disease – meant that many soldiers also simply deserted, as some of the disappearing Boulogne pioneers undoubtedly did. However, the war's toll of death and illness was clearly appalling. Even avoiding the immediate war zone did not always guarantee protection from the perils of military service. When the bulk of Henry's great army of 1544 returned to England before Christmas, 'the soldiers coming from Calais and Boulogne were dying along the road from Dover to London, and along the roads from London to every quarter of the kingdom, while trying to go home. After they had come home those who were well fell sick and those who were sick got worse, and from this sickness and feebleness and pest they died in every part of England.' Even allowing for some exaggeration, this report accurately reflects both the danger of veterans bringing home disease and the heavy burden of sickness and crime which was borne along the road from Dover to London whenever soldiers returned from France.[24]

As well as causing enormous misery at home and abroad – especially for Scottish and French civilians who lived in the war zones – Henry's wars showed the limitations of England's military power. Although English forces consistently had the upper hand against the Scots, the full deployable force of the realm was barely sufficient to seize and hold one small French port in 1544. When France turned a greater proportion of its own military power – although by no means its full capacity – against England in 1545, Henry's government was forced to pull out all the stops to defend the realm and even then it was a very close-run thing. Whether the realm could have sustained another full campaign season during the summer of 1546 can only be a matter of conjecture.

One sign of the terrible strain which the war imposed on England's military structures was a sudden shift in the means by which soldiers were raised for service abroad. Henrician England operated two distinct but overlapping and often contradictory systems for raising troops. Armies for defending the realm were raised by calling out the militia of individual counties. By law, all men aged 16 to 60 were required to possess various pieces of military equipment according to their wealth and were supposed to practise with it, although many did not. This universal service requirement was the theoretical basis of the militia, although in reality county officials only designated a pool of able-bodied men for active service if the militia were called out. The county militia could serve outside its own county borders 'where necessity requireth', but could not legally be forced to serve overseas.[25]

For recruiting the armies which he sent abroad, Henry used a separate and curiously archaic system of dispatching letters under the royal signet to selected individual landowners, requesting them to raise soldiers from their own tenants, servants and other dependants. The curious point about this 'quasi-feudal' system is that Henry had created it in 1511 on the eve of his first war with France, even though it was considerably less flexible than the practice of issuing indentures (i.e. recruitment contracts) to would-be officers which had been used since the time of Edward III. Henry's 'quasi-feudal' system meant that he went to war in 1544 accompanied by a large part of the landowning class and an unprecedented number of their tenants and servants. However, the system was critically dependent upon sending out scores of letters to suitable recipients and upon the latter being able to raise worthwhile numbers of men. Even at the best of times, many letters went astray or were sent to gentlemen who lacked the ability to 'make men'. This might be acceptable for England's traditional raiding strategy, but it was ill-adapted to multi-year campaigning. When Henry needed fresh troops in a hurry to help defend Boulogne in September 1544, it was apparent that the 'quasi-feudal' system could not produce them quickly enough, if at all. In desperation, the government abandoned custom and ordered the muster

check
anthony Lee

commissioners of 12 counties to select a total of 4000 militia men for immediate despatch to France. Military necessity could no longer permit the luxury of raising troops by a system which was socially congenial, but cumbersome and unsuited to generating a steady supply of reinforcements. Henceforth, it would be the militia system which would provide most of the troops for service overseas, although confusion between the two systems would persist until the end of the century, despite an attempted rationalisation in 1558.[26]

The crumbling of England's expeditionary force-style recruitment system also forced it to rely more heavily upon large numbers of foreign troops. Henry was only willing to attack France in the first place because Charles V provided him with auxiliary troops free of charge who could make up for England's shortage of heavy cavalry and infantry armed with pikes and handguns. Henry also hired more foreigners at his own expense and subsequently launched a huge effort to recruit thousands more mercenaries when Charles recalled the auxiliaries after the Treaty of Crépy. Unlike the green troops provided by fresh drafts of Englishmen, mercenaries were hardened fighters and familiar with the new style of warfare which was emerging in Europe as handguns and artillery began to proliferate.

Although more English soldiers were starting to use arquebuses and pikes, most of Henry's troops were equipped with bills and longbows, which were outranged by the newer weapons and required considerable skill, fitness and courage to wield effectively. The longbow, in particular, suffered badly from improvements in armour design, which had progressively reduced the range at which arrows could pierce enemy helmets or shoulder and chest armour. During the Boulogne campaign, Henry's cavalry had to draw French horsemen 'within a stick's throw of the bowmen' to ensure their arrows did real damage to the enemy, and attacks required equally close contact. According to the French officer Blaise de Monluc, 'we who were accustomed to fire our arquebuses at a great distance ... thought these near approaches of theirs very strange, imputing their running on at this confident rate to absolute bravery.' However, English élan was not easily sustained for extended periods, especially when exhaustion and sickness took their toll and enemy guns had killed the boldest soldiers. Traditional English weapons and tactics perhaps

changes in weapons 1540s

longbow v.
armour.

mercenary
skills learnt

remained more serviceable on the northern borders because campaigns there were short and English troops remained supremely confident in their superiority over the Scots, even though the ranks of Scottish pikemen proved an increasingly tough nut to crack. Even at Flodden, where England won a crushing victory in 1513, the arrow storms which had been so deadly against the French in the Hundred Years War proved alarmingly ineffective against Scottish infantry wearing modern armour.[27]

Mercenaries added valuable skills and experience to Henry's armies and reduced the problems of finding enough English and Welsh recruits. This made the recruitment of adequate numbers of mercenaries a matter of vital importance. During early 1545, Charles V deliberately obstructed Henry's attempts to recruit troops in Germany, the largest market for mercenaries. English agents also had to compete against rival recruiters for France, which had long relied upon foreign infantry. This caused special difficulties because England's traditional raiding strategy meant that it lacked the network of military contacts in Germany which France had developed during the fifteenth century. Some unscrupulous mercenaries took advantage of Henry's desperation to swindle his agents out of large sums of money. The most outrageous was Friedrich von Reiffenberg, whose promises to provide 3000 horsemen and 10,000 foot for the defence of Boulogne in 1545 came to nothing, but milked a mind-boggling £80,000 from the hapless English recruiters. Other military contractors were genuinely unable to transport their men to English territory or switched sides after arrival in the war zone. Nevertheless, despite such difficulties, Henry was increasingly successful in hiring mercenaries in the large numbers which he needed. However, the financial burden imposed by such large-scale employment of mercenaries was heavy. Quite apart from the costs incurred in recruitment and transport (let alone unforeseen losses due to swindling), mercenary infantry were usually paid 8d per day, whereas English foot received only 6d. Mercenary horsemen were paid three times as much as English cavalry. Although mercenaries were expected to provide their own equipment, the disparity in pay sometimes caused severe tensions between English and mercenary troops and allegedly dispirited English soldiers, who resented risking their lives for lower pay.[28]

1544/5 mercenaries brought new skills but greater costs. Old methods OK on northern boundaries. 31

New weapons

The Glory of War

Far and away the greatest strain which Henry's wars imposed upon England was financial. The events of the 1530s had revolutionised royal finances and permitted the accumulation of reserves of perhaps £1 million in cash and movable goods by war's eve. Henry's finance ministers anticipated that the French campaign of 1544 would last three months and cost £250,000, including a small reserve for contingencies. With limited borrowings in the money market at Antwerp and the sale of lead stripped from monasteries and small amounts of ex-monastic land, they reckoned that the war could be funded without even touching the crown's reserves. In fact, the war cost £650,000 in 1544 and £1.3 million by late 1545. Calculations made in the reign of Edward VI produced even more terrifying figures. By the time of Henry's death in 1547, his wars in France and Scotland, together with the costs of the navy and new fortifications at Boulogne and elsewhere, exceeded £2.1 million. This disastrous explosion of expenditure was fuelled by the unexpected duration and intensity of the war and the fact that it was waged not only in France but also in Scotland, on the seas and along the coast of England itself. It was a far cry from England's traditional strategy of despatching expeditionary forces to fight for a few months before returning home. From late September 1544, without Charles V to subsidise his war effort by providing extra troops and ready access to supplies from Flanders, Henry had to bear the full cost of fighting by himself – including hiring extra mercenaries to replace the departed imperial soldiers. Moreover, virtually every last item necessary for war, including the staves for making longbows – the quintessentially English weapon – had to be imported from abroad. Henry's very success at Boulogne also made it impossible to secure a speedy end to the war and locked him into a vicious circle of expenditure: the more he spent on defending and fortifying Boulogne, the more important it became to protect his investment there, which forced him to spend even more money defending the town. The sole prize of Henry's final wars therefore proved remarkably burdensome. Having spent approximately £590,000 to capture Boulogne, Henry was forced to spend another £320,000 garrisoning it and over £120,000 (by 1550) on new fortifications there – perhaps £1 million in total by 1547. Henry's wars against Scotland cost another £350,000, while naval expenditure reached £265,000.[29]

Cost of wars.

The real impact of these wartime costs was even worse than the figures suggest. While crown income, especially taxation, was often painfully slow to come in, the demands of war meant that Henry's government had to raise very large sums of cash very rapidly and with precious little warning. This made life a nightmare for his privy council. Failure to find the necessary money would not only infuriate the king, but might provoke a military disaster, with soldiers at the front line suddenly being left short of arms, victuals or reinforcements. Keeping England in the war therefore required extraordinary measures to raise money quickly. Perhaps £1 million was borrowed in the money market at Antwerp. In early 1544, it was anticipated that Henry's chief agent there, Stephen Vaughan, would need to borrow £20,000. By October 1546, Vaughan alone had arranged loans worth £272,000. Bearing 12–14 per cent interest and expiring after only a few months, these loans provided only brief respite before they required repayment and the negotiation of new loans. As a result, the crown was forced to sell far more ex-monastic lands than it had ever intended. This brought in cash and relieved the king of payments to the ex-religious, but also eroded the crown's landed estate for the future, ensuring smaller revenues in subsequent years. Various forms of taxation, both those approved by parliament and otherwise, ultimately covered a quarter or a third of the costs of war in the 1540s. This required the highest levels of taxation experienced in England since the fourteenth century. Since these imposts involved a succession of separate payments, taxpayers were hit by a kind of 'compound taxation' which had a dramatic cumulative impact on their assets. For the clergy, this was a painful education in what it meant to be members of a nationalised Church headed by the king, while urban merchants were drained of their working capital, which fuelled unemployment in towns. The wealthier landowners were also hit hard by the various imposts, even though they were already struggling to provide men and arms for the war.[30]

Nevertheless, the most dramatic and painful expedient for raising cash was the debasement of the coinage. This involved both diluting the precious metal content of gold and silver coins (debasement proper) and simply increasing the face value of coins. Open and large-scale changes to the coinage began in 1544 and were soon manipulated to produce enormous profits to the crown, with gold and silver coins suffering further degradations in 1545 and 1546. The hundreds of thousands of pounds which these procedures generated were so important to Henry's finances that Lord Chancellor Wriothesley described them as 'our holy anchor'.[31]

Although it offered short-term financial salvation, plundering the coinage had disastrous effects upon the realm as a whole. Most importantly, debasement severely exacerbated inflation in the price of food and goods, although its full impact only hit home in the latter stages of Henry's reign and during the reign of Edward VI. Besides eroding the real value of the crown's tax and land revenues – even though the former were already unsustainably high and the latter were being sold away for quick cash – inflation also savaged the budget of every significant landowner in the realm. While prices rose sharply, landed incomes were largely based upon rents and fines and lost half their real value within five years, heightening tensions between landowners and their tenants. This hit directly at the social class most intimately involved in raising soldiers and the very tenurial relationships upon which most recruitment had formerly been based. Ironically, if the crown had not also been unconsciously applying deflationary forces to the realm's economy by sucking up money through taxation and sending large amounts of coin overseas to pay soldiers, buy supplies and repay loans, the price rise and its impact on society would have been even worse. Yet the benefits of these deflationary pressures were hardly apparent to taxpayers. Although the very poorest members of society were excluded from paying, many subjects who did have to pay taxes were forced to sell assets to acquire the necessary cash. In fact, the chronic shortage of coin in early modern England meant that the realm's economy was always based less upon cash than upon networks of credit. Inflation and debasement – which forced buyer and seller to agree their own value for a coin, since its face value had been rendered untrustworthy – inevitably put powerful new strains on this credit economy.

The relative scarcity of coins (despite the brief but massive outpourings of debased coins after 1544) also meant that money had social and cultural resonances which modern scholars are only beginning to appreciate. In this light, the debasement clearly had a

[handwritten margin notes: "Good of psychological effect of debasing coin and this immediate image" and "Good."]

profound psychological impact upon the realm. Coins were the most widespread and pervasive symbols of royal authority, displaying the king's name, royal style and physical appearance to his subjects. What, then, must the people of England and Wales have thought when the king's own government repeatedly devalued and, as it were, defaced these images of the king? Although this was an age of state-sponsored iconoclasm, meddling with the coinage was, ironically, perhaps the greatest act of defacement of all. In the short term at least, such uncertain times may have encouraged stronger attachment to the unifying figure of Henry himself. Nevertheless, the more lasting impact of Henry's desperate efforts to fund his wars in the 1540s was undoubtedly negative, undermining popular trust in the very 'imperial' kingship which those wars had been supposed to consummate.[32]

Somerset's War, 1547–49

The death of Henry VIII on 28 January 1547 brought the crown to his 9-year-old son, Edward VI, but the real power in government was the new king's uncle, Edward Seymour, earl of Hertford, who promptly took on the mantle of lord protector and became duke of Somerset. Somerset had unfinished business with the Scots and was determined to bring about the marriage of Edward VI with Mary Queen of Scots which had proved so elusive since 1543. He also believed that military success in Scotland would win him popular acclaim in England and cement his hold on power. As a result, Somerset was anxious to avoid open conflict with France, even though the latter also had a new king, Henri II, who was bent upon recovering Boulogne and avenging his defeat there in October 1544. The willingness of the English government to ignore French provocations rather than risk open war on the Continent and the sheer strength of the new defences at Boulogne – the sight of which made Henri weep with frustration when he viewed them in October 1547 – meant that Somerset could concentrate England's military resources against Scotland to an unprecedented extent.[33]

Somerset believed that he could succeed where Henry VIII had failed because he planned to adopt a new strategy against Scotland.

Instead of launching large and expensive expeditions which merely caused the Scots short-term pain and hardened antagonism towards England, he planned to occupy Scottish territory permanently by building and garrisoning new forts in key parts of the Scottish lowlands. These bases would not only protect the north of England from attack and allow English forces to range deep into Scottish territory, but would also overawe the local inhabitants and encourage them to ally themselves with England. In effect, the strategy was designed to create a new English 'Pale' in southern Scotland to match those around Calais in France and around Dublin in Ireland – enclaves on foreign soil which survived by virtue of English fortifications and troops. To encourage Scots to accept this new Pale, Somerset launched a hearts-and-minds campaign in which his propagandists lauded the idea of a new, openly Protestant 'Greater Britain' which would embrace both realms. As fellow 'Britons' rather than hostile English and Scots, the people of the two kingdoms would embrace the Protestantism which the new Edwardian regime espoused and fulfil God's design for 'Britain' by supporting the union of their royal houses. However, if the concept of 'Britain' did not produce the desired results, Somerset could always fall back on the impregnability of his new fortresses. Recent history had shown that the Scots had trouble besieging even old-fashioned castles. Somerset planned to raise the stakes still further by building his new forts according to the latest cannon-resistant designs which he had observed at Boulogne – structures collectively known as *trace italienne* and characterised by low-angled bastions and massively thick earth walls.[34]

Somerset launched his invasion in early September 1547. While a small army threatened to attack Scotland from Carlisle in the west, the main English force of about 12,000 foot, 5000 horse and 1400 pioneers headed north along the traditional eastern route from Berwick. These troops included a sizeable number of mercenaries, as well as English veterans drawn from the garrisons at Calais and Boulogne. Since even 900 carts were insufficient to carry all the essential supplies and equipment, extra stores and another 6000 soldiers were carried aboard a fleet of 80 ships. Scotland responded with a full mobilisation, producing an army of about 26,000 men, including several thousand Highland archers but only 1500 light cavalry.

Berwick   Richard Lee

1547

PINKIE

Somerset's troops penetrated most of the way towards Edinburgh
before they finally located the main Scottish army, which was drawn
up in a strong defensive position at Inveresk. The next day, 10
September, Somerset planned to move up in preparation for an
assault, but was surprised to discover the Scots crossing the River Esk
and advancing to meet him. Although their counsels were divided, as
so often, the Scottish leaders had decided that their troops could not
stand being bombarded both by Somerset's cannon and by the
English fleet, which had drawn in close to the shore and begun to
pound the Scottish left wing.

The result of this decision was the battle variously known as Pinkie
or Musselburgh. While the English infantry struggled to move from
marching columns into battle formation, the Scots surged forward
until slowed by a cavalry charge. This attack by the Gentlemen
Pensioners and other English heavy cavalry suffered a bloody
repulse, failing to break the massed ranks of Scottish pikemen,
despite bitter fighting. However, once they halted to fend off the cavalry, the Scots were bombarded by English cannon and blasted by
mercenary Spanish and Italian arquebusiers. Lacking adequate cavalry of their own (which had been routed in a skirmish the previous
day), the Scots could not fight off these withering attacks and
promptly burst into retreat as the main body of English infantry
began to engage them with arrows and bills. The retreat soon became
a rout as the English horsemen sought a bloody revenge upon the
fleeing enemy. Abandoned Scottish pikes lay 'like a wood of staves
strewed on the ground as rushes in a chamber', while the fields were
covered with hideously mangled dead bodies. Some 6000–10,000
Scots were cut down or drowned in trying to escape across the Esk,
while another 1500 were taken prisoner. Perhaps 800 had been killed
on the English side, although many of the horsemen carried bloody
wounds. Lord Grey, the English cavalry commander, 'receaved a
greate wownde in the mouthe with a pyke, sutche as clave one of his
teethe, strake hym thowroghe the tongue, and three fyngers deepe
into the rouff of the mouthe'.[35]

Although it was the most disastrous defeat since the catastrophe of
Flodden in 1513, enough Scots escaped towards the safety of
Edinburgh Castle to form the nucleus of a fresh army. However,

Somerset disregarded this future threat and began to set up his new forts. The first, at Eyemouth, just north of Berwick, had actually been begun even before Pinkie. Gradually, a chain of forts was constructed, supported by outlying encampments to extend their reach. The most northerly was Broughty Craig, just outside Dundee, which was surrendered to an English naval expedition by a local aristocratic collaborator. Many other Scots also 'assured' themselves to England in these early months, but the good will soon turned sour. Other weaknesses of Somerset's strategy also quickly emerged. Even in October 1547, there were shortages of horse fodder and difficulties in keeping horses fit for service. Without adequate mounts, the light cavalry based in the new forts would be immobilised and the garrisons themselves rendered unable to control the surrounding countryside, which negated the whole purpose of the forts and turned them into sitting ducks. The forts also suffered from the perennial problems which bedevilled military logistics on the northern borders, with wagons struggling to reach inland garrisons over muddy roads and bases on the coast depending on favourable winds for resupply. Life for the troops soon became thoroughly miserable and desertion was rampant, especially as Somerset sought to save money by keeping the garrisons' pay three or four months in arrears.[36]

At an even more basic level, Somerset's plan went awry because the intimidating impact of the new *trace italienne* forts proved politically counter-productive. Instead of encouraging compromise from the Scots, the apparent impregnability of the English forts drove the Scots to seek massive aid from France. Worse, they purchased this support by pledging the hand of Mary Queen of Scots in marriage to Henri II's heir, reaffirming the auld alliance in the most emphatic – and potentially permanent – way possible. This dramatically raised the stakes, threatening England with a nightmare scenario which had never quite come to pass in Henry's reign – the prospect of fighting French armies not only across the Channel but also on England's northern borders. Once again, the dream of military glory was turning to ashes.

From early 1548, therefore, the character of the war in Scotland changed radically. Instead of seeking to tame the Scots, the race was now on to build new forts to keep the French at bay. The most

Scots - Fr. alliance.

important of this new wave of forts was Haddington, 18 miles south of Edinburgh, which was fortified in June 1548 and garrisoned with no less than 2500 troops – a mini-army in its own right. However, an attempt to intercept the French army at sea was bungled and more than 12,000 enemy troops landed safely in Scotland on 19 June. Many of the French troops were foreign mercenaries and the inclusion of 2000 cavalry in the force posed an especially grave threat to England's declining cavalry arm.[37]

It soon became clear that the main French target was Haddington, which now became the focus of a bitter siege. Although a powerful defensive position, Haddington lay several miles from the coast and was difficult to supply with all the stores which its large garrison required. The first attempt at relieving the siege proved a disaster, virtually destroying the main English cavalry force in Scotland and consequently sapping the life blood of the whole garrison system. The English government was now forced to raise a full army for the task – 11,000 foot and 1800 horse, including a large number of foreign mercenaries. The French, who had suffered heavy losses during the siege, withdrew and the English commander, the earl of Shrewsbury, finally relieved Haddington at the end of August. Although Shrewsbury was able to resupply Haddington and reinforce its depleted garrison, he felt unable to risk attacking the French and the whole costly expedition achieved little of lasting value.

Even a new fort which was hurriedly built as a supporting base for Haddington proved to be more of a costly liability than an asset. Nevertheless, Shrewsbury's expedition reflected the new tone of the war. The increased proportion of mercenaries and arquebusiers among his soldiers signified the greater resources which were required to combat the French. Yet the cost of this effort was so high that Somerset almost gambled on cutting the army by 2000–3000 men to save money – a risk which Shrewsbury refused to accept. Equally ominous was the extreme difficulty which Shrewsbury had experienced in raising cavalry, which suggested that four years of war, taxation and inflation were now sapping the ability of English landowners to provide suitable horsemen.[38]

If Henry's wars had resulted in the literal meltdown of royal finances, Somerset's supposedly cheaper war against Scotland continued the process. More crown lands were sold and the new properties which were seized from religious charities at the end of 1547 were also quickly liquidated. However, the English government found itself simply unable to pay for war without throwing out the 'holy anchor' of debasement. By the summer of 1549, the government was so dependent upon profits from the Mint that payments to the troops had to wait until a fresh shipment of bullion was converted into debased coins. Somerset's war therefore locked England into more of the same social and economic problems which had begun to plague the realm after Henry's debasements, even though some royal officials actually identified a connection between government actions and these problems.[39]

Ironically, the government itself lit the fuse which caused these problems to explode. Although it realised that the war could not be sustained without debasement, the government believed that it could reduce its impact and ensure continued popular support by blaming inflation upon the greed of landowners, who allegedly displaced tenant farmers to raise sheep. This spawned a moral crusade for agrarian reform which dovetailed with the regime's broader reform agenda of instituting Protestantism in England. Enclosures and excessive sheep-rearing were publicly blamed for unsettling rural society and denuding the realm of men fit for military service by forcing rural workers off the land. Perhaps partly because of its increasing difficulties in recruiting troops for the Scottish war, Somerset's government launched a commission of enquiry into enclosures in the summer of 1548 and promised serious action with new commissioners in 1549. This alarmed landlords – who continued to suffer from inflation and the burdens of war – and excited unrealistic expectations among the increasingly angry commons.[40]

During the spring and early summer of 1549, the rejuvenated Scots and newly reinforced French nibbled away at England's hold on Scotland. The small garrisons at Home and Fast Castles and Ferniehurst were overwhelmed and, in June, a bloody amphibious assault destroyed the new English base on the island of Inchkeith, near Leith. Haddington was again besieged. Meanwhile, events in England now conspired to prevent Somerset using the new troops which he had gathered for a counter-offensive. Between May and

August, popular discontent exploded into the open across the realm. Mass gatherings of the peasantry protested about the alleged abuses of greedy landowners, composed petitions to the government and vented their fury on local enclosures. Anxious to avoid entanglements which might impede his new campaign in Scotland, Somerset zealously tried to appease this chorus of complaint. However, in two regions these mass exercises in collective bargaining went horribly wrong.

In Cornwall and Devon, unlike elsewhere, there was a genuine rebellion. Although there was anger about the local impact of a new tax on sheep, the main thrust of the rising was opposition to the government's new Protestant prayer book, which became the only legal form of religious worship in England on 10 June. When the heavy-handed response from a local Protestant gentleman provoked violence, the protesters formed a peasant army and began a siege of Exeter in early July which ultimately lasted five weeks. More typical of the 'stirs' of 1549 were the 20,000 protesters who congregated outside Norwich, the realm's second-largest city. Their leaders styled themselves 'the king's friends and deputies' and instituted a people's court under an oak which they called the Tree of Reformation. When negotiations with the city authorities broke down and a royal herald proclaimed them as traitors for refusing to disperse, the rebels stormed Norwich on 22 July, before withdrawing to their camp outside the walls. The support which they received from some of the city's inhabitants shows that popular discontent in 1549 also extended to the towns. A government relief force of 1500 men under the marquis of Northampton entered Norwich on 31 July, but was promptly attacked by thousands of rebels, enraged that local officials had let the soldiers into the city. After more than 24 hours of bitter street fighting, Northampton's surviving troops were finally forced to flee for their lives. The defining moment in the struggle had come when Northampton's deputy-commander, Lord Sheffield, was captured by the rebels and beaten to death by men who were furious at the privileges of the aristocracy and the suffering of the poor.[41]

The killing of Lord Sheffield and the subsequent sacking of Norwich represented the realisation of a collective nightmare for members of the land-owning class – the loss of control, destruction of property and mob rule. Across the realm, gentlemen experienced echoes of the same popular anger and lack of respect. In the south-western rising, captured gentry at Bodmin had been taunted by cries of 'Kill the gentlemen!'. In Oxfordshire, demonstrators slaughtered all the deer in Sir John Williams's deer parks at Thame and Rycote.[42] It is hard to overstate the impact of this experience on the landed class and their socially inferior counterparts who served as the mayors and aldermen of the realm's towns. Memories of the 'camping time' of 1549 – and the bloody events which followed in Norfolk, Devon and Cornwall – would cast a long shadow over English government at all levels until at least the end of the century. Even in the 1590s, when few of those who had lived through the events of 1549 remained alive, the fear of reviving massive popular discontent would constrain the Elizabethan war effort and encourage efforts to cushion the burden on the common people.

Somerset's government was stunned by the outpouring of popular anger. To compound matters, Henri II declared war on England on 8 August and began attacking English positions around Boulogne. Urgent action was now imperative. Lord Russell had finally relieved Exeter on 6 August, aided by the redoubtable Lord Grey. Despite commanding an army of 4000 men, including 1500 mercenaries, Russell took three days to fight his way through to the city, killing 1000 rebels in the process. The final act came on 17 August near Sampford Courtenay in the west of Devon, where 2000 die-hard rebels were overwhelmed and slaughtered by Russell's troops. Events soon followed a similar course in Norfolk, where operations were commanded by John Dudley, the former lord admiral who had been created earl of Warwick. Warwick assembled an army of about 3000 horse and 6500 foot, including 1100 German mercenaries, many of whom had recently fought with Russell. Most of the English troops, especially the cavalry, were provided by the gentry and nobility. Warwick made a final, forlorn offer of pardon to the rebels on 23 August, which was met by a boy who 'showed his bare buttocks and did a filthy act'. Warwick stormed into Norwich the following day and fought off a fierce rebel counter-attack in the city streets. By 27 August, he felt secure enough to turn against the main rebel camp, which had now been transferred to an open – and indefensible – field named Dussindale. Once the opening volley from the *landsknechts* had thrown the rebels into chaos, Warwick unleashed his large force of cavalry on the rebels. Even more than at Sampford Courtenay, the result was a massacre rather than a battle: perhaps 3500 rebels were killed. With this effusion of blood and the exemplary executions which followed, the rising was finally smothered, although the resentments which had fuelled it smouldered on.[43]

By early September, order had been reimposed across the whole realm. However, the consequences of the summer's turmoil on the military situation continued to unfold. In Scotland, the great base at Haddington was finally abandoned. The remaining English garrisons in the north were in a poor state, so starved of men and money that they could barely defend their own positions, let alone threaten the Scots and French. At Boulogne, the English outposts had fallen, but the main defences remained stubbornly defiant, much to the fury of Henri II, who was leading the offensive in person. Nevertheless, the council was so desperate for fresh troops to reinforce the town that they ordered local authorities to impress vagabonds and ringleaders in the recent 'stirs' for service in France in mid-October.[44] The conditions of military service were therefore now so poor that even the government saw it as a punishment or, at least, a dangerous ordeal by which social undesirables might prove their worth. Within the English government itself, the blame for these disasters – and, above all, for the shocking unruliness of the commons – was levelled at Somerset. After a power struggle which lasted several weeks, he was arrested on 11 October and sent to the Tower three days later. His place as the king's dominant councillor was soon taken by Warwick.

The fall of Somerset and the military deadlock which set in over the winter opened the way for peace with France and Scotland. Formal negotiations began in January and the Treaty of Boulogne was signed on 24 March 1550. Boulogne was returned to France at once, but Henri II was forced to pay a ransom of 400,000 crowns (£140,000) – far less than had been agreed in 1546, but far more than he wanted to pay. Matters with Scotland were more complex, but the last two English forts in Scotland were finally abandoned and demolished after the agreement of a subsidiary treaty at Norham in June 1551. Shortly afterwards, it was agreed that Edward's abortive engagement

Poor troops by 1550
vagrants be

Treaty at Norham June 1551
Scots fort demolished [43]

to Mary Queen of Scots should be supplanted by his betrothal to Elizabeth, the 6-year-old daughter of Henri II. These agreements finally concluded the wars which Henry VIII had launched in 1542 and 1544, and which Somerset had partially renewed in 1547. They reflected the utter defeat of every English ambition except defence of the realm itself: expanding English territory on the Continent by even a single small French port had proved unbearably demanding; Scotland had defeated every effort to draw it within England's orbit and had instead become a virtual satellite of France; and England itself now began to dance awkwardly to France's tune. This comprehensive failure had also come at a terrible price. Henry's wars had cost well over £2 million and the military expenses of Edward's reign – principally from Somerset's revival of Henry's wars – were reckoned at over £1.3 million by late 1552, excluding another £170,000 spent on maintaining English rule in Ireland. Somerset's war in Scotland had swallowed £600,000 (almost twice what Henry had spent there, 1542–47), while even the suppression of the 1549 risings cost over £27,000. The human cost, and the indirect effects of such vast expenditure upon the realm, cannot be quantified. However, the result of Henry's wars was plain enough. Even before the events of the summer of 1549, Sir William Paget had warned his colleagues on the council of the realm's growing demoralisation: 'all thinges in maner goinge backewarde and unfortunately and every man almoste out of harte and corage, and our lackes so well knowen as our enemies despise us and our frendes pitie us'. It was a far cry from Henry VIII's bellicose optimism of 1543–44.[45]

Military Exhaustion, 1550–57

Peace provided a blessed relief for the battered Edwardian regime, especially as the realm continued to be troubled by rumours of imminent new 'stirs' at home and tensions abroad with Charles V over England's Protestant Reformation. The challenge now was to maintain some kind of national military capability despite the shambolic state of the crown's finances and the realm's economic and political woes. Warwick's government was not helped in this task by the run of bad harvests which struck between 1549 and 1551, forcing up the

Norham
1551

cost of food, and the fierce outbreak of sweating sickness which hit the realm in 1551.[46] England's great export trade in woollen cloth, which was worth twice the value of royal revenues and linked the economic fortunes of London and Antwerp, also collapsed in 1551–52 – in part, because of the cumulative impact of debasement, which had slashed the relative cost of English cloth and stimulated over-production. In the longer term, one result of this dramatic slump was to encourage London merchants to diversify their business activities, spawning a new interest in long-distance, and even transoceanic, trade and exploration. This would have profoundly important consequences during the reign of Elizabeth. In the short term, however, the crash of the cloth market merely added to the realm's economic misery.

By 1551, Warwick and his colleagues finally recognised the necessity of ending debasement and stabilising the coinage. This involved minting new coins with a higher silver content and recognising the lesser value of the old debased coins by 'crying down' their official value. Unfortunately, the announcement of lower values for debased coins was badly bungled. The need to build new fortifications at Berwick and Calais also encouraged the government to seek one last desperate windfall from debasement – worth £114,500 between April and July 1551 – before issuing new coins with an increased silver content in October. The whole process was clumsy, at best a partial success (since the base coins remained in circulation, encouraging the hoarding of good coins) and testimony to the terrible burden which even reduced military spending still placed upon royal finances. Nevertheless, it meant that future English governments would have to fund major military spending without the 'holy anchor' which had proved both such a blessing and a curse. Paying for wars and repaying foreign loans would henceforth depend ever more heavily upon selling more of the crown's dwindling supply of ex-monastic lands and taxing a population which was now becoming decidedly tax-averse.[47]

The remainder of Edward VI's short reign demonstrated that this financial strait-jacket, drawn even tighter by the need to repay accumulated war debts, would permit only limited military expenditure. Some foreign mercenaries were retained to bolster the garrisons at

Berwick and Carlisle on the northern borders, but defences along the southern coast were deliberately run down. Spending on the navy seems to have been fairly consistent, but many of the king's warships were hired out for commercial use to save money, especially after the outbreak of war between Charles V and Henri II in late 1551 ended any immediate threat to England. The regime's boldest military initiative, after months of debate, was the creation in February 1551 of a permanent corps of 850 cavalrymen for protection of the king, 'the staie of the unquiet subjectes, and for other services in all eventes'. Although paid quarterly by the crown, these so-called 'gendarmes' would serve in separate bands recruited and controlled by 12 aristocrats, ten of whom were members of the council. Paraded in London in December 1551 and May 1552, 'ther cottes in brodery of yche lord's colors', these soldiers gave the government the nucleus of an army to confront an enemy invasion and the means to prevent a repeat of the events of 1549. Yet even this precious resource soon had to be sacrificed for the sake of economy. As a result, when the sudden death of Edward plunged Dudley (who had been created duke of Northumberland in October 1551) into a struggle for the throne with Princess Mary in July 1553, he lacked the immediate military muscle to overawe Mary or to dissuade large numbers of noblemen and gentry from joining her cause, egged on by a groundswell of popular support. Although Northumberland finally scraped up 1500 men to march against Mary's host in East Anglia, his force was so badly outnumbered and demoralised that he could not risk a battle and meekly surrendered on 24 July. This failure cost him his head on 22 August.[48]

Despite the tide of enthusiasm which swept Mary to the throne, her government found itself facing the same basic problems which had bedevilled the Edwardian regime. For all Northumberland's economies during 1552–53, Mary still inherited a debt from Edward VI of £185,000, which required further cuts in military expenditure, including reductions in the garrisons of the Pale around Calais. These financial problems were made more difficult because Mary also granted away lands and revenues to the Church as part of her drive to reverse her brother's religious policies and to reunite England with the Church of Rome. A major overhaul of the crown's financial administration in 1554 made little immediate impact on the situation and serious improvement required the steady repayment of foreign loans, heavy taxation in 1555–57, peremptory demands for 'loans' from wealthier subjects in 1556–57 and further retrenchment. There was even another small burst of debasement, although it was carefully restricted to Ireland. Despite these impositions, Mary's privy council was deeply aware that they oversaw a battered realm which was still struggling to overcome the effects of war. These concerns were powerfully reinforced by the impact of terrible harvests in 1555–56 and a virulent 'new ague' (probably influenza) which exacted a calamitous toll upon the realm. The years 1557–58 and 1558–59 saw the highest per capita levels of mortality in English history between 1541 and 1871.[49]

Mary's reversal of Edwardian religious policies also extended to the realm's diplomatic orientation. Her marriage to Philip of Spain, the son of Charles V, which was foreshadowed in late 1553 and celebrated in July 1554, ended England's alienation from the Habsburgs which had lasted, off and on, since Crépy in 1544. The match proved highly controversial because it raised the prospect that England would become subservient to Spain in the same way that the intended marriage between Edward VI and Mary Queen of Scots might have subordinated Scotland to England. In the event, Mary failed to conceive an heir and Philip proved content to abide by the marriage treaty which protected English interests. However, the fear of excessive Spanish influence prompted a dangerous rebellion in January 1554, which reached London before it was overcome.

 Unlike the risings of 1549, Sir Thomas Wyatt's rebellion was driven by disaffected members of the landed élite. Some of the leaders were also veterans of the old garrison at Boulogne. When 600 men of the London militia were sent into Kent to crush the insurrection, the militia captains refused to attack their old comrades in arms and instead brought their troops over to Wyatt's side. Although aristocrats and gentlemen loyal to Mary scrambled together more than 2000 of their own troops to defend London, uncertainty about the loyalty of many of the government's forces sparked wild rumours of treason when the leading rebels simply marched past the soldiers and cannon arrayed at St James's fields and approached the City gates.

Perhaps only the fear of Londoners that the Kentish men might sack the City and Mary's own determination not to flee, despite the urgings of her councillors, ensured that Wyatt finally met resolute resistance. Although a few dozen of his followers were killed in clashes, Wyatt chose to surrender rather than risk a pitched battle without local support. Mary's government had survived, but her realm's lack of enthusiasm for the Spanish match, which the rebellion had revealed so alarmingly, remained a source of anxiety until the end of the reign. Mary's marriage to Philip also put the realm on course for fresh conflict with France, with whom Charles V was already at war. England remained aloof from this conflict, but the French reinforced their hold on Scotland when Mary of Guise – the mother of Mary of Scots – became regent there in April 1554. Henri II also offered some support for English exiles who plotted to depose Mary and replace her on the English throne with Princess Elizabeth.[50]

In response to this potential French threat and because his own strategic interests required a strong English naval presence in the Channel (to protect the sea route between his territories in Spain and the Low Countries), Philip encouraged Mary's government to begin improvements to the navy. At the time of Henry VIII's death in 1547, the crown had owned 53 ships of all sizes, displacing a total of 11,265 tons. By late 1555, the fleet was down to 30 vessels. However, this decline was not as disastrous as it appears, since much of the reduction reflected the disposal of ships which were no longer worth the cost of their upkeep. More importantly, this retrenchment was balanced by the revival of naval construction, beginning with two new large warships – the *Philip and Mary* of 500 tons and the *Mary Rose* of 600 tons. This was critical because the navy had endured a virtual 'procurement holiday' since the furious building and purchase programme of 1544–46. Given the government's straitened circumstances, it was a clear sign of national priorities.

The commitment to laying down new warships is also significant because it shows that the revitalisation of the fleet had begun before Philip's dramatic intervention with the privy council in September 1555. When the council declared that no warships were available to escort Charles V's ship through the Channel, Philip exploded in fury and lectured the councillors on the critical importance of English

48 Elizabeth's Wars

seapower. Since 15 ships were ultimately provided as an escort, it seems that the problem was less about naval readiness than cost. Although it is difficult to chart Philip's precise role in the (literal) rebuilding of the navy, it is likely he played an important part in triggering an overhaul of its administration. During the closing years of Henry VIII's reign, unexpected deaths and the pressures of war had encouraged the creation of a new board of officials to oversee naval administration with proper salaries and clear lines of responsibility – the 'admiralty' or 'council of the marine', which later became known as the Navy Board. This streamlined the running of the navy and ensured that the fleet was administered by experienced seafarers rather than distant bureaucrats, but provided insufficient clarity about how the growing naval budget was to be spent. In the wake of Philip's tirade to the council, new checks were imposed on naval expenditure, culminating in a major change on 8 January 1557. Henceforth, the navy would receive a fixed budget for repairs and building instead of irregular allocations for specific purposes, permitting confident forward planning. However, the treasurer of the navy now also became directly responsible to the lord treasurer, who alone could authorise warrants for the navy, while the lord admiral could only offer 'advice' on expenditure. In effect, the navy would now report to the lord treasurer and the effectiveness of a lord admiral – who retained oversight of operations and maritime justice – would depend upon striking a partnership with the lord treasurer. This was a very telling reflection of the central importance of financial administration for military operations.[51]

Mary's War, 1557–58

By 1557, Philip had succeeded to many of his father's dominions and was locked in war with France. He expected English aid in this war, but few of the privy council shared Mary's enthusiasm for supporting Philip's cause. This changed after a small band of English exiles landed at Scarborough on 23 April under the leadership of one Thomas Stafford, who called upon Englishmen to throw off the Spanish yoke. Stafford was promptly arrested, tried and executed, but the blame for the insurrection was directed at France, from whence he had sailed.

Although Henri II protested his innocence, previous French involvement in conspiracies against Mary made the charge seem credible and the privy council quickly endorsed the queen's decision to declare war. There are many curious features about Stafford's bizarre voyage to Scarborough, and it seems entirely possible that he was only able to land in Yorkshire because agents of Mary's government wanted an overt act of violence which could be used to justify a declaration of war on France. If the landing was the result of an English 'special operation', it performed its function perfectly, although the realm seems to have greeted the new war with little real enthusiasm.[52]

Ironically, one of the few groups in England which genuinely welcomed the war were those men who had previously won disfavour from Mary's government, such as the surviving family and followers of the late duke of Northumberland and some Protestants like the earl of Bedford. For them, military service offered a path to rehabilitation. Many of these men joined the force of soldiers and pioneers which was raised to reinforce Philip's great multinational army in June and July. Like Henry's force of 1544, this expeditionary force, which was commanded by the earl of Pembroke, was composed of aristocratic retinues – the last time that an English army was sent abroad entirely based upon the 'quasi-feudal' system. Although they did not reach the front line at St Quentin until after the French had already been defeated, the English contingent participated enthusiastically in the final assault which captured the town. About 18 per cent (1299 men out of 7128) were wounded, invalided or prematurely discharged through sickness by the time the campaign was over.

There was less opportunity for glory on the border with Scotland, where the summer and autumn were punctuated by alarms about French or Scottish troops preparing to invade northern England. In the end, much to the despair of the French, the Scots mustered but refused to launch an invasion. Like the English, they were profoundly weary of war. Nevertheless, England's northern borders seemed distinctly vulnerable, especially as the French now threatened Berwick with a powerful fort which they had built on the ruins of the old English base at Eyemouth. Fortunately, the onset of winter seemed to guarantee several months' respite from serious action.[53]

Scotland 1557 1558.

This assumption was proven wrong in dramatic fashion when the French duke of Guise launched a surprise attack on Calais with an army of over 30,000 men on 1 January 1558. Although English reinforcements had been sent to Calais during the summer of 1557, these had been withdrawn to save money over the winter, allegedly leaving a garrison of only 500 soldiers and 200 armed townsmen. Surprise and frozen marshes enabled the French to seize Rysbank, the fortress which controlled sea access to Calais, on 2 January. This cut Calais off from any reinforcement by sea, rendering the desperate efforts in England to ready ships and men almost irrelevant. In the event, no serious effort was made to ship across large numbers of troops to relieve or recover Calais until 9 January, when a storm hit the Channel. The storm lasted for days and was so fierce that sailors complained 'the devil was raised up and become French', forcing the abandonment of relief efforts. Philip might have sent aid to Calais by land, but the only troops he sent – a mere 200 arquebusiers from neighbouring Gravelines – were repulsed on 6 January. Calais Castle fell the next day, despite desperate English efforts to recover it, and the governor of Calais, Lord Wentworth, felt compelled to seek terms the same night. Overwhelming numbers, well-handled siege guns and a bungled defence allowed the French to achieve in a week what had taken Edward III eleven gruelling months in 1346–47.

Elsewhere in the Pale, the fortress of Hammes was abandoned on 10 January, but Guisnes (which had newly rebuilt fortifications) held out grimly under the veteran Lord Grey until 21 January. The fighting there was so fierce that when Grey's son Arthur went to parley with the French, he had to scramble over a bulwark covered with 'naked and new slayne carckasies, som of them yet sprawlyng and grownyng under owre feet'. It was later claimed that 800 Englishmen and over 4000 French troops were killed before Grey surrendered the fortress in return for honourable passage home for all the surviving defenders, except the officers.[54]

The sudden loss of the Calais Pale shocked England. The London undertaker Henry Machyn spoke for many when he described the news as 'the hevest tydyngs to London and to England that ever was hard of'. Like the burnings of Protestants which had now become so unpopular, the loss of Calais was widely blamed upon the Spanish, who were accused of failing to save Calais and inducing the queen to enter this unnecessary war in the first place. Although unfair, such sentiments reflected the stirrings of a virulent Hispanophobia in England which would become enormously powerful during Elizabeth's reign. In strategic terms, the fall of Calais meant that England had lost its most heavily fortified base, which had served as both its gateway into France and its chief bastion against French aggression. Only the Tower of London was more important – barely – for national security and the business of government. The vast stocks of arms and munitions at Calais, together with its mint, harbour and wool market, were now gone. There was also a deep psychological impact. Calais had been the last remaining prize of the Hundred Years War and its loss represented the final collapse of the tradition of successful war against France which Henry VIII had sought to revive and embellish only 14 years earlier. Henry's wars had demonstrated that England was not strong enough to expand its beachhead in France, but Mary's war had lost that beachhead altogether. For the first time in centuries, the sovereign of England now held no territory in Continental Europe.[55]

Given Calais' extraordinary importance to England, Mary's government made surprisingly little effort to recover it. Although orders were issued in mid-January for English troops to be raised for a joint operation with Philip's army, the whole venture soon fizzled out. Far fewer troops than were required actually turned up at Dover and those who did were poorly equipped and very different from 'the handsomest and best picked men' that had been requested. In one contingent of 1000 men at Dover and Sandwich, fewer than 200 had armour and weapons.[56] One immediate result of this fiasco was an effort to improve England's ability to man and equip armies. While it was relatively easy to revitalise the navy, since the crown itself owned and operated the warships, overhauling army structures was a political and financial problem of an entirely different order, involving the vital interests of the nobility, gentry and town corporations, and affecting nearly every subject in the realm. Inevitably, any changes were conservative and required compromise.

After much debate, new laws were passed through parliament 'for the having of horse, armour and weapon' and 'for the taking of musters'. The latter act reinforced the penalties for subjects failing to attend musters and officials corruptly excusing men from service, while the former introduced a new income scale which specified which weapons must be owned by all subjects worth at least £5 a year. However, in seeking to solve old problems, the parliament created new anomalies. Although they still controlled considerable wealth, the clergy were exempted from the requirement to provide weapons, while an even heavier burden was placed upon the nobility and wealthy gentry. There were contradictory provisions about the control of musters and no provision at all was made for raising money to pay for training costs or the filling of community armouries (for the use of men worth less than £5 a year). The new arms requirements also ensured that most subjects would be equipped with old-fashioned bows and bills and that only a limited proportion of the militia would be equipped with guns and pikes. The 'horse, armour and weapon' act also merely blurred the distinction between the militia and the 'quasi-feudal' systems and did nothing to resolve the contradictions between them. In many ways, therefore, the Marian reforms were distinctly unsatisfactory and would cause serious difficulties during the reign of Elizabeth. Nonetheless, the acts did ensure that the realm retained an irreducible minimum level of military capability and marked an improvement on the former arms requirements which dated back to 1285.[57]

Although they were debated with urgency, the new arms and musters statutes brought little immediate benefit to England's struggling war effort. When Philip's representatives tried to revive English interest in a combined campaign to recover Calais in late January, they were shocked by the privy council's sense of pessimism. 'How desirous soever we be to recover Calais', the council informed Philip, raising and sustaining 20,000 troops for the new operation was entirely beyond England's capacity. Not only were there insufficient men available, but funding the effort – which would add £170,000 within five months to war costs which already included £150,000 a year for existing garrisons and £200,000 a year for the navy – would require politically dangerous levels of taxation. According to the council, all the realm's resources were needed simply to defend its coastline and northern borders. These claims of England's enfeeblement were undoubtedly exaggerated – partly out of irritation with Philip's demands and partly out of demoralisation – but they reflected real problems. Most obviously, the realm was being wracked by the combined effects of dearth and disease, which killed perhaps 200,000 people between 1557 and 1559 and must have incapacitated many more for extended periods. God, it seemed, was punishing England and the loss of Calais was merely another sign of divine disfavour. With the demands of work and food production taking immediate priority, local communities were unwilling to release many of their healthy men for military service. When the government did manage to raise men to serve at sea or on the Scottish borders, an alarming number of them promptly deserted.[58]

Despite these problems, however, the navy at least continued to perform well. English warships helped to thwart a French advance on Gravelines in July, sailing close to the shore to bombard the enemy troops with their cannon. Shortly afterwards, the fleet even launched a major offensive operation with Philip's forces, when 7000 troops were landed for an attack on the French port of Brest. The intention was that Brest could be seized as a bargaining chip to win the return of Calais, but the local defenders offered such stout opposition that the operation had to be abandoned.[59] This extinguished Mary's last faint hope of recovering Calais. By the time she died on 17 November 1558, it was already clear that diplomacy could not succeed where English arms had failed. As Mary's successor, Elizabeth I would now have to confront a hostile France without the shield of Calais and all that it represented.

2   The Burden of War: operations and developments, 1558–c.1572

Elizabeth I came to the throne in November 1558 accompanied by a bow-wave of adulation and relief, but her realm remained demoralised by the effects of war and anxious about the prospects of further conflict. Although fighting had been suspended and peace talks had begun, England was still technically at war with France. Its relationship with Philip II of Spain – the realm's king-consort until Mary's death and sovereign of a vast agglomeration of Habsburg territories in Spain, Italy, the Low Countries and the New World – was also distinctly uncertain. It was a sign of how far English perspectives had changed since the giddy optimism of 1544 that one observer likened the kingdom and its unmarried new queen to 'a bone thrown between two dogs' – the object of contention between western Europe's two superpowers whose ultimate reward would be the toothy embrace of the victor.[1] In fact, this may have exaggerated England's importance, especially to Philip, who had more urgent concerns in the Mediterranean. The most immediate danger to England emanated from France, which retained its hold on Scotland and had a direct interest in Elizabeth's crown after Mary Queen of Scots – Elizabeth's cousin and heir apparent – married Henri II's heir, Francis, in April 1558. If Elizabeth died or was toppled from power, France now had both motive and means to intervene. For Philip, Henri II's bitter rival, this was an unpalatable prospect. However, Philip was also appalled by the new Elizabethan regime's determination to abandon England's Catholic revival and to reimpose the Protestantism of Edward VI's reign. Philip ultimately put his rivalry with France ahead of matters of religion during the critical early years of Elizabeth's reign. But, at the time, the fear that Spain might become openly hostile or even join France in seeking to reimpose Catholicism on England seemed very real.

Elizabeth's government finally made peace with France as part of the Treaty of Cateau-Cambrésis of April 1559 which ended the war between Philip and Henri. The cost of peace was signing away Calais, although the treaty contained the face-saving clause that France would return Calais to England in eight years' time in return for payment of 500,000 crowns. Henry VIII had conceded a very similar clause concerning Boulogne in the the Treaty of Camp of 1546, confident that it was merely window-dressing by which French diplomats could disguise the permanent loss of Boulogne. At Cateau-Cambrésis, the boot was on the other foot. However, unlike the French with Boulogne in 1546, no one – including Elizabeth and her privy council – seriously believed that England might be able to reconquer Calais. Cateau-Cambrésis was also important because the willingness of Europe's two great Catholic powers to make peace was seen by many Protestants as signifying the start of a new crusade against the Protestant communities which were now emerging as a significant political force in France, Scotland and the Low Countries. Although erroneous, this belief – that there was an international Catholic conspiracy against Protestants which superseded even the bitter dynastic rivalry between France and Spain – reflected the new mode of ideological politics which was beginning to dominate European affairs.

This had profound implications for Elizabeth's government. In a world in which Catholics fought Protestants, there could be no compromise over whose interpretation of God's 'truth' was correct. Such wars would be long and cruel and could not be ended merely by a token victory which satisfied a sovereign's royal ego. Despite occasional tactical truces, religious wars would have to continue until one side was able to extirpate the 'heresy' of its enemy. It was also apparent that the coming conflicts would not simply be between rival realms, as in the past. Although England officially became a Protestant state again at virtually the same time that it signed the Treaty of Cateau-Cambrésis, the other Protestant communities of north-western Europe lived within the territory of states which were officially Catholic. For them to take up arms would entail rebellion against their prince. This posed an acute dilemma for Elizabeth, to whom these Protestants soon began to look for support. While she was concerned about the fate of fellow Protestants, Elizabeth also shared her father's preference for dealing with fellow anointed sovereigns – and hence disliked all rebels on principle – and recognised the practical dangers of being seen to condone rebellion abroad when so many of her own subjects still remained Catholics.[2]

The emerging new world of ideological warfare and dissident minorities made England's obvious military and financial weakness a matter of critical vulnerability. Elizabeth's government therefore took immediate steps to import military necessities from the Continent. The key role in this operation was played by Thomas Gresham, Elizabeth's chief agent in Antwerp, who arranged large purchases of arms and munitions in the Low Countries and Germany and oversaw their transportation to England. This was an especially delicate task because it had to be done in secret. Unlicensed arms exports were illegal in the Low Countries and Elizabeth's government was anxious to conceal its urgent need for weapons. Many of Gresham's arms were routed through Germany and shipped home in small consignments. Elaborate precautions were taken to ensure secrecy in England, while foreign customs officials were systematically bribed to turn a blind eye. As Gresham explained: 'well fares that peny geven that saves one hundred!'. By 1560, his purchases amounted to a staggering £108,956 and included 18,000 corslets, 33,000 assorted guns, 6000 pike heads, 16,000 bowstaves, 60,000 weight of match and 420,000 weight of gunpowder. Gresham's full shopping list shows that England was still dependent on imports for virtually every item needed for war, including the essential components for making gunpowder. The huge scale and cost of these purchases – which reached £139,000 by 1562 – emphasise how desperately weak England's defences had become after almost two decades of draining warfare. Despite inheriting a debt of almost £300,000 from Mary, Elizabeth and her council felt compelled to spend over £100,000 in a crash programme to restock the realm's armouries, even though it required raising massive new loans in Antwerp to cover the cost.[3]

False Dawn: Scotland, 1559–60

The need for Gresham's costly new supplies was underlined in May 1559, when Scottish Protestants rose in rebellion against Mary of Guise, the French regent who controlled Scotland while her daughter, Mary Queen of Scots, remained in France. Two months later, Henri II was killed in a jousting accident, which brought his young son to the throne as Francis II and made Mary Queen of Scots the queen of France. This opened the way for the duke of Guise and his brother, the cardinal of Lorraine – Francis II's uncles by marriage – to take effective control of France. Guise had been scarred in the face by an English lance at Boulogne in 1545 and had exacted his revenge by seizing Calais in 1558. He was also a Catholic zealot and eager to advance Mary Queen of Scots' claim to the English throne, encouraging her to adopt heraldic devices which asserted that she – and not Elizabeth – was the rightful queen of England and Ireland. Elizabeth therefore faced a serious threat from France which seemed destined to spark another war, as well as the more immediate problem of how to respond to appeals for help from the Scottish Protestants. Given the battering which England had taken in the last war against France, the realm's lack of military supplies and the continuing impact of influenza and plague, initiating a new war seemed a desperate prospect. However, failing to prevent a French victory over the Protestants in Scotland would not only unleash terrible repression there, but also give France a secure base to invade England across its weakly fortified northern border. Despite increasingly urgent efforts to strengthen the defences at Berwick in recent years, professional military opinion held that England's key fortress in the north was still far too weak to resist a serious attack by the French.[4] This meant that England could not simply ignore events in the north and trust in its own defences, even if Elizabeth overlooked the fate of fellow Protestants.

Elizabeth's response to this terrible dilemma was to adopt the sort of indirect approach which would become typical of the new wars of religion. Covert aid was sent to the Scottish rebels in the form of money – initially only in French coins, to avoid suspicion – and arms. Larger sums were given as loans, but the queen's agents were instructed to arrange things 'as of your selve[s] . . . so as the quene shuld not be a partie therto'. When the Scots sought experienced offi-cers for their army, Sir William Cecil, the queen's secretary of state and the chief advocate of an aggressive policy in Scotland, suggested that English officers might go as volunteers, but only as individuals who pretended that they had been denied employment at home. Like the rest of the operation to aid the Scots, the emphasis was upon ensuring that Elizabeth could deny involvement if anything went wrong – what is today known as 'plausible deniability'. As Cecil told Sir Ralph Sadler and Sir James Croft, the two men in charge of the operation in the north, 'ye must compass this matter indirectly by practise [i.e. deception]'. However, this sort of covert support became increasingly inadequate as the French began to regain the upper hand and the Protestants lost heart. Matters became even more acute in December 1559, when it was reported (erroneously) that French forces were reoccupying the fort at Eyemouth. This alarmed the privy council because Eyemouth was 'Berwick's chief enemy' and its reoccupation would be in direct contravention of Cateau-Cambrésis, suggesting that the Scottish war was about to escalate into a full-scale conflict between England and France. This prospect finally ended the bitter debate over intervention in Scotland which had divided the privy council. Sir William Winter was now ordered to sea with 34 warships and instructed to deliver supplies to Berwick, before sailing north to the Forth of Firth. There he was to impose a blockade and prevent French reinforcements reaching Scotland, under the pretence of acting on his own initiative. This stretched plausible deniability to breaking point, but the ruse succeeded long enough to serve its purpose. Four thousand troops were also ordered to Berwick. This was explained to the French regent in Scotland as a purely defensive measure, but the privy council intended this deploy-ment to prepare the way for an attack on Leith, where most of the 3000 French troops in Scotland were awaiting reinforcements from home. The council hoped that Winter's blockade would hold long enough for English and Scottish forces to overwhelm Leith in the same way that the French had overrun Calais two years earlier.[5]

Orders to put this plan into effect were issued on 25 December 1559, but Elizabeth cancelled them three days later. Instead of a where van Hunsdon ?

lightning strike in the dead of winter, she ordered the forces gathering on the northern borders to delay any offensive action. Elizabeth may have been correct in this decision because the winter weather made it impossible to assemble sufficient cavalry until the end of January. More importantly, though, she harboured deep misgivings about embarking upon any kind of serious military operation. In the light of recent history, she was understandably anxious about the outcome and cost of the campaign. She also recognised that going to war would require her to delegate her royal authority to distant commanders and weaken her control over events. As an intelligent, but unmarried, young woman – a status which would have placed her under the tutelage of a male relative, had she not been queen – the extent to which she could control events was profoundly important. Elizabeth had already shown that she deeply resented being lectured to by her male subjects and was beginning to feel her way towards a style of man-management which encouraged a certain amount of jostling for her favour among the councillors and courtiers, preventing them from forming a united front to push her into policies which she did not like. However, war presented an insidious challenge to her control of affairs. Not only was war the quintessential 'men's business', but its successful prosecution also required unity of purpose, which risked encouraging a collusive solidarity between the privy council and the commanders at the front, since men experienced in war might presume to have a better grasp of events than their female sovereign. Going to war therefore involved a potential battle of wills between Elizabeth and her male advisers and commanders – and virtually every campaign during her reign would demonstrate the reality of these fears. For Elizabeth, waging war would always entail a more subtle domestic struggle over the exercise of royal authority, as she sought to dictate the actions of her distant commanders and the privy council sought to inhibit her from making unrealistic demands upon the commanders or from undermining their confidence by excessive criticism for failing to meet those demands.

Elizabeth's last-minute decision to delay action in Scotland and seek a diplomatic solution was undoubtedly seen by some councillors as female hesitancy. Cecil, in particular, took it very badly. For

Lee sent to explain affairs at the front.

him, the Scottish operation was not merely a response to the French threat, but also a unique opportunity to implement the sort of 'British' policy which he had first espoused when he served as the duke of Somerset's secretary. As he had urged Croft earlier in the year, 'kindle the fire [in Scotland], for if it be quenched the opportunity will not come again in our lifetime'. Cecil was so dispirited by Elizabeth's decision that he drafted a letter asking her to release him from further involvement in Scottish affairs. Although the details remain obscure, Cecil remained at his post, but failed to change the queen's mind. It was only in mid-February, after it was clear that the latest French attempt to ship reinforcements to Scotland had been defeated by bad weather and Winter's ships were in control of the Forth, that Elizabeth permitted her agents in the north to negotiate a treaty at Berwick which committed England to open intervention on behalf of the Scottish Protestants. By then, she undoubtedly also knew that Protestants in France were about to launch a *coup* against the Guise family, although it is unclear whether she or her ambassador to France actually encouraged the action. The so-called Tumult of Amboise was a total failure, but it helped to ensure that no more French troops could be spared for Scotland. Elizabeth also learned from the envoys whom she sent to Spain that she had nothing to fear from Philip II. Far from making common cause with France against Protestant England, Philip was so hostile to France – and so anxious to keep the English Channel open to ships sailing between Spain and the Low Countries – that he even offered military assistance if England were attacked. Nevertheless, it was not until 28 March that an English army of 6000 foot and 1200 cavalry finally marched into Scotland under the old war-horse Lord Grey and headed for Leith.[6]

Grey, who had been freed after the fall of Guisnes in 1558 by payment of a ransom, was vastly experienced, but lacked the self-confidence required to cope with the conflicting demands placed upon him.[7] On the one hand, Elizabeth still sought a diplomatic solution, even though this required negotiation with Mary of Guise and the avoidance of precipitate action, whilst fuelling Scottish fears that the English would abandon them. On the other hand, Grey received letters and messengers from the court and from the duke of Norfolk at Berwick which urged him to deal with Leith quickly. Grey also had to face a redoubtable French opponent who used his large garrison to launch frequent and unsettling sorties against the English. The defences of Leith itself, which had been rebuilt by the French, were enormously strong. Even though the English and Scottish forces grew to over 8000 men (although the queen was actually paying wages for over 12,000), the besieging army remained too small to sustain multiple siege batteries, which allowed the defenders to concentrate their efforts against a single point of attack. 156①.

The result of this combination of contradictory pressures was perhaps inevitable. When Grey was finally given unambiguous directions to capture Leith in late April, he responded to the demand for speed by rushing preparations for an assault upon a single inadequate breach. The assault was launched early on 7 May 'with greater courage than preparacion'. Although the attackers struggled in the breach for over an hour, its defenders were too strong and the failure to neutralise firing positions around its flanks exposed the English troops to 'a very hell: nothinge was sene but fire and smoake, nothinge was heard but roareing of shot'. Elsewhere, attacking troops found that their assault ladders were at least six feet too short, leaving those who climbed them as easy targets even for 'the Frenchmen's harlots', who helped the garrison by hurling stones, wood and 'burning fire' at the attackers. By the time they retreated, perhaps 500 English troops had been killed out of the 7000 men who took part. Despite the courage of individual soldiers, the whole action was 'marvellously ill handled' by Grey and his officers – exhibiting the same chronic lack of professionalism which had been evident earlier in the campaign, when a lengthy consultation was required before English gunners were allowed to fire back at French cannon emplaced in church steeples. When the news of the débâcle reached court, Cecil was mortified and Elizabeth exploded in fury, but all agreed that the siege must continue. Reinforcements were sent and Grey prepared to starve the defenders out, aided by Winter's continuing naval blockade. Within weeks, the French garrison was reduced to gathering shellfish from nearby beaches. The death of Mary of Guise on 11 June further disheartened the garrison. Cecil subsequently travelled north and negotiated a formal peace. According to the Treaty of Edinburgh, signed on 6 July, all French and English

attack of Leith. failed
siege succeeded.

[handwritten: 6 July 1560 Treaty of Edinburgh.]

troops were to leave Scotland, the French fortifications at Leith, Dunbar and Eyemouth were to be demolished and the regency of Scotland would pass to a council of 12 Scottish noblemen. When a Scottish parliament subsequently enacted a Protestant Reformation during August, the collapse of the French position in Scotland was complete.[8]

This success finally allowed Elizabeth's government to tackle the long-postponed task of reversing the effects of debasement under Henry VIII and Edward VI by withdrawing the base coins from circulation and converting them into new coins which had the higher silver content of pre-1544 currency. The process began in September 1560 and was largely completed by the end of 1561. The revaluation of the currency gave a fillip to trade – and hence to royal customs revenues – and the conversion process itself brought the crown a tidy profit (despite public claims to the contrary).[9] However, the chief impact was psychological. By this action, Elizabeth's government reversed the most egregious example of the damage which had been done to England by the wars of the 1540s and 1550s. If the debasements of Henry and Edward had literally devalued the royal image and sent shockwaves of uncertainty through the tangled webs of debt and credit which sustained the realm's cash-starved economy, Elizabeth's restoration of the coinage was an assertion that those dark days were over and that the nation's honour had been revived.

[handwritten: Revaluation of Coinage]

Fiasco in France, 1562–63

Although it staved off a crisis and cleared the way for reforming the currency, the close-run victory in Scotland did not solve England's problems with France. Indeed, French plans to reverse their defeat in Scotland were not finally shelved until Francis II sickened and died at the end of 1560. This broke the Guise stranglehold on power in France and left Mary Queen of Scots a youthful widow, ultimately resulting in her reluctant return to take up the reins of government in Scotland in August 1561. In France, the manoeuvring over power increasingly edged towards civil war between moderate and hardline Catholic parties (the former focused on the crown, the latter led by the Guise family) and their Protestant enemies, led by the prince of

Condé and Admiral Coligny. Inevitably, the leaders of the French Protestants (known as Huguenots) sought support from England, especially after the duke of Guise massacred those attending a Protestant service at Vassy in March 1562. Elizabeth was very wary of becoming entangled in French affairs and again looked for a diplomatic solution. However, the Guisans were in no mood for compromise and the Huguenots looked increasingly vulnerable. For Cecil, this raised the prospect of a Catholic victory and a nightmare scenario in which the duke of Guise would not only renew his push for Mary Queen of Scots to supplant Elizabeth as queen of England, but would also link up with Philip of Spain to crush Protestantism across northern Europe.

Cecil had previously argued against open involvement in French affairs, recalling the disastrous consequences of England's adventure at Boulogne: 'God forbid that she should enter into the bottomless pit of expense of her force and treasure within the French king's own mainland.' Now he and the rest of the privy council urged the queen to aid Condé before it was too late. Elizabeth received similar advice from Robert Dudley, a son of the late duke of Northumberland and the queen's favourite courtier. The intensity of Dudley's personal relationship with Elizabeth had caused a scandal in 1560, forcing them to pull back for the sake of propriety. Now Dudley's stout support for Condé provided him with a platform to make his mark in public affairs. In October 1562, he was appointed to the privy council, where he would continue his staunch advocacy of English aid to Protestants abroad – from September 1564, as earl of Leicester – for the next quarter-century.[10]

Faced with a consensus among her advisers in favour of supporting the Huguenots, Elizabeth gradually moved towards intervention in France in the same fashion she had in Scotland. Again, the initial concern was to ensure plausible deniability. In July 1562, English warships were ordered to patrol the coast of Normandy under the cover of apprehending pirates. With the connivance of English authorities, bands of English (and Scottish) soldiers began to join the Huguenot defence of Rouen as individual 'volunteers'. By October, there were probably 500 of these soldiers of fortune in Normandy. Small sums of money were also delivered to the Huguenots by semi-official

1562

agents of the queen. Nevertheless, Condé needed far more substantial help and appealed to Elizabeth for a loan to hire German mercenaries. This opened the way for serious haggling during July and August which shaped the terms of official English intervention in France. According to a treaty signed with Condé's representatives at Hampton Court on 20 September, Elizabeth would loan the Huguenots 140,000 crowns (£42,000). As security for this loan, the Huguenots would give the English control of Havre de Grâce (modern Le Havre, but called Newhaven by the Elizabethans), a Norman port which Francis I had built for his wars against Henry VIII and which controlled access up the River Seine to Rouen and Paris. The queen would also supply 6000 troops, half of which would garrison Newhaven. The other 3000 would be available to support the hard-pressed Huguenot defenders at Rouen. Although Elizabeth had serious misgivings about committing troops in France, no doubt recalling the shambles at Leith two years earlier, she was convinced by her advisers of the need to act and was captivated by the prospect that Newhaven could be held as a bargaining chip to secure the return of Calais. This made the intervention in Normandy very different from that in Scotland. Instead of merely aiding their co-religionists to counter the menace of Guisan aggression, Elizabeth and her council hoped to use the French civil war to reverse England's humiliation of 1558.[11]

It was not long before the central contradiction in English policy – supporting the Huguenots as allies and yet expecting them to acquiesce to the national disgrace of returning Calais – was exposed. Even before the treaty was signed, many Huguenots were unhappy at the idea of the English again occupying French territory. This prospect became even less appealing after English troops began arriving in France in October, but failed to save Rouen. After a siege lasting five months and which ultimately involved over 30,000 besiegers, the city walls were breached and Catholic forces began an orgy of killing and plunder. Only a few hundred English and Scottish troops reached Rouen before the final assault, most of them independent volunteers. Although the surviving soldiers in official English pay may have been ransomed, many of the volunteers suffered for their lack of formal status and were promptly executed or sent to the galleys. By the time

Le Have – Newhaven

the bulk of the English army arrived in France under the command of Ambrose, earl of Warwick (Robert Dudley's older brother), there was precious little scope for positive action. Although a subsidiary garrison was established at Dieppe, it was quickly withdrawn because the town proved indefensible. Matters became even more confused after the main Catholic and Huguenot armies clashed in a bewildering and bloody battle at Dreux in December, which saw Condé captured. In one of the most bizarre episodes of the French Wars of Religion, Condé and the duke of Guise actually spent the night in the same bed because there was only one bed available befitting their illustrious noble rank, even though they were bitter enemies. Condé subsequently began to negotiate with his Catholic captors, while Admiral Coligny, who remained free, demanded more English aid. Two months later, the duke of Guise was mortally wounded, removing the most zealous opponent of peace between Catholics and Huguenots. By the end of March 1563, the two warring sides had agreed a temporary reconciliation and began to turn against the English intruders. A combined French army massed to recover Newhaven by force.

Bed.

The fundamental weakness of the English position now became painfully apparent. Although reinforcements were desperately rushed to Newhaven to strengthen Warwick's garrison, the town's defences had been designed to resist attack from the sea rather than a landward assault. Trusting in the support of their Huguenot allies, Warwick's troops did nothing to improve the defences until it was too late. Even worse, persistent problems with pay and supplies were now compounded by the outbreak of plague. By the end of June, the garrison was reduced to below 3000 and lost 500 men a week to desertion and disease. A month later, after enduring three days of bombardment, the position had become utterly hopeless. The town's walls were collapsing, while a major naval effort to relieve Warwick's force was thwarted by foul weather and French guns were making it impossible for warships to enter the harbour. On 28 July, Warwick surrendered on generous terms which allowed him to take home all his surviving men and their equipment.[12]

The Newhaven expedition was an unmitigated disaster. Although it may perhaps have buttressed the Huguenot position at a critical period, the attempt to regain Calais by holding Newhaven alienated even England's Protestant allies and resulted in a costly new embarrassment for English arms which compounded the humiliation of 1558. Warwick's returning troops – demobilised as rapidly as possible to save money – also brought the plague back to England with them, adding thousands of civilian deaths at home to those who had already died in France. Over 20,000 died in London alone. If this terrible toll were not bad enough, the peace treaty which was agreed with France in April 1564 effectively ended English claims upon Calais, in return for a token payment of 120,000 crowns – less than Elizabeth had lent the Huguenots, let alone what she had spent on military operations.[13]

Despite its demoralising outcome, the Newhaven expedition confirmed new procedures by which English and Welsh men were impressed for military service abroad. Although the Marian legislation of 1558 effectively reiterated the legal ban on members of the county militia – in effect, all men aged between 16 and 60 – being forced to fight overseas, Elizabeth's government simply ignored this embarrassing impediment and acted on the presumption that the crown could override such statutory limitations by virtue of military necessity. Crucially, an overwhelming majority of aristocrats, landed gentlemen and town officials agreed with, and supported, this policy. Levies of men for military service abroad therefore combined a proportion of volunteers, who presented themselves to recruiters (who announced their arrival in a town by the sound of a drum), and a far larger number of men who were involuntarily conscripted ('pressed') by the local authorities, in order to fill out their required quota of fresh recruits. During the final weeks of the siege of Newhaven, when the pressure to raise new soldiers quickly was most intense, London officials even pressed inmates of Newgate prison to help meet their quota. In contrast to the Henrician levies of the 1540s, when militia troops had been sent to France or Scotland under the leadership of local landlords and in the company of their neighbours, the Elizabethan system focused upon local authorities meeting specific numerical targets, almost regardless of how the recruits were raised. The new recruits also served under captains who were appointed by the privy council and, consequently, often strangers to the county.

This recruitment system was far from ideal in military terms and generated endless complaints by the privy council and by commanders in the field, but it worked, albeit imperfectly and sometimes with difficulty. Although an attenuated version of Henry VIII's old 'quasi-feudal' system still survived in the form of aristocratic officers raising cavalry units and small numbers of footmen for their own retinues, it was the legally questionable system of impressment which provided the great mass of raw human material for the armies sent abroad during the remainder of Elizabeth's reign.[14]

The Cost of War, 1559–69

By the time the Newhaven expedition was wound up, Elizabeth's expenditure on military emergencies had reached almost £750,000 in only four years. In addition to the £139,000 spent on Gresham's arms purchases, the intervention in Scotland in 1559–60 had cost about £230,000 (including £85,000 for the navy), while strengthening Berwick and maintaining a large garrison there cost £103,000 between 1560 and 1563 (and would cost another £153,000 before the watch on the northern borders was reduced in 1567). The Newhaven venture cost £250,000, excluding the £42,000 loan. Such enormous expenditure was only possible because of massive borrowing on the Antwerp money market – £306,113 by April 1562 and almost £500,000 by 1564. This level of indebtedness was clearly unsustainable, especially when tensions between Elizabeth and Philip's regent in the Low Countries began to threaten England's financial standing in Antwerp. However, repaying the debts was not easy. Although the crown lands had shrunk alarmingly over the past decade or so, the demands of war and creditors required fresh sales – £260,000 worth by 1565, alienating £12,000 a year of income.

On a more positive note, Elizabeth benefited from a controversial decision by Mary's government in May 1558 to boost the value and reach of customs duties. This added about £50,000 a year to the crown's revenues. In the longer term, it also gave the Elizabethan regime greater incentive to avoid open war, since conflict simultaneously reduced customs dues and demanded heavy spending, whereas peace fostered taxable trade. Most of the queen's extra income was

early debts until 1574 ensured
that parsimony became ingrained.

raised by taxation, thanks to new parliamentary subsidies granted in 1559 and 1563, which produced almost £500,000 by 1566. Nevertheless, royal finances remained so stretched that the government sought a new subsidy from parliament in 1566, even though this breached the convention that a subsidy would only be granted during wartime. This request was ultimately approved, but the turmoil in parliament about Elizabeth's continuing refusal to name an heir or marry prompted her to remit a third of the expected yield of the new tax, forcing the government into fresh economies. This confirmed what had already become apparent – that the huge early expenditure on war, and the burden of debt which it had created, now required England's government to operate within a tight financial strait-jacket. By the time the last of the queen's debts were finally cleared in 1574, this enforced economy had become a deeply ingrained habit, ensuring that parsimony remained a dominant characteristic of the Elizabethan regime.[15]

Given the hefty debt it inherited from Mary, Elizabeth's government had always tended towards frugality. In the early months of her reign, for example, the 'ordinary' navy budget (which had been set at £14,000 per annum in 1557) was cut to £12,000 and the garrison in Ireland was trimmed back to reduce annual expenditure there from £27,000 a year to £20,000. The desire to contain costs also helps to explain why neither Grey's army in Scotland nor Warwick's at Newhaven included any foreign mercenaries. Nevertheless, the sweeping post-war cuts of the mid-1560s demonstrated a new and enduring concern for economy. In 1563, warship construction was halted and the 'ordinary' navy budget was slashed to £5714 in February 1567 by removing victuals to a separate account. It remained at this level, nominally at least, until 1587. Expenditure in Ireland, which ballooned to £47,550 by 1566–67, was cut by two-thirds by 1568–69, although such limited spending could not be sustained for long. Expenditure on Berwick, which averaged over £36,000 a year 1560–67, was reduced dramatically by cutting the garrison by two-thirds and curtailing further improvements to the fortifications. From 1567 until the end of the reign, spending on Berwick remained at £15,000 a year. Even the queen's own household was not immune from the quest for economy. Although swingeing cuts

corruption in the ordnance.

proved difficult to implement, regular crackdowns on 'waste' ensured that the household budget was pegged under £50,000 a year until at least the mid-1570s.[16]

One of the indirect legacies of the Newhaven campaign was therefore a pervasive sense of financial stringency and a concern to avoid incurring new liabilities. More obviously, the bitter experience of Newhaven reinforced Elizabeth's doubts about the efficacy of open warfare, especially as English troops had again performed poorly. It also made her deeply sceptical about the promises of foreign Protestants who sought English aid. In contrast to some of her leading councillors, who believed that England was unavoidably involved in an undeclared struggle with the Catholic powers, Elizabeth refused to frame her policies in religious terms. Chastened by the experience of Newhaven, she resolved always to minimise risk and to shape her future actions according to calculations of *realpolitik* rather than religious solidarity. Nevertheless, the queen's strategic and religious interests meant that she could not simply abandon the Protestants of France (or the Low Countries): their defeat would surely expose England to the attentions of ambitious Catholic conquerors. The lessons of 1562–63 therefore encouraged a return to the sort of indirect and deniable actions which had preceded open intervention in Scotland and Normandy. Over the next two decades, Elizabeth would occasionally provide loans to Huguenot or Dutch leaders, including almost £70,000 to the Huguenots in 1568–69 alone – a telling sign of the queen's determination to prevent the defeat of her co-religionists, notwithstanding her straitened financial circumstances. More typically, though, Elizabeth's government simply permitted French or Dutch exiles living in England to offer private assistance to their comrades abroad. Some of the queen's more 'forward' (i.e. zealous) subjects also shared in this effort. Despite the gruesome fate of those captured at Rouen, a steady stream of English volunteers went to fight in France, a trend which Elizabeth's government studiously ignored and tacitly encouraged. Among these Protestant adventurers were young men like John Norris and Walter Ralegh, for whom the French wars were a nursery of martial experience. They would feature prominently in the later wars of Elizabeth's reign.[17]

John Smyth:

Poor performance of English troops

For their part, French (and later Dutch) Protestant leaders encouraged English support by issuing letters of reprisal which gave English merchants and gentleman investors a legal fig-leaf for otherwise naked piracy against the ships of their Catholic adversaries – an increasingly lucrative activity in which the English government could technically deny any involvement. Although officially neutral and consistently anxious to avoid open entanglement in Continental conflicts, Elizabeth's regime sought to protect its strategic interests and to aid its co-religionists abroad by turning a blind eye (and occasionally even extending a helping hand) to unofficial, low-level involvement in the European wars. These were Elizabethan England's 'unofficial' wars, characterised by private initiative and semi-covert support for Protestant dissidents in states with which England was formally at peace.[18]

Ireland, 1534–76

If Elizabeth's government had re-learned the lesson that England could not risk open warfare against Continental enemies, it also experienced the difficulties and frustrations of fighting a very different sort of war in Ireland. The English crown controlled only about a third of Ireland, including the Pale which centred upon Dublin, but aspired to control the whole island, especially after Henry VIII laid claim to be 'king of Ireland' in 1541. Ideological, economic, religious and strategic reasons reinforced this aspiration, but it put English soldiers and settlers on a collision course with the many Gaelic lordships which occupied the rest of the island. Although numerous schemes were advanced for the total Anglicisation of Ireland – most of them originating from authors based in Ireland, who stood to benefit from the subjugation of the native Irish – there was no consistent government policy of conquest. Except in moments of crisis, Ireland always ranked very low among the priorities of the English government and the idea of outright conquest seemed neither practical nor necessary. Instead, successive English governors in Ireland sought to extend the authority of Dublin into the Gaelic territories in a piecemeal fashion, utilising a fluctuating (and often counter-productive) mix of diplomacy, legalism and military intimidation.

The low priority accorded to Ireland not only reflected how little events there seemed to affect England, but also the poor prospects which it offered for easy success. Beyond the lowlands of the Pale, much of Ireland was covered in hills, bogs and woods, which greatly reduced the effectiveness of heavy cavalry, pikes and longbows. Such terrain made straggling columns of footmen (unless escorted by cavalry) dangerously vulnerable to attack from light horsemen or native infantry armed with javelins and unencumbered with armour. Even more than in Scotland, major military operations in Ireland were also susceptible to supply problems, since the English-controlled portion of the island lacked sufficient grain, horses, arms or money to support a large army. Serious campaigning was critically dependent upon a steady flow of supplies across the Irish Sea – a task which stormy weather and organisational problems could all too easily make a logistical nightmare. Frequent shortages of supplies and pay meant that English troops in Ireland were notoriously ill-disciplined and prone to desertion. These problems were made even worse by the chronic corruption of English military officers in Ireland, who were often happy to exploit their position in the same way that the officers of Boulogne were alleged to have done – holding back soldiers' pay for their own benefit, arranging the cheapest possible food, regardless of its quality, and claiming pay for more men than actually served in their ranks, leaving the unit dangerously under-strength if it ever faced combat. The captains enjoyed unusual freedom of action because English troops in Ireland were usually dispersed into separate small garrisons and because senior military officials were equally irresponsible, holding their posts for life and determined to squeeze the maximum financial benefit from them, despite the military consequences. The fact that a corrupt, incompetent and openly Catholic official such as Jacques Wingfield could retain charge of the ordnance office – responsible for the supply and maintenance of all artillery in Ireland – from 1558 until 1587, despite regular absenteeism, and still be allowed to arrange the transfer of the office to a friend underlined how little the government in England really cared about military efficiency in Ireland. Although complaints to the English government about the conduct of officers and officials in Ireland were legion, they were usually stifled by the intervention of courtiers and councillors anxious to protect their friends or relatives. Except when some emergency arose, the overriding concern of Westminster was minimising the cost of the garrison in Ireland. So great was the desire to cut costs in Ireland that debasement of the coinage began there years earlier than in England and continued until the Elizabethan revaluation of 1561. With the end of debasement, cost-cutting became even more important in the relentless quest for economy.[19]

The English garrison in Ireland was more like a heavily armed police force than an army of conquest. Before the mid-1590s, there were rarely more than 1500 or 2000 troops in the queen's pay in Ireland. These numbers were occasionally doubled or tripled when the English authorities in Ireland became involved in a serious conflict with an Irish lord – what the English crown termed a 'rebellion' – but the reinforcements were withdrawn as quickly as possible to save money. Irish leaders could often field larger numbers of soldiers than the English lord deputy, although not for long periods. Most Irish soldiers were light infantry called *kerne* (from *ceatharnaigh*: 'warband'), who fought 'naked' – that is, without armour, but also sometimes almost literally unclothed – using swords and javelins. The governments of Henry VIII and Protector Somerset, desperate for additional troops to fight the French and the Scots, had employed some of these men in the 1540s, but found it necessary to train them as arquebusiers to make them fully effective in open warfare. Even so, firearms did not become common in Irish armies until late in the century. The heavy infantry in Ireland were known as 'gallowglasses' (*gallóglaigh*: 'foreign warrior') and were originally Scottish mercenaries who had settled in Ireland. They traditionally wore helmets and armour and used two-handed swords and long axes, but increasingly began to use the pike, imitating the shift which had occurred in Scotland at the start of the sixteenth century. Like their counterparts in Scotland, gallowglass infantry were highly effective against native horsemen, who placed a higher premium on mobility than armour. Riding on light horses and without stirrups, Irish cavalry wielded their spears overhand, rather than couched like a lance. Irish lords in Ulster, in particular, were also able to supplement their forces by hiring extra mercenaries from the Highlands and Western Isles of

Scotland. Unlike the gallowglasses, these so-called 'new Scots' or 'redshanks' stayed in Ireland only for the fighting season. Like the *kerne*, the redshanks were light infantry who fought bare-legged, although a higher proportion of them seem to have wielded the short bows which were common to Scotland and Ireland (in contrast to the longbows of Wales and England). Renowned as doughty fighters, the redshanks were also available by the thousand, making them a serious problem for the English government. Indeed, one of the few demands which England made in return for its support of the Scottish Protestants in 1560 was their support in stemming the seasonal flow of redshanks into northern Ulster. However, Elizabeth's government failed to grasp the opportunity to stifle the activities of the redshanks, despite the willing support of the earl of Argyll, and suffered the consequences for the remainder of the century.[20]

The establishment of a substantial English garrison in Ireland was a result of the Kildare rebellion of 1534–35, which destroyed the long-standing English policy – in effect since the 1470s – of delegating royal authority in Ireland to the local earls of Kildare and removed the protective buffer which Kildare's lands and soldiers had provided between the English Pale and the Gaelic Irish. By the end of Henry's reign, this produced conflict with the O'Mores and O'Connors in Leix and Offaly, who became the chief target for the Irish version of Somerset's 'garrisons' policy in 1547. This resulted in the invasion of these territories and the establishment of Forts Governor and Protector (later renamed Philipstown and Maryborough) and other less elaborate new fortifications in 1548. The costs of defeating the Irish in Leix-Offaly and maintaining these new garrisons meant that the aggressive policies of the Edwardian government soon became unsustainable, especially as they spurred Irish overtures to France, sparking rumours of French intervention in 1550–01 which required expensive preparations for coastal defence. This forced the English government into sharp economies and it was not until late in Mary's reign that a new effort was launched to clear the region for English settlement. The legal groundwork for the new plantation was laid by the simple expedient of declaring the O'Mores and O'Connors as rebels in June 1557, making their land forfeit to the crown. However, continuing resistance meant it was not until the mid-1560s that the most recalcitrant clansmen had been hunted down and English land-lords and soldier-settlers seated in their place. Even then, the planta-tion continued to be an active war zone until the last O'Mores were treacherously massacred by English settlers in 1578. The running sore of Leix-Offaly is significant not only because it was the largest colonising venture by the crown during the middle of the century, but also because it typified the experience of the English army in Ireland, with persistent guerilla warfare, punitive raids and summary executions. For the military officers who led these brutal sweeps, the business of 'colonisation' was highly attractive: under martial law, those commissioned to execute the law were entitled to one-third of the possessions of dead 'rebels', which gave them a distinct incentive to increase the body-count of 'suspected traitors'. Local collaborators had a similar incentive to boost the death-toll because they received a set fee for every dead 'rebel' as 'head money'.[21]

In addition to such police actions against relatively weak (albeit stubborn) opposition, the English in Ireland occasionally encoun-tered more formidable enemies. In the early years of Elizabeth's reign, the greatest threat was posed by Shane O'Neill, whom the crown refused to recognise as earl of Tyrone because he was not the heir of the previous earl according to English law, even though he was recognised as 'the O'Neill' by the members of his clan. Shane aspired to dominate Ulster and was the target of costly campaigns by English troops in 1560, 1561 and 1563, which achieved nothing beyond slaughtering thousands of cattle. Despite his willingness to fight openly against Irish enemies, Shane consistently avoided a pitched battle with the English. This was deeply frustrating because he posed a serious threat. Not only was he bullying the other clans of Ulster and raiding the Pale, but he also renewed overtures to France, offering the crown of Ireland to Charles IX in return for French assis-tance to expel the English and defend Catholicism. The size of Shane's army – which allegedly included 1000 horsemen and 4000 foot – forced Elizabeth to boost the forces of her new lord deputy, Sir Henry Sidney, to over 3000. Sidney launched his offensive in September 1566. While a naval force entered Lough Foyle and landed 700 troops to establish a new fort in Shane's rear at Derry, Sidney himself marched into Ulster from the south with 200 cavalry, 1200

English foot and 300 gallowglass mercenaries, cutting a swathe of destruction through Shane's heartland. Both actions severely dented Shane's prestige, especially when his furious assault on Derry was repulsed with very heavy casualties. Ironically, the fort was destroyed by mischance when its powder magazine exploded in April 1567, forcing its abandonment and the evacuation of the survivors. However, this misfortune was matched by Shane's own disastrous defeat against the O'Donnells a month later. Unwisely, he turned for aid to his old enemies, the MacDonnells, who promptly killed him. An Irish knife achieved what years of serious campaigning by English forces had failed to accomplish. Perhaps 3500 men had been killed and £100,000 been spent in fighting Shane. Yet this terrible price purchased little satisfaction. Shane's title as the O'Neill passed to Turlough Luineach, who prepared for a new round of conflict with the English by marrying the sister of the Scottish earl of Argyll, thereby gaining ready access to a steady supply of redshanks and laying the basis for a future alliance with the MacDonnells.[22]

The death of Shane O'Neill had barely permitted some relief for Elizabeth's exchequer before growing English pressure on southern Ireland provoked a backlash in Munster. In the absence of the earls of Desmond and Ormond, who had been held in England since 1565 for engaging in a private war, followers of both earls became increasingly anxious about their own futures and were infuriated by the landgrabbing activities of English adventurers like Sir Peter Carew, Humphrey Gilbert and Richard Grenville, who had established private settlements on lands confiscated from the Irish for their allegedly 'defective' legal titles. In the summer of 1569, James Fitzmaurice Fitzgerald, the 'captain' of Desmond's soldiers, led 2000 men to destroy Grenville's settlement at Kerrycurrihy, before marching to besiege Cork. A parallel rising further east around Carlow, Kilkenny and Wexford was led by Sir Edmund Butler, Ormond's brother, partly out of antipathy towards Sidney and Carew and partly as a family power-struggle against Ormond himself. However, neither force was able to capture a town and, despite committing numerous atrocities against their enemies, the Butlers were soon forced to surrender to Ormond, who rushed home from England and demonstrated his loyalty to Elizabeth by executing over 160 of the former rebels.

Fitzmaurice's force also soon melted away as a vengeful Sidney marched to the relief of Cork. The whole of Munster was placed under martial law and Humphrey Gilbert slaughtered men, women and children, piling up their severed heads outside his tent to terrify visitors. Sir John Perrot executed another 800 Irish between 1571 and 1573. Yet, despite such brutality, Fitzmaurice remained at large. In the end, Fitzmaurice only submitted when he learned that Desmond had been released to return home. In 1575, he fled abroad to seek the military support from foreign Catholic powers for which he had waited in vain during his rebellion.[23]

The Fitzmaurice rebellion caused enormous suffering across southern Ireland, but things could have gone much worse for the English if Turlough Luineach had kept his secret promise to Fitzmaurice to raid the Pale when Sidney marched south. However, such restraint did not prevent Turlough Luineach from becoming a target of the so-called 'enterprise of Ulster'. This scheme involved private investors being given royal grants to occupy selected parts of Ulster, with the multiple aims of creating settlements which would bring landed wealth and status to the investors, inhibiting the seasonal flow of redshanks into Ulster from Scotland, weakening the power of the O'Neills and, ultimately, bringing the Irish those 'benefits of civilisation' which could be derived from working a plough rather than herding cattle. Unlike in Munster, where men like Carew, Gilbert and Grenville operated against a background of strong English influence, the settlers in Ulster would have to seize control of their designated lands 'at their own charge and perils', like English conquistadors. In effect, the English government had reacted to the burdensome costs of Ireland by privatising the future penetration and settlement of Ulster.

The first of these private colonial enterprises was launched in 1571 by Sir Thomas Smith, the former Edwardian councillor who had been recalled to serve Elizabeth. Although Smith and his investors recruited 800 soldiers for their venture, delays and desertions meant that only 100 remained when Smith's son landed on the Ards Peninsula in August 1572. By the time Smith's son was killed in October 1573, it was apparent that the expedition was a failure. Two further expeditions in 1573 and 1575 fared even

English settlements in Ireland

worse. Despite this, Walter Devereux, first earl of Essex, sought to launch a far larger 'enterprise' in 1573. Rallying support from many of England's aristocratic families, and accompanied by many of their younger sons, Essex launched a huge effort to occupy Antrim. Mortgaging his English lands to the queen for £10,000, he recruited and armed over 1000 men. Yet even this force proved inadequate for the task of controlling the land when faced with resolute local opposition. Like earlier English expeditions into Ulster, Essex found the Irish unwilling to offer battle, but adept at springing ambushes. Essex appealed to Elizabeth for aid and was reinforced for 1574 by 300 veterans of the war in the Low Countries and a similar number of raw recruits, all paid for by the crown. Essex's total force approached 3000, including 700 cavalry. Yet the new campaign again achieved no decisive success and Essex resorted to desperate measures to break the Irish resistance before his finances collapsed and his army fell apart. In October, he treacherously arrested Sir Brian MacPhelim O'Neill at a feast and ordered one of his captains, John Norris, to massacre 200 of the Irish chieftain's unarmed followers. Essex again lashed out in desperation in July 1575, using three of Francis Drake's ships to ferry Norris's troops to Rathlin Island, where the wives and children of the MacDonnells had been sent for safety. When the 200 defenders surrendered, they were massacred by Norris's men, who subsequently swept the island, killing another 300 men, women and children, as well as 300 cattle, 3000 sheep and 100 stud mares. Such brutality reflected both the soldiers' frustration at being unable to strike a decisive blow against the Irish and Essex's realisation that these expeditions would cost him many of his ancestral lands in England. By the time Essex died of diarrhoea in Dublin in October 1576, none of the 'estates' which he had tried to plant were viable and the Ulster venture had proved a catastrophic failure for the earl and his investors, not to mention his Irish victims. The whole exercise had not even saved the crown money: in trying to support Essex's private wars, the queen had been forced to spend no less than £87,000. The experiment of relying upon private enterprise to fight Elizabeth's wars in Ireland had proved to be a disaster.[24]

Essex 1st Earl *senior* affairs in Ireland.

Public Investment and Private Enterprise

The resort to private wars in Ulster demonstrated the belief of Elizabeth's government that Ireland was a burdensome sideshow which warranted severe (and ultimately counter-productive) cost-cutting. However, the experiment had also seemed like a logical extension of the partnership between private enterprise and the state which characterised many activities of the era, especially those concerning England's aggressive maritime expansion in the 1560s and 1570s. In part, this expansion was driven by the efforts of English merchants to find fresh opportunities after the slump of the cloth market at Antwerp in the early 1550s, which encouraged new trade with Russia and the Baltic (the only source of many commodities essential for ship-building), as well as the Levant, Italy, the Barbary coast and West Africa. This urge to diversify trade became even stronger after Philip II's government in the Low Countries sought to punish England for its support of foreign Protestants by imposing a ban on English wool and cloth in 1563–64. This caused severe distress in both countries, but weakened England's remaining economic dependence on Antwerp and inadvertently helped to radicalise politics in the Low Countries.[25]

The brief trade war also confirmed the belief that England's security required government action to stimulate the local manufacture of products essential to its economic and military capacity. In an age of religious war, national self-sufficiency in strategic materials seemed a vital goal, even if it could never be fully achieved. A range of schemes were advanced during the 1560s which sought to combine local raw materials with imported expertise to manufacture products under the protection of royal monopolies. Most of these ventures involved the active participation of privy councillors and courtiers, who were able to secure the necessary grants from the queen and hoped to combine national benefit with personal profit. Although efforts to mine alum (used in dyeing cloth) proved a failure, German metalworkers were employed to produce copper wire (used for carding wool) and brass (used for armaments and domestic ware). Another German, Gerard Honrick, was contracted in 1560 to build gunpowder mills, introducing a hitherto secret technique to manufacture

Home production of armaments

saltpetre from local materials. This helped to reduce England's chronic dependence on imported supplies, but it was insufficiently productive to obviate the need for continuing secret imports of saltpetre, such as those from Morocco during the 1570s. A slightly different form of state intervention was the enactment of legislation in 1563 which mandated the eating of fish on Wednesdays – known mockingly as 'Cecil's fast' because of Cecil's vocal advocacy of the measure. This was intended to bolster the fishing industry and consequently to boost the number of vessels and seamen which the realm could mobilise in time of war.[26]

By far the most successful example of state-sponsored industrial development arose from the earlier efforts of Henry VIII to establish cannon manufacture in England. Although the best cannon were made from bronze, these were very expensive and (despite the mining efforts launched in the 1560s) dependent upon imports of copper. This had presented a real problem when the new coastal fortifications of 1539–40 and the build-up of warships required an unprecedented number of new guns. The solution came from a technical breakthrough which enabled Henry's gunfounders to make iron cannon, which were vastly cheaper. By 1543, William Levett, the rector at Buxted in Sussex, had mastered the process for large-scale production and was able to accept an order in 1545 for 120 guns to be delivered over two years. By 1549, there were about 20 blast furnaces and 28 forges operating in Sussex. There were about 50 furnaces and 60 forges in the realm by 1574. Henry's wars therefore created a major armaments industry. By Elizabeth's reign, the cost and quality of English iron cannon – thanks to the secret technique of vertical casting – created a lively export market, although much of it breached the official monopoly on exports which was granted to Ralph Hogge in 1567. Illegal exports raised the prospect of guns being acquired by England's Catholic enemies rather than its Protestant allies, but the trade helped to keep the realm's forges and furnaces active. Iron was not suitable for making the big guns of royal warships, which continued to be made of bronze, but it produced perfectly serviceable small and medium guns – the sort of weapons which were needed in the greatest numbers for war and which could also be mounted on merchant ships. England's unique ability to produce good affordable

which Company? Cannon

iron cannon enabled English merchants and privateers to arm their ships more easily – and heavily – than their foreign counterparts.[27]

This proliferation of iron cannon was especially important for a second element of English maritime enterprise – piracy. Although endemic in the west country and south Wales, this had taken on a life of its own after Henry VIII issued a general licence for English ships to attack French and Scottish merchant vessels in December 1544. Piracy proved so profitable to English shipowners and the many gentlemen investors who took a financial stake in these expeditions (like Walter Ralegh's father) that even the cessation of hostilities failed to curb the seizure of foreign ships. Since the enforcement of royal policies depended upon unpaid local officials, most of whom were actively involved in the business themselves, the central government had little chance of stamping out the practice.[28]

By the 1560s, the growing tensions between Elizabethan England and the Catholic powers helped to make piracy against French and Spanish ships seem patriotic and part of the 'unofficial' wars which Elizabeth's government formally disavowed. Anti-Catholic piracy helped to create a common cause – and often fostered strong personal ties – between English captains and investors and Huguenot (and later Dutch) seafarers. This international community of Protestant adventurers not only constituted a lobby which had strong political influence in England, but also encouraged intrusions into the New World, which had been reserved exclusively for Spain and Portugal by a papal treaty of 1494. Such a monopoly was intolerable to Protestants on religious, economic and strategic grounds. Following the lead of Huguenot sailors, Englishmen began to enter the Caribbean in voyages which combined commerce with piracy. Most famously, John Hawkins launched a series of transatlantic expeditions between 1562 and 1568 in which he bought or captured slaves in West Africa and sold them to Spanish colonists in the Caribbean. Since this trading contravened Spanish law, the transactions were often conducted under the pretence of being 'forced' upon the 'unwilling' colonists by English guns. The success of these voyages therefore depended upon the hazy distinction between 'war' and 'peace' which obtained in a region far distant from Europe. The ventures were so profitable that Elizabeth herself invested in them, even providing two of the nine ships in Hawkins's expedition of 1567–68, including his flagship. This was an open affront to Philip II, but the prospect of a boost for the queen's inadequate finances seemed difficult to resist. However, Philip was determined to demonstrate that such flagrant intrusions into the New World would no longer be tolerated. When Hawkins's battered fleet arrived in San Juan de Ulúa in Mexico in September 1568, it was caught between the port's defenders and a pursuing Spanish fleet. After a prolonged stand-off, the Spanish suddenly attacked, sparking a bloody battle which resulted in the loss of all but two of the smaller English ships – one captained by Hawkins and the other by his protégé Francis Drake.[29]

Spain and the Spectre of War, 1567–72

The battle at San Juan, like the queen's willingness to seek a profit at Philip's expense, underlined the increasingly fraught relations between England and Spain in the late 1560s. While the Spanish complained about rampant English piracy and intrusion into the New World, English opinion was outraged by the arrest of English sailors by the Inquisition in Spain. More importantly, England and Spain were set against each other by events in the Low Countries, where years of tension over the centralising policies of Philip's government there fuelled a popular Protestant uprising in August 1566. Twelve months later, a Spanish army under the command of the duke of Alba arrived to reassert Spanish control in the region and extirpate Protestantism. Alba's arrival raised fears that his army might soon be employed against England, while the brutal repression orchestrated by the 'Council of Blood' confirmed the worst fears of Protestants about 'Spanish cruelty'. For Elizabeth, the problem of how to respond to events in the Low Countries was soon compounded by the behaviour of Mary Queen of Scots, who lost her throne in Scotland and fled into England in May 1568. This effectively opened up a new 'home front' in the undeclared struggle between England and its Catholic adversaries. Mary was still the heir apparent to the English throne and her arrival encouraged feverish plotting by courtiers anxious to protect the realm – and themselves – against the uncertainties stemming from Elizabeth's continuing lack of a husband. For some die-hard

Catholics, Mary's arrival even offered the prospect of displacing Elizabeth by force and re-establishing Catholicism in England. The likelihood of Spanish support for this sort of action – previously slim because of Mary's ties to France – became dramatically stronger in December 1568 after Elizabeth seized the contents of a ship carrying money to pay Alba's army. The ship and its companions had put into English ports to avoid storms and Huguenot pirates. Rather than allow the money to reach Alba, Elizabeth claimed the money – at least £85,000 worth. While she was deciding whether or not to keep the money, Alba ordered the seizure of English goods in the Low Countries, which not only confirmed Elizabeth's course of action, but triggered the retaliatory seizure of Spanish goods in England.[30]

The new trade war was far more serious than its precursor of 1563–64 because it represented an open conflict between England and the whole Spanish world, rather than merely between England and Philip's government in the Low Countries. Despite the problems over piracy and the urgings of some of their councillors who saw politics in ideological terms, Elizabeth and Philip had both sought to preserve a measure of amity between their states. By 1569, the conjunction of events meant this no longer seemed possible and both governments began to recognise the other as a real or potential enemy, initiating a cold war between England and Spain. Across the realm, general musters were ordered to check the readiness of the county militias during the late spring and summer.

From the English perspective, the hostility of Spain seemed palpable after a rebellion which occurred in the north of England at the end of 1569. The so-called Northern Rising broke out after months of furtive meetings among the Catholic members of the gentry and frequent rumours that Mary Queen of Scots would marry the duke of Norfolk. When the marriage plan collapsed in the face of Elizabeth's adamant opposition, Mary's chief supporters in the far north, the earls of Westmorland and Northumberland, feared they would be punished for their involvement. Both men also felt aggrieved about how their families' traditional influence in the north had been consistently undermined by government actions. Their leading followers, who urged them to action, felt this lost prestige and power even more acutely. When Elizabeth demanded that the earls appear at court to explain their conduct, the combination of fear and anger tipped them into a rebellion. They declared their stand by celebrating mass at Durham on 14 November and soon gathered over 5000 men, almost a third of them horsemen. However, despite its avowed intention of restoring Catholicism, the rising drew relatively little popular support, even from among Northumberland's own tenants. Although the rebels marched south towards York, it was soon apparent that they had no real plan and lacked appeal outside the northeast. One contingent seized the port of Hartlepool in the hope that troops sent by the duke of Alba might be able to land there, but they waited in vain for Spanish intervention. By late November, loyal noblemen, including the earls of Sussex and Warwick and Lord Hunsdon, were assembling a royal army which approached 20,000. As the queen's forces began to move north, the rebel force retreated and dissolved. Unwilling to confront the lumbering royal army, the northern earls returned home and then fled into Scotland, where they sought shelter with their fellow Catholic supporters of Mary across the border.[31]

While hundreds of rebels were executed in an orgy of government fury, many of Hunsdon's troops remained poised for action, in case the Marian Scots failed to hand over the fugitives. This costly display of military might seemed especially timely when the pro-English earl of Moray, who acted as regent for the infant James VI and had detained the fugitive earl of Northumberland, was assassinated in January 1570. Shortly afterwards, Leonard Dacre, a claimant to the Dacre barony, instigated the only serious battle of the northern crisis by trying to ambush Hunsdon near Naworth. Failing to wait for support from his Scottish borderer allies, Dacre attacked Hunsdon's force and was decisively beaten. Despite their 'proud' charge, several hundred of Dacre's men were killed or captured. With the fugitive rebels still being sheltered by Mary's supporters and Moray dead, Elizabeth's government launched a large raid into Scotland in April 1570 to devastate the lands of Dacre's ally, Lord Hume. English troops also accompanied the Anglophile earl of Lennox when he returned to Scotland to replace Moray as regent and joined his campaign against the Marians. When Mary's supporters still refused to recognise the authority of Lennox's pro-English Protestant regime,

Edinburgh
Castle

1570

another destructive raid was launched into Scotland in August,
which ultimately forced them to give way. One result of the crisis created by the Northern Rising was therefore the termination of any
hope that Mary might be restored to the Scottish throne and the reinforcement of England's ties with the Protestant regime in Scotland.
Even though the Marians were not finally neutralised until after the
earl of Morton succeeded Lennox as regent in 1572 and 1500 troops
had to be sent to help Morton's government capture Edinburgh
Castle in 1573, England's northern border was effectively protected by
the actions of 1570.[32]

However, by far the most important consequences of the
Northern Rising concerned Catholicism, the future religious com-
plexion of Elizabeth's regime and the threat posed by Spain. The
seizure of Hartlepool and the later interrogation of Northumberland
revealed that the rebels had been in contact with the Spanish ambassador in England, Don Guerau de Spes, and had ultimately pinned
their hopes on Spanish military support. Although de Spes's promises proved to be empty and none of Alba's troops stirred from
Flanders, the Northern Rising demonstrated that England now faced
the real prospect of a Spanish invasion. This danger seemed even
more pressing after it was learned in mid-1570 that Pope Pius V had
issued a papal bull deposing Elizabeth on the grounds of heresy and
absolving Catholics from loyalty to her government. In effect, this
meant that good English Catholics must become traitors to
Elizabeth. This was a political disaster for Catholicism in England,
raising the spectre of Romanist fifth-columnists aiding a foreign
invasion. Although Elizabeth herself remained willing to trust
Catholics who proved their loyalty, the danger encouraged her councillors to treat the realm's large remaining pockets of Catholicism as
a threat to national security and to reconstruct the regime along
increasingly Protestant lines. In many parts of the realm, Catholic
gentlemen were steadily squeezed out of local office and replaced by
reliable Protestants. Many Protestant gentlemen – and women – also
conscientiously supported puritan ministers, whose Calvinist theol-
ogy was despised by the queen, but who had the virtue of being viru-
lently anti-Catholic. The puritans became the most insistent
preachers of the anti-papal, anti-Spanish message which was central

to a new Protestant 'super-patriotism' which emerged in England during the 1570s.

If Elizabeth and her councillors – not to mention the great mass of her subjects – still harboured any doubts about the danger posed by Spain, they were dispelled by the revelation of the 'Ridolfi Plot' in October 1571. This conspiracy involved plans of baroque complexity for the arrest or assassination of Elizabeth, the marriage of Mary to Norfolk (or, alternatively, Don John of Austria), a diversionary landing of Spanish troops in Ireland, a mass rebellion orchestrated by Norfolk and other lords to restore Catholicism in England, and the use of English ships to transport Spanish soldiers into England from Spain and the Low Countries. The whole unwieldy scheme – or, rather, series of schemes – was probably betrayed to Cecil (who was created Lord Burghley in February 1571) from the outset by Thomas Stukeley and the Florentine banker, Roberto Ridolfi. Almost certainly, the offer by John Hawkins to defect to Spain with a fleet of ships was also a sham, intended only to secure the release of his men who had been captured at San Juan de Ulúa. Once the prisoners were freed, Hawkins immediately informed Burghley how his offer to betray Elizabeth had been approved by Philip himself. Yet, however empty of substance these plans might have been when they were first mooted, the consequences of Philip and his councillors taking them seriously were profound and long-lasting. Thanks to de Spes's enthusiasm and Philip's own sympathy for Mary and impatience with Elizabeth, Spain had clearly committed itself to toppling Elizabeth, even if it required her assassination – and Elizabeth and her councillors now knew it. Although Elizabeth refused to put Mary on trial for her part in the conspiracy, despite howls of fury from the parliament which met in 1572, Norfolk was executed for his involvement in the affair and de Spes was expelled from England.[33]

Another consequence of the crisis of 1568–71 and the Spanish hostility towards England which the Ridolfi Plot had revealed was greater English maritime aggression towards Spain. In part, this was a result of the Spanish embargo on English ships and goods, which forced merchants to pursue profit by other means. However, English maritime penetration of the New World, in particular, was also driven by open hostility towards Spain. At least 13 new expeditions were launched into the Caribbean between 1570 and 1577. The goal of these voyages was no longer trade. Weighed down by their increasingly heavy batteries of iron cannon, English ships now set out to plunder Spanish ships and settlements. By far the most notorious of these privateers was Francis Drake, whose insatiable quest for loot and revenge for the events at San Juan de Ulúa encouraged him to make repeated sweeps along the Panama isthmus, where huge quantities of silver and treasures from South America were brought across from the Pacific coast on mule trains for shipment to Spain. Drake attacked Nombre de Dios, the silver trail's Caribbean terminus, in 1572 and again in 1573. Although the raids brought him little profit, they caused grave alarm in Spain because the finances of the whole Spanish monarchy depended upon the safe arrival of American treasure. The danger seemed so acute that Spain was forced to spend substantial sums to reinforce its defences in the region.[34]

The desire to wrest a greater share of this vast wealth from Spain also encouraged more ambitious schemes. Although earlier Huguenot colonies had been brutally destroyed by the Spanish, potential investors lobbied the queen for permission to establish English enclaves which could tap the land and riches of the New World and provide strategic bases for intercepting Spanish treasure ships. Significantly, many of the advocates of these schemes, such as Richard Grenville and Humphrey Gilbert, were also involved in the various attempts to colonise Munster and Ulster. This helps to explain the piratical nature of English private adventurers in Ireland, who expected easy profits and quickly resorted to extreme brutality when the Irish proved unwilling to comply with their demands. However, Elizabeth was much less willing to approve the establishment of colonies in the New World than in Ireland. Although Grenville was granted approval in 1574, the queen swiftly reversed her decision. This underlined the schizophrenic nature of the cold war with Spain. Despite the brazenness of Drake's privateering, such actions were entirely unofficial and even illegal. Elizabeth was willing to connive at Drake's piracy because it suited her strategic interests, produced money for the royal coffers and remained 'deniable'. By contrast, granting a royal patent to establish English settlements in territories claimed by Spain and Portugal – however unreasonable

those claims might seem to Protestant minds – breached the requirement for plausible deniability and pushed the 'unofficial' conflict
between England and Spain too close to the threshold of open war.[35]

The Low Countries, 1572–74

Calculations of national interest and acceptable risk proved far more
difficult to establish in relation to the Low Countries, where the
stakes were much higher and consensus among the queen's advisers
correspondingly more elusive. During the late 1560s, Elizabeth was
prepared to allow Dutch Protestants to launch attacks on Spanish
shipping from English ports and to ferry men and munitions across
the Narrow Seas. However, the most conspicuous group of Dutch
seafarers, the Sea Beggars, proved increasingly troublesome, provoking loud complaints from foreign merchants and even attacking
English ships. The growing alliance between the Dutch Protestants
and the Huguenots was also worrying because it raised the prospect
of excessive French influence in the region, especially when the
Dutch leader, William of Orange, agreed a plan with Admiral
Coligny and Charles IX for a full-scale French invasion of the Low
Countries in 1572. Although the earl of Leicester and Sir Francis
Walsingham (then English ambassador in France, but soon to be
appointed secretary of state) were passionately committed to the idea
of an international Protestant cause and were willing to support the
scheme for the sake of destroying Alba's bloody regime and 'liberat-
ing' their Dutch co-religionists, other key advisers such as Burghley
and the earl of Sussex shared Elizabeth's profound alarm at the idea.
For them, permitting English Protestants to assist the Huguenots in
their civil wars in France and providing sanctuary for Dutch exiles
was one thing, but allowing the Huguenot alliance with Dutch
Protestants to trigger a French occupation of the Low Countries was
quite another. Given her difficulties with Spain, Elizabeth was eager
to ensure that England itself enjoyed good relations with France – a
diplomatic initiative which resulted in the Treaty of Blois in April
1572 – but the idea that France might control the whole Continental
coastline around England was utterly unacceptable. Quite apart from
reducing future English diplomatic options and imperilling the

restoration of trade with Antwerp, this would leave the realm almost surrounded by a power which had a far longer and deeper history of conflict with England than Spain. The recent tensions with Spain still paled in comparison with the bitter wars which England had fought with France during the previous 50 years.

Elizabeth was consequently very wary when the Sea Beggars shattered Alba's control of the Low Countries and unexpectedly reignited the Dutch Revolt by occupying the ports of Brielle (Den Brielle) and Flushing (Vlissinghen), following their expulsion from England in March 1572. Glad to be rid of the Dutch trouble-makers, she initially restricted support from England to that provided by Dutch exiles. Although 300 English and Welsh volunteers were at Flushing by the start of June, it was not until early July – when French forces were flooding into the region – that Sir Humphrey Gilbert took a larger contingent of 1200 troops to join the fray. England's unofficial intervention in the Low Countries was not so much to aid the Dutch – although the soldiers who went may have believed this was their goal – but to forestall French domination. While Walsingham, in particular, hoped that Gilbert's arrival would be merely a prelude to full and open support for the Dutch, Elizabeth was worried the imminent French invasion might sweep away Alba's regime and take control of the region. Given the choice between French or Spanish domination – a third option, Dutch independence, was still utterly impractical – Elizabeth preferred the devil she knew. Such was her concern to prevent French dominion over the Low Countries that Burghley suggested offering Alba English military support against the French invasion and Elizabeth herself raised the idea with an informal agent of the duke. For their part, the Francophile leaders of Flushing remained (rightly) wary of Gilbert's troops and initially refused even to admit them into the town.[36]

The looming Anglo-French crisis in the Low Countries was averted by the actions of Charles IX, who repudiated his recent dealings with the Huguenots in the most emphatic manner by unleashing the notorious St Bartholomew's Day (24 August) Massacres in Paris and a dozen other cities, in which several thousand French Protestants died. This eliminated the immediate French threat in the Low Countries and plunged France itself back into civil war. Animated by sympathy for their fellow Protestants and a desire to inhibit further French interest in invading the Low Countries, Elizabeth's government once again permitted – and perhaps quietly encouraged – unofficial, deniable forms of aid to the Huguenots. English volunteers again streamed into France and the comte de Montgomery was able to assemble a relief convoy for the besieged Protestant stronghold of La Rochelle in English ports. This support had to be delicately managed because, despite its profound disgust at the St Bartholomew's Day massacres, Elizabeth's government maintained its official amity with France, even renewing the Blois accords with the new French king – the conspicuously Catholic Henri III – in March 1575. This dismayed many of the queen's more ardently Protestant subjects, who were convinced by the events of August 1572 that all Protestants were threatened by the implacable blood-lust of Catholic powers. However, it was critically important for England to avoid any risk of confrontation with France when the situation in the Low Countries remained so threatening.[37]

The collapse of French invasion plans in August 1572 immediately allowed the full force of the Spanish army to be turned against the Dutch rebels and their motley collection of German, French, English and Scottish allies. The result was a northern European *reconquista* which was pursued with deliberate brutality in the hope of encouraging a speedy end to the rebellion. When rebel towns were recaptured, the surrendering garrisons were regularly put to the sword or drowned and the inhabitants severely punished, even massacred. Alba knew that Spain was already locked in a major war against the Turks in the Mediterranean and hoped to crush the Dutch before the combined cost of both wars drove the Spanish monarchy into bankruptcy. Elizabeth's government sought to defeat this bloody campaign, but deliberately restricted English aid to deniable actions which would not imperil a future *rapprochement* with Spain. Gilbert was ordered to act 'as thoughe he and his companies departed out of England thether without her Majestie's assent' and Elizabeth later made a show of banning English aid to the rebels altogether. Although another 1500 troops went to the Low Countries in 1573, the drift of official English policy was towards repairing relations with Spain, especially after Alba's experiment in terror failed and Philip replaced him with a more moderate viceroy. By the end of 1574, England and Spain had agreed an end to their trade war, even though the conflict in the Low Countries still ground on, with the rebels still grimly clinging to much of Holland and Zealand and the Spanish army beginning to falter for lack of money.[38]

By the time the cold war between England and Spain thawed into some semblance of renewed cordiality, most English soldiers had left the Low Countries. A few of those who remained, such as the Welshman Roger Williams, even changed sides and joined the Spanish army. Nevertheless, the experiences of the volunteers who fought for the Dutch rebels in 1572–73 are significant because they reveal the characteristic strengths and weaknesses of English soldiers during the first half of Elizabeth's reign. The initial 300 men who landed at Flushing in 1572 under the command of Thomas Morgan were mainly veterans of combat in France, Scotland and Ireland, and included an unusually high proportion of gentlemen adventurers (including Williams). Not surprisingly, this tough unit acquitted itself well in its early actions. By contrast, Gilbert's companies seem to have been relatively green troops. Even when stiffened by some of Morgan's men, Gilbert's force exhibited a combination of enthusiasm and raw inexperience. When ordered to relieve the desperately besieged city of Mons, Gilbert allowed himself to be absorbed for days on end in clumsy attempts to seize Sluis and Bruges, never getting close to Mons before it fell. A subsequent amphibious operation to capture Ter Goes, an outpost of the main Spanish maritime base at Middelburg, went horribly wrong when its garrison proved far larger than expected. Both sides suffered heavy casualties before the rebels withdrew, but the defeat drew such scorn from the people of Flushing that Gilbert's troops were shut out of the city upon their return. The ban was only lifted after they defeated an enemy surprise attack which sought to take advantage of the troops' lack of fortified defences. The Spanish were so confident of success in this attack that they carried halters to hang the survivors: when the attack was beaten off, many of the captured enemy were hanged by their own nooses. After this success, a second attempt to capture Ter Goes was launched in mid-September, employing a total rebel force of over 3000 men – perhaps a quarter of them English – and a battery of siege guns. Despite the greater resources, the operation was hampered by a lack of munitions and by disagreements between Gilbert and the governor of Flushing. Both commanders absented themselves from the camp after the failure of an ill-prepared assault which Gilbert had only permitted in order to prove 'that hyt was not cowardlyness that causyd hym too gaynesaye thys enterprise'. Despite acts of courage by the soldiers, the whole siege was woefully mismanaged – 'our ignorant poore siege', Williams later called it. It collapsed completely when the famous Spanish soldier, Cristóbal de Mondragon, led 3000 veteran troops on a gruelling wade through flooded fields to attack the besiegers from the rear. The rebel force panicked and fled towards the safety of the small ships hovering offshore, many of them drowning in the process. Perhaps 200 Englishmen were killed or captured. Stricken by the disaster and disillusioned by his experience of war in the Low Countries, Gilbert soon returned home, taking many of his men with him.[39]

The actions of 1572 showed English troops could fight with considerable spirit, but also that they were inexperienced, had limited staying power and were gravely handicapped by poor leadership. They were fortunate that most of the enemy soldiers whom they fought against before the disaster at Ter Goes were almost equally unskilled. Nevertheless, as engagement followed upon engagement, the troops who stayed in the Low Countries (or returned after finding the calm of England no longer to their taste) became steadily more experienced in war, benefiting greatly from the cross-pollination of ideas among the diverse mix of nationalities who fought for the Dutch. The cosmopolitan mix also encouraged English and Welsh soldiers to measure themselves against the other combatants and to prove their relative worth in combat. During 1573, when Thomas Morgan brought another 1500 men over to join the effort to relieve the siege of Haarlem, some English troops found themselves in action against Alba's main army, rather than the regional forces they had faced in 1572. The result was a painful lesson in the efficiency of the Spanish army – made all the worse by the loss of unit insignia and news of the mass execution of Haarlem's garrison (including a few score English troops) after its surrender on 13 July. However, the value of such experience was evident even by the time Morgan withdrew most of his regiment to England later in the year. When Morgan paraded his 700 remaining men for the queen (a number which suggests both heavy attrition among his ranks and that many men chose to remain in the Low Countries), they included, according to Williams, 'the first perfect harguebushiers [arquebusiers] that were of our nation' and the first English troops to adopt the musket, a new and bulkier form of firearm which was becoming popular on the Continent because it fired a heavier bullet. Not surprisingly, Elizabeth's government were eager to ship many of these men to Ireland, where they were intended to boost the earl of Essex's flagging fortunes in Ulster. Although the small number of English troops remaining in Dutch service after 1573 and the parlous state of the Protestant cause made it difficult to repeat the exercise for many years, Morgan's men marked the first significant instance of English troops being 'schooled' in the Low Countries before being deployed for service elsewhere. This practice would later become a cornerstone of the Elizabethan war effort.[40]

Schooling troops
in Low Countries
for service
elsewhere.

3   The Spectre of War: operations and developments, c.1572–1585

The daunting array of threats to England's national security which emerged in the late 1560s prompted important changes to the realm's defences in the early 1570s. Most immediately, a new programme of warship construction was initiated. The *Foresight* was launched in 1570, the *Dreadnought, Swiftsure, Achates* and *Handmaid* in 1573 and the *Revenge* and *Scout* in 1576–77. The old *Bull* and *Tiger* (both originally built in 1546) were also extensively rebuilt in 1570. In comparison with the major warships built at the start of Elizabeth's reign, the new vessels were notably smaller and better suited to escort duties in European waters. Whereas the *Triumph* (1562) was rated at 1000 tons and the *Elizabeth Jonas* (1559) and *Victory* (1562) at 800 tons, even the largest of the new ships – *Dreadnought, Swiftsure* and *Revenge* – were rated at only 400–500 tons.

The new ships also reflected a very different design from their forebears. With the *Dreadnought*, or perhaps the remodelled *Bull* and *Tiger*, English warships were designed with lower 'castles' fore and aft (especially the forecastle) and longer, sleeker lines which gave the vessels greater speed and manoeuvrability and a longer gundeck. Despite their smaller size, these 'race built' ships carried a heavy armament. Instead of the profusion of light anti-personnel guns which had characterised warships in the 1540s, the new vessels carried most of their firepower as large cannon which were designed to smash enemy ships. The *Dreadnought*, for example, carried 35 bronze cannon weighing over 30 tons, 17 of which can be classified as 'heavy' guns. The *Revenge* was even more heavily armed. Only 92 feet long at the keel and 30 feet wide at the lower deck, it carried 42 cannon (weighing almost 40 tons) in two gundecks. Twenty-two of these guns fired heavy projectiles weighing 17–30lb, eight fired shot of 8–9lb and ten fired shot of 4–5lb, in addition to various light anti-personnel weapons.[1]

The combination of unprecedented nimbleness and firepower gave Elizabeth's new warships the ability to out-sail an enemy ship and to pummel it from a distance without having to risk close-in combat. Nevertheless, this was an option which most Elizabethan captains still preferred to eschew – what technology permitted was one thing, but what habit and profit suggested was quite another. Although their new low-cut ships were less than ideal for grappling with large foreign ships (which now towered above them), the lure of plunder meant that English seamen still instinctively sought to board an enemy vessel whenever possible. With this in mind, the *Revenge* complemented its heavy guns with an arsenal of personal weapons comparable to that of the *Mary Rose* in the 1540s. In 1591, it carried 110 muskets, 70 calivers, 50 longbows, 100 sheaves of arrows and many pikes, bills and swords. Even in the late 1590s, Sir Walter Ralegh urged the need for a greater supply of swords and shields on the queen's warships.[2]

All designs inevitably involve compromise and the 'race built' galleons were no exception. The price to be paid for such combat power and sailability was that the new ships were very crowded and short of space for storing supplies – especially as victuals for four men for 28 days required a ton of stowage space. The *Revenge's* full complement of 300 men therefore required 75 tons of stores per month. Victuals for three months left barely half the ship's carrying capacity available for everything else which it needed to carry, including cannon, munitions and the crew itself. This was acceptable if the fleet operated simply as a short-range defensive force, sailing in the waters near the British Isles. Insofar as the queen and her councillors understood the practical implications of naval design, this probably seemed like no great limitation, given the realm's overwhelmingly defensive posture in the 1570s. However, Elizabethan England was building these ships at the very time that privateering voyages to the New World were encouraging men like Hawkins and

Drake to contemplate revolutionary new concepts for long-range, oceanic warfare. When the time came to put such plans to the test in the late 1580s and 1590s, the queen's warships proved far from ideal for these operations, much to the frustration of their proponents. Although the greatest difficulties arose from victuals, operations in the Atlantic put a great strain on the masts and rigging of vessels the size of the queen's main warships. Ralegh also complained they carried an excessively heavy weight of cannon for oceanic navigation. In his experience, English ships were 'so over-pestred & clogged with great ordeinance . . . that much of it serves to no better use but only to labor & overcharge the shipps in any grand seas & foule weather'.[3]

During the 1570s and 1580s, however, the 'race built' warships proved so successful that their design principles were gradually standardised across the royal fleet through a steady programme of building new ships and rebuilding old ones. Wealthy and well-connected investors in privateering, such as the earl of Leicester, also began to construct their own vessels in similar fashion: the earl's *Galleon Leicester* of 1578 was apparently even built from the same plans as the *Revenge*. In an era when other ships were still built individually under the direct supervision of a master shipbuilder, this ability to create a blueprint for the construction of several new ships from the same design – a class of ships, rather than a series of one-offs – underlined the technical sophistication of the queen's shipwrights, permitting construction without the designer's own presence and the introduction of incremental improvements to successive ships in the same class.[4]

The naval rearmament of the 1570s and 1580s also marked a decisive break with the retrenchment of the 1560s in terms of government spending on the navy. This spending was made possible largely by the willingness of parliaments to approve regular grants of peacetime taxation, breaking the former convention that subsidies would normally only be voted in time of war. These grants themselves reflected a deep-seated fear of the international 'Catholic threat'. Even if Elizabeth herself refused to accept such conspiracy theories, many of her leading subjects – including privy councillors such as Sir Walter Mildmay – believed them implicitly. In urging the House of Commons to approve a fresh subsidy in 1566, Mildmay warned his audience that 'when we see our neighbours' houses on fyer, it is wisedom to provide

and forsee how to kepe the smoke and sparkes of the same as farre
from our owne as we can'. In his view, the cause of 'this hostilite and
garboyle abrode' was patently obvious: 'the malice of the ennemyes
and adversaries of Godde's ghospell'. The ominous events at the end
of the 1560s seemed to confirm Mildmay's diagnosis and subsequent
parliaments continued to vote new peace-time subsidies throughout
the next decade and a half. Once the last of the crown's foreign debts
were finally paid off in 1574, an even greater proportion of this revenue could be devoted to preparing defensive measures against the
alleged 'malice' of international Catholicism. Although she viewed
foreign policy in far less ideological terms, Elizabeth was happy
enough to take the money.[5]

Between 1574 and 1584, expenditure by the treasurer of the navy
averaged £10,379 a year, while the surveyor of victuals (whose spending reflected operations rather than construction and maintenance)
averaged £4151 a year. Total naval spending therefore ran at over
£14,500 a year during this period. This loosening of the purse strings
represented a sustained commitment by Elizabeth's government to
building the best equipped navy the realm could afford. Nevertheless,
the unremitting financial burden of naval rearmament meant that
the government was eager to contain costs by making economies
elsewhere. In October 1579, the crown entered into a five-year 'bargain' with John Hawkins, by which Hawkins contracted to maintain
and repair the queen's fleet for an annual sum of £4000 – almost
£2000 less than the notional budget – supplemented by separate
contracts for mooring and caulking the fleet. Inevitably, this degree
of cost-cutting caused fierce controversy among navy officials, but
Hawkins's efforts proved successful enough to secure a second 'bargain' in 1585. This follow-on contract was accompanied by plans for
a rolling programme of major refits for the queen's ships extending
as far ahead as 1597 – a remarkable degree of forward-planning for
the sixteenth century. In the event, such plans were overtaken by the
outbreak of war and Hawkins ultimately resigned his contract in
1587, when he was no longer able to make a profit from his maintenance work.[6]

The recognition by Elizabeth's government that sea-power, rather
than armies and fortresses, constituted the realm's first line of

defence – especially now that England no longer possessed a forward base at Calais – also encouraged major efforts to gather information about the nation's maritime resources. A list of merchant ships available for defence in July 1570 proved so sketchy that Lord Burghley ordered a comprehensive survey of England's shipping in 1571–72. Subsequent surveys during the 1570s added more detail. By February 1580, the privy council was able to specify which 22 merchant ships, displacing a total of 4860 tons and manned by 2790 sailors, would reinforce the queen's 20 warships to confront an invading fleet. An expanded survey of 1582 included all vessels down to 80 tons and provided exact information about the number and location of the mariners who could be drafted into military service. London, for example, had 143 masters, 991 mariners, 957 ferrymen and 195 fishermen, while Yarmouth had 42 masters and 380 seamen. Such relentless gathering of data meant that Elizabeth's privy council not only knew more about its national maritime resources than any other European government of the time, but also more than subsequent English governments until the twentieth century. The Elizabethan council was therefore able to refine its plans for maritime defence and to have confidence that they would work. The emphasis upon regularly updating information and upon contingency planning meant that Elizabethan England was able to delay its mobilisation against an imminent invasion until almost the last minute, which sharply reduced the period for which the crown would have to pay wages on a large scale. Since Elizabeth could not afford the sort of prolonged alert which her father had mounted in 1545, the regular information-gathering and planning of her council ensured that the cost of national defence could be kept to a minimum without sacrificing security.[7]

Militia Reform and the Demands of Training

Despite the heavy investment in maritime defence, the prospect of confronting soldiers of the Spanish army on English soil meant it was imperative to upgrade the county militias. As Burghley (then still Sir William Cecil) had himself observed in 1569: 'the realm is become so feeble by long peace as it were a fearful thing to imagine, if the enemies

were at hand to assail the realm, of what force the resistance would be.'
Although various schemes were floated for creating a new national
corps of arquebusiers to spearhead the realm's defences, the stumbling
block remained the question of who would pay for such a force. Given
its continuing expenditure on the navy and memories of the failed
experiment of the gendarmes of 1551–52, the crown was both unwilling and unable to foot the bill. To make matters worse, the shortcom-
ings of the militia legislation passed at the end of Mary's reign were
becoming increasingly obvious. Most of the weapons which the arms
act of 1558 prescribed now seemed out-of-step with the needs of the
battlefield – longbows, bills or halberds and old-fashioned armour.
Even arquebuses had changed, evolving into the heavy musket and
the lighter (and cheaper) caliver, which was rapidly becoming the
basic form of firearm. The privy council was forced to use 'persua-
sion' (i.e. frequent hectoring letters) to encourage the gentry and
town corporations to pledge more of the most critical arms –
especially guns, pikes and horses – than they were legally required to
provide by the statutes of 1558. These efforts brought considerable
success in boosting the realm's declared stocks of weapons in the
1560 and 1570s, but apparently reached the limits of subjects' generosity during the 1580s. However, even if the number of weapons
was increased, the problem of training remained because neither the
arms act of 1558 nor the parallel musters act created proper arrangements for training men, let alone provided the means to pay for such
training.[8]

With firearms and pikes, training – and especially training as
whole units rather than merely as individual soldiers – was now far
more critical than it had been when troops were armed only with
bows and bills. The latter were weapons which essentially demanded
a great deal of individual skill – especially the longbow, which
required years of practice at the butts to use effectively – but only
fairly rudimentary teamwork. By contrast, the complexities of firing
and reloading a caliver in combat not only required rigorous training, but also careful coordination among soldiers in the same unit to
prevent accidents. Pikes were perhaps even more demanding in
terms of coordination. Unless a body of pikemen fought together,
these very long weapons rapidly became more of a hindrance than a

help. If even a few of its members failed to do their duty, the whole unit became very vulnerable to the enemy. As numerous contemporary engagements showed, a pike phalanx which lost its cohesion was a recipe for defeat and disastrous casualties. It was also critically important for pikemen and troops armed with guns to work together because their weapons were complementary. Troops with firearms needed the protection of pikes because they were slow to reload and vulnerable to cavalry attack, while pikemen needed the support of arquebusiers to blast away at enemy ranks and break them up before fighting came to the 'push of the pike', and to prevent enemy arquebusiers from doing the same to them. In short, the new weapons simply could not be used in a militarily useful way without regular training and demanded a strong emphasis upon unit coordination and discipline.

The privy council's solution to the training problem was to direct the county militias to focus their limited resources on equipping and training only a small proportion of their men. These so-called 'trained bands' would include the best potential soldiers, leaving the rest of the militia to supplement the trained men in an emergency or to serve as pioneers. The scheme was first tested in London in March 1572, when 3000 of 'the most likely and active persons' from the City militia were chosen to serve as pike and shot, and subsequently demonstrated the benefits of their intensive new training in a wargame staged for the queen on May Day. The success of this experiment led to its nationwide adoption in 1573. However, the new system soon encountered serious problems, mostly arising from the new costs which it imposed upon the counties. The authorities in Devon informed the council that 1000 of the 10,000 men in the county might be suitable for training, but the fall-off in trade meant they could not afford to pay for it. Officials in Derbyshire reported their county could only afford to train 500 of the 4000 suitable men there. Such responses were understandable. Creating trained bands meant that local officials had to find money to pay the wages of all the men being trained (8d each per day – the same as soldiers on campaign), pay one or more expert muster-masters to oversee the training, pay for all the arms and armour needed to equip men who did not already own the appropriate equipment themselves (and few did), pay the cost of storing these arms between musters, and pay the cost of powder, match and shot expended during the training itself. Taken together, these costs placed a heavy financial burden upon a county, especially as they would recur every year and there was no explicit legal mechanism for levying the county's inhabitants. Nevertheless, the privy council renewed the scheme in 1577 and refused to accept non-compliance by the county authorities. Specified numbers of men were to be trained for ten days a year – for four days after Easter, four days after Whitsuntide (seven weeks after Easter) and two days after Michaelmas (29 September). Moreover, these were to be 'meet and able husbandmen and farmers' sons that are likely to continue in the place' and not 'such artificers as commonly are removing'. In other words, the trained bands were to be manned by the relatively well-to-do – men who could be relied upon to be available when needed, but also who had something to protect against both foreign invaders and native-born rebels.[9]

Despite the council's determination to create militarily useful trained bands as rapidly as possible, progress demanded many compromises and a blizzard of paperwork about the number of men appearing for each year's training and the state of their weapons. With far too few guns and pikes available to equip the required numbers, most counties included many men armed with bows and bills among their trained bands. Although it sought to eliminate bills in favour of the pike, the council had little choice but to accept the continuing use of bows as an adjunct to guns and pikes. The high costs of annual training – £320 to train 400 men according to officials in Lincolnshire in 1577, £350 to train 500 men according to those in Norfolk – meant that the wholesale purchase of guns, pikes and matching armour was simply unaffordable, even if sufficient arms had been available. As it was, the realm remained short of weapons and the increased demand raised prices. Expert opinion also still tended to endorse the continuing military utility of the longbow, despite its abandonment by English volunteers fighting in France or the Low Countries. The council therefore required the trained bands of Devon to provide 1200 shot, 800 archers and 1000 pikemen in 1584 (they actually mustered 1202, 804 and 1172 respectively), while Hampshire was to provide 800 shot, 200 archers and 500 pikemen (they mustered 800, 203 and 498 respectively). Even without the added cost of replacing longbows, the burden which these trained bands placed upon their counties was very high. The estimates for annual training costs which had been offered to the council in 1577 ranged from 14s to £1 per head. If accurate, these estimates meant that the 3000 men of Devon cost the county £2100–£3000 a year, while the 1500 men of Hampshire cost £1050–£1500. Such large sums could only be collected by taxing the county community in the same way as a parliamentary subsidy, which had the benefit of being famil-iar and giving the impression of due process, even though the system technically operated by authorisation from the privy council rather than on a statutory basis.[10]

The creation of the trained bands produced a military force of dis-tinctly variable quality, ranging from the 3000 well-equipped and adequately trained troops of London to the patchier forces fielded by most other counties. Ten days of training each year provided a mod-est level of military competence, but its annual repetition and steady improvements in the provision of muster-masters produced a grad-ual increase in the bands' war-fighting capability, albeit rising from a fairly low base. However, the creation of the trained bands also meant that the queen's subjects best suited to soldiering were now earmarked strictly for home defence. In the long-run, this may have helped to reduce tensions about the conscription of ordinary militia men for service abroad by demonstrating the crown's respect for the idea that the counties should not be stripped of their fundamental means of self-defence for the sake of foreign wars. This was a basic principle which had shaped the statutory limitations on the employ-ment of the militia outside their home county. By reserving the trained bands for home defence, the crown paid deference to this deep-rooted local concern and made it easier for the county authori-ties to participate in ignoring the legal restrictions on pressing other militia men for service abroad. It also ensured the counties could be confident that their heavy investment of resources in the trained bands would not be simply diverted away to other purposes which lay beyond their control or interest. This was critical for ensuring that the counties actually complied with the council's demands for ever greater investments of time and money in the trained bands.

Nevertheless, this policy had profound effects upon Elizabethan war-making.

Even more than the design of the new heavily armed but short-legged warships, the policy of reserving the trained men for home defence underlined the overwhelming priority which Elizabeth's government attached to protecting the realm: any troops sent overseas would have to be either volunteers or men who were regarded as unsuitable for the trained bands. The very structure of Elizabethan military organisation therefore ensured that future expeditionary forces would consist very largely of poor quality troops, severely limiting their effectiveness. To address this problem, the privy council put great store in the ability of experienced officers to turn unpromising human material into competent soldiers. As Burghley's son Sir Robert Cecil observed of a force sent to France in 1591, 'I hope well of the matter yf our rawe troupes bee well conducted.'[11] Officers who had served successfully as volunteers in France or the Low Countries were regarded as a critical national asset and councillors like Leicester, Burghley and Walsingham made a special point of keeping in touch with them. For their part, the captains were eager to curry favour with such powerful patrons in the hope of one day securing a post from the queen.

The gradual creation of an experienced cadre of officers would prove one of the great unheralded achievements of Elizabeth's reign, but officers alone could not provide the whole solution to the weakness of English armies which had been so glaring in the 1560s. Recovering the effectiveness of English armies would also require solving a critical problem which the reforms of the 1570s still failed to address: the lack of any means for supplying experienced common soldiers. Veteran troops were essential to effective military operations, especially in small-unit actions such as those which characterised the war in the Low Countries, where rival forces fought highly localised but intensive campaigns which put a premium on discipline, efficient weapons handling and resilience under enemy fire. The duke of Alba argued that any troops could fight a battle, but only veterans could win a skirmish. In Ireland, rebels did their best to 'avoid the old soldiers' and focused their attacks on the still-bright uniforms of 'the newe come ignorant men', knowing that the latter posed less danger and often panicked under fire. Having survived the rigours of earlier campaigns, veterans knew how to look after themselves in the field and suffered vastly lower attrition from sickness or desertion than green troops. Because of their skills and because far fewer of them fell by the wayside, veteran troops kept their fighting power during a campaign much better than freshly recruited soldiers, whose numbers and effectiveness fell away precipitously after only a month or two of service.

During the reigns of Henry VIII and Edward VI, England had been able to obtain veteran troops largely by hiring foreign mercenaries, whose presence had been critical to the success of English armies. Mary's government only sought to hire mercenaries after the loss of Calais and then suffered the misfortune of seeing Philip divert them into his own army, after England had paid for them. Under Elizabeth, the recruitment of mercenaries ceased altogether, except when she hired German troops as 'deniable' aid for her French or Dutch allies. This loss of fighting power was compounded by the implications of the loss of Calais. In addition to hiring mercenaries, England had been able to raise some veteran troops of its own from the garrisons which it maintained at Calais, Guisnes and Hammes (and briefly also at Boulogne). These frontier garrisons had provided a steady stream of (mainly) native-born professional soldiers who could spearhead English expeditions into France or Scotland and acted as a filter for new military ideas and tactics, which were absorbed through regular contact with England's allies in Flanders or the French. The loss of the Pale of Calais meant that Elizabeth's armies were deprived of the benefits of these garrisons at the very time when they were also denied support from foreign mercenaries. Moreover, neither Berwick nor the garrison in Ireland proved an adequate substitute for Calais. Although it provided the core of Hunsdon's army at Naworth and 300 of its troops were sent to France in June 1563 as part of the desperate effort to defend Newhaven, Berwick's garrison was too small to generate similar contingents for service elsewhere after 1567. As the main focus of official English military activity between 1563 and 1585, Ireland provided an introduction to war for many of Elizabeth's army officers. Yet even veteran officers from Ireland often faced a steep learning curve when confronted with the more intense campaigns

fought on the Continent. The wars in Ireland also consumed common soldiers, rather than trained them for combat in other theatres.
In this light, it is hardly surprising that the expeditionary forces
which went to Scotland and Newhaven in the early 1560s performed
so poorly. Although many of their officers were experienced, these
were raw troops who lacked the leavening of veteran soldiers which
had been considered indispensable in the armies of Henry VIII and
Edward VI, and they performed accordingly.[12]

The initiatives of the 1570s failed to address the need for a steady
supply of veteran soldiers. The most the privy council could hope for
was that the queen might be able to call upon some of the English
volunteers fighting in France or the Low Countries, as indeed happened in the mid-1580s. However, it was not until England found a
replacement for the garrisons of the Calais Pale that Elizabethan
armies began to develop a new cadre of veteran soldiers which
allowed them to face the Spanish army on something approaching
equal terms. Far more than the displacement of bows and bills by
calivers and pikes, the key to military success for English arms would
be the creation of a system which could generate a steady supply of
'old' soldiers: it was not weapons, but the men who used them that
made all the difference.

England Besieged, 1577–84

In the mid-1570s, England's strategic position improved considerably, thanks to the failure of Alba's *reconquista* in the Low Countries,
the restoration of trade with Spain, the deadlock in the French civil
wars and the consolidation of Morton's Anglophile regime in
Scotland. However, things worsened again as the decade drew to a
close. In the Low Countries, despite the apparent basis for a peace settlement offered by the Perpetual Edict of February 1577 and the subsequent withdrawal of Spanish troops, open war soon flared again
and ended all hope of compromise. Although Spain now found itself
facing a regional alliance which embraced most of the provinces of
the Low Countries rather than merely the rebels of Holland and
Zealand, the new coalition and its central organ of government, the
States-General (usually reduced to States in England), was riven by

tensions between Catholics and Protestants. There was also much controversy about the role of William of Orange ('William the Silent'), the pre-eminent Dutch leader whose association with the Calvinists and widespread support from the common people fuelled the hostility of would-be rivals. By early 1579, the coalition broke in two, with the provinces of Hainault and Artois forming the Union of Arras and returning to Spanish authority *en masse*, while the rival Union of Utrecht (consisting of Holland, Zealand, Utrecht, Friesland, Gelderland and Ommelanden) remained committed to waging war against Spain until they had secured their independence from Spanish authority.[13]

The revival of war in the Low Countries created a crisis for England and gave fresh urgency to the efforts to improve its defences. Not only did the war return the Spanish army to the region, but the appeals of the States-General for aid revived the possibility of French intervention, especially after the sixth bout of civil war in France came to an end in September 1577. Elizabeth was unable to decide how to respond to the situation and her council divided on the issue. Twice – in the autumn of 1577 and again a year later – Elizabeth toyed with the idea of openly committing English troops to the conflict, only to withdraw the offer. With the incalculable costs and risks of combat, the danger of provoking open war with Spain and the alarming volatility of politics in the Low Countries, she decided England could not afford to pursue the military option, much to the chagrin of the earl of Leicester, who had hoped to lead the expeditionary force. Instead, the queen sought to aid the Dutch and pre-empt the French by hiring 10,000 German mercenaries from John Casimir, son of the elector of the Rhineland Palatinate. Like her previous use of Casimir to aid the Huguenots in France in summer 1575, this gave Elizabeth 'deniability', but it cost £40,000 and still failed to stop the States-General from appointing the duke of Anjou, the brother of Henri III of France, as 'Defender of Belgic liberty' in August 1578. Anjou's intrusion into Dutch affairs was soon complicated and delayed by his intervention in English affairs, when he sought Elizabeth's hand in marriage. Although there had been discussion of a match between Elizabeth and Anjou during the Anglo-French *rapprochement* of 1570–72 which resulted in the Treaty of Blois, it had not progressed far. The revival of Anjou's suit over the winter of 1578–79 was very different. This was clearly Elizabeth's last chance to marry and produce an heir who could keep Mary Queen of Scots off the throne. Marriage with Anjou would also give England influence over the duke's involvement in the Low Countries and forge a new alliance with France, strengthening its position with Spain. Yet Anjou was a Catholic and implicated in the St Bartholomew's Day Massacres. Elizabeth's own nagging uncertainty about whether Anjou would really make a suitable husband was both reflected and reinforced by the sharply divergent opinions of her councillors and courtiers, who began to form factions for and against the marriage.[14]

Anjou's suit crystallised opinions about the oldest and most explosive issue in Elizabethan politics – whom should the queen marry? It also coincided with what seemed like the steady revelation of a vast international Catholic conspiracy against England, as threats began to crowd in from every side. In the Low Countries, the new Spanish viceroy, Alexander Farnese, prince (later duke) of Parma, succeeded in detaching the Union of Arras from the States-General in May 1579. A nephew of Philip II and, at the age of 33, already an experienced soldier, Parma would soon prove to be the greatest general of the age. Two months later, James Fitzmaurice Fitzgerald returned to Ireland with Italian and Spanish troops and established a fort at Smerwick on the Dingle peninsula. Although involving only a small fraction of a force which had originally been intended for an invasion of England, Fitzmaurice's landing carried the blessing of Pope Gregory XIII and was proclaimed as the start of a Catholic crusade against Elizabeth's regime. Fitzmaurice's arrival soon provided the spark for large-scale rebellion in Munster.

In September 1579, Esmé Stuart, sieur d'Aubigny, arrived in Scotland from France and began to win favour with his cousin, James VI, who was now 13 years old. A member of the hard-line Guise family, d'Aubigny – soon created earl and then duke of Lennox – was seen by Elizabeth's government as an instrument of international Catholicism, employed to undermine Morton's regency and to make James a Catholic. Although Lennox was probably more concerned to secure advancement for himself, these fears accurately reflected the hopes of the pope and the duke of Guise, especially after Lennox secured Morton's arrest for murder in December 1580.

At the beginning of 1580, the king of Portugal died without an obvious local heir and Philip II promptly invaded to claim the throne for himself – an ominous foretaste of what might occur if Elizabeth died unmarried and childless. The acquisition of the Portuguese empire reinforced Spain's hold on the New World. It also added a network of trading bases which stretched from Africa to India and Southeast Asia and a fleet of warships which significantly increased Spain's naval strength in the Atlantic. By the time the final Portuguese resistance was crushed with an amphibious landing in the Azores, Spanish confidence reached such heights that some boasted that 'even Christ was no longer safe in Paradise, for the marquis [of Santa Cruz, Philip's admiral] might go there to bring him back and crucify him all over again'. Such large additions to Spanish wealth and strength made many in Europe wonder if there was any limit to Philip's ambition, especially as he celebrated his triumph with the motto *Non sufficit orbis*: 'the world is not enough'. England itself also felt the impact of what now seemed to be the whole of international Catholicism on the move against it, when Robert Persons and Edmund Campion launched the first Jesuit mission to England in June 1580. Although other missionary priests had been slipping into the realm for several years, the Jesuits sought to foment rebellion against Elizabeth and prepare the way for a foreign invasion to restore Catholicism by force.[15]   *Lee - execut. Campie-*

The end of the decade saw Elizabeth's government struggling to *1581* cope with these multiple, and often interconnected, challenges. The most difficult for Elizabeth personally was Anjou's suit, which she almost accepted at the end of 1579, before putting him off in early 1580 and finally declining marriage in 1581. This spared the realm even greater dissension than had arisen when her sister Mary had married a foreign prince – Philip – in the 1550s, but it left Mary Queen of Scots still only a heartbeat from the throne. This guaranteed that Catholic extremists would continue to plot against Elizabeth and that the realm would face civil war if she became seriously ill, with the Protestant gentlemen who now dominated local and central government seeking to prevent Mary's succession at all costs. The failure of the Anjou match also meant that Henri III was distinctly unreceptive when Elizabeth pressed him for an Anglo-French alliance in 1581 to balance the newly swollen power of Philip's Spain. Another setback came in Scotland. Although she approved the massing of troops at Berwick in the spring of 1581 for military intervention to topple Lennox and save Morton, Elizabeth finally cancelled the operation and left Morton to his fate. To the dismay of Morton's supporters in England, she recognised that such an invasion lacked adequate support within Scotland and might simply ensure James's conversion to Catholicism, reviving the old strategic nightmare of an enemy to the north. In the event, a Protestant *coup* drove Lennox into exile in August 1582, but Anglo-Scottish relations were only really stabilised in 1585–86, when James was granted an annual pension by Elizabeth and encouraged to believe that he would be her successor (now that she was well past child-bearing age) if he remained England's ally. Although James would occasionally toy with secret overtures from Catholic powers, the lure of being invited to succeed Elizabeth ultimately proved sufficient to guarantee Scottish amity towards England and ensured that the realm did not have to face a hostile northern neighbour during the remainder of the queen's reign.[16]

If open military intervention proved impossible in the Low Countries and Scotland, it was an urgent necessity in Ireland, where the landing of Fitzmaurice's small band of papal crusaders stirred a major rebellion. Although Fitzmaurice himself was killed in August 1579, the earl of Desmond's brother had 2000 men in the field by autumn and was so confident of his superiority over the queen's forces that he risked a pitched battle. On 3 October, fewer than 1000 English troops engaged the rebel army at Monasternenagh, near Limerick, and succeeded in breaking its hard core of 1200 'choice' gallowglasses. Although they 'valiantlie resisted' two attacks spearheaded by close-range fire from English arquebusiers and the outcome of the battle 'stood verie doubtfull', the Irish finally cracked when the English 'so fiercelie and desperatelie set upon them afresh with the third volée'. This hard-fought victory was a tribute to the fortitude and effectiveness of experienced officers and men, even though outnumbered. Desmond himself was proclaimed a traitor and the suppression of the rebellion became an exercise in reducing the earl's strongholds one by one, ravaging his lands and forcing the submission of his suspected allies, while a naval task force prevented any foreign reinforcements arriving from abroad. The task was expected to be completed over the summer of 1580 by a new lord deputy, Arthur Lord Grey (whose father had commanded at Guisnes and Leith), who brought over 2000 fresh reinforcements – the largest single draft since the 1530s. However, Grey's plans were dented by an unexpected rising in Leinster. Although this rebellion soon collapsed, 600 new Spanish and Italian troops arrived at Smerwick in September, benefiting from the temporary withdrawal of the queen's ships for resupply and maintenance. The decisive action now focused on Smerwick.[17]

In mid-October 1580, Elizabeth's forces in Ireland totalled 6500 men and another 1300 were on the way – a costly commitment that showed how seriously she and her government viewed the situation there. By early November, Grey was able to surround the small earth fort at Smerwick and royal warships (including the *Revenge*) were in position to join the bombardment from the sea. The warships alone carried over 150 cannon. Hopelessly out-matched, the defenders surrendered within days, even though Grey promised them nothing. Grey proved as good as his word. Although the Spanish officers were spared, the other defenders were promptly executed, much of the killing being done by troops commanded by Walter Ralegh. The systematic brutality of this action – so reminiscent, ironically, of Alba's failed *reconquista* in the Low Countries – reflected Grey's hatred of Catholicism and a desire to shock the Irish into submission. In this latter aim, Smerwick proved little more successful than other English massacres in Ireland. Even a year later, the slashing of troop numbers to save money – 3300 men were demobilised between November 1581 and January 1582 alone – proved distinctly premature. Despite (or perhaps because of) the devastation of the countryside which caused widespread famine and Grey's boast that he executed almost 1500 'chief men and gentlemen, . . . not accounting those of meaner sort', between September 1580 and August 1582, Desmond's force grew again to over 2000 by autumn 1582. Elizabeth finally turned the campaign over to Desmond's old enemy, the earl of Ormond, who steadily undermined Desmond's support and finally hounded him to his death, at the hands of vengeful Irishmen, in November 1583. By then, the crown's costs approached £300,000 and the toll of death and destruction was enormous. Yet this spending and suffering had actually been prolonged by the Elizabethan regime's aversion to sustained expenditure and systematic campaigning (which seemed too costly). By withdrawing so many troops over the winter of 1581–82, the government inadvertently rescusitated the rebellion and was forced to keep paying for its suppression for another two full years.[18]

Money also helps to explain Elizabeth's enthusiasm for Francis Drake's unexpected feat of circumnavigating the globe, from which he returned safely in September 1580 after three years at sea. The genesis of this voyage remains somewhat obscure, although it seems Drake told his backers (including the queen, who made an in-kind investment of £1000) that he would simply round Cape Horn and explore the Pacific coast of South America, with the costs of the venture being covered – and, hopefully, much exceeded – by brazen piracy against Spanish possessions in the region. In the event, he failed (or was unable) to turn back and ended up making the Tudor equivalent of a successful lunar landing. Only Magellan had undertaken such a feat before and the idea that it could be achieved by a ship from England, which was still barely finding its feet in oceanic navigation, seemed extraordinary.

With this success, even the East Indies, which had previously seemed exotic and impossibly distant from England, now came into focus as a target for trade and piracy. Suddenly, it seemed that English seafarers could achieve anything and they began to spawn wildly ambitious new ventures, their imaginations fired by the apparent weakness of Spanish colonial defences and the mind-boggling scale of Drake's plunder of Spanish ships and settlements. Officially, his ship returned with treasure worth £307,000 – equivalent to the crown's entire revenues for 1579 or 1581 – but the real value was probably twice as high. Success of this magnitude had a profound strategic impact. Although various plans had been mooted for offensive maritime war against Spain before, Drake's circumnavigation now seemed to prove that English ships could strike at long range and reap financial rewards on a scale which could simultaneously cripple Spain and enrich England. Philip and his advisers had long been determined to avert this threat, which forced Drake's backers to shroud his plans in secrecy when he set out and perhaps explains why Drake changed the name of his main ship from *Pelican* to *Golden Hind* just before he entered the Pacific: while the former name honoured the queen, who used the pelican as a royal symbol, the new name instead associated the voyage with the queen's councillor, Sir Christopher Hatton, providing a certain 'deniability' for Elizabeth.[19]

In the wake of Drake's triumphant return, official English concern to appease Spain's outrage proved patently insincere. Elizabeth eagerly received a large cut of the treasure, brushing off Spanish protests, and knighted Drake himself in April 1581. By her command, Drake's ship was permanently docked at Deptford and became a tourist attraction. Yet the circumnavigation also ensured a more serious response from Spain to the threat now posed by England's maritime predation. The landing of fresh Spanish and Italian troops in Ireland in September 1580 was approved by Philip in direct retaliation for Drake's piracy. Philip also authorised the building of nine new galleons which would later form the core of the *Gran Armada* of 1588. The king's ambassador in England also warned Elizabeth that Spain would declare war if she permitted Drake and other English adventurers to join an international fleet being raised for an expedition to the Azores by Dom Antonio, a pretender to the Portuguese throne. Talk of 4000 English volunteers fighting for Dom Antonio and a financial contribution from Elizabeth herself was soon squelched. Despite the euphoria of Drake's success and the new strategic possibilities which it opened up, the queen remained determined to avoid war with Spain.[20]

The Low Countries, 1578–84

The difficulties of Elizabeth's position were even more evident in the Low Countries, where her desire to defend vital national interests and yet avoid entanglement in open war against Spain forced her into a zigzag of different (and even contradictory) policies which sometimes bewildered her councillors. In 1578, she hired Casimir to aid the Dutch and permitted more English 'volunteers' to join those already fighting for the States-General. When this failed to stabilise the

Dutch cause or stem French intervention, she changed course and sought cooperation with France, either by backing Anjou or making a formal alliance with France itself. For a time, both of these options were subsumed in the larger (and, in English eyes, more important) question of whether Elizabeth should marry Anjou in the hope of prolonging the Tudor dynasty. When the queen's decision not to marry also killed off the option of an alliance, she put her money and support behind the duke. Anjou received a 'loan' of £30,000 to pay his private army in September 1581 and was promised another £60,000 during a visit to England in December – greater sums than the king of France was prepared to invest in his brother's success at the time. When Anjou left England in February 1582 to be installed as 'sovereign' of the Low Countries in place of Philip II, Leicester and a host of other English luminaries accompanied him to the celebrations, emphasising the queen's endorsement. Yet Anjou proved an utter failure both as a political figurehead and a military leader. Denied sufficient money and power by the States and overshadowed by William of Orange, he finally tried to force his will on the Low Countries by launching a *coup* in February 1583 – the so-called 'French fury' – which proved a bloody fiasco. He returned to France for good a few months later and died in May 1584.

The failure of Anjou's 'reign' was all the more disastrous for the Dutch – and alarming for Elizabeth – because it coincided with renewed pressure from Parma, whose campaign to reconquer the Low Countries for Spain gathered momentum in 1582, thanks to the return of Spanish and Italian troops who had served in the conquest of Portugal in 1580–81. These veteran troops helped Parma to achieve dramatic success in 1583, capturing most of the Flemish seaports, including Dunkirk and Nieuport, and key towns on the Scheldt estuary. Boosted by regular infusions of cash from Spain, Parma completed his conquest of Flanders (except Ostend) in 1584 and moved into Brabant, forcing the surrender of Brussels in February 1585 and tightening the noose around Antwerp, the greatest prize of all.[21]

Parma's apparently unstoppable advance seemed especially ominous after the assassination of William of Orange in July 1584. This vastly compounded the leadership vacuum created by Anjou's failure and removed the only Dutch leader who had broad national and

Leicester's Triumph

international support. The steady collapse of the Dutch cause also threatened disaster for England. Not only would Elizabeth lose all hope of being repaid the money she had loaned to the Dutch – £100,000 by late 1583 – but Parma's victorious army would be in position to invade England itself. To avert defeat, the Dutch would need money and military support on a large scale. Elizabeth would not risk such massive extra investment without cast-iron guarantees of eventually being repaid, for which the only realistic collateral could be English control of one or more Dutch ports. Yet this would require English troops to garrison the ports and could only be interpreted by Spain as an open act of war. After Orange's death, Elizabeth desperately tried to pursue other options for aiding the Dutch, even those which had failed in the past. Casimir was approached about raising a new army and overtures were made to Henri III for reconsideration of an Anglo-French pact. These options failed to get off the ground, but one final hope of securing third-party support for the Dutch remained, thanks to a request by the States that Henri III should succeed his late brother as 'sovereign' of the Low Countries. In the past, the prospect of French domination of the region had represented an unacceptable threat to English interests, but Elizabeth was now sufficiently desperate for a means to stop Parma without risking war with Spain that she was willing to withdraw her objections. Yet even this offer of a drastic reversal in English policy was insufficient to secure a definitive answer from Henri III, who left the Dutch – and England – in uncertainty for the remainder of 1584.[22]

Despite Elizabeth's own profound reluctance to become too openly involved in the Low Countries, England had become ever-more obviously entangled in the fighting there in the late 1570s. In July 1578, the States' forces had included more than 3000 English and Welsh 'volunteers' (and 4000 Scots). Shortly afterwards, English and Scottish troops won a notable victory for the Dutch at Rijmenant, where they held off the full weight of the Spanish army for a whole day and forced them to withdraw with heavy casualties. The engagement gave a huge boost to Dutch morale and won international fame for John Norris, who now began to emerge as the most capable English officer in the Low Countries. However, the usual terrible 'wastage' suffered by fresh troops meant that the English companies

John Casimir - not a lot else.

had lost 50 per cent of their men by September. The ramshackle finances of the States-General left the survivors without pay and desperately scratching for food. In fact, it would be a full decade before Norris was finally paid for the service of his troops during this campaign. During the 'reign' of Anjou, the financial shambles grew worse and matters were further exacerbated by the increasingly bitter rivalry between English officers, each desperate to secure status and money for himself from the fresh burst of recruiting which accompanied Elizabeth's support for the duke. Although Norris was technically 'colonel-general' of the English volunteers, Colonel John North tried to undermine his authority – on the grounds that he should be the senior commander because of his more eminent lineage. North even brawled with officers loyal to Norris, on one occasion stabbing a captain twice in the chest. Colonel Thomas Morgan also tried to poach men from Norris's regiment to make good the short-fall in his own unit. These tensions were magnified by the way companies from rival English regiments were often assigned to garrison the same town. The explosion finally came at Aalst (near Ghent) in November 1583. By then, the circumstances of the troops were so bad – they had not been issued bread for three months, let alone pay – and the acrimony among the commanders was so great that a group of anti-Norris officers finally sold the town to the Spanish in return for food and a month's wages. Although most of the common soldiers seem to have been surprised by this action and quickly deserted back to Norris, the town was lost to the enemy.[23]

The betrayal of Aalst helped to clear the path for Parma's advance on Ghent and caused bitter recriminations between the Dutch and the English. It also showed how dangerous the quarrels of rival officers could become if there was no adequate authority to keep them in line. However, the underlying cause of the disaster was the appalling conditions faced by foreign soldiers in Dutch service in the early 1580s, which often made Spanish silver more effective than siege guns. The shambolic finances of the States meant its army was falling apart and that they urgently needed both reinforcements and money to stave off defeat. As one English captain complained to Walsingham, troops were forced to shelter in 'rotten houses' and sleep on the bare earth, which caused terrible losses through disease and desertion: 'for anything I can see, the States are beggars and not able to give us entreatment for our service'.[24] The military situation therefore mirrored the diplomatic scene. Fresh troops to reinforce the Dutch might be found in Germany or Scotland, but only France or England could provide both men and money.

The Outbreak of War, 1584–85

By autumn 1584, the deteriorating situation in the Low Countries and continuing uncertainty about Henri III's intentions meant Elizabeth might soon have to choose between direct intervention to support the Dutch or abandoning them and devoting her resources to armed isolationism. Informal discussions about this question had begun immediately after the death of William of Orange, but the privy council did not meet to argue the matter as a group until 10 October. Although the balance of opinion favoured prompt action to support the Dutch, the debate would ultimately last several months, until Elizabeth herself made a final decision. While some councillors pleaded for immediate intervention, others urged the queen to cut her losses and revert to wary neutrality, arguing England should not waste its precious resources on support for foreign rebels. They feared the war in the Low Countries would prove a bottomless pit for men and money, while its sprawling and untidy nature – with its endless small skirmishes and sieges, mutinies and betrayals – would contaminate those soldiers who fought there, undermining England's tradition of patriotic service to the sovereign. By 18 March 1585, when another meeting was held to discuss the issue, disagreement among the councillors had reached such a pitch that those who urged the queen 'to shunne this unnecessary warre' incurred 'great displeasure and ill will among the military sort of men, as persons inclining to the Spaniard's party, degenerate and faint-hearted cowards'. This bitterness reflected the magnitude of the issues at stake and the growing urgency of the situation across the Narrow Seas. It also underlined the frustration caused by the queen's continuing inability to make a decision.[25]

Yet Elizabeth had reason to hesitate over her decision and those who feared the impact of war with Spain were not simply 'cowards'.

War offered few benefits, but entailed enormous risks and brought immediate and obvious costs. The crown would not only have to confront vast new demands for money if war broke out, but also faced a collapse in key sources of revenue. Elizabeth's income relied heavily on customs duties – almost 25 per cent of her receipts in 1584 came from this source – and the system of farming out the collection of customs dues to private contractors in return for guaranteed 'rents', which had emerged in the 1570s, could only remain attractive if trade continued undisturbed. The most immediate casualty of war would be commercial ties with Spain itself, which had boomed since the end of the trade war in 1573–74 and created a healthy flow of revenue to the crown. The merchants involved in this trade constituted a powerful political lobby and used their connections to argue against war, just as they had often previously argued for the maintenance of good relations with Spain and the muzzling of pirates like Drake. In Burghley's mind, at least, open conflict might bring more general economic damage, with potentially disastrous consequences: 'if England have no other war but a stay of vent [i.e. foreign trade] then the realm would not, nor could not, long endure to yield either obedience or profit to her Majesty'. In other words, the dislocation of England's external trade would be sufficient by itself to foment the sort of widespread rebelliousness and unwillingness to provide men and money for the crown which Burghley remembered from the worst days of Edward and Mary.[26]

However, despite such forebodings, most councillors (probably including Burghley) still believed it was better for Elizabeth to risk war in alliance with the Dutch than to wait for Spain to turn against England with a victorious army and all the maritime resources of the Low Countries. They believed Philip harboured 'insatiable malice' towards Protestant England and war with Spain was unavoidable. By acting now, Elizabeth would at least be able to ensure the coming war was fought overseas, rather than on English soil.

This was a difficult argument to dismiss. The meeting in October 1584 came only a few weeks after Walsingham had finally learned the full extent of Catholic planning in 1582 for an invasion of England by way of Scotland. Once an army of 6000–8000 'good and trayned soldiers' had been landed at Dumbarton, thousands of Scottish

[handwritten: Not Sept 1584.]

Catholics (including James VI, it was hoped) would have been recruited to march south and displace Elizabeth from the English throne in favour of Mary Queen of Scots. The plan had failed when Lennox was toppled from power before the operation could begin. The full story allegedly reached Walsingham when two Jesuits and another priest were arrested in the Netherlands at the beginning of September 1584. One of the Jesuits supposedly tried to tear up an incriminating document he was carrying, but the wind blew most of the pieces back aboard the ship, allowing it to be reconstructed. This information was all the more unsettling because it fitted into a pattern which showed that England's Catholic enemies – the papacy, Jesuits, the duke of Guise and agents of the king of Spain – were determined to organise an invasion of England and had been working towards that end for several years. The potential of these plots had been revealed in November 1583, when Francis Throckmorton was arrested and tortured for information about his dealings with Mary Queen of Scots. As expected, Throckmorton admitted a plan to rescue Mary from government custody, but he also revealed that the duke of Guise had intended to launch a surprise invasion by landing at Arundel in Sussex. This came as a terrible surprise because the privy council had received no warning from its informers – if Guise had gone ahead with his plan, no ships or soldiers would have been waiting to counter the invasion.[27] *[handwritten: Bossy what were Lees preparat.]*

The shock of this revelation was compounded by learning that the so-called 'Throckmorton Plot' was sponsored by the Spanish ambassador in England, Don Bernardino de Mendoza, and involved a range of English Catholic aristocrats, including Lord Paget and the earl of Northumberland. Mendoza was promptly expelled from England for his part in the affair. This was the second time an accredited Spanish diplomat had been caught plotting against Elizabeth – de Spes had also been expelled in the wake of the Ridolfi Plot – and it ended ambassadorial ties between England and Spain for the rest of her reign. Henceforth, political contacts between the two crowns would be by irregular means and there would no ambassadors on hand to ease tensions between them.[28] *[handwritten: 1584 Page]*

The fate of the Low Countries therefore seemed to be part of a larger picture, in which Spanish efforts to subdue the Dutch were merely

[handwritten: hadn't been at Court since 1579???? Admin]

a preliminary step towards the invasion and forcible re-Catholicisation of England. The Jesuit who had been captured with invasion plans in September had allegedly boasted that 'the delayinge of the interpryse [i.e. invasion] is only untyll suche tyme as the king of Spayn have ordered the Low Countryes to obedience.' The prevailing mood of the council at the time of the debate in October 1584 was clearly evident by their decision to remove the incentive for Mary Queen of Scots' supporters to seek Elizabeth's death by creating the Bond of Association. Signed by Protestant lords and gentlemen across the realm, the Bond was effectively a pledge to slaughter Mary and all her followers if Elizabeth died an unnatural death – a kind of reverse St Bartholomew's Day Massacre ready to be unleashed. Drafted by Burghley and Walsingham, this extraordinary measure raised danger- ous issues about the succession and underlines how much further the council was prepared to go than the queen to protect the realm against the consequences of potential Catholic subversion.[29]

The uncertainty about the Low Countries was ended on 27 February 1585, when Henri III finally refused the Dutch offer of sov- ereignty. This forced Elizabeth's hand and cleared the way for nego- tiations about official English intervention. Nevertheless, the queen's obvious reluctance still created uncertainty and helped to make the privy council's meeting on 18 March a heated one.

Elizabeth's doubts about confronting Spain were evident in her repeated vacillations over a new expedition planned by Sir Francis Drake. In the days following William of Orange's assassination, she had given approval for Drake to raid the East Indies and had agreed to meet almost half the cost in cash and kind. Other investors includ- ed key members of the council such as Leicester, Hatton, Walsingham and the new lord admiral, Lord Howard of Effingham, as well as courtiers like Sir Walter Ralegh and Sir Philip Sidney and important London and Plymouth merchants. However, the queen changed her mind and Drake's force of more than 20 ships remained in port during the spring of 1585, still waiting for the order to sail or disband. On the other hand, she permitted a small expedition organ- ised by Ralegh and commanded by Sir Richard Grenville to sail for the newly christened territory of 'Virginia' in April. This set out to establish the first English settlement in the New World, the ill-fated

Roanoke colony, whose unfortunate location was chosen in the mis-apprehension that it would provide a secret, but easily accessible and self-supporting, base for raids on the Caribbean. Despite the notorious opposition of Spain to rival European colonies in the New World, especially those founded by Protestants, Elizabeth apparently decided that permitting the departure of Grenville's handful of ships might bring major benefits and was less provocative than releasing Drake's high-profile expedition.[30]

In late March, Elizabeth was given further cause for thought when it was learned that the duke of Guise's Catholic League in France had secretly signed a treaty with Spain. Henri III subsequently agreed to cooperate with the League in a new round of religious conflict against the Huguenots. Instead of becoming an ally against Spain, it now seemed France would plunge back into civil war and might even emerge as an enemy to England. This reinforced Elizabeth's desire to limit her commitment to the Dutch and ensured that negotiations during June and July were restricted to a provisional treaty concerning a limited force to relieve Antwerp. Meanwhile, dramatic news arrived in early June from Spain, where all northern European ships in their harbours (except French vessels) were suddenly arrested. This raised fears in England that the ships might be used for a Spanish invasion and seemed to confirm a Franco-Spanish conspiracy (in fact, French ships were excluded simply because they tended to be smaller than vessels from other countries, which had further to sail to reach Spain). Philip's real concern was to seize Dutch ships, in the hope of crippling their war effort, but he opted for blanket coverage and the later release of non-Dutch ships for reasons of administrative efficiency.

This policy reckoned without the precarious state of Anglo-Spanish relations. The arrests provoked howls of outrage from the English merchants who traded in Spain and Portugal – the very group which had done most to argue the case for accommodation with Spain – and prompted immediate calls for retaliation. Elizabeth responded by imposing an English embargo on trade with Spain, granting letters of reprisal for English merchants to seek recompence from Spanish ships and authorising the seizure of the Spanish fishing fleet working the Grand Banks off Newfoundland.[31] She also cleared the way for Drake to set sail, although he had now changed his target from the Portuguese Moluccas to Spain's colonies in the West Indies. Drake's fleet finally sailed from Plymouth on 14 September, effectively beginning the naval war against Spain.

In the meantime, after much hard negotiation, a provisional treaty was agreed with the Dutch on 2 August, by which England would provide 4000 foot and 400 horse to assist in the relief of Antwerp. Elizabeth would pay these troops for an initial three months and the Dutch would pledge Ostend or Sluis as security for repayment of this expenditure (£18,670). The commander of the force was John Norris, whom the privy council had quietly directed to begin recruiting officers and troops towards the end of June. As a result of this stealthy head-start, he was able to land the first 2000 foot and 450 cavalry at Middelburg on 21 August – far faster than the Spanish could have expected. Yet even this rapid response proved too late for Norris's men to reach Antwerp before its surrender. With the fall of Antwerp, the position of the Dutch looked more parlous than ever, but Elizabeth recognised that she could not pull back. Instead, she agreed a fresh treaty on 4 September which increased her commitment to 5000 foot and 1000 cavalry, in addition to 1400 troops to garrison the ports of Flushing and Brielle – the so-called 'cautionary towns' which were placed under English control as pledges for the repayment of Elizabeth's war costs in the Low Countries, which were now expected to total £126,000 a year. The commander of the queen's forces would also act as governor general in the Low Countries – with wide, but imprecisely defined powers – and two Englishmen would sit on the Dutch Council of State, enabling them to demand an overhaul of Dutch finances, which seemed dangerously disorganised to English eyes. Elizabeth's increased aid therefore came with significant strings attached and made the Low Countries a virtual protectorate of England. These conditions were not intended to facilitate English sovereignty over the Dutch – which Elizabeth had consistently refused – but to protect her investment. Before she fully committed herself to the Dutch cause, the queen was determined to ensure that she would be able to recover the money which she was about to spend on their behalf.[32]

Henry continue to hold yearly tournaments with for. ambass.

4 The Perils of War: operations and developments, 1585–1588

By September 1585, England was effectively at war with Spain. On the same day that Drake's fleet finally put to sea – 14 September – Norris mustered over 3400 English troops at Utrecht, while 600 more occupied the key port of Ostend. Shortly afterwards, the queen's soldiers began garrisoning the 'cautionary towns' of Flushing and Brielle. Another 3000 English 'volunteers' also served in the States' pay. If these deployments were not sufficient to constitute acts of war, Drake's fleet – which included the queen's ships *Elizabeth Bonaventure* and *Aid* – arrived off the north-western coast of Spain on 27 September and spent ten days terrorising the region before continuing its voyage towards the West Indies. However, neither England nor Spain made a formal declaration of war – and none would be issued by either side during the 19 years of conflict which followed. In contrast to the days when Henry VIII or Mary sent a herald to the French court to initiate conflict by proclaiming their 'defiance' of France, Elizabeth and Philip slid into war without observing the medieval diplomatic niceties. In part, this was because neither side really wanted the war, which made them refrain from public commitments which would make future compromise impossible.[1]

Although his approval of the Ridolfi Plot and implication in subsequent plans to bring down Elizabeth's regime gave the privy council ample reason to believe that he harboured 'insatiable malice' towards her realm, Philip had generally been hesitant about seeking confrontation with England. In comparison with Pope Gregory XIII, the duke of Guise or even Mendoza, his own ambassador, Philip was notably less bellicose, balancing the heavy cost of tackling the 'English problem' with his empire's existing commitments and already overstretched resources. Although he responded to news of Drake's circumnavigation by sending a token force to Ireland in 1580 and building a new squadron of galleons, his involvement in the plans for invading Scotland and England in 1582–83 was distinctly half-hearted and ultimately prevented the operations going ahead: without generous Spanish support, neither the pope nor Guise had sufficient resources to proceed on their own. Philip did not fully trust his allies and he was more concerned to complete the conquest of Portugal than to begin a new adventure. Fighting a two-front war – against the Turks in the Mediterranean and against the Dutch in the Low Countries – had driven the Spanish monarchy into bankruptcy in 1575 and Philip was determined not to repeat the experience. When a truce with the Turks enabled him to slash his military expenditure in the Mediterranean, he was able to provide better funding for the Army of Flanders when the war resumed there in late 1577. However, Spanish naval expenditure began a long-term decline, interrupted only by the campaigns to secure control of Portugal and its possessions. Although the marquis of Santa Cruz was able to launch successful amphibious operations in the Azores in 1582–83, the fleet and army which accomplished these tasks – precisely the sort of force needed for war against England – were quickly dismantled. Moreover, the move from naval operations in the Mediterranean to those in the Atlantic was not accompanied by the creation of a suitable infrastructure on the Iberian Peninsula to match that left behind in Italy. Spain was therefore woefully ill-equipped in 1585 for the maritime war which conflict with England would inevitably entail. After so many years of shadow-boxing and 'deniable' initiatives, Elizabeth's sudden willingness to risk open confrontation with Spain came as an unwelcome surprise to Philip.[2]

For her part, Elizabeth saw the war as an unpleasant necessity – and one from which she hoped to extricate herself as quickly as possible. Her strategy was that the arrival of English troops in the Low Countries would prevent the Dutch from being defeated and demonstrate her determination to prevent a successful *reconquista*. While Philip's hopes were being thwarted on land, Drake's fleet would take the offensive at sea by raiding Spanish colonies in the Caribbean and threatening the transatlantic flow of silver which underpinned Philip's finances. Encouraged by the proponents of naval warfare, she hoped that Drake's expedition could not only seize sufficient booty to force Philip to the negotiating table, but also cover the costs of the voyage and even subsidise the rest of England's war effort. Elizabeth's chief war aims were sensibly limited and reflected her desire for a speedy return to normalcy. Apart from warding off any immediate threat to the realm, she sought to force Philip into a negotiated settlement for the Low Countries, which reflected her long-standing goals of removing the Spanish army from the region and permitting the practice of the Protestant faith, whilst keeping the French out. In addition, she sought the repayment of her war costs by the Dutch and a return to peaceful coexistence between England and Spain. The difficulty with these goals was that they failed to resolve the problems which had plunged Spain and England into war in the first place: if almost 20 years of conflict and huge loss of life and treasure had not driven Philip to accept a compromise in the Low Countries, how could England apply enough pressure to force his hand without making itself a prime target for Spanish retaliation in the process? Even if Philip did agree a settlement, how could England trust an apparently 'insatiable' Spain not to revive the war in years to come? Experience would show there were no easy answers to such questions.

The most immediate problem with Elizabeth's strategy for a rapid resort to negotiation lay in the unwillingness of her generals and soldiers to accept such a passive role for her army in the Low Countries. Although the queen instructed him to adopt a defensive posture, Norris initially could not find enough suitable towns to garrison all his troops. He also believed – probably correctly – that at least a pretence of launching field operations was necessary to stall Parma's momentum. In mid-October, Norris sought to probe Spanish defences near Arnhem, but 'such was the unskilful fury of our soldiers as in a great hour they could not be drawn back, although the place was nothing suitable nor by no means to be entered'. Despite the futility of the attack, Norris praised the élan of his troops: 'I never knew raw soldiers more forward in service, so that in short time they will be able to do anything against the enemy that is for men to do.' Although the casualties were low, Elizabeth was furious with Norris's initiative and demanded that he withdraw immediately. When he complied, the Spanish promptly crossed the river and routed the Dutch troops which had been left to guard the position. The 'storm' over Norris's desire for aggressive action reflected what would become a familiar tension between Elizabeth and her generals. While she wanted to restrict military operations to minimise risk, cost and casualties, commanders at the front repeatedly strained – or even ignored – the limits of their instructions to undertake bolder actions which seemed necessary in the light of local circumstances and more in keeping with the 'glory' of war. In large measure, this tension reflected a clash between the queen's preoccupation with the political and material cost of war and the more narrowly focused military concerns of officers who thought in terms of tactics and the morale of their troops. While Elizabeth was usually prepared to accept explanations based on urgent necessity, she always remained profoundly suspicious of male pretensions to martial glory, believing that the human and material costs of gratifying men's egos would ultimately end up being borne by her purse and crown. Such fears were often justified, but her frustration at not being able to control events so far from the action – and the corresponding resentment of officers who received orders which seemed unrealistic or out of date, but which they were expected to obey – ensured that the queen's dealings with her generals were frequently acrimonious. Elizabeth's brief indignation at Norris would prove to be a mild foretaste of what was to come in the years ahead.[3]

By the time the earl of Leicester arrived in the Low Countries in early December 1585 to assume command of the enlarged army promised by the second treaty with the Dutch, Norris's initial force of 4000 men had been severely depleted by sickness and desertion. By New Year, one senior officer feared that 'the flower of the pressed English bands are gone'. Although Leicester had brought reinforcements with him, these seemed poor-quality troops and woefully unprepared for combat, 'most of them (especially the shot) being so unskilful that if carried to the field no better trained than they are, they would prove much more dangerous to their own companions than serviceable upon their enemies'. One-third of the company commanders were also new to war. The problems of inexperience were compounded by that of numbers. Twenty-six of the 49 foot companies in the queen's pay were immediately absorbed by garrison duties, leaving a mere 23 companies to face Parma. Leicester consequently encouraged the States to boost the allied field force by recruiting large numbers of volunteers in England in the early summer of 1586. Although this increased the strength of the combined Anglo-Dutch army, it had disastrous effects on the States' budget and, ultimately, on the finances of the whole English intervention in the Low Countries. Leicester also felt frustrated over the provision of cavalry. He himself had pledged to recruit the army's horsemen and sent out over 200 letters to his friends and followers requesting their assistance. However, Elizabeth delayed the process and only three-quarters of the 1000 horsemen required arrived by early January. These 750 cavalrymen represented some 199 different retinues, ranging in size from a single man to the 50-man contingents provided by the earl of Essex and Burghley's eldest son, Sir Thomas Cecil. Larger groups were themselves composed of various sub-retinues. The 50 lances provided by Sir Thomas Cecil, for example, included 28 of his own men, 17 horsemen set out by seven of his gentlemen friends and five men from his father's household. As a whole, Leicester's cavalry represented the largest and most expensive 'quasi-feudal' force despatched overseas during Elizabeth's reign. It was also a powerful reminder of the extent of Leicester's own personal and political investment in the forthcoming campaign.[4]

Despite the earl's best efforts to mobilise English and Dutch resources, his command had fundamental structural problems. The rickety financial and military structure of the States' war effort meant that Leicester's administration had to divert money to prevent the Dutch army (which now included large numbers of English volunteers) from mutinying for lack of pay. This was entirely contrary to Elizabeth's financial planning, but was both a military necessity and an inevitable consequence of Leicester's own Janus-like position as the queen's commander and the States' governor general. The financial tangle which resulted from this diversion of funds was compounded by uncertainties about whether certain costs should be borne by the Dutch or the queen – in part, a result of the English intervention being based upon two separate treaties – and by the chronically poor administration of the English army itself. Sending troops to the Continent was one thing, but maintaining an army there proved to be quite another. After an absence from war on the Continent of so many decades, the administrative structures of Leicester's army, including the basic arrangements for pay, discipline and supply, had to be virtually reinvented piecemeal. The result was not merely confusion, but also massive corruption. The privy council's attempt to prevent corruption by creating a pay system whereby money would be paid to the troops themselves, rather than to their captains, simply made the officers more determined to skim off whatever benefits they could, whilst the chronic lack of cash (since so much of the money sent to pay the queen's troops was diverted to the Dutch) forced the soldiers to rely upon credit from their officers or local merchants and to endure ruinous interest rates. The inevitable irritations which arose from such dealings, and widespread theft by troops who soon became hungry and ragged, helped to poison relations between English units and the towns where they were quartered. Finally, Leicester's army was plagued by quarrels among its officers. The arrival of Leicester and his staff reduced Norris to the status of a subordinate commander and many of the officers whom he had recruited earlier in 1585 found themselves being squeezed out by new appointees of the earl. The result was an even more poisonous atmosphere than had existed among the volunteer officers during Anjou's time.[5]

Leicester was instructed by Elizabeth 'rather to make a defensive then an offensyve warr and not in any sort to hazard a battaile without great advantage'. Although Leicester and the many young aristocrats who had accompanied him to war might have craved the chance to take the offensive, the persistent shortage of money, the rawness of his troops and fraying relations among the officers meant that the army was in no fit state to do so. Instead, Leicester chose to assert his control of affairs at a political level, by dealing with the States General to make himself the effective successor to Anjou as 'absolute governor general' of the Low Countries. This was in clear violation of the spirit, if not quite the letter, of his instructions. When

Elizabeth belatedly learned what he had done, she exploded in royal fury. Although Leicester desperately pleaded that the Dutch needed a single figurehead to coordinate their war effort, Elizabeth saw his action as entangling England – and herself – in the internal politics of a country whose sovereignty she had already refused, which cast her in an awkward light and potentially raised a huge impediment to future negotiations with Spain.

Even worse, Leicester's grand installation as governor general on 25 January reflected the nightmare of any sovereign, but especially a queen – that of a military commander using the army and authority which she had entrusted to him to create an independent power-base for himself. The fact that it was Leicester, her oldest and dearest favourite, who was now exalted as 'His Excellency' also made it a peculiarly personal betrayal. Elizabeth responded by showering Leicester with such blistering criticism that his friends at home and most of the privy council had to come to his defence, pleading with the queen that forcing Leicester to resign the governor-generalship or sacking him as military commander would irreparably damage cooperation with the Dutch. At one point (echoing his behaviour of a quarter-century earlier), Burghley threatened to resign as lord treasurer if the queen insisted on undermining the joint war effort in this way. Such collective pleading finally prevented Elizabeth from forcing Leicester's resignation, but the earl's authority in the Low Countries and among his officers was badly damaged.[6]

While Leicester sought to recover from his bruising confrontation with the queen, Parma opened the new campaign season by attacking the town of Grave. Leicester scraped together 3000 men under Norris and the German Count Hohenlohe to defend the town. The allied force was put to the test in early April, when Spanish troops attacked and drove defenders back along a muddy dike. As fresh English and Dutch troops joined the fray, the tiring Spaniards were halted and pushed back. In the end, about 3000 men from each side became locked in a ferocious battle in heavy rain which rendered firearms useless and turned the ground into mud. After almost two hours of desperate struggle, the Spanish withdrew with heavy casualties and Hohenlohe was able to resupply Grave the next day.[7] Leicester was overjoyed at the victory and celebrated by staging extravagant festivities for St George's Day at Utrecht. He even bestowed a knighthood on Norris. However, Parma now took the field himself and renewed the siege of Grave, which surrendered almost immediately. He also swiftly captured the other towns along the river Meuse, before attacking Neusz on the river Rhine. Here the defenders put up stout resistance, but their only reward was to be massacred when Parma's troops broke in. The town was virtually demolished in the orgy of destruction which followed.

Leicester tried to relieve Neusz, but he was crippled by lack of money. After months without pay, his troops were on the verge of mutiny and reduced to wearing rags. When new drafts arrived from England in the summer of 1586, 500 men deserted within two days, although 200 of them were captured. Several were hanged as a deterrent to others. As Leicester himself admitted, 'our old ragged roggues here hath soe discouraged our new men as, I protest to you, theie looke like dead men'. The privy council managed to ship another £45,000 in cash to Leicester in July and August, but even this only paid the infantry until 11 April 1586 and most of the cavalry remained unpaid. The feuding among the officers also grew worse, with partisans of Norris and Leicester coming to blows. Norris's brother even had to flee for his life from one drunken dinner. Leicester's step-son, the earl of Essex, was alarmed at these 'private warres', which seemed 'more dangerous then the annoyaunce of any enemy'. Nevertheless, the whole army was buoyed by the daring capture of Axel in mid-July. Led by Sir Philip Sidney, Lord Willoughby and Maurice of Nassau, several hundred English and Dutch troops launched a surprise attack on the town in the dead of night. Once a few men swam the moat, climbed the ramparts and opened the gates, the main force stormed into Axel and slaughtered the garrison. After this success, Leicester decided to halt Parma's offensive by threatening the town of Zutphen on the river Yssel. Fielding 7000 foot (5000 of them English) and 2000 cavalry, he captured the weakly defended town of Doesburg at the end of August. However, Parma acted quickly to defend Zutphen itself.[8]

Early on the morning of 22 September, Leicester sent Norris and Sir William Stanley, a veteran of Ireland and fierce partisan of the earl, to intercept a Spanish convoy heading for the town. Norris and

Stanley had 200 cavalry and 300 pikemen, but they were joined at the last minute by a bevy of aristocratic officers – including Essex, Willoughby, Sidney and others – who were spoiling for a fight. With their squires, this group consisted of perhaps 50 heavily armoured knights. When the morning fog began to lift, the ambushers suddenly found themselves facing a vastly larger convoy than expected, including 600 cavalry and 2500 foot, many of them Spanish veterans. Rather than retreat, the English attacked head-on. Time and again, the English horsemen battered into the Spanish lines, their heavy armour deflecting enemy bullets and their lances, swords and axes inflicting heavy losses on those enemy who came within arm's reach. The effectiveness of the English lancers clearly came as a nasty shock to the Spanish, who had abandoned the use of heavy cavalry in 1572 and gone over to light horsemen suitable for patrolling and small skirmishes rather than frontal assault. However, the Spanish commander kept his head and concentrated on escorting the supply wagons into the town, a task which he finally accomplished after almost two hours of skirmishing, albeit at the cost of alarming casualties – perhaps 200 men, including several experienced officers, had been killed or captured. English losses totalled about 60 men, although many horsemen had hair's-breadth escapes when their (unarmoured) horses were brought down by enemy fire.

Although it failed to prevent the revictualling of Zutphen, the skirmish provided welcome evidence that English troops – albeit the army's most highly skilled and motivated men – could fight the best enemy troops on level terms. Leicester celebrated this success by bestowing more than a dozen knighthoods, including one to the Welsh veteran, Sir Roger Williams. Four noblemen were also made knights banneret, including Essex and Willoughby. Nevertheless, this self-congratulation soon faded when it was realised that a wound to Sir Philip Sidney – the nephew of Leicester and son-in-law of Walsingham, governor of Flushing and hero of Axel – was mortal. His death on 17 October triggered such an outpouring of tributes in England that Zutphen became one of the most famous battles in early modern English history. His grand funeral at St Paul's cathedral in London on 16 February 1587 would also serve as a propaganda vehicle to whip up flagging public support for the war.[9]

One final piece of heroism occurred on 6 October, when English troops stormed one of the Spanish forts defending Zutphen. While the assault was still in the balance, Edward Stanley clambered into the breach by himself and fought nine or ten defenders at a time in full view of the whole army, 'first with his pike, then with the stumpes of his pike, and afterward his sword'. This inspired his men to win the day and impressed Leicester so greatly that he knighted him on the spot and gave him £40 in gold and a lifetime pension of £66 a year. Stanley's feat underlines the power of personal example and how (as in most wars) much of the serious fighting was actually done by a small minority of those involved.[10]

While Leicester's army maintained a largely defensive posture, the main offensive thrust of Elizabeth's war with Spain in 1585–86 was embodied in Drake's expedition to the West Indies. Significantly, this was a largely private-enterprise endeavour, with the queen's contribution being less than a third of the total cost of the venture (and even less in terms of cash). This eased the burden on the exchequer and enabled Elizabeth to maintain a degree of deniability during the early months of the war. For his part, Drake revelled in the opportunity to pursue profits for himself and his investors, rather than following strict instructions which might inhibit his piratical instincts. As Elizabeth observed in March 1586, 'yf nede be, . . . the gentleman [Drake] careth nott yf I shold dysavowe hym'.[11]

By the time Drake sailed in September 1585, his force consisted of about 25 ships. He also had at least eight pinnaces (over-sized row-boats which could carry a sail) for in-shore work and 2300 men, including 12 companies of infantry under the command of Christopher Carleill. After hovering off the Spanish coast long enough to obtain extra supplies, Drake sailed south to the Canary and Cape Verde Islands. On the way, he learned from a French ship that he had already missed the chance to intercept the Spanish treasure ships sailing home from the New World. In the Cape Verde Islands, he landed 1000 men to seize the town of Santiago, which he burned after the inhabitants failed to offer a suitable ransom. He then headed across the Atlantic, reaching the West Indies a week before Christmas, after an 18-day passage. However, the landing at Santiago had exposed the fleet to 'a lamentable and grevous sycknes' which soon killed several hundred men and left many more chronically weakened for long periods. Despite this, Drake headed for Hispaniola and its capital of Santo Domingo, which was captured with little resistance after Carleill's troops executed a surprise night landing several miles to the west. They occupied the city for a full month and destroyed much of it in the pursuit of plunder – news which caused terror around the Caribbean and fury in Spain. The troops re-embarked at the end of January and Drake headed for Cartagena, which was even richer and more important than Santo Domingo. By now, Spanish settlements in the region were aware of the English presence and the inhabitants of Cartagena had constructed new fortifications to defend their city. Nevertheless, Drake's force conducted another textbook combined-arms operation, landing troops in the dark and coordinating their attack with cannon fire from the ships. Demonstrating the benefits of drill by attacking 'with pikes roundly together', Carleill's soldiers quickly routed the local militia. Once again, Drake's men ruthlessly scoured the city for booty, but much of the city's wealth had already been spirited away, leaving Drake and his men with a disappointingly modest haul.[12]

The occupation of Cartagena lasted two months and Drake seriously considered holding it as a permanent English base, but his officers were eager to head home and the army could no longer provide an adequate garrison. An earlier plan to attack Nombre de Dios and Panama (reviving his tactics of the early 1570s) was also no longer practical. Drake therefore skirted Cuba and headed north to the Atlantic coast of Florida, where he attacked and demolished a Spanish fort. Continuing north, the fleet reached the fledgling English colony at Roanoke on 9 June. The settlement was already beleaguered and, although Drake offered supplies, many of the colonists ultimately chose to sail home with the fleet. Drake's ships finally reached England at the end of July 1586, almost 11 months after they had left. About a third of those who had set out – some 750 men – failed to return.[13]

The terrible mortality of the voyage was not redeemed by financial success. Based upon the declared plunder, the queen and other investors only recovered 75 per cent of their costs. The intoxicating prospect of waging a self-funding – or even profit-making – war, which had been raised by Drake's circumnavigation of 1577–80, had not been realised. However, despite this disappointment, the value of the expedition was not measured by contemporaries solely in material terms. Above all, the expedition had done huge damage to Spanish honour. This ensured that it influenced the course of the Anglo-Spanish conflict to a far greater extent than the fighting in the Low Countries. Philip II recognised that the financial cost of this and future raids on the Caribbean would be heavy, but the cost to his royal authority if he failed to stem English aggression would be even greater. His response was to strike at the root of the threat by targeting England itself. For their part, English proponents of oceanic warfare saw the West Indies voyage as sufficiently successful to justify new plans to attack Spanish interests from the sea. Given the extraordinary success of Drake's amphibious landings, it seemed that, with a little more luck, great things might be achieved next time. Drake himself went to the Low Countries in October 1586 to lobby Leicester and the Dutch for support in his next venture. Reviving old plans to back Dom Antonio's claim to the throne of Portugal, Drake proposed that a combined Anglo-Dutch force should land the pretender in Portugal or the Azores to stir up rebellion against Philip. Despite the mixed results of fighting in 1586, England's offensive at sea promised to become even more aggressive in 1587.[14]

The War Goes Sour, 1586–87

Despite the optimism of Drake and his backers, England's war effort was in sorry shape by the end of 1586. Although Elizabeth was contractually bound to spend only £126,000 a year on the war in the Low Countries, actual spending topped £150,000, while the costs and debts of the States ballooned alarmingly. The latter directly affected English soldiers in Dutch pay – whose numbers peaked at 7500 foot and 500 cavalry in September 1586 – and forced the illicit diversion of money earmarked for the queen's troops, which left both parts of the allied army desperately short of money. As the full magnitude of the financial shambles began to emerge during the early months of 1586, Elizabeth became increasingly angry that Leicester's military administration could not provide accounts to explain where the money was going. For a sovereign who disliked substantial spending at the best of times, this continuing inability to track or adequately contain expenditure was infuriating. After paying out £45,000 in July 1586, Elizabeth became so averse to spending more money that no further cash was sent until the end of October. Leicester consequently was forced to slash the military establishment. Although it was deeply unpopular with officers and troops alike, 24 of the 50 infantry companies in the queen's pay were dissolved and their troops were redistributed among the remaining 26. Yet even this did not bring all the companies back to full strength, which suggests how heavy the year's losses had been from combat, disease and desertion. For their part, the States were forced to dissolve almost 50 companies of Dutch troops and 12 units of cavalry. Most of the English troops were also paid off over the winter. However, even these reduced establishments proved financially insupportable, especially as Elizabeth refused to send more money until February. With the exception of the garrisons at Flushing and Brielle (who benefited from new financial arrangements with local merchants), the army was left destitute over the winter.[15]

If this were not bad enough, the alliance between England and the Dutch was rocked in January 1587 by the sudden surrender to Spain of the fort at Zutphen (which had been so hard-won in October) and the nearby town of Deventer. The English commanders of these garrisons, Sir William Stanley and Rowland York, also took most of their men with them into Spanish service. In English terms at least, this was defection on an unprecedented scale. Although Stanley's regiment consisted of Irishmen, his officers were largely Welsh and Stanley himself was a relative of the earl of Derby and a prominent follower of Leicester. Such connections had enabled him to recruit his own officers and men, which ensured their loyalty to him at the decisive moment. For the remainder of Elizabeth's reign, Stanley would be an ardent advocate of Catholic plans to invade England and his Irish regiment (which also attracted English Catholic exiles) would become one of the most renowned units in the Spanish army. Stanley therefore became a bogeyman figure in the eyes of Elizabeth's government and seemed to confirm all their worst fears about the loyalty of the queen's Catholic subjects.[16]

Stanley's betrayal encouraged anti-English sentiment among the Dutch towns and made life even more miserable for English soldiers, who were already despised by the local inhabitants for their poverty and were now regarded as untrustworthy. This wave of anger killed Drake's plans for an Anglo-Dutch expedition and encouraged a new assertiveness in the States which made Leicester's position precarious – especially as he had publicly staked his reputation on Stanley during the 'private warres' among his officers. It required months of negotiation before Leicester, who had returned home for the winter, was able to return to the Low Countries. However, the broader context for Dutch mistrust of English intentions was provided by Elizabeth herself, who had consistently pursued secret contacts with Parma in the hope of arranging formal peace talks. Although a direct approach to Parma was cancelled in deference to Dutch sensitivities in September 1585, a variety of contacts were pursued at the queen's insistence during 1586 by Sir James Croft and other councillors. Walsingham, and especially Leicester, were at first kept in the dark, although the merchants who acted as intermediaries were so indiscreet that their dealings became widely known. Despite loud complaints from the States about the rumours, Elizabeth continued to push ahead during 1587, believing that she was making progress towards a compromise with Parma and that the latter acted with Philip's blessing. Indeed, as the financial crisis of the allied armies in the Low Countries worsened and their military weakness became increasingly apparent, Elizabeth believed the pursuit of peace was imperative.[17]

This belief was reinforced when Parma besieged the port of Sluis in June. Although its defenders – including 800 English troops – put up a heroic defence against overwhelming odds for seven weeks, Leicester proved unable to mount a serious relief operation. Despite bringing 4600 new reinforcements from England and £30,000 in cash, he could not mobilise troops or ships from the Dutch. He also showed little confidence in his own troops' ability to save the town, which was understandable given the rawness of the new arrivals. After enduring a bombardment of unprecedented intensity – 4000 heavy rounds on one day alone – and fighting back repeated assaults by Parma's best troops, the garrison finally surrendered on 4 August.

More than half the defenders had been killed. Despite heavy casualties of his own, especially among his officers, Parma allowed the surviving defenders honourable and unmolested passage home. Yet even the praise which Parma lavished upon Sir Roger Williams and other English officers could not disguise the fact that a port had been lost which might assist an invasion of England and that the allied war effort was now chronically dyspeptic. Indeed, it emerged that the 4600 extra troops sent to rescue Sluis had been raised on the erroneous assumption the Dutch would pay them. Although these units were soon dissolved, the error underlined the shambolic nature of the army's administration and helped to ensure English spending in the Low Countries between November 1585 and November 1587 topped £313,000 – almost 25 per cent more than planned. These experiences made Elizabeth more determined than ever to pursue negotiations with Spain. She even forced Leicester to approach the States about joining her quest for a peace conference. The Dutch refused and Leicester's efforts to claw back his lost authority in the Low Countries during the remaining months of 1587 merely made things worse. Although Leicester returned to England for good in December, the crisis between the allies persisted well into 1588.[18]

Elizabeth's determination to secure peace with Philip was also sharpened by reports of naval preparations in Spain and Portugal, which many of her councillors regarded as evidence of a planned invasion. Although she placed her greatest trust in negotiation, Elizabeth recognised the need to counter these ominous preparations – as long as doing so did not jeopardise her dealings with Parma. In mid-March, Drake was instructed to disrupt the Spanish naval build-up in any way he could and was given four royal warships to form the core of his fleet. Drake and other investors (including the lord admiral) readied seven more ships, while a syndicate of London merchants provided another ten. Once again, national strategic interests were expected to coincide with the pursuit of private profit. Whether deliberately or not, the new expedition also provided further 'deniability' for Elizabeth. Only days after the fleet set sail, the council issued new orders for Drake which banned him from attacking Spanish territory. Drake was certainly tipped off about the queen's likely change of heart and the fact that the new instructions never reached him – even though he was able to send regular reports back to England – suggests that Drake's backers saw the benefits of simultaneously preserving his freedom of action and giving Elizabeth an excuse to 'dysavowe' him if anything went wrong. After Drake's return, the revised orders enabled Elizabeth's government to safeguard the peace talks by claiming she had been 'unwitting, yea unwilling' to approve Drake's actions and was 'greatly offended with him'.[19]

Drake arrived off the Iberian coast in mid-April and soon learned that a large number of merchant ships were in Cadiz harbour, protected by only a few galleys. When the fleet arrived off Cadiz on 19 April, Drake ordered an immediate attack, even though it was already late in the afternoon. Believing the English fleet to be Spanish vessels, the defenders were taken by surprise when the new arrivals opened fire. The harbour defences proved ineffective and the galleys were soon driven off, leaving Drake's ships to overwhelm two large merchantmen which offered brief resistance. Most of the other ships in the harbour were unmanned and the English were able systematically to seize, plunder or burn the dozens of vessels riding at anchor. On the morning of 21 April, after spending some 30 hours in the harbour, Drake withdrew and headed northwards up the coast. At Lagos and Sagres, the fleet landed several hundred troops, but little was achieved except the destruction of a small fort and the desecration of local Catholic churches.

Although the focus of Spanish naval activity was the Portuguese capital of Lisbon, the defences there were too strong to attack. Drake contented himself with destroying local Portuguese fishing boats and vessels carrying supplies necessary for barrel-making, judging that these would deprive the Spanish of fish rations and the barrels needed for storing them. At the end of May, Drake's fleet was dispersed by storms, but most of his ships accompanied him to the Azores, where they captured the *Sao Phelipe*, a large Portuguese carrack making its way home from the East Indies. Even allowing for goods which quickly disappeared into the hampers and trunks of Drake and his men, the treasures from this ship (worth £108,000) brought the expedition the sort of bumper profit which had been hoped for in the West Indies voyage. Elizabeth – never prone to splashing cash around – allowed all the ordinary seamen an extra two months' pay as a bonus, while those aboard the ships which actually took the *Sao Phelipe* also received a further six months' pay. Drake's raid on Cadiz therefore not only witnessed the 'singeing of the king of Spain's beard', as legend has it, but also revived enthusiasm for the potential profits to be made from taking the offensive at sea. However, Spain's furious reaction to Drake's voyage would ensure that it would be another two years before the next major English maritime expedition could be launched.[20]

The 'Enterprise of England', 1585–88

The phrase 'the enterprise of England' – meaning a concerted effort by Spain and its Catholic allies to overthrow Elizabeth's government and replace it with a more congenial regime – was apparently coined in May 1569 by Guerau de Spes, the Spanish ambassador in England who first urged Philip to support secret plots to replace Elizabeth with Mary Queen of Scots and was ultimately expelled for his involvement in the Ridolfi conspiracy. In the years that followed, Philip showed intermittent interest in pursuing this 'enterprise', but refused to commit substantial resources to the task. The king's attitude finally became fixed at the end of 1585, when Drake landed on the Spanish coast before heading towards the West Indies. News of the subsequent sacking of Santiago, Santo Domingo and Cartagena reinforced Philip's opinion, confirming fears about the chronic vulnerability of Spain's global empire that had been excited by Drake's circumnavigation five years earlier. As the king's chief foreign policy adviser, Don Juan de Zuniga, put it: 'to fight a purely defensive war is to court a huge and permanent expense because we have to defend the [East and West] Indies, Spain and the convoys travelling between them.' Reasons of both honour and economy demanded that Philip should meet the English challenge head-on by attacking England itself.[21]

This dramatic, but secret, shift in Spanish strategy had huge military and diplomatic implications, which meant it was not until mid-1586 that 'the enterprise of England' was launched fully. Philip's two senior military commanders, Parma and Santa Cruz, initially offered rival plans which emphasised their own role in affairs. While Parma suggested a surprise invasion launched from Flanders, arguing that his army could be easily shipped across the Narrow Seas in barges, Santa Cruz advocated the despatch of an immense naval task force from Spain and Portugal. Faced with this conflicting advice, Philip chose to combine their strategies. Using a much smaller fleet than originally suggested, Santa Cruz was to invade Ireland. Once the English were completely distracted by events there, the Spanish fleet would dash into the Channel and rendezvous with Parma's army, which would already have put to sea after surprising the enemy with a rapid embarkation. Covered by the fleet, Parma's flotilla would land in Kent and head straight for London. This decision reduced the burden on Spain and Portugal, which lacked sufficient ships, supplies and seamen to create the vast fleet which Santa Cruz had wanted, but it also meant the two main elements of the operation would be planned and prepared by separate staffs hundreds of miles apart – by Parma in Flanders and Santa Cruz in Lisbon, with Philip overseeing progress from Spain – and that its success would require a miracle of coordination. Although he believed that God would provide this miracle, Philip recognised that victory would be more likely if Elizabeth's government suffered a failure of nerve or was distracted by internal rebellion. To that end, Philip turned up the heat on English exports, which soon faced bans not only in Spain and Portugal, but also (thanks to Spanish diplomatic pressure) in France, Flanders and Hamburg. From his new base in Paris, Mendoza encouraged plots by Catholic extremists in England, resulting in the arrest of Anthony Babington and his co-conspirators in August 1586. The failure of this plot brought disaster upon Mary Queen of Scots, who was executed in February 1587 for approving Babington's plan to kill Elizabeth. This caused uproar across the whole of Catholic Europe and added the motive of revenge to Philip's grand 'enterprise'. However, Mary's death also ensured that Spain's costly exertions would not end up installing a pro-French Catholic on the English throne.[22]

Philip hoped to launch his invasion of England in the summer of 1587, but this ultimately proved to be impossible. Santa Cruz's naval build-up had already been delayed by the panic which followed

Drake's West Indies voyage and the raid on Cadiz caused even more problems. Drake's attacks along the Iberian coast destroyed precious supplies and his sortie towards the Azores forced Spanish warships to set sail in pursuit. More importantly, the confusion and anger arising from Drake's repeated landings on Spanish soil encouraged a series of policy oscillations by Philip himself which bewildered Parma and Santa Cruz. Unwell but desperate to proceed with the invasion, the king issued a stream of orders which paid little heed to reality. Chopping and changing plans, he briefly even reverted to Parma's original suggestion of a simple surprise attack by troop-carrying barges. With the element of surprise long since lost, however, Parma's troops could not risk putting to sea without naval escort, even if his army had been ready (which it was not). Santa Cruz's warships were also unable to take the lead because they did not return from vainly pursuing Drake until the end of September. By then, the season when the weather was most likely to permit an invasion had almost passed and the ships were unfit for fresh operations. The invasion therefore had to be postponed until 1588.

At a cost of 30,000 ducats (approx. £7500) a day – twice the cost of Parma's Army of Flanders – the continuation of naval preparations for another year was an enormous burden on Spain. The experiences of 1587 also shaped the events of the following year in other ways. In September, Philip's last-gasp effort to launch the invasion in 1587 saw him simplify the plan by removing the diversionary landing in Ireland and ordering the fleet to head straight into the Channel to cover the landing of Parma's flotilla in Kent. This made coordination between the fleet and army even more critical than before, whilst lessening the opportunities for communciation between the two forces. Success would now require a greater miracle than ever. After the confusion of 1587, Philip also decided there could be no deviation from his instructions in 1588. In effect, Spanish planning went from one extreme to the other: instead of the bewildering fluidity of constant changes, there would now be rigid obedience to an unalterable plan.[23]

As Drake's Cadiz voyage demonstrates, the Spanish preparations soon became obvious to Elizabeth's government. Indeed, the intelligence assets of Walsingham and other councillors ultimately produced so much information about the scale, pace and purpose of the

Spanish build-up that it caused considerable uncertainty about how England should prepare its defences – too much intelligence, especially when it was inconsistent, became almost as disconcerting as too little. Nevertheless, the obvious threat provoked increasingly frantic action. Although the *Rainbow* and *Vanguard* (500 tons each) were launched in 1586 and the *Ark Ralegh* (800 tons) was bought from Sir Walter Ralegh and renamed *Ark Royal* in 1587, the main change to the queen's fleet in the mid-1580s was the acquisition of small vessels suitable for scouting. Between 1584 and 1587, nine new vessels of 40–90 tons were built or bought for the queen. These additions reflected the realisation that it was less important to expand the battle fleet than to ensure the queen's existing warships could engage the enemy effectively. On land, relatively minor repairs were made to fortifications along the southern and eastern coasts. Although the coastal defences which Henry VIII had built were now largely decayed, lack of time and money prevented more elaborate building work. Many vulnerable areas instead received temporary fieldworks which were cheap and required only spadework – the Elizabethan equivalent of 1940-style barbed wire and pill-boxes. The traditional system of warning beacons was overhauled and a constant watch was maintained between spring and autumn. Regional munitions stores were created and detailed plans were drawn up for the destruction of local bridges and food supplies in the event of a landing. Other precautionary measures concerned the treatment of Catholics, whose loyalty the government mistrusted (ironically, a doubt which Philip also shared). Although known Catholics had been disarmed in 1586, the example of Stanley and York encouraged a policy of internment for prominent Catholics in 1587–88. The government also took an increasingly ruthless line with captured Catholic missionaries, executing 86 priests and their helpers during the period 1586–91, 31 of them in 1588. This was the most intense bout of persecution in the whole reign and reflected the government's acute fear of potential Catholic fifth-columnists.[24]

The most dramatic developments in the face of the looming Spanish threat involved local administration and the county militias. Between 1585 and 1587, the military resources of each county were placed under the control of a lord lieutenant. Lords lieutenant had been appointed during periods of crisis in the past – for example, during the 'camping time' of 1549 and during the Northern Rising of 1569–70 – but the demands and duration of the war with Spain would ensure the office now became permanent. Lieutenants functioned as the queen's chief agents in the counties and ensured that the central government could directly harness local resources to the demands of national security. Aided by his deputy lieutenants, a lord lieutenant would supervise the raising of money for military purposes, levy troops for service abroad, oversee the regular mustering of the county's trained bands and, if necessary, lead the latter into battle. In many counties, the deputies were especially important because the lieutenant was a member of the privy council and hence often absent. Burghley, for example, was lord lieutenant of Lincolnshire, Hertfordshire and Essex, while the lord admiral was lieutenant of Surrey and shared the lieutenancy of Sussex with his fellow councillor, Lord Buckhurst. Such appointments ensured the privy council had direct oversight of military affairs across large swathes of the realm and that most councillors were intimately aware of the local consequences of their orders. The lieutenancy system therefore not only reflected (and made possible) the council's desire to enforce greater uniformity and centralised control over the county militias, but also anchored council instructions in what was practicable.[25]

The council's awareness of how far local gentlemen and communities could be pushed was critically important in forcing through controversial and expensive changes to the county militias in 1587–88. Drill for the trained bands was stepped up and special training camps were introduced in which large numbers of troops received intensive instruction for two or three weeks at a time. A committee of expert military advisers which met at the end of November 1587 also helped to initiate a change of strategy which was implemented during the spring of 1588. Instead of trying to defend the whole coastline, deployments were planned around likely landing places, most of which would be covered by trained bands from two or more counties. This required pre-planned coordination between neighbouring lieutenancies and marked the end of the ancient practice of simply rushing to confront an invading enemy on the beaches. This more professional and systematic approach to national defence reflected the influence of officers such as Sir John Norris and Sir Roger Williams, whose advice was based upon their enormous collective experience of war in Ireland and the Continent. The more sophisticated tasking of the militia completed the logic behind creating the trained bands in the first place – if only a minority of a county's militia were trained for combat, it followed that extra trained troops would have to be drawn from nearby counties to make up for the reduced number of soldiers available to face the enemy.

However, even careful planning could not compensate for the realm's chronic shortage of (relatively) trained soldiers. In April 1588, the trained bands of England and Wales numbered only 48,127 foot and 4716 cavalry. The privy council therefore ordered lieutenants to bolster their bands by adding large numbers of armed but untrained men. London, for example, was required to add 4000 new men to its 6000 trained troops, while Cornwall (which seemed a prime target for invasion but had very few troops) added 2100 to the 1500 men already in its trained bands. By distributing them among the existing bands, it was hoped the new men could learn quickly and would take courage from their more practised comrades if required to fight. This emergency measure boosted the total number of 'trained' infantry to 87,199 and enabled the privy council to plan for the creation of multiple armies to defend the realm.[26]

Planning such changes was one thing, but implementing them was quite a different matter. Altering the strength and deployment areas of trained bands upset many country gentlemen who served as militia officers, especially in cases where units were reduced in size, which was regarded as an affront to the commander's honour. Local gentlemen were also aggrieved when they found themselves receiving orders from officers whom the privy council had employed as expert military advisers. Although seasoned by war on the Continent, these advisers were often seen locally as outsiders and socially inferior. The new strategy of using troops from several counties to defend specific landing sites also raised fears among the soldiers that their homes might be left unprotected. Above all, the changes to the trained bands placed an enormous extra financial burden on the counties.

Boosting the number of training days and the number of men to be trained greatly increased the wages bill and required large new purchases of arms, armour and munitions. These items were already in short supply, but the nation-wide scramble to equip extra troops drove up prices further. Even without the expense of adding new men to the trained bands, according to one Kent JP, the cost of training 300 horse and foot for 16 days was £300. Such hefty costs ensured that many members of the trained bands continued to be armed with old-fashioned bows and bills and made the question of who should pay, and how much, a matter of burning importance. In Burghley's opinion, 'the reportes which I heare out of sundry contreys of the reiteration of unsupportable charges towardes musters do trouble me as mutch as the expences of the queen's tresur.' He was especially concerned that 'thes demandes for musters, for powder and new weapons' were now being levied even on the urban poor: 'I se a generall murmur of people, and malcontented people will increase it, to the comfort of the enemy.'[27]

Burghley was not alone in fearing the consequences of the realm's defences resting too heavily upon the commons. The whole privy council was deeply alarmed about the economic and social impact of the war, fearing a repetition of the nightmare of Edward VI's reign. In 1586, a poor harvest increased food prices, while the huge new demand for food to supply the queen's troops in the Low Countries siphoned large quantities of grain and meat out of the realm. This drove up prices for the stocks that remained and caused acute unrest. In Ipswich, angry locals hijacked a shipment of meat destined for the army. In Hampshire, a group of disgruntled weavers, tailors and clothiers – victims of a simultaneous slump in the cloth industry – became so angry at the high price of bread that they planned to fire a signal beacon to raise the militia and begin a 'commotion' in the manner of 1549. This fighting talk came to nothing, but the council learned of the plan and investigated it with a thoroughness which underlined its concern about popular restlessness. Large quantities of rye were hastily imported from the Baltic to help meet the demand. In January 1587, the council also instigated new price controls on local grain supplies, which simultaneously reduced popular anger over alleged profiteering and made it easier for contractors to secure

supplies for military victuals at consistent prices. Further relief came
from a bumper harvest in 1587. Nevertheless, the balance between
what was militarily desirable and what the realm could provide without undue discontent remained a delicate one, especially before the
new harvest came in. In February 1587, the navy victualler Edward
Baeshe planned to purchase 1000 quarters of wheat, 1000 quarters of
malt and 100 barrels of butter from Norfolk. 'For the ease of the cun-
try', the lord lieutenant of the county, Lord Hunsdon, intervened to
halve the amount of wheat and reduce the butter to 60 barrels. This
was still too much in the opinion of local JPs. Baeshe ultimately had
to settle for 500 quarters of wheat and 600 quarters of malt and had
to turn to Suffolk for the butter.[28]

Despite their anxiety about the dangers of overburdening local
communities, Elizabeth and her councillors believed that the almost
unmanageable demands imposed upon the exchequer gave them no
choice but to shift as many war costs as possible away from the
queen to her subjects. Although years of scrimping had ensured that
the treasury held reserves of £270,000 in 1585, the huge cost of the
war in the Low Countries and the threat of invasion swiftly consumed this surplus. Even with income of almost £150,000 from taxation in 1587 (and £200,000 in 1588), there was a constant shortage of
cash. By the start of 1588, the government was forced to cut the budget for the army in the Low Countries by 8 per cent, while 2400 of the
queen's richest subjects were commanded to contribute towards a
forced loan of £75,000 and the City of London was asked to loan
another £30,000.

This was still not enough to cover the cost of the war. The council
therefore decided to transfer much of the the cost of naval defence to
port towns, which were each ordered to provide and pay for specific
kinds of ships to bolster the queen's fleet. This sparked widespread
dismay, but mayors and town councils did their best to comply.
King's Lynn, for example, was required to provide two ships of more
than 60 tons each and a pinnace, armed and victualled for two
months. With most of its larger vessels recently departed for the Low
Countries or Iceland, the best the town could offer was a pinnace and
one ship of 150 tons. However, manning and supplying these vessels
would require financial contributions from neighbouring towns,

over which the mayor of King's Lynn had no jurisdiction. Getting the town's two vessels to sea required a further intervention by the council with the authorities in the neighbouring communities.

The privy council's sudden demand for ports to provide ships caused much bewilderment, but the greatest concern created by this heavy new burden was the same as that caused by changes to the trained bands – that some individuals and communities might be forced to pay too much (with severe consequences for the most vulnerable inhabitants), while others escaped paying altogether. The key to overcoming these complaints was the privy council's ability and willingness to force neighbouring communities to spread the burden. Without the regular interventions by the council in favour of local cooperation, the sense of inequity created by the council's own demands for war-related expenditure in the localities might have generated disastrous social and political tensions.[29]

Such problems reinforced Elizabeth's continuing dismay at the cost of the war and made her more determined than ever to secure a negotiated settlement with Spain. After months of indirect communication, she finally convinced Parma to hold a formal peace conference at the start of 1588. A high-powered English delegation arrived at Ostend in February, but Parma and his representatives argued about the location of the talks (ultimately held at the nearby village of Bourbourg) and never got beyond raising basic questions about a potential cease-fire. Although it became apparent that Parma was not interested in making serious progress, Elizabeth was desperate for peace and forced her delegates to keep negotiating. They were still there when the Spanish fleet arrived off Cornwall in mid-July. In reality, the peace talks were a deliberate attempt by Philip to conceal his invasion plans. Parma's instructions were to maintain the deception as long as possible, whilst actually preparing his army for the invasion. Once the decision to launch 'the enterprise of England' had been taken, Philip's only interest in Elizabeth's peace-feelers lay in exploiting her hopes to reduce English defensive preparations and undermine the Anglo-Dutch alliance. The result of this policy was that Elizabeth would never be able to trust Spanish talk of peace again and the war would consequently continue until both Philip and Elizabeth were dead.[30]

Despite her fervent desire for a diplomatic settlement, Elizabeth recognised the importance of preparing for the worst, especially as the flood of intelligence about preparations in Spain and the Low Countries made the privy council increasingly sceptical about the prospects for peace. By the summer of 1588, the realm's defences were more or less ready. Plans were made to create four separate defensive armies. One force would shadow the Spanish fleet as it sailed up the Channel, ready to respond to a landing. Another army under Lord Hunsdon would protect London and the queen's person, while Leicester commanded a third army which covered Kent and Essex, its troops straddling the Thames estuary. A fourth army, led by the earl of Huntingdon, would guard the north. In addition to the trained bands, the manpower for these armies would come from the servants and tenants of the nobility, courtiers and clergymen and from some 2000 infantry recalled from the English garrisons in the Low Countries. Although it caused further ill feeling with the Dutch, the return of the latter troops was especially significant because it showed the 'cautionary towns' had now assumed the role formerly held by Calais. When the crown needed to confront a dangerous enemy, the garrisons in the Low Countries could release a substantial number of veteran troops to provide the backbone for a new army – a military resource which had been missing since 1558. The 16,000 men raised by the nobility and royal servants constituted the remnants of the 'quasi-feudal' system which Henry VIII had relied upon for his invasions of France. Although the old system had virtually collapsed during 1544–45 and was now useless for sending soldiers overseas, it remained a useful supplement to the trained bands for national defence because these troops were paid by the men who raised them rather than by the crown. This was critically important to Elizabeth's government in 1588.

By contrast, the trained bands had to be paid by the crown once they reached their designated assembly areas, which gave Elizabeth a strong incentive to mobilise them for the shortest possible time. This explains why none of the four armies was allowed to reach full strength. More than 20,000 men joined the 'shadowing' army at various stages during the Armada's advance up the Channel, but they never formed a single force. Hunsdon received only about 5000 of the 29,000 militia troops scheduled to join his army (although all the 'quasi-feudal' soldiers were called out) and Huntingdon mobilised only 2700 men in the north before cancelling the order. Even Leicester's army, which would have constituted the main force to counter an invasion in Kent and which peaked at 17,000 troops, was not fully fleshed out. This reflected a conscious gamble by the queen that partial mobilisation could provide sufficient insurance against a Spanish landing and that, if necessary, full mobilisation could still be achieved quickly enough to save the day. For Leicester at least, this economy seemed too great a risk: 'I beseech you assemble your forces and play not away this kingdom by delays.' Nevertheless, it was a sign both of how overstretched the queen's finances had become and how efficiently the trained bands could respond that Elizabeth took such a gamble.[31]

The strategy of partial mobilisation also reflected a decision made in the autumn of 1587 that the realm's first line of defence would involve engaging the enemy at sea, rather than allowing them to land. Faced with two obvious threats – the fleet mustering in Lisbon and the barges being gathered for Parma's army in Flanders – the initial plan for naval defence entailed creating two separate fleets. While the lord admiral commanded the main force near Dover to cover Parma and protect the most likely area for invasion, Drake would lead a smaller fleet in the west. Drake's plan was to repeat his success of the previous year by attacking the Spanish fleet before it left port. However, his force was too small to tackle Lisbon and Elizabeth refused to let him sail because she harboured hopes of a peace agreement, especially when news arrived that Philip's chief admiral, the marquis of Santa Cruz, had died. Frustrated at his enforced inactivity, Drake wrote to the council on 30 March and demanded reinforcements and permission to depart, pointing out that Parma could never risk putting to sea unless supported by the Spanish fleet. Drake's letter was a plea for virtual *carte blanche* to attack Spain and his strategic analysis was distinctly self-serving. Nevertheless, his argument was also correct – without protection from the Spanish fleet, Parma's army and all the expensive preparations which he had made for launching an amphibious assault would be rendered irrelevant.

Ironically, Drake's appeal triggered an overhaul of English strategy which was so profound that it actually cost him his independent command. Following debate among the council and approval by Elizabeth, Lord Admiral Howard was instructed to leave only a covering force in the Straits of Dover and move the bulk of his fleet to join Drake's ships at Plymouth. This combined force (with Drake now as second in command) would immediately set sail for Spain to engage the enemy fleet in its home waters. Although risky, this strategy appealed because attacking the Armada while its location was still known seemed easier than trying to defend against an assault which might fall almost anywhere in England, Wales or Ireland. It also promised a shorter – and hence cheaper – campaign.

Once Howard's main fleet had relocated to Plymouth, the problem of victuals reinforced the need to strike quickly. Already low on food (as a result of shortage of money and available supplies), Howard's force found itself unable to obtain extra provisions in the west country. Every day the winds kept the fleet in port left it with fewer supplies for the voyage to Spain, making it imperative to settle the matter swiftly, before the fleet was incapacitated for lack of food. Three times the fleet set sail for Spain – on 30 May and 19 and 23 June – and three times the winds changed, driving them home again. On the last occasion, the fleet had almost reached the Spanish coast when the weather turned.[32]

Although the English did not know it, the last of these winds which drove the fleet back to Plymouth in mid-July was finally pushing Philip's *Gran Armada* ('Great Armed Fleet') towards England. The Armada had endured terrible supply problems of its own and suffered severely from the same unseasonable weather which had plagued the English. Leaving Lisbon on 18 May, it had been forced to seek shelter in Corunna on 9 June and spent a month there repairing the damage. Reports reaching England suggested that it would not be able to leave Corunna. The appearance of the Armada off the Cornish coast on 19 July came as a nasty surprise to the English fleet, which was still licking its wounds after its latest attempt to reach the Spanish coast. Surprise and confusion therefore marked the opening of a naval campaign which represented uncharted territory for both sides. The new Spanish commander, the duke of Medina Sidonia, was urged by some of his subordinate officers to attack the English fleet while it was still trapped in Plymouth Sound and desperately trying to put to sea in the face of a contrary wind. Medina Sidonia declined to do so because Philip's instructions required him to head straight for the expected rendezvous with Parma's sea-borne army at 'the Cape of Margate' (i.e. the Downs). The Armada was also not equipped for engaging an enemy fleet covered by shore batteries, especially as its four galleys (the oared vessels which the Spanish regarded as essential for amphibious operations) had failed to make it across the Bay of Biscay. Medina Sidonia stuck to his orders and headed eastwards, allowing the English to get to sea and begin probing attacks.[33]

To English eyes, the Armada seemed enormous and its adoption of a tight crescent formation (with the wings projecting forward) seemed ominously well disciplined. In reality, the Armada was a large convoy rather than a battle-fleet. Of the 140-odd ships which left Corunna, only 23 were galleons (i.e. front-line warships), while another 70 ships were large merchantmen. The Armada carried fewer than 8000 seamen, but approximately 20,000 soldiers. In response, Elizabeth's government ultimately mobilised 16,000 seamen and soldiers and almost 200 vessels, mostly small auxiliaries. The main burden of defence rested upon the queen's warships (21 of which were rated at 200 tons or more) and another 30-odd ships of similar size (but slightly reduced firepower) provided by port towns and private individuals. The 34 vessels owned by the queen carried 6300 men, of whom only 1492 were soldiers. They also carried 883 cannon and 555 specialist naval gunners to fire them, whereas Spanish warships generally carried fewer big guns and relied upon ordinary soldiers to service them.

Such numbers underline the different nature of the two fleets and explain their contrasting tactics. The Spanish crescent formation was the product of galley-warfare and was intended to protect the vulnerable transports from English gunfire by allowing the warships on the Armada's wings to surround, grapple and board any enemy vessels which came too close to the transports. The English were aware of this danger, recalling that the Spanish had used grappling tactics to overwhelm the international fleet which supported Dom Antonio in the Azores in 1582. Howard's captains sought to maintain a safe distance

by using their manoeuvrability to close rapidly on the enemy warships stationed along the Armada's flanks, successively discharging
their heavy bow guns and smaller broadside guns, before tacking
away, firing their large guns in the stern and withdrawing to reload in
safety. This minimised exposure to enemy counter-fire, virtually
eliminated the risk of being grappled and boarded by enemy soldiers,
and forced a handful of Spanish warships to endure a steady succession of bombardments.

Nevertheless, the initial result of these contrasting tactics was a
stalemate. Although the Spanish were frustrated by their inability to
get to grips with English ships and were stunned by the intensity of
their cannon fire, they suffered little damage. For their part, the
English remained wary of approaching too closely and tended to
shoot from too great a distance to be effective. Although Howard's
warships fired off most of their shot and powder and had to seek
resupply, the advance of the Armada was barely impeded.[34]

Medina Sidonia's orders required him to proceed to the Downs to
meet Parma's army without becoming entangled in sea battles on the
way, but did not explain how Parma was to reach the Armada.
Medina Sidonia himself was not briefed on Parma's preparations at
Dunkirk and Nieupoort until the beginning of May and, even then,
he still believed the 300 boats and barges which Parma had gathered
would be sufficient to break the Dutch blockade in the shallow
waters off Flanders. With this in mind, Medina Sidonia was prepared
to bend his instructions by seeking an anchorage off the Isle of Wight
and waiting for news of Parma there, rather than heading straight for
the Downs. He also repeatedly tried to play upon English eagerness
for plunder by using warships to masquerade as stragglers, hoping to
trick the English into a grappling fight. His aim was to inflict sufficient damage on Howard's force to draw away the enemy ships facing Parma. However, the English fleet drove the Armada past the Isle
of Wight and refused to take the bait for close combat. Doubly
thwarted, Medina Sidonia had to settle for anchoring off Calais on 27
July. Still believing that Parma's fleet could cross the Straits by itself,
he asked his colleague for extra munitions and reinforcements for
the decisive naval battle with the English fleet which he expected
would precede the landing of Parma's troops. Such requests reveal

Medina Sidonia's complete lack of understanding of events. Parma's major warships were trapped at Antwerp and his invasion force consisted of small vessels which were critically vulnerable to fire from the Dutch shallow-water craft, let alone from the English squadron which patrolled deeper waters. The barges were also limited to calm seas. Even with the Armada at Calais, the 30 miles of shallow water which separated Medina Sidonia's ships from Parma's flotilla would have proved extraordinarily dangerous to cross. The psychological effect of such heavy losses on those soldiers who survived the crossing, not to mention on Parma himself, could only be imagined.

With no galleys and scores of large transports, Medina Sidonia lacked any means of providing support to Parma. Problems of coordination also worked against the operation. Although he managed to embark almost 30,000 men in less than two days, Parma only received news of the Armada's approach on the 27th and did not complete loading until 31 July. By then, the Armada would have had to hover off Calais for four days, which the worsening weather would have made impossible. Even if the enemy blockade could have been broken, the rough seas would have proved an impenetrable barrier to Parma's overloaded barges (and remained so for several weeks to come), while the main body of the Armada itself would probably have been blown into the North Sea. The central element of Philip's plan – the junction of the Armada and Parma's army – was impractical from the outset, but Medina Sidonia's restrictive instructions and lack of naval experience, coupled with vigorous enemy counter-action and inclement weather, ensured there was no realistic possibility of improvising a viable alternative.[35]

When his attempt to halt at the Isle of Wight was thwarted by an English attack which threatened to drive the Armada into dangerous shoals, Medina Sidonia decided to anchor off Calais in a final (but futile) effort to prepare for Parma's break-out. This stop made the Armada a sitting target and allowed Howard to attack it with fireships on the evening of 28 July. Fire at sea represented every sailor's nightmare, but the impact of eight burning ships being inexorably blown towards the moored fleet was all the greater because so many of the Spanish ships were merchantmen heavily laden with supplies and soldiers and crewed by sailors who had never volunteered for the voyage. The result was panic and the scattering of the Armada. The next day, while the Spanish struggled to regain cohesion, the English fleet was finally able to close with the enemy and fire their cannon at short range. The bombardments were prolonged and furious. One Spanish warship allegedly received over 1000 hits and another was 'riddled with shot like a sieve'. This fearful pounding killed and wounded hundreds of Spaniards, but it only sank one ship outright. Two more vessels were so badly crippled that their crews ran them aground and many others suffered substantial damage.

For a while, it also seemed the battered Spanish fleet would be driven into the shallows off Flanders, but the wind changed and the Armada managed to escape northwards, pursued by Howard. This pursuit was essentially a bluff since the English fleet had again exhausted its supplies of shot and powder and was running out of victuals (the sudden appearance of the Armada having prevented resupply after the fleet's last effort to sail to Spain). Nevertheless, the chase was continued because it seemed the enemy fleet might still land in northern England or Scotland or seek shelter for the winter in Scandinavia or Germany. The extent of the damage inflicted on 29–30 July was not realised. Nor was it apparent until several days later that Medina Sidonia had decided to head home around the north of Scotland and down the west coast of Ireland. This hazardous journey took a heavy toll on the Armada. Almost one-third of the fleet failed to reach Spain, most of these ships being wrecked along the coast of Ireland where English troops (and many Irish) gleefully slaughtered the soldiers and sailors who struggled ashore.[36]

Ironically, the plight of English seamen was little better. By the time Howard and his advisers broke off the pursuit on 2 August, the supply problem had become acute and disease was beginning to decimate the crews, many of whom had been aboard ship since early May. The *Elizabeth Jonas* soon had over 200 dead from its complement of 500 men. One estimate puts the total death toll at almost 8000 by the end of the year. Just as in 1545, when England had faced a French equivalent of the Armada, prolonged and intense naval operations sparked an infection which spread through the exhausted and malnourished sailors like wildfire. Despite the pleas of Howard and other naval officers for emergency supplies of food and clothing, little was done for the returning seamen, who were essentially left on the quayside to fend for themselves once the process of demobilisation began. This was not simply a matter of official indifference to the suffering of returned servicemen, but also a symptom of the government's acute shortage of money. Even before the Armada's arrival, Burghley had been fretting about the unbearable cost of the campaign, hoping that deaths would provide a useful saving for the crown's wage bill: 'I marvell that, wher so many ar dead on the seas, the paye is not dead with them, or with many of them.' The appalling mortality which followed the Armada's defeat therefore offered the prospect of financial relief for the exchequer. The failure to provide properly for the returned mariners was also a result of the speed of demobilisation – which was itself driven by the need to save money. With wages and victuals for the fleet costing £13,000 a month in mid-August, it was decided to dispense with all but the queen's own warships and 11,500 men were dismissed within a fortnight, even though the treasurer of the navy lacked sufficient money for the task.[37]

Despite such expedients and the wholesale transfer of military costs to the localities during the spring and summer, payments from the exchequer between October 1587 and October 1588 topped £400,000. Spending on the navy alone in 1588 exceeded £150,000 – almost as much as the crown's entire expenditure in the pre-war years. By the end of 1588, the treasury was virtually empty. All that remained of the reserves was £3000 in cash and some bonds worth £1200. Although public celebrations for the victory continued into September and captured Spanish banners were hung from London Bridge, the queen and council were perhaps almost as relieved that the worst of the spending was over as that the enemy had actually been defeated. However, the war itself was far from over. Once the celebrations had finished, it remained to be decided how England should seek to prevent Spain from launching another invasion in the future – and how the realm could pay for such counteraction. Many of Elizabeth's subjects also burned for revenge against the enemy. In the meantime, the coastal towns were left to struggle with the human cost of the Armada campaign, even though the war effort had drained them of the money and supplies which were needed to relieve suffering on such a large scale.[38]

5   *The Depths of War:*
operations and developments,
1589–1595

The defeat of the *Gran Armada* and the thwarting of Parma's invasion plans created a unique window of opportunity for Elizabeth and her government. Philip had stripped his dominions of so many ships, mariners and supplies to create the Armada that the Iberian coast and Spain's links to the New World were left virtually undefended, and would remain so until the returning warships could be repaired and re-equipped. Elizabeth's immediate impulse was to take advantage of this situation by directing the lord admiral to intercept Spain's incoming treasure fleet, the *flota* ('fleet'). The annual convoy which brought American riches to Europe was a hugely attractive target because it sailed a predictable route – from Havana to Cadiz via the Azores – and arrived in Spanish waters at the end of each summer or early autumn. It also carried enormous wealth, especially by English standards. Capturing even a few of the treasure ships could transform the queen's war-ravaged finances. The loss of this treasure would also be a crippling blow to Philip, who depended upon American silver to service his debts and guarantee the continued operation of his government.

Intercepting the incoming silver fleet had been the subject of English mariners' fantasies since at least 1570 and rapidly became the central focus of their emerging oceanic strategies. As the proponents of sea warfare envisaged it, ambushing the treasure ships would bring unprecedented wealth and power to the queen (and her seamen), forcing Spain to its knees and allowing Elizabeth to dictate terms to Philip. This strategy was later likened to that of the mythical

Jason – defeating Philip 'by fetching away his golden fleece'. Even more optimistic scenarios imagined Elizabeth diverting the transatlantic flow of silver to England permanently, making herself 'Empress of the Oceans' at the expense of all her European rivals. This was sheer fantasy, but the appeal of plundering a silver convoy remained undeniable. Drake had hoped to achieve this goal at the outset of his West Indies voyage in 1585 and the prospect that he might lie in wait for the *flota* off the Azores after his raid on Cadiz in 1587 had caused the Spanish such concern that Santa Cruz's warships were sent out to pursue him. The failure of Philip's 'enterprise of England' finally seemed to offer the opportunity to realise this long-cherished dream.[1]

Despite Elizabeth's eagerness to refill the exchequer with a haul of captured Spanish silver, it was soon obvious that the Armada campaign had left her fleet in no condition to accomplish the task. This meant the mission would have to be postponed until 1589, which would give Spain time to revive its defences. To prevent this and to thwart any new invasion plans, England needed to destroy the remnants of the Armada in its home base at Lisbon as soon as possible. Once this was achieved, English ships could await the next treasure convoy at their leisure. If the queen's fleet also seized the Azores, the *flota* would have no means of escape. This was a logical plan, but it threatened to place an unsustainable burden on the exchequer because neutralising the land defences at Lisbon and seizing the Azores would require a substantial army. Faced with a military operation which was unaffordable, the queen and council chose to make the expedition attractive to private investors by allowing the landing of troops at Lisbon to serve the secondary purpose of asserting Dom Antonio's claim to the Portuguese throne. This was an old idea which Elizabeth had never liked, but Dom Antonio's cause had huge commercial appeal in London, thanks to the prospect of breaking into Portugal's East Indies trade. So great was the allure of Portuguese riches that the expedition swiftly became a mirror image of the 'enterprise of England' – a counter-Armada bent upon invading Portugal and sparking a rebellion against Philip to place a tame pretender upon the throne there. Unlike the Spanish venture, however, this would be a largely private-enterprise operation. By late

September 1588, it was agreed the crown would only have to invest £20,000, together with a few ships and cannon, while a syndicate of 'adventurers' organised by Sir John Norris and Sir Francis Drake carried the rest of the burden.[2]

In contrast to earlier expeditions, such as those by Drake in 1585 and 1587, the heavy reliance on private funding did not serve the secondary purpose of allowing Elizabeth to 'dysavowe' the venture. Philip's deception at Bourbourg and the launching of the Armada had finally ended any concern about deniability. The private-enterprise character of the counter-Armada was essentially a matter of resources – Norris and Drake claimed they and their backers could mobilise ships, supplies and men in quantities which the crown deemed unaffordable after its recent financial exertions. However, such massive private investment brought consequences of its own. Since the investors expected to make a profit, the expedition's commanders (who were themselves investors) would inevitably prefer to take actions which maximised the opportunities for financial reward. The very magnitude of the investment also gave the 'adventurers' powerful political leverage. Since she could hardly allow the expedition to fail, Elizabeth would find it difficult to deny the 'adventurers' further concessions if they later claimed these were essential for success. Such tendencies had been evident in Drake's voyages and in the disastrous 'enterprise of Ulster' in the 1570s, but the counter-Armada raised the problem of private investment and control far more acutely because of the scale and strategic importance of the operation.

The tension between the queen's strategic interests and the investors' financial concerns became obvious during October 1588, when fresh intelligence revealed that the remnants of the Armada had not returned to Lisbon, as expected, but had limped into the ports of northern Spain. This immediately decoupled the objective of destroying Spain's warships from that of invading Portugal on Dom Antonio's behalf. Even at this stage, however, the momentum behind the Portugal venture was so powerful that Elizabeth could not cancel or significantly change the operation. Preparations continued towards an early February departure. Nevertheless, things soon began to go wrong. Norris's efforts to secure ships, soldiers and arms from the Dutch ran into problems and his attempt to pick the best troops out of the English forces in the Low Countries caused a storm of protest, not least from Lord Willoughby, Leicester's successor as the English commander there. Willoughby was furious that Norris was trying to plunder his command. The States were even more hostile to the withdrawal of English troops. This wrangling ensured that no Dutch warships and few Dutch infantry joined the expedition and that Norris received only 1800 English veterans from the Low Countries. The 600 English cavalry which Norris requested also turned out to be so inadequate that their units were broken up, despite the expense incurred in shipping them home.

These were serious problems because Norris had counted upon large numbers of shot from the Low Countries so he could economise on his arms purchases by equipping most of the new recruits whom he was raising in England with pikes. Even worse, the weapons and troops from the Low Countries did not reach England until March. While the army and fleet waited for these critical reinforcements, the investors allowed the force to grow larger, calculating that a bigger army would improve the chances of success. These delays and the ballooning size of the force strained the venture's finances and forced the investors to demand an immediate injection of cash and victuals from the crown. By the time the fleet finally sailed in early April, the cost to the queen had grown to almost £50,000.[3]

Although she grudgingly approved this additional expenditure, Elizabeth remained concerned that the expedition would fail to achieve what she regarded as its primary task – destroying the remnants of the Armada – before heading for Portugal. Accordingly, she gave Norris and Drake strict instructions to this effect and even sent a clerk of the privy council to keep a record of their actions. Her worst fears were soon realised. Instead of attacking the Spanish ships known to be at Santander, the fleet headed for Corunna, where the Armada had stopped on its way to England. Norris and Drake found few Spanish ships there, but Norris's army stormed the weakly defended lower town and began besieging the upper town. Although the siege was a costly failure and wasted precious time, the army officers were eager to prove their troops could rout the local Spanish militia, as they did on several occasions. After so many years of striving to match the Spanish army in the Low Countries, it was clearly important to officers like Norris to assert their military superiority over the Spanish in Spain itself. The misconceived and unnecessary attempt to capture the upper town at Corunna suggests that Norris and his subordinates got carried away by this sentiment. For their part, the common soldiers were more concerned to supplement their inadequate supplies by pilfering Spanish wine and apparel which had been abandoned by Spanish seamen. Unfortunately, these clothes had been cast off because their owners had been invalided out of the Armada and the diseases which they carried were soon transmitted to the English. By the time the fleet withdrew from Corunna after almost a fortnight's activity there, 2000 men had abandoned the voyage.

These losses explain why Norris and Drake chose to head for Portugal even though they had learned that ships from the Armada were being repaired in nearby ports for a planned new attack on England or Ireland during the summer. Given the alarming attrition in the army, they clearly believed they had to launch the Portugal operation before they lost the means to act at all. As it was, they already lacked the strength to attack Lisbon directly. On 16 May, the fleet headed for Peniche, 45 miles north of Lisbon, where the army landed amid heavy seas and in the face of opposition from Spanish troops waiting on the beach. The first wave fought for two hours, 'even to the very pike', before Norris could land reinforcements and the enemy fled inland. Once they had recovered from these exertions, the troops marched for Lisbon. The army had now shrunk to 6000 effectives, and six days of marching in summer heat while wearing armour reduced numbers further. Morale suffered from constant shadowing by enemy troops and the conspicuous absence of the promised local support for Dom Antonio. By the time it reached Lisbon, the army was in no condition to besiege the city, even if it had brought siege guns with it. Although a sally by the defenders was repulsed after fierce fighting on 24 May, Norris's army could not sustain itself near Lisbon for long. On 26 May, Norris accepted the inevitable and led the army down the river towards Cascaes, where Drake's fleet had been busily seizing scores of German merchant ships.

Frustrated by the unwillingness of the Spanish to confront them in open battle, Norris sent a trumpeter to challenge the enemy, while the earl of Essex offered to meet Spanish officers in single combat. Neither gesture brought any success and Norris and Essex failed to secure the martial glory which they so desperately craved. The frustration continued even after the army re-embarked. Contrary winds thwarted the plan to sail to the Azores and kept the fleet pinned against the Iberian coast for a fortnight. Short of supplies, Norris landed 2000 soldiers near Vigo on 19 June, but all they captured for their efforts was more wine – always a dangerous commodity for English soldiers and sailors, who were accustomed to large daily rations of beer. The only option now was to head home, although Drake still planned to take 20 ships to set an ambush off the Azores. However, the weather again intervened and the whole fleet was blown back to England, reaching Plymouth and other southern ports at the beginning of July.[4]

Although its commanders sought to put a brave face on things, England's counter-Armada had been a disastrous failure. The remnants of the Armada had not been destroyed, Dom Antonio's claim to the Portuguese throne had been revealed as hollow boasting and the fleet had not even approached the Azores, let alone intercepted the *flota*. The investors in the expedition, including the queen, saw precious little return for their investment, although those officers who survived the experience may have secretly benefited from the massive pilfering of captured goods which occurred during the voyage. Subsequent government investigations revealed the magnitude of the problem, but failed to recover much of the booty. The Portugal voyage also caused very heavy casualties. At the muster taken before departure on 8 April, the expeditionary force had supposedly totalled over 23,000 men, including 17,000 soldiers and 1500 gentlemen and their servants, and 180 vessels of all sizes. One contemporary claim suggested 11,000 of 21,000 men died on the voyage. A more realistic estimate of the army on the eve of departure was 13,400, including officers, which would imply a total force of about 17,500. However, even the most favourable contemporary estimate of those who returned – 6000 soldiers and another 3000 deserters – would suggest about 5500 died on the voyage (assuming a 33 per cent mortality rate among the mariners). Less optimistic estimates would imply a death-toll approaching 8000. Although most of those who died succumbed to disease, a bungled assault on the upper town at Corunna cost 300 lives and many officers were noted as being wounded during the campaign. Indeed, almost a third of the captains and colonels ultimately died on the voyage. This represented a grievous loss of military experience, especially as England depended so heavily upon veteran officers to train and lead its raw recruits.[5]

The political and strategic consequences of the failure of the Portugal expedition were profound. England's chance of delivering a knock-out blow to Spanish naval power had been lost. Philip was not only able to repair many of the Armada's ships, but he was also able to launch a crash programme of naval construction. These new, English-style warships would soon erode English superiority at sea and spark renewed fears of invasion. Events in Portugal also destroyed forever the credibility of Dom Antonio as a challenger to Philip. To be fair, the Spanish had been able to arrest potential Portuguese dissidents and prepare for the arrival of the English fleet because details of the expedition's plans had been betrayed to the enemy, but the fact that these spies included members of Dom Antonio's own household only reinforced English doubts about the Portuguese.[6]

In terms of English strategy, the most dramatic consequence of the voyage was the discrediting of large-scale amphibious expeditions. Elizabeth felt her misgivings about the venture had been amply justified and she was determined not to be caught out again. Not only had the expedition failed in its objectives and cost her thousands of pounds, but Norris and Drake had played fast and loose with her orders. Both commanders were subsequently investigated for their conduct, but Drake was the bigger loser because his reputation had been based upon aggressive naval operations of the kind which the queen was now unwilling to support. It would be fully five years before Drake secured another command.

Ironically, the biggest winner from the débâcle in Portugal was Robert Devereux, second earl of Essex, who ran off to join the expedition in blatant defiance of Elizabeth's prohibition. Following the death of the earl of Leicester (his step-father) in September 1588, Essex had emerged as Elizabeth's new favourite. However, Essex saw himself as a soldier and was determined not to be trapped at court, as

Leicester had been for so many years. Although Drake had served the earl's father, Essex probably became involved in the schemes surrounding Dom Antonio through Leicester. He was certainly in cahoots with Drake by early 1588. Essex later claimed that he arranged – presumably with Norris – for more than two dozen of the captaincies and colonelcies in the Portugal army to be bestowed upon his friends and servants, 'so as I might authoritie and party enough when I would'. Essex's participation in the Portugal expedition represented a calculated gamble that he could prove himself more than the bold horseman he had been at Zutphen and win a fortune from the venture's success – and that the queen would forgive him for his flagrant insubordination.

Essex failed to win any riches on the voyage, but his heroism and willingness to risk his future at court for the sake of his martial aspirations won him a large following among officers and soldiers and showed he was a very different man from his late step-father. When he and Sir Roger Williams leaped into shoulder-deep water at Peniche to lead the first wave ashore, Essex literally made a splash which would ripple through English political and military affairs for the next decade. Within a few short years, the qualities which he demonstrated in Portugal – careful pre-planning, personal courage and a willingness to risk everything once the action was underway – would make Essex both the most dynamic figure in England's war effort and the most controversial figure at Elizabeth's court.[7]

Privateering and the War at Sea

The price which England would pay for failing to impede the recovery of Spanish naval power in 1589 became increasingly evident during 1590. By the spring of that year, spies were reporting that a dozen large new galleons which had been laid down for Philip in Bilbao and Santander – the so-called 'Twelve Apostles' – were rapidly nearing completion. Designed in the English manner with low forecastles and heavy cannon armament, these new galleons were up to twice the size of the *Revenge*. Along with another dozen large warships built in Ragusa (in modern Croatia), the 'Apostles' represented the start of a massive build-up of Spanish naval power in response to the defeat of 1588. By 1600, the Spanish crown would build or purchase 69 new warships. Many more were constructed for private owners. For most of the 1590s, the Spanish Atlantic fleet would number between 40 and 60 vessels and operate as three separate squadrons: the Indies Guard Armada, based at Cadiz and designed to escort ships sailing to (or from) the New World in the seas between the Spanish coast and the Azores; the Portuguese Armada, based at Lisbon; and the main fleet, the Ocean Armada, based at Ferrol. Together, these ships constituted a battle-fleet which was far more capable than the *Gran Armada* of 1588 and significantly larger than Elizabeth's fleet, both in numbers of ships and tonnage. Philip's new Atlantic fleet, in fact, became the largest sailing navy yet seen in Europe.[8]

England could not afford to match this massive naval construction programme. All that could be afforded in the immediate aftermath of 1588 was six small vessels and three new front-line warships, two of them copies of the *Revenge* and one 'which shall carie the countenance and forme of the Revendge, but excedinge her in burthen [by] 200 tonnes'. Another four minor warships were built between 1592 and 1595, while two more front-line ships (*Warspite* and *Due Repulse*) were launched in 1596, both significantly larger than the *Revenge*. Further naval construction was then suspended until 1601. Perhaps in compensation for this trickle of royal shipbuilding, the bounty which the crown had previously paid to builders of large private ships on a discretionary basis was transformed into an entitlement in 1594. The result was a significant flow of money to private shipbuilders, who built an average of 20 vessels a year which could serve as auxiliary warships during the next nine years.[9]

In 1590, the imminent debut of the 'Apostles' and the queen's lack of money both encouraged a fresh attempt to intercept the homebound Spanish treasure fleet, before Philip's new ships could make an impact. The plan for 1590 repeated the new strategy of a 'double blockade' which had been attempted in piecemeal fashion during the early autumn of 1589. Elizabeth had been furious when she learned that Drake and Norris had returned from Portugal without even attempting to intercept the *flota*. As a result, Sir Martin Frobisher was hurriedly sent out to patrol the Spanish coast, where he effectively acted as a back-stop to the earl of Cumberland, who had previously taken a small private fleet to the Azores. Both forces had frustrating narrow-misses and captured only a few prizes. Nevertheless, the principle of a 'double blockade' seemed proven and it was repeated in more coordinated fashion in 1590. While Frobisher took one squadron to the Azores, a second squadron under Sir John Hawkins patrolled the waters off Spain and kept an eye on the enemy fleet at Ferrol. However, this vigorous (and expensive) blockade proved to be in vain. Thanks to attacks by English privateers in the Caribbean and delays in concentrating its ships at Havana, the home-bound Spanish convoy never sailed in 1590. Hawkins and Frobisher were also thwarted by a new Spanish tactic which saw Philip's precious annual shipment of silver sent home separately aboard two fast frigates (*fregatas* or *galizabras*).

Thanks to the diversion of large warships in 1587–88 into what became the *Gran Armada*, the Spanish authorities had experimented with loading the king's silver aboard much smaller ships which relied upon speed for their safety, rather than size. Sailing alone across the Atlantic, they by-passed the Azores and avoided the slow and cumbersome convoys, whose comings and goings were familiar to every pirate in Europe. This made interception almost impossible, except by blind luck. The new system proved such a success that the frigates became the standard means of carrying Philip's treasure home from the New World. From an English perspective, the silver frigates were a frustrating innovation, but the home-bound treasure fleets still carried enough merchandise and private treasure to remain a hugely attractive prize. Given the elusive nature of the frigates, the *flota* represented the only viable target for large-scale interception. The continuing quest to attack the incoming fleets made sense because the obvious place to ambush them, the Azores, also gave waiting ships an opportunity to intercept the other great prize of the oceans, the huge Portuguese carracks which sailed to Lisbon from Goa in India. A few such ships made this voyage every year and carried goods of enormous value. While poorly armed, the sheer size of these monsters and the infrequency of their arrival made them a difficult target. Nevertheless, as Drake had shown with the capture of the *Sao Phelipe*, a Portuguese carrack made an admirable substitute for intercepting a silver frigate or returning *flota*.[10]

The magnetic attraction of the treasure fleet and the erroneous belief that it – or a carrack – must soon appear perhaps explains why Hawkins moved his ships away from Ferrol and closer to the Azores in early September. Quite apart from seeking profit for himself and his subordinates, he must have realised that Elizabeth would be angry if he failed to cover the cost of the year's operations. However, Hawkins found no treasure ships and his wandering allowed a Spanish fleet to leave Ferrol and land troops in Brittany. This was a disastrous lapse and rectifying the mistake would cost England dearly in the years to come.

The utter failure of 1590 resulted in the replacement of Hawkins and Frobisher for the next season's campaign by Lord Thomas Howard, a distant cousin of the lord admiral and the queen. With the 1591 fleet from Havana including ships from 1590 and carrying two years' worth of goods and treasure, Elizabeth was doubly determined to intercept it. However, efforts to secure ships for Howard from the Dutch and the port-towns of England brought little success and he ultimately sailed with a single fleet built around eight royal warships, including five front-line galleons, and 20 privately-owned ships, only three of which were rated at more than 150 tons. By contrast, Philip's fleet to escort the treasure convoy on its final leg between the Azores and Spain totalled 60 ships, half of them genuine warships and five of them 'Apostles'. By late August, Howard's exhausted fleet had been at sea for over four months and had been patrolling the Azores since the start of June. On 30 August, Howard's force was anchored off Flores, its depleted crews frantically scrubbing and fumigating their ships' storage and ballast spaces. The English fleet could hardly have been more vulnerable when news arrived that enemy vessels were approaching. A desperate race began to re-ballast the ships and get to sea before the Spanish could attack. Remarkably, all of the English ships won the race – except the *Revenge*, whose captain, Sir Richard Grenville, allegedly delayed to recover sick crewmen from ashore.

The *Revenge* could still have escaped, but Grenville decided to attack the closest enemy ships, which he bombarded from close range before heading out to sea. This manoeuvre cost valuable time and the *Revenge* was soon overhauled by the two fastest 'Apostles', the *San Felipe* and *San Bernabe*. The *San Felipe* was more than twice the size of the *Revenge* and rammed her in preparation for boarding, but the heavy guns of the *Revenge* inflicted so much damage that the *San Felipe* was quickly put out of action. The *San Bernabe* was more successful and grappled the *Revenge*, opening the way for hours of intermittent musketry and hand-to-hand combat. The *San Cristobal* subsequently attempted to board the *Revenge* from the stern, but the latter's large stern-guns caused such destruction that the *San Cristobal* had to withdraw to avoid being sunk. Two more Spanish ships rammed the *Revenge* during the night and lashed themselves to its bow. One of these vessels was so badly damaged by the *Revenge's* bow guns that it sank, while the other ship sank later the next day. By morning, after a day and a night of close-range combat, Grenville was mortally wounded and had to be forced to surrender by the remnants of his crew. Two-thirds of the 250 men aboard the *Revenge* were dead or dying and the ship had been dismasted and was leaking badly. Spanish casualties had been very heavy, but the admiral agreed to repatriate the survivors to England in return for possession of the ship and her valuable cannon. Although some of the cannon were transferred to other ships (and the remainder were salvaged by the Spanish in 1603), the *Revenge* sank a few days later when the Spanish fleet was hit by a storm. Grenville himself died two or three days after the battle, still cursing his men for surrendering. Ironically, Grenville's father had drowned on the *Mary Rose* in 1545, creating a tragic link between the two great disasters of Tudor naval history.[11]

The last fight of the *Revenge* brought a calamitous end to the English naval campaign of 1591, although Sir Walter Ralegh tried to put a brave face on matters when he published a tract about the incident. Ralegh celebrated the courage of Grenville (his friend and relative) and instanced the long struggle off Flores as evidence that raw English courage would always be worth more in battle than Spain's superior numbers. This exercise in 'hero-making' proved incredibly successful and created a jingoistic myth which has persisted through the intervening centuries. Yet, however bravely Grenville and his men fought once the shooting began, the decision to risk battle rather than join the rest of the fleet in escaping a vastly superior enemy force seems foolhardy. Despite the propaganda image created by Ralegh, Grenville's contemporaries such as William Monson and

Arthur Gorges clearly viewed his behaviour as irresponsible, even a dereliction of duty. In part, this divergence of opinion reflects the difference between professional mariners like Monson, who made their careers in the navy and recognised the value of living to fight another day, and gentlemen like Grenville (and Ralegh), who had limited experience of naval warfare and owed their command to connections at court and were determined to squeeze every last ounce of fame from their brief periods at sea.

The catastrophic outcome of Grenville's quest for honour proved a salutary lesson to his contemporaries. Even the ambitious gentlemen who sought to accomplish some notable action to win acclaim from the queen and their peers did not want to cost Elizabeth another warship. The loss of the *Revenge* also demonstrated what might have happened in 1588 if Medina Sidonia had succeeded in luring the English ships within grappling range of the Armada. Despite their devastating effectiveness in the early minutes of the battle, the *Revenge's* cannon were fired very sparingly after the *San Bernabe* secured itself alongside, perhaps because the gun crews were preoccupied with repelling boarders. The long struggle which followed was principally a battle between soldiers and sailors using pikes, calivers and swords, rather than a contest of naval gunnery. In this sort of battle, even a model of contemporary naval technology such as the *Revenge* could not prevail against the large numbers of soldiers carried by Spanish ships.[12]

After the loss of the *Revenge* and the obvious resurgence of Spanish naval power, the queen's warships refrained from further sweeps into the Atlantic in search of treasure ships. The renewed threat of invasion, which had already caused scares in 1590 and 1591, kept the royal fleet close to home. Instead, the hunt for treasure ships was left to privately owned ships. Privateering had been a prominent feature of the war against Spain from the outset. Indeed, the expectation of plundering Spanish ships had made some Englishmen welcome the conflict. As Sir George Carey, governor of the Isle of Wight, had observed to a friend, 'we shall have better booties, richer spoiles and braver robberies hereaboutes in one daie then yow shall have in Wales in seven yeares.'[13]

Every year after 1588, 100–200 privateers put to sea to attack enemy shipping. Most of these vessels were under 100 tons, and many less than 50 tons, but they infested the waters around Spain, the Azores and even the Caribbean. In the summer of 1590, the presence off Cuba of ships belonging to Carey and the London merchant John Watts kept the Spanish treasure fleet 'corralled' in Havana and humiliated the local governor. One of Carey's ships, the 30 ton *Content*, even had the temerity to engage in a day-long battle with the main Spanish fleet in the region, including four large galleons, and got away unscathed after taunting the Spaniards by singing psalms at them. Other private expeditions were conducted on a larger scale. Cumberland's 1589 voyage involved the queen's warship *Victory* and included an amphibious landing in the Azores at Horta to capture a Spanish fort. Yet Cumberland missed capturing six ships of the *flota* by a whisker and his chief prize from the voyage sank off the Cornish coast before he could get it home. Local gentlemen secured most of the spoils by scouring the beaches for flotsam. Such frustrations strained the earl's finances almost to breaking point but, as with most privateers, the prospect of a major success next time around encouraged him to keep trying. Between 1589 and 1591, the efforts of large and small privateers secured some 300 prizes worth about £400,000. In 1598, when pickings were decidedly poor, the haul was worth about £75,000. A rough estimate suggests that privateering in the 1590s normally brought £100,000 or more into England each year and constituted about 15 per cent of the realm's total imports. This was slightly more than the value of the trade with Spain and Portugal which had been lost with the outbreak of war.[14]

The scale of the privateering industry – for that is what it became – meant that it embraced a substantial cross-section of English (and Welsh) society and played a key role in many coastal communities. Country gentlemen and merchants invested in privateering voyages to supplement their other activities, while mercantile syndicates and profit-hungry courtiers like Cumberland, Carey and the lord admiral built and operated small fleets of their own. The demand for new and longer-range ships created a boom in shipbuilding, while the need for more cannon kept the iron furnaces roaring. Both activites contributed to the continuing deforestation of England. Thousands of common seamen also chose to brave the dangers of these voyages in the hope of sharing in any profit. This represented a desperate gamble by men who saw little alternative prospect of escaping poverty: 'no kinde of men of any profession in the common wealth passe their yeres in so great and continuall hazard . . . [and], of so many, so few grow to grey heires'. Despite the discomfort and danger involved, the willingness of so many sailors to join privateers exacerbated the problem of finding enough crewmen for the queen's warships. In early 1586, the crown increased sea wages from 6s 8d per month (the level set at the end of Henry VIII's reign) to 10s a month. Although this worsened the burden on the exchequer, it still failed to attract sufficient seamen away from the privateers and royal commanders were forced to resort to impressing men even from inland counties, who had no experience of the sea. Not surprisingly, the queen's warships suffered constant problems with desertion while they remained in port. Given the high mortality which prevailed on both royal and private vessels, the crown and private entrepreneurs were competing for a relatively restricted pool of experienced seamen. Although large numbers of men put to sea, many died while voyaging, while others returned too weak or sick to sign on for a new expedition.[15]

Despite the competition for sailors, privateering brought many benefits to the queen. The efforts of privateers kept constant pressure on Spanish trade and shipping and inflicted significant losses upon Philip's subjects. Elizabeth also levied customs duties on prize goods, while the lord admiral received a 10 per cent share of all the prizes which his officers could identify. The queen's continuing investment – in effect, speculation – in privateering expeditions also brought occasional windfall profits. The most spectacular example was the taking of the carrack *Madre de Dios* by a pack of English ships off the Azores in July 1592. At 1600 tons, the *Madre de Dios* only succumbed after a prolonged battle, but its contents may have been worth as much as £500,000. In the feeding frenzy which followed its surrender, vast quantities of jewels, spices, silks and scents were pilfered by the victorious crews and their officers. By the time the carrack was brought back to England, a mere £140,000 worth of goods remained for the investors. Although holding only a 10 per cent share in the voyage, Elizabeth seized about £80,000 for the exchequer and left the remainder to be divided among Cumberland, Ralegh, Hawkins and various London merchants.

Elizabeth believed her exorbitant war costs entitled her to take such actions, but it infuriated her fellow investors, even though they were unable to complain too openly. By contrast, many foreign victims of English privateering complained very loudly about the unscrupulous behaviour of the queen's subjects. The illegal seizure of foreign merchantmen caused regular diplomatic protests from the French, Dutch, Danes and the Hanse, which required careful handling to prevent English merchants suffering retaliation from aggrieved foreign governments. These complaints of piracy also prompted endless suits in the court of admiralty, where the wheels of justice turned with frustrating slowness. It sometimes took years for the court to produce a verdict, which infuriated the merchants who had been deprived of their ships and cargoes. Even if a suit was upheld, debate about compensation and the value of the cargo seized could produce further bitter wrangling. In such cases, the final beneficiaries of privateering were often the lawyers.[16]

The Netherlands after Leicester

The English army in the Low Countries struggled for lack of funds during the Armada crisis. Even in the spring of 1587 – well before the real cost of defending against invasion began to bite – it was obvious that insufficient cash would be available from England to keep the army paid properly. As a result, a system was instigated whereby soldiers were paid weekly 'imprests' or 'lendings'. These were advances on the soldiers' pay which would be deducted when a proper pay was finally made and were intended to provide soldiers with the bare minimum to pay for food, gunpowder and other necessities. The real purpose of the system was to ensure cash sent to the Low Countries was 'drawne to as great length as might be', whilst allowing the crown continually to postpone the settling of 'full pay' and the large release of cash which this entailed. In this way, payments from the exchequer for the army in the Low Countries were restricted to £70,000 between Michaelmas 1587 and Easter 1588, and a mere £36,000 in the crucial period between Easter and Michaelmas 1588.

For the soldiers, however, the system meant survival on bare rations for the indefinite future, with every slight diminution in the

money which they received through their captain's hands, or escala-
tion in the price of basic necessities, pushing them below subsistence
level. They could not even afford to repair or replace arms which had
been damaged – like the purchase of new shoes or hose, these outlays
required specific advances from their captains, who were themselves
caught between the chronic lack of cash and the expectation that
they should look and behave like gentlemen. Further problems arose
with the privy council's decision in March 1588 to reduce the export
of coin by contracting for the supply of military apparel with merchants based in England. Not only did these contractors cut corners
to maximise their profits, but the council itself tried to reduce royal
expenditure in the wake of the Armada campaign by paying for only
110 suits of apparel for every company of 150 men. This cost-cutting
ultimately proved to be excessive and the allowance was raised to 127
suits in 1591.[17]

These arduous conditions triggered a mutiny among the garrison
at Ostend in August 1588. Having endured 'great penury' for many
months, the soldiers took action when a new batch of rations seemed
inedible and the victualler, Henry Cox, charged excessive prices.
While the meat and cheese on offer were unpalatable and the beer
was spoiled, Cox demanded a price for wheat five times higher than
that in England. Many of the troops had not received a full month's
pay in over two years and subsisted entirely on lendings which
would no longer stretch to cover Cox's prices. The soldiers held Sir
John Conway, their commander, as a hostage and petitioned the
queen for redress. Elizabeth agreed to forgive the commotion and the
privy council investigated the complaints. When 1500 fresh recruits
arrived in the Low Countries, many of the long-serving troops at
Ostend were moved elsewhere and replaced with new men, but further troubles arose in October when the soldiers' hopes of receiving
a 'full pay' were dashed. After another month of escalating tensions,
Conway finally arranged with loyal officers and soldiers to arrest the
ringleaders in the middle of the night. Thirteen soldiers were ultimately executed and others were ejected from the town.[18]

Given the circumstances in which Elizabeth's soldiers served, it is
perhaps remarkable that a major upheaval such as that at Ostend
was a rare occurrence. Compared with other contemporary armies

(especially the Spanish Army of Flanders, in which mutinies virtually became a ritualised form of collective bargaining), English armies mutinied very little. Moreover, when troubles did occur, the trigger was usually bad food or beer (a critical part of the soldiers' rations), rather than pay. Although it is possible they simply became inured to the parsimonious policies of a government which consistently tried to limit the payment of cash, it is more likely that the (relative) placidity of English troops reflects the efforts of captains to look after their men. Elizabethan army officers have traditionally had a black reputation for unscrupulously exploiting their charges for the sake of profit. To some degree, this image is warranted, especially in Ireland. However, the reality of dealings between captains and their soldiers tends to be distorted by the nature of the surviving evidence, which preserves endless complaints against captains, but contains only fleeting examples of the sort of assistance provided by officers which never warranted being committed to paper. Although some captains were unscrupulous, no army can function for long without an effective working relationship between soldiers and their officers. Most Elizabethan captains were undoubtedly characterised by paternalistic attitudes towards their men. When the earl of Essex ordered his own expensive belongings be thrown out of his carriage to make room for sick soldiers during the march on Lisbon in 1589, this was an extreme example of an officer's concern for his men. Other captains clearly shared the sentiment, although they acted upon it in much less extravagant ways. By contrast, the mutiny at Ostend, where extremists even talked of gaoling their officers, reflected a serious breakdown in the usual cooperation between officers and soldiers.[19]

Despite the distractions at Ostend, English troops played a critical role in defeating Parma's first offensive after the defeat of the Armada. In mid-September 1588, Parma began besieging the strategically important town of Bergen-op-Zoom, which had a weakened Anglo-Dutch garrison and whose food stores had been repeatedly depleted by officers determined to feed their starving soldiers. The only reinforcements available were from other English garrisons. Willoughby himself had to purchase fresh arms and supplies on his own credit – almost £2000 worth. However, Parma was unable to prevent river access to the town and the gradual build-up of reinforcements and supplies gave the defenders confidence and (from Parma's perspective) made them disconcertingly aggressive. Parma was therefore receptive when two English soldiers entered his camp and offered to betray the town's north fort for money. In fact, the offer was a stratagem approved by Willoughby and Count Maurice of Nassau, a son of William of Orange who was beginning to emerge as the chief Dutch military leader. When the Spanish tried to enter the town on the night of 10 October, they were ambushed and several hundred of Parma's best men were killed. After this disaster, Parma abandoned the siege. For the first time, Parma – widely acknowledged as the best general of his day, leading Europe's most famous army – had been defeated in open battle. The elation which followed this victory was dented in the following spring by news that German troops in the service of the States (not English troops, as is often asserted) had surrendered the town of Geertruidenberg to the enemy. Nevertheless, Parma's defeat at Bergen was a major blow to the myth of Spanish invincibility.[20]

Although Willoughby only assumed command of the queen's forces in the Low Countries at the end of 1587, his dealings with the States became so rancorous that he returned home for good in March 1589. In Dutch eyes, Willoughby was too closely associated with Leicester and compounded the problem by antagonising such influential Dutch leaders as Maurice and Jan van Oldenbarneveldt, the advocate of Holland. Willoughby's departure, following upon Leicester's death in September 1588, reflected the final failure of Leicester's policy of interference in Dutch politics and opened the way for a new relationship with the Dutch. Although the treaties of 1585, which treated the Low Countries as an English protectorate, were still in force and the queen still maintained 6400 troops there, the political balance between England and the Dutch was beginning to change. One sign of the transformation was that Willoughby's command (itself a lesser version of Leicester's old governor-generalship) was effectively subdivided between the governors of the towns under English control, the queen's chief diplomatic agent in the Low Countries, Thomas Bodley, and Sir Francis Vere, who was appointed as serjeant major-general of the English field forces (i.e. non-garrison troops) in July 1589. Although a cousin of the earl of Oxford, Vere was not a nobleman like Leicester and Willoughby (or even Lord Burgh, the governor of Brielle) and was a generation younger than Sir John Norris. By 1590, his field force totalled only 1400 men. Instead of aspiring to be a supreme commander, Vere functioned as a subordinate to Maurice. This reversed the previous relationship between English and Dutch commanders, but it proved to be a far more stable and productive partnership. Under Vere, English troops became increasingly integrated with the Dutch army and played a central role in Maurice's military success during the 1590s.[21]

The turn-round in Dutch military fortunes, which became possible after the victory at Bergen, really began with the capture of Breda in February 1590. Using a boat carrying turf as a Trojan horse, Maurice smuggled troops inside the town and seized it in a night attack. Vere and 600 English troops formed part of Maurice's assault force. In 1591, Maurice launched a major offensive which won Zutphen, Deventer and other towns during a drive up the Ijssel river, before capturing Hulst and Nijmegen. The following year, he overwhelmed the Spanish garrison at Steenwijk. Bit by bit, Maurice began to reconquer the territory which had been lost to the Spanish in the 1580s. Vere's troops played a conspicuous part in most of these operations. In the process, they became trained in the new style of warfare which Maurice was developing and which ultimately made the Dutch Republic 'the schoole of war' for the whole of Europe.[22]

Maurice's desire to make the States' multinational army more effective – and the need to ensure inter-operability among its different nationalities – encouraged the institution of what were effectively 'best practice' drills across the whole army. As one English officer noted, the daily routine for the English troops in the Low Countries, like the rest of the Dutch force, became centred around 'exercising our men with the remembrance of old Roman exercises'. Although some critics complained that gunpowder negated the usefulness of classical Roman and Greek precedents, the fabled professionalism and success of Rome's legions offered basic lessons about tactics and training. By studying Roman military manuals and histories, Maurice and his advisers invented the notion of weapons-handling drills which were practised relentlessly (firing and reloading a musket, for example, was broken down into 42 separate actions). They also introduced manoeuvres such as the countermarch, which permitted successive lines of musketeers to fire a volley and retire to reload while the next rank moved forward into firing position. These drills allowed Maurice to break his forces into smaller and more flexible sub-units and to employ linear formations in battle (using formations only ten ranks deep), instead of the old Spanish-style squares, in which many soldiers made no direct contribution to the fight. Standard drills gradually forced the standardisation of weapons and ammunition, while the greater discipline required of soldiers spilled over into improved relations with civilians, who became less disparaging of soldiers when they saw the results of the new emphasis on orderliness. The connection between troops and Dutch taxpayers was reinforced by a 'repartition' of military finances, which committed individual provinces to support specific units rather than an abstract (and unpopular) national budget. Maurice also emulated the Roman practice of expecting soldiers (rather than pioneers or civilians) to wield the spade and pick. This permitted him to construct elaborate fieldworks during sieges and gave engineers an even more central role in military operations, but rankled with the old-style soldiers such as Lord Burgh, who scorned 'these idle moles whom with undeserved fame the spade hath raised'. Vere certainly shared Burgh's yearning to fight in the heroic knightly fashion. In contrast to Maurice's command from the rear, Vere was usually to be seen at the front of his troops, wearing bright red. Nevertheless, he recognised the value of Maurice's more scientific and disciplined approach to war and sought to inculcate the new mind-set in his subordinates. As a result, Vere's officers and veteran troops became increasingly professional in their approach to war, creating a cadre of soldiers who could form the backbone of new English expeditionary forces. This confirmed the pattern which had been created by the calling home of Low Countries veterans in 1587 and 1588. Although it distressed the Dutch, who lost combat power whenever substantial numbers of English troops were withdrawn, the ability of Elizabeth's government to call upon 'old soldiers' in times of crisis meant the Low Countries became the definitive replacement for the sort of military training and experience which had once been offered by the English garrisons of the Pale of Calais.[23]

France and the Descent into 'Deep War', 1589–94

Despite the achievements of Maurice and his circle, the remarkable recovery in the military fortunes of the Dutch would have been impossible without Philip II's decision to divert Parma's Army of Flanders into France in 1590. This was a consequence of Philip's alliance with the duke of Guise's Catholic League and the tit-for-tat assassinations of Guise and his brother in December 1588 (on the orders of Henri III) and of Henri himself seven months later. The death of Henri III resulted in the event which Guise and Philip had sought to avoid since Anjou's death in 1584: the accession of the Protestant Henri of Navarre as Henri IV of France. A survivor of the St Bartholomew's Day Massacre and occasional recipient of aid from Elizabeth, Henri came to the throne facing bitter hostility from the League and a general unwillingness among many of his other subjects to obey a Protestant. While the League rallied to drive him from the throne, Henri found himself unable to raise money and faced with mass desertions from the French royal army. For Elizabeth and her government, the crisis confronting Henri raised the prospect of the pro-Spanish League taking control of France and supporting Philip in a new 'enterprise of England'. Just as in 1585, therefore, the imminent collapse of a friendly power forced Elizabeth to commit troops to war on the Continent. The recognition of a 'common cause' with Henri IV meant England would have to raise extra men and money in addition to those already being absorbed by the war in the Low Countries and at sea.

In combination with the failure of the Portugal expedition, the contested succession of Henry IV brought a new and ominous character to England's strategic outlook. If the triumph of 1588 had encouraged thoughts of striking a crippling blow against Spain and dictating terms for peace, the events of mid-1589 dashed those hopes. Although it reduced pressure on the Dutch, the emergence of France as the new prime area of conflict dramatically expanded and escalated England's war against Spain. Indeed, the latter half of 1589 marked the start of what might be termed 'deep war', when no end to the fighting seemed in sight and Elizabeth's regime could only seek to endure, as new threats and commitments mounted up on all sides.

English resources now became so stretched that Elizabeth was forced to resume selling crown lands on a scale not seen since the dark days of the early 1560s.[24]

In September 1589, Lord Willoughby was ordered to reinforce Henri with 3600 troops hastily levied in south-eastern England. Anxious to restrain costs, Elizabeth agreed to pay for only the first month of her troops' service – if they served beyond the end of October, they would be dependent upon Henri. Inevitably, Willoughby's green soldiers suffered terribly from this arrangement. After fighting in the king's unsuccessful attempt to seize Paris, they made a long series of marches which took them south and west almost as far as the River Loire, before heading north towards Le Mans and Falaise. Most towns quickly declared for the king and Henri's polyglot army of French, Swiss, Scots and English rarely had to make a fight of it. When action was required, Willoughby's force performed extremely well, thanks to his insistence on officering his untried levies with 'the best experimented captains that have served in the Low Countries'. At Le Mans, the ingenuity of their officers saw English troops unexpectedly cross a river on a make-shift bridge of ladders and barrels, while at Alençon an improvised machine was used to hook down a drawbridge, allowing the English to storm part of the town's outer defences. However, the predominant characteristics of Willoughby's expedition were gruelling marches in winter weather and, because the troops had advanced so far from the coast, scanty communications with England and inadequate supplies. These conditions exacted a heavy toll of sickness and misery. By 20 December, Willoughby's force was reduced to 800 effectives.

When Henri released the English troops after Christmas, the survivors returned to England in a terrible state. Some of those who disembarked at Rye were 'wonderful sick and weak, some wounded, some their toes and feet rotting off and some lame, the skin and flesh of their feet torn away with continual marching, all of them without money, without apparel to cover their nakedness, all of them full of vermin'. All had to be washed and re-clothed by the town. The worst of them required intensive care, but 'the persons in whose houses they were lodged and dieted, and the women that did attend and watch them, are for the most part fallen very sick and every day there

dieth four or five of them with the infection they had from these soldiers.' As so often, the miseries of war were not restricted to the soldiers or the battlefront. Nevertheless, England and Wales were more
fortunate than Continental countries, where the need to defend land
borders ensured that large bodies of troops were permanently quartered on the population and caused year-round problems.[25]

In the months which followed the return of Willoughby's force,
the French king's prospects brightened considerably. By summer
1590, he was once again pressing on Paris. Henri's success against the
League enabled Elizabeth to avoid committing further English
troops, but it also prompted Philip to order Parma's army into France
in July. Parma soon defeated Henri's hopes of taking Paris. However,
the Spanish army suffered almost as badly in the French mud as
Willoughby's had done 12 months earlier and was forced to withdraw for the winter.

For England, the danger posed by Parma's French expedition was
compounded by news in November that Spanish ships had taken
advantage of Hawkins's departure from the waters off Ferrol to land
3000 troops at Blavet in southern Brittany. This opened a new front
in the war in France and posed a direct threat to England, since
Breton ports would be a perfect springboard for a future 'enterprise
of England'. Elizabeth's government responded to the new danger
with vigour. An amphibious assault was planned against Blavet for
the spring of 1591 to destroy the Spanish force before it could be reinforced. Sir John Norris (finally forgiven for his failure in Portugal)
was placed in command and orders were issued to withdraw 3000
veterans from the Low Countries and to levy 1500 new men for
training in England – if necessary, even taking men from the trained
bands to ensure quality troops. These aggressive plans fell apart over
the winter 1590–91. The Dutch refused to release so many men and
the 1500 troops trained in England were ultimately sent to the Low
Countries to replace a similar number of veterans, many of whom
were subsequently diverted to the defence of Dieppe. To make matters worse, the latter mission was commanded by Sir Roger
Williams, who had become a bitter rival of Norris. Norris had to settle for a fresh levy of raw recruits and a much depleted core of veterans. The whole idea of attacking Blavet was abandoned and Norris

was reduced to establishing a bridgehead in northern Brittany, based around Paimpol, a fishing village which lacked even wharves. The prevailing south-easterly winds which made Brittany such an attractive base for Spain also hindered resupply efforts from England. By late summer, Norris's troops were in such poor shape that he chose to march inland in search of winter quarters, even though it left the Breton ports nearest to England exposed to enemy attack.[26]

Norris's difficulties partly reflected his reduced status as a military commander after 1589, but his chief problem was that Brittany became a sideshow after Elizabeth accepted Henri's plan for a combined campaign in the summer of 1591 to capture the city of Rouen in Normandy. Normandy was far more important to Henri than Brittany, while Elizabeth was attracted to the venture by the promise that her war costs in France and loans to Henri would be repaid from Rouen's substantial customs revenues. Elizabeth pledged 4000 men (including the 600 veterans already at Dieppe under Williams) and pay for two months. Since Henri promised to lead the campaign himself, command of the English force was given to the earl of Essex, who had been furious when Norris won the Brittany command. Now Essex had the last laugh. However, despite his enthusiasm for the 'common cause' and vigorous style of generalship, Essex soon found the realities of campaigning in France deeply frustrating. Under extreme pressure from Elizabeth to complete the campaign quickly and cheaply, he found himself waiting endlessly for the French king's arrival. Although Essex cemented a firm friendship with Henri by making a four-day ride through enemy territory to meet the French king, the latter was determined to act according to his own priorities, not those of England. This infuriated Elizabeth, who vented her frustrations in bitter reprimands to Essex. Little was achieved by the time the queen's pay ran out in October and Essex had to pay the army from his own pocket until he could negotiate an extension of royal funding.

Although the siege of Rouen began in mid-November and Henri finally arrived a few days later, even reinforcement by 1000 English veterans from the Low Countries in December failed to bring significant results. As exhaustion, winter weather and erratic supplies took their toll, Essex's force dwindled to 1400 men. Essex and his troops performed well in combat, but the siege of Rouen was mishandled from the start. Henri's unwillingness to risk major damage to the city – which led him to reject Essex's advice to attack the city walls directly – meant little headway was made by the time Parma advanced to relieve Rouen. Once Henri departed to face Parma and the siege fell away, Essex could no longer resist Elizabeth's demands for his return to England. By the time he handed over command to Williams in early January 1592, Essex's 'army' in Normandy had withered to fewer than 1000 combat-worthy troops.[27]

The Rouen campaign was a bitter experience for all concerned. Elizabeth's hopes of a quick, cheap and profitable victory soon turned to ashes and her mistrust of Henri IV – already excited by his exploitation of Willoughby's men and his lack of support for Norris's troops – now became increasingly pronounced. The futility of the operation also made the appalling casualties harder to bear. However, the alarming decline in Essex's numbers – despite his best efforts to hold his army together – was by no means unique to the queen's forces. All armies suffered terribly once they moved away from towns where they could receive regular supplies, especially during winter. Parma's army, which entered France in November 1591, declined from 30,000 men to barely 10,000 three months later.

The Rouen campaign also proved a painful lesson for Essex, whose commitment to the venture not only crippled his own finances, but cost the life of his only brother. Although he gained precious military experience, he also discovered how uncomfortable it could be to serve as Elizabeth's general without assured support at court. Although the privy council generally sought to deflect the queen's furious outbursts against him, enough fulminating letters crossed the Channel to convince the earl that he could not rely upon the support of others in the future. His response was to reinvent himself over the next few years to become an influential privy councillor in his own right, whose expertise in foreign and military affairs compelled the queen to take his advice seriously and placed him at the centre of England's war effort. Nevertheless, some of Essex's actions in Normandy hinted at difficulties which his subsequent political transformation temporarily concealed. Essex's friendship with Henri IV was far too close for Elizabeth's liking and their shared habit of leading their armies from the front reflected a common concern for soldiers' morale and aggressive action which did not suit her preference for limiting her realm's involvement in war. Elizabeth was also appalled by Essex's mass dubbing of 24 new knights on 8 October. For Essex, such knightings recognised courage and a shared commitment to martial honour, whereas Elizabeth fumed that Essex's new knights lacked sufficient wealth to maintain themselves in appropriate style and owed their advancement to Essex, rather than herself. The peculiarly masculine bond of knighthood represented a potential threat to Elizabeth's 'man-management' and she always took great care to limit the distinction. Essex's insistence that the battlefield should be a place of reward for gentlemen who risked their lives to serve with him directly challenged the queen's stand on knighthoods and would become a regular source of friction between them for the remainder of the decade.[28]

Norris's troops in Brittany had been starved of supplies while priority was given to operations in Normandy. Fortunately, their adversaries suffered similar problems and neither side could strike a serious blow until May 1592, when League and Spanish forces took advantage of the betrayal of an Anglo-French plan to besiege the town of Craon. The result was a two-day engagement in which Norris's men stoutly resisted the enemy until they ran out of ammunition, which left the English pikemen defenceless against enemy gunfire. Although Norris repeatedly tried to stem the enemy advance using pikes alone, the task was impossible and the whole royalist army was scattered. Perhaps 1500 royalists were killed, a third them English, who also suffered another 200 wounded. After this disaster, the privy council ordered the urgent despatch of fresh reinforcements, but quibbling by Williams and the Dutch meant that Norris received only a few hundred untrained 'volunteers'. The Spanish and their League allies, however, were too short of money to capitalise on their victory. It was not until early 1593 that Norris received more veterans from the Low Countries to boost his force to 3000 – a strength which soon began to decline again as the rugged conditions took their toll.[29]

By 1593, the whole strategic situation in France was being transformed. Parma's death in November 1592 severely dented Spain's military standing in France and the Low Countries. The whole nature of Spanish intervention in France also changed. Instead of propping up the Catholic cause, it was now increasingly obvious that Philip sought to win control of the French throne for his own family, a prospect which increased desertions from the League and brought a flood of support for Henri IV when the latter announced he would convert to Catholicism in July 1593.

Henri's action was a political master-stroke, but it infuriated Elizabeth, who saw it as further proof the French king could not be trusted. As a royal clerk observed, 'if the king of Spayne were dead, wee are like enoughe to care little for France'.[30] In the months following Henri's announcement, Elizabeth withdrew the last English troops from Normandy and repeatedly sought the evacuation of Norris's men from Brittany, only to be convinced to delay by the pleas of Norris, the privy council and French envoys. In the end, Norris's command was saved by intelligence that the Spanish might attack the port of Brest, whose vast harbour and maritime infrastructure would make it a perfect base for a future Spanish Armada. In April 1594 news arrived that Spanish troops were building a fort on the Crozon peninsula to cut seaward access to Brest – the first step towards besieging the port itself. The prospect of Brest falling into Spanish hands seemed so appalling that Elizabeth and her government acted with extraordinary urgency. Within weeks, siege equipment was despatched to Norris, while 1100 English veterans from the Low Countries were landed in Brittany by mid-June. This response thoroughly out-paced the Spanish, who struggled even to re-supply their new fort – christened 'El León' ('The Lion') – and were virtually paralysed by the disintegration of League support in Brittany. For a while, Elizabeth contemplated escalating the war in Brittany still further, designating Essex to lead a new army of 6000 men and the lord admiral to command most of the royal fleet in a combined offensive against the fort. By August, however, it was apparent that an effort on this scale was unnecessary, sparing Elizabeth considerable expense and Norris the prospect of becoming Essex's subordinate. Instead, Norris received 2000 fresh recruits, boosting his force to a nominal total of 5500. Significantly, half of this force were veterans, whose skill and perseverance proved critical in the tough campaign which followed.

The attack on 'El León' began with the arrival in early September of a naval squadron under Sir Martin Frobisher, which blockaded the seaward side of the fort and began intermittent bombardment. The army's need to march overland and constant bickering between Norris and Marshal Aumont, who commanded some 3000 royalist French troops, meant the landward investment was not completed until several weeks later. Tenuous supply lines and winter rains ensured the Anglo-French forces soon began to drop like flies. Ferocious resistance from the fort's garrison of 400 Spaniards and rocky ground which made trench-digging virtually impossible also contributed to the besiegers' gloom. By November, Aumont was sick and eager to abandon the siege, but Norris and his officers demanded one last chance to storm the fort. The all-out attack was launched on 7 November and lasted most of the day. The French, in particular, suffered heavy casualties, but repeated assaults finally exhausted the defenders' ammunition. The gate was opened and Frobisher was able to storm into the fort with a party of his seamen. What followed was an orgy of killing, mainly conducted, it seems, by English soldiers and sailors. Barely a handful of the Spanish garrison survived the slaughter. Four hundred Frenchmen were killed in the assault, but only 60 English (although others, including Frobisher, later died of their wounds). However, Norris's losses from sickness and desertion during the whole campaign amounted to 1500 men and his troops were in no condition to follow up their victory by attacking the main Spanish base at Blavet, as Aumont suggested. Although the failure to neutralise Blavet would cause considerable anxiety in the coming years, the long and costly English campaign in Brittany was effectively over.[31]

The Continent or Ireland? The Costs and Choices of War

After their victory near Brest, Norris and his battered veterans were ordered to Ireland, about 1200 of them finally arriving there by April 1595. This decision deeply distressed the earl of Essex, who had hoped they would be available for further operations on the Continent. In his mind, Elizabeth's determination to complete the withdrawal of English soldiers from France represented a spiteful rejection of Henri

IV, who had reaffirmed his commitment to the common struggle against Spain by declaring war against Philip – something which Elizabeth had never done. Even worse, the transfer of Norris and his troops signalled a major shift in the deployment of English military resources. Future operations on the Continent would now have to compete for men and money against what Essex thought was a 'miserable, beggerly' sideshow in Ireland.[32] Essex believed this spelled disaster for the 'common cause' with Henri (and the Dutch) and risked allowing Spain to recover the military initiative after a string of recent defeats in Brittany, Picardy and the Low Countries. However, with Elizabeth and Burghley both thoroughly mistrustful of Henri IV and Burghley strongly supportive of action in Ireland, Essex's pleas for new combined operations with the French and Dutch made little impression on the queen. Once the victory at Crozon enabled England to escape from 'deep war' and restored Elizabeth's ability to limit her involvement in the conflict, Essex's arguments in favour of expensive new actions overseas became distinctly unappealing. Nevertheless, Essex continued to argue his case, believing passionately that only he could save the queen from making a terrible mistake.

Essex's disconcerting persistence in arguing with Elizabeth and Burghley against disengagement from the war in France and in favour of greater intervention on the Continent strained relations at court and the council table. These arguments also generated heat because they raised basic questions about England's war effort. Since Spain had shown itself to be England's mortal enemy, could Elizabeth afford to redirect her forces away from the war against Spain to combat Irish 'rebels'? How serious was the threat to English control in Ireland and could Irish restiveness actually be neutralised without the large-scale commitment of troops? Did limited national resources require Elizabeth to choose between operations on the Continent or in Ireland? Indeed, how much longer could Elizabeth's subjects bear the cost of war at all? Essex's answers to these questions were far more aggressive than Elizabeth or Burghley, whose chief concerns lay in defending the integrity of the queen's own dominions and avoiding the sort of popular tumults which had accompanied prolonged war in the late 1540s. By contrast, Essex was not born until

1565 and his boyhood companion had been the son of the Huguenot leader Montgomery. Essex's defining experiences were not the threat of French invasion or the 'camping time', but the enmity of Spain and the sense of purpose which he felt when soldiering.[33]

Although Essex urged that the war with Spain must take priority over everything else, events in Ireland soon thoroughly justified the transfer of Norris and his veterans. Since the late 1580s, trouble had been brewing in Ulster, where English attempts to reconstitute County Monaghan antagonised the great lords of the province, including Hugh O'Neill, second earl of Tyrone. Although he had strong ties to England, Tyrone became increasingly alienated from the queen's government and plunged into open war with the crown in 1595 – two years after the opening rounds of what later became known as the Nine Years War. Tyrone proved a uniquely dangerous enemy because he not only combined the titles of earl and 'the O'Neill', but was also tied by marriage to many of the other chieftains of Ulster, including Hugh Roe O'Donnell, who became his chief ally. No longer could the English hope to divide and conquer by exploiting local feuds. Even worse, Tyrone had built upon the foundations created by Shane and Turlough Luineach O'Neill to create a substantial army. Although it still included some of the traditional gallowglass and redshank troops and could be augmented by the 'rising out' of raw tenants, Tyrone's army was remarkable for its large numbers of Irish volunteers who effectively served as professional soldiers, depending upon Tyrone for pay and upon his lands and tenants for food and lodging. Often misnamed 'bonnaghts' by the English (from *buannacht*, 'billeted men'), these Irish troops were equipped in modern fashion with pikes, calivers and muskets, and were drilled by English, Irish and Spanish veterans of the Continental wars.

Although it imposed a heavy burden on Ulster, Tyrone's army changed the whole nature of England's war in Ireland, as became apparent when Sir Henry Bagenal resupplied the English fort at Monaghan in May 1595. Bagenal's force numbered 1700 men (including some of Norris's veterans and some raw recruits) and constituted the largest English force in Ireland. After brushing up against Irish forces on his journey to Monaghan, Bagenal found his homeward path blocked by Tyrone's army, which occupied a ridge overlooking bogs near Clontibret. As Bagenal's men sought to cross the broken ground and skirt Tyrone's position, they found themselves running a gauntlet of Irish skirmishers. They also confronted units of Irish pikemen, who refused to approach to the 'push of pike' but whose presence forced them to assume defensive formations which were then peppered by redshank archers, javelins thrown by horsemen and 300 Irish shot – the latter wearing red coats 'like English soldiers'. Since they wore less armour than the English, the Irish foot were able to avoid a decisive engagement. The presence of large numbers of Irish horsemen further demoralised Bagenal's men. At one point, the English ground to a halt, their powder almost gone and their pikemen close to panic. They were only saved by a desperate charge of 40 horsemen in the direction of Tyrone himself, who was unhorsed and nearly killed before making good his escape. By nightfall, Bagenal's force had lost 300 men and expected to be overrun on the following day, but the final assault never came and they were able to reach the safety of Newry. After the near-disaster of Clontibret, Bagenal demanded his troops be evacuated by sea, fearing that his command would not survive even the short march to Dundalk. The size and composition of Tyrone's army had proved a very nasty surprise, while the earl's ability to coordinate thrusts by light horse and flanking fire by muskets and calivers severely rattled the English authorities in Dublin. Fortunately for the queen, Tyrone lacked the siege guns necessary for offensive operations against royal garrisons and his secret appeals for aid from Spain brought little response. However, the scale of Tyrone's military commitment boded ill for the future. In terms of numbers and personal weaponry (if not discipline), Tyrone's army was virtually equivalent to English forces in the Low Countries. The strategic implications of this development would have a decisive effect upon the closing years of Elizabeth's reign.[34]

If Tyrone was prepared to force heavy burdens upon Ulster to sustain his large and costly army, the apparent unwillingness of England and Wales to sustain Elizabeth's wars was a cause of growing anxiety for the queen and her council in the mid-1590s. Receipts from parliamentary taxation continued to show a sharp decline and government efforts to make up for the shortfall by boosting the tax-rates in

1593 and 1597 sparked acrimonious debate in the House of Commons and merely underlined the magnitude of the problem. Much of the decline arose from the systematic under-assessment of the income of the wealthiest members of society. Lord Burghley, for example, claimed his income remained static at £133 from the time of his ennoblement in 1571 until his death in 1598, while many JPs were also assessed at unrealistic levels. Tax returns from the City of London, where much of the realm's wealth was concentrated, declined even faster than the national average. In 1602–03 , the subsidy there yielded only 40 per cent of the value of the equivalent grant in 1571–72.[35]

In part, this chronic tax evasion was a result of the other heavy demands which the war placed upon gentlemen and wealthy merchants. Regular local imposts to levy and equip fresh troops for service overseas and the constant high costs associated with the trained bands hit the counties and towns hard. During the crisis of 1588, Burghley feared these charges might cost 'as much as 4 subsydyes'. In the case of London, at least, this claim was entirely accurate: parliamentary taxation on the City netted £8815 in 1588, but military exactions cost it £31,609. Such heavy burdens made the reuse of subsidy assessments to calculate the payment of local militia rates a huge incentive for gentlemen and wealthy merchants to minimise their tax liability by conniving with their friends, relatives and neighbours who served as subsidy commissioners. This practice had the disastrous double effect of eroding the crown's income from taxation whilst simultaneously shifting more of the burden for local war costs to the poorer members of society. Although the privy council sought to limit the impact of this trend by demanding that JPs be assessed at a minimum of £20 per annum and directing lords lieutenant to use their own knowledge of the wealth of local gentlemen when levying *ad hoc* charges, the inequities of war finance became increasingly obvious.[36]

The recognition that urban and county communities were being hit hard by the costs of war made both the privy council and local authorities extremely sensitive about signs of popular restiveness, especially given the socially regressive manner in which taxes and imposts were being levied. One particular cause of concern were the very men who constituted the queen's armies and fleets, who were always regarded as potential trouble-makers when they were not controlled by their officers. Many of those who went abroad were unwilling conscripts and liable to desert while marching to their port of embarkation or cause trouble at the port, especially when contrary winds prevented their departure and left them without adequate supplies or money. Chester, which served as the chief base for operations in Ireland, witnessed regular disturbances involving soldiers in the 1590s, despite the best efforts of the mayor and the appointment of two trouble-shooters by the privy council in 1596.

Soldiers and sailors were deemed even more of a threat after they were discharged. Many ex-servicemen allegedly failed to return home and instead adopted a life of vagrancy and crime. Sometimes they even banded together to protest their lack of pay. In August 1589, hundreds of angry veterans of the Portugal expedition converged on London and 'so rudely behaved themselves about the countrey, about the court and elsewhere' that the lord mayor had to mobilise 2000 men of the trained bands. Several protesters were hanged. Elizabeth herself had to order one band away from the court at Westminster. The mounting fear of disorder by such 'masterless men' encouraged the widespread appointment of provost-marshals to arrest suspicious vagrants and (if necessary) enforce martial law. Originally officers charged with enforcing military discipline on campaign, provost-marshals were first appointed to control civilians in Ireland in the 1550s, but were also occasionally employed in England. By 1588–89, the degree of military activity in England meant that provost-marshals were appointed across much of the realm and they became a fixture of late Elizabethan local government, scouring the highways for rogues and trouble-makers and handing them over to the local JPs for punishment.[37]

The mid-1590s also saw more serious signs of unrest. In June 1595, London was rocked by a dozen separate disturbances, culminating in a large-scale riot on Tower Hill which involved apprentices and ex-servicemen, some of them armed. Martial law was immediately declared, but the council was careful to ensure the provost-marshal did not use his powers of summary execution. Although five men were hanged, all were pointedly condemned under civilian law. In November 1596, the council learned of an aborted plan for a popular rising in Oxfordshire, where high grain prices had been made even worse by the government policy of diverting grain to London to dampen discontent there. The council chose to make an example of the Oxfordshire plotters, deliberately twisting the law to ensure they were executed as traitors. The contrast with the Hampshire beacon plot of 1586, when an intensive investigation resulted in no executions, underlines how anxious the privy council had become to prevent popular 'stirs' like those of 1549. This fear was all the greater because the realm suffered poor harvests in 1594 and 1595 and disastrous harvests in 1596 and 1597 – the worst succession of harvest failures in the entire sixteenth century.[38]

Moreover, the council was acutely aware that disquiet was not restricted to the commons. In late 1595, questions about Elizabeth's continued longevity and the royal succession burst into the open. The lieutenant of the Tower was even dismissed from office for conspiring to hold the Tower in the event of the queen's death. In June 1596, an embittered veteran soldier, Sir John Smythe, made an extraordinary speech during musters at Colchester, condemning the government's right to conscript men for service overseas and calling Burghley a traitor. Smythe was fortunate to escape treason charges, but spent 18 months in the Tower and the rest of Elizabeth's reign under house arrest. The council was itself also increasingly troubled by Essex's growing rivalry with Burghley and his son Sir Robert Cecil.[39]

In light of such problems and the alarming developments in Ireland, it is not surprising that Elizabeth and Burghley were eager to avoid further entanglement in France. Nevertheless, events soon gave Essex the opportunity to press his case for taking the war to Spain. By the middle of 1595, Essex's intelligence sources had convinced him that Spain was preparing to try again to do what it had failed to do in 1588. At first, his claims about a new Spanish Armada made little impression on the queen. Other councillors, including Burghley and Cecil, argued (correctly) that this was an alarmist interpretation. Nevertheless, opinions changed dramatically after four Spanish galleys from Blavet launched a minor raid against Cornwall on 24 July, burning the villages of Mousehole, Newlyn and Penzance. For the first time, Spanish soldiers had landed on English soil. Now it seemed the whole realm was perilously vulnerable to Spanish attack and Essex's fears were justified after all. This perception helped to secure the queen's approval for the long-delayed expedition of Sir John Hawkins and Sir Francis Drake, which was intended to interdict the flow of silver to Spain from the New World by seizing and garrisoning Panama. With luck, this might distract the expected new Armada and cripple Philip's finances. However, given the difficulties of defending England and Wales, let alone Ireland, the best option for resisting an invasion seemed to be a pre-emptive strike against the Spanish fleet before it could put to sea – the same strategy which had been attempted, but thwarted, in 1588. By the end of 1595, Essex was still unsuccessful in his efforts to revive English intervention in France, but his relentless advocacy of waging offensive war against Spain ensured that the pin-prick raid on Cornwall sparked a revival of amphibious operations on a scale not seen since 1589. Although the situation in Ireland was teetering towards disaster, England's main effort in 1596 would be against Spain and would largely be shaped by Essex.[40]

6 The Limits of War:
operations and developments,
1596–1604

England's return to the offensive in late 1595 reflected the genuinely transatlantic scope of the conflict with Spain. This was war on a completely different geographical scale from anything envisaged in the 1540s and 1550s. In its original conception, the new expedition planned by Drake and Hawkins was intended to seize and hold Panama, the central node which connected Spain's South American colonies (and silver mines) with its possessions in the Caribbean and Mexico. This extraordinary plan probably exceeded the limits of Elizabethan logistics and certainly underestimated the likely Spanish response, but its daring – and the prospect of massive profit at the enemy's expense – seemed powerfully attractive.

In early 1595, when Elizabeth's withdrawal from France seemed most disheartening, Essex himself apparently toyed with joining the venture. However, the prolonged gestation of the voyage and the size of the force involved – which included six of the queen's major warships and 1000 infantry officered by veteran captains – meant it lacked the vital element of surprise. The Spanish naval preparations which Essex's agents claimed to be a new Armada were actually a response to intelligence about the plans of Drake and Hawkins. This misperception of Spanish intentions helped to transform the expedition when the raid on Cornwall reminded Elizabeth's government of the realm's vulnerability to seaborne attack. The raid was intended as retaliation for an English privateer's recent occupation and sacking of Recife in Brazil, but it convinced Elizabeth and her council that Spain's seapower had become so threatening that it required urgent action. Drake and

Hawkins, who would be taking away 25 per cent of the queen's entire front-line fleet, became caught up in the sharp debate which followed. In light of the apparent Spanish threat, Essex modified his previous advocacy of the Panama expedition and urged Elizabeth to both strengthen the force and change its target to the ships gathering in Spanish ports. Essex probably hoped to lead this operation himself, but the plan was opposed, apparently by Burghley and the lord admiral, with 'great distemper of humures on both sides for a few dayes'. In the end, Elizabeth was swayed by fresh intelligence from the West Indies. Enticed by news that a Spanish treasure ship was stranded at San Juan in Puerto Rico, she ordered the expedition to continue, but changed its target to Puerto Rico and insisted that it return within six months so its ships could be used in the strike against the Spanish fleet which was now planned for the spring of 1596.[1]

Drake and Hawkins finally sailed at the end of August 1595. Elizabeth provided the six largest vessels in their fleet of 27 ships and paid two-thirds of the expedition's cost, with the rest being met by the commanders and other private investors. It soon proved to be a poor investment. As co-commanders, Drake and Hawkins exemplified all the worst problems of divided command, being 'men of so different natures and dispositions that what the one desireth the other would commonly oppose against'. These clashes were all the sharper because both were now old men (by Tudor standards) and embittered by their enforced inactivity during recent years. After much disagreement, the fleet tried to land in the Canary Islands in late September to seize fresh supplies, but heavy surf and Drake's dithering ensured that Spanish troops were waiting on the beach and the landing had to be abandoned. Even worse, the diversion to the Canaries wasted time and allowed the Spanish to take prisoners, who confirmed the fleet's objective. By the time Drake and Hawkins had crossed the Atlantic and prepared for action, five Spanish frigates had already rushed reinforcements to Puerto Rico.

When the English fleet approached San Juan on 11 November, they found the town on full alert. To make matters worse, Hawkins, who had been sick for some time, died the next day. Drake responded by ordering an attack on the Spanish frigates in the harbour. Using the cover of night, soldiers were rowed past the defending cannon to attack the enemy ships with incendiaries. The attack was pressed home with vigour, but the boats were 'excedingly lardid' by enemy fire and the incendiaries proved so ineffective that only one frigate caught alight. Two hundred Englishmen were killed or wounded. After this reverse, the attack on Puerto Rico was abandoned and the fleet headed southwards, utimately occupying the small town of Rio de la Hacha in the hope of extorting a ransom from its inhabitants. This wasted almost a month and brought no reward. With all hope of surprise now gone, Drake gambled on reviving his original plan of attacking Panama. Occupying Nombre de Dios on 27 December, he ordered the infantry commander, Sir Thomas Baskerville, to make an overland approach, rather than heading up-river by boat. Since it was the rainy season, Baskerville's men had a terrible time, struggling with knee-deep mud and dampness which ruined their food and gunpowder. Eventually, they encountered enemy troops entrenched behind stout timber defences and protected from outflanking by the terrain. Baskerville's exhausted troops tried to break through, but 60 or 70 were killed and wounded and the effort had to be abandoned. The soldiers trudged back to Nombre de Dios and the fleet set sail again, after burning the town, on 5 January 1596. Not only had the golden dream of seizing Panama turned to ashes, but the fleet was now racked by disease. Drake himself died from dysentery on 28 January. Like Hawkins and so many others, Drake's body was buried at sea. Baskerville and the other surviving officers, however, were desperate to salvage something from the voyage and decided to plunder the town of Santa Marta, which lay near Rio de la Hacha. Yet even this proved impossible. As the fleet headed for Santa Marta, they encountered enemy warships which had recently arrived from Spain to intercept them. Several hours of inconclusive skirmishing ensued before the English ships managed to escape. Dispersed and battered, the survivors of the expedition finally struggled home in April and May.[2]

Calais, Cadiz and the Spanish 'Armada' of 1596

The disastrous failure of Drake and Hawkins's expedition and the deaths of two such famous naval commanders came close to panicking Elizabeth into cancelling the strike against Spain which was almost ready to sail when the first survivors reached England. Originally planned by the lord admiral as a naval operation, the voyage to Spain became something quite different when Essex was appointed as co-commander by early in 1596. Under Essex, the landing force grew into a sizeable army and the whole venture gained extra momentum. Although this was a military operation of the crown and much of the shipping was provided at the expense of coastal communities, Elizabeth's desire for economy meant that Essex and the lord admiral both had to subsidise the expedition out of their own pockets to ensure it would proceed in the manner they believed necessary. Lord Admiral Howard offered to equip 1000 soldiers and pay off 2000 men after the expedition returned home, while Essex armed 1500 soldiers, paid the wages of 1000 men and provided 100 lancers. Essex also encouraged hundreds of gentlemen volunteers to serve the queen without pay. When news from the Continent and the Caribbean caused Elizabeth to suspend the expedition, Essex spent £1250 a week for a whole month to keep the army in being while she decided whether or not to proceed.[3]

Elizabeth's hesitations were driven not only by the failed expedition of Drake and Hawkins, but also by the sudden thrust of Spanish troops towards Calais at the end of March. This raised the alarming prospect of Spain controlling a port which had once been the outer bulwark of England's national defences and had been a magnet for the *Gran Armada* of 1588 even when still in French hands. Essex and Howard were diverted to prepare a relief operation and 6000 men were hurriedly conscripted in the south-eastern counties. In London, the emergency levy was conducted by locking the doors after the start of the Easter Sunday service, when the whole population was required to attend church.[4]

Despite such extraordinary measures, Elizabeth hesitated about authorising the despatch of troops. At first, she demanded that Henri IV guarantee English control of Calais as the price for her intervention – a demand which he refused. When she finally decided that she needed to act even without this concession, it was too late. As the English had discovered in 1558, the defences of Calais were no match for a determined attack by a large modern army. By the time Essex was ordered to embark his troops on 15 April, the final resistance at

Calais had already collapsed. Although the flow of news from across the Channel was confusing, the fall of Calais showed Elizabeth at her worst as a war-time leader, issuing contradictory orders and adopting a stop-go approach which drove even Burghley to despair. It also further poisoned relations with France, where Elizabeth was blamed for the disaster. Although it actually jolted Elizabeth into approving the negotiation of a new alliance with Henri, the fall of Calais symbolised how precarious their uneasy partnership had become.[5]

The shambles of Calais also convinced Essex – if he did not think so already – that a queen could not wage a war without firm male guidance. Elizabeth's subsequent vacillation over the expedition to Spain seemed to confirm this opinion. On 16 May, she finally cancelled the operation, only to reverse her decision an hour later. After the events of the last 18 months, Essex already planned to use this expedition to revive England's commitment to war on the Continent, but Elizabeth's behaviour made him even more determined to act. In his opinion, 'princes that are once in warres, when they do little, must suffer much'. Minimising the realm's 'suffering' therefore required circumventing the queen's 'doing little'. While the fleet prepared for departure, Essex drafted a letter to his colleagues on the council. He argued England could only be protected from the enemy if the war were transferred to Spanish soil by seizing a defensible port and forcing Philip to concentrate his army against it. With regular supplies and reinforcements shipped from home, England could create 'a continuall diversion' which would hobble Philip like 'a thorne sticking in his foote'. This argument revived some of the ideas advanced to support the Portugal expedition of 1589, but was entirely contrary to the queen's instructions in 1596. In effect, Essex intended to subvert the new expedition and turn it to his own purposes, not those approved by Elizabeth. As he admitted to one of his secretaries, 'I know I shall never do her service butt against her will'. Not surprisingly, he ensured the letter was not delivered until the fleet was beyond recall.[6]

Essex's secret plans meant that he threw himself into preparing the new expedition with a passion. While the lord admiral and naval officials took charge of the fleet, Essex directed his formidable energy towards the formation and organisation of the army. Months of planning and feverish preparation ensured the expedition was the

Esset 1596 conjay

best-organised force yet sent abroad by the Elizabethan regime. The fleet consisted of 100 ships divided into four squadrons, backed up by 18 substantial Dutch ships and a host of smaller vessels, many of which were privateers hoping to share in the spoils of victory. Although most of the fleet were armed merchantmen, 17 of the vessels belonged to the crown, including 11 of the queen's front-line ships – almost half the royal battle-fleet. The army totalled 6300 men, grouped into eight regiments, each consisting of 750 men in seven companies (except Essex's own regiment, which had 1050 men in eight companies). A third of the troops were veterans whom Sir Francis Vere had brought from the Low Countries, with the remainder being new recruits. The Dutch squadron also carried 2000 Dutch veterans, while 500–1000 English gentlemen volunteers sailed aboard the queen's warships. The volunteers were especially important because their high level of motivation (including the fear of dishonour) made them a disproportionately valuable addition to any army. In Essex's view, 'those gentlemen and adventurers thatt serve withowt pay shall do more service in any fight then the whole troupes besides'. The high number of veterans and gentlemen volunteers meant that a large part of Essex's force reflected a similar mix to that seen in the Spanish army, whose *tercios* were built around 'old soldiers' and élite volunteers (*particulares*). Given Essex's fascination with the enemy and the long-term championing of Spanish methods by Sir Roger Williams, who acted as the earl's chief military adviser until his death in November 1595, this similarity was no accident. However, the organisation of the army into small regiments also showed that Essex understood the new model of soldiering which Vere and his troops had learned under Maurice of Nassau.[7]

The new expedition also reflected other benefits of hard-won military experience. Although relations between Essex and Howard were increasingly fraught, both worked hard to avoid a repetition of the difficulties which had plagued Drake and Hawkins. Extraordinary efforts were also made to ensure that the expedition's objective remained secret until after the fleet finally put to sea on 30 May. As a result, the Spanish government was taken by surprise when the fleet arrived off Cadiz on 20 June, even though the lord admiral had been considering an attack there for at least a year. Although foiled in its

1596 Lee followed fleet for three days

initial attempt to land on the seaward side of the port, the fleet entered Cadiz Bay on 21 June. There lay a large merchant convoy bound for the New World, protected by a squadron of galleys, four of the 'Apostles' and a variety of other warships. The latter positioned themselves in a narrow channel which forced the leading English warships to approach them virtually in single file, while exposing the attackers to fire from the town defences. Essex, Ralegh, Vere and other senior officers vied with each other to put their ship in the lead, where the defensive fire was heaviest – and the honour was greatest. The cannonade continued for several hours until the tide allowed the English ships to close with the Spanish, who were swiftly pulverised by English gunnery. Subsequent inventories show that the English gunners expended extraordinary quantities of gunpowder and shot in the battle. While the smaller Spanish ships were able to flee into shallower water, the huge 'Apostles' and large Ragusan galleons could not escape. Two 'Apostles' (the *San Andres* and *San Mateo*) and a Ragusan were captured, but the others were destroyed. The poet John Donne, who served as one of Essex's gentlemen volunteers, described the terrible choice of the Spanish defenders between burning to death or jumping overboard and drowning.

While Howard was still trying to comprehend the magnitude of the victory, Essex ordered the leading regiments of his army into boats for an assault. In an echo of his landing at Peniche in 1589, Essex was first to reach the shore. The veteran troops quickly put the local militia to flight, pursuing them back to the city gates. The attackers soon found ways of climbing the walls – even Essex boosted himself over, after first aiding a servant, who 'stode on th'erle's handes as th'erle helped him up'. Once the gates were flung open, English troops poured in and resistance was swiftly snuffed out everywhere except the citadel, which surrendered the next day. By the time Howard and Ralegh caught up with Essex in the marketplace, the most spectacular English success of the war with Spain was already won – and with negligible casualties on land or sea. The only blemish was that the merchant fleet, which Essex had expected Howard to secure, was burned by the Spanish before the English could seize it.[8]

The capture of Cadiz opened the way for Essex to execute his plan by persuading Howard and the other senior officers to garrison the city. Flushed with victory, they initially agreed to the proposal, although it contravened the queen's explicit instructions. However, such a drastic step soon encouraged second thoughts. Once the officers and soldiers had finished gathering up their piles of booty, the appeal of an early return home also became overwhelming. In the end, the city was burned and abandoned – and Essex's hopes along with it. Although the fleet subsequently raided several small Spanish towns, the huge haul of plunder taken at Cadiz encouraged a steady drift homewards. Even the prospect of heading for the Azores to ambush the home-bound *flota* failed to generate sustained interest, much to the despair of Essex, who still hoped for greater success to placate the queen's inevitable fury. By early August, the whole fleet was back in English ports. Vere's veterans were promptly ordered back to the Low Countries and 1000 of the newly blooded recruits were despatched to Ireland, while the rest were dismissed.[9]

Essex's brazen attempt to hijack the Cadiz expedition infuriated Elizabeth and consolidated opposition to him at court. In attempting to 'serve' the queen 'against her will', he convinced many observers that he was a dangerous maverick whose hatred of Spain had led him to treat his own sovereign with disrespect. Elizabeth was also enraged that Essex and the lord admiral dubbed almost 60 new knights after the victory. Further ructions followed the earl's attempt to make political capital out of the expedition by secretly scheming to publish a 'True relation' which glorified his role in the battle. To prevent such claims and counter-claims, the council banned all publications about Cadiz altogether. Perhaps worst of all (in Elizabeth's eyes) was the massive peculation which followed the fall of Cadiz, which saw vast quantities of loot disappear into private hands, depriving the queen of what she had hoped would be a spectacular windfall for the exchequer. She was especially angry because the merchant fleet which had been burned in Cadiz Bay was worth an estimated £3.5 million – ten times her ordinary annual income and more than enough to re-finance England's whole war effort. An inquisition into the stolen booty was launched under the auspices of Burghley and Cecil, which Essex interpreted as an attack on himself, even though he had studiously left the great bulk of the loot for his subordinates. Although the commanders were cleared and some plunder was recovered, the investigation, and the uproar over the mass knightings, convinced Essex and his friends that soldierly honour – and the rewards which supposedly went with it – was under attack by 'mushroom men' who remained safely at home and profited from military contracts or the bribery which accompanied them. The indignation felt by the Essexians was evident in Lord Willoughby's private description of auditors who criticised fighting men as 'harpies' and inimical to common sense and the needs of the state. Events soon dampened down these fierce murmurings, but the episode set the scene for martial 'honour' to become an explosive political issue in later years.[10]

The post-Cadiz investigation vindicated Essex, but his full rehabilitation was confirmed by the very event which the Cadiz expedition had been intended to prevent – the launching of a new Spanish 'Armada'. Although the victory at Cadiz caused an international sensation and forced the Spanish crown to renegotiate its debts, it left the bulk of Spain's warships untouched at Lisbon and drove Philip to desperate measures to redeem his royal honour. Philip was even more determined to act because England and France signed a new treaty in May and the agreement was expanded to include the Dutch – creating the Triple Alliance – in October. From Spain's perspective, this seemed like a strategic nightmare, with all of its chief enemies coordinating action against it. In reality, Elizabeth strictly limited her commitment to France to 2000 men – a quarter of the number promised by the Dutch – and stipulated they could only perform garrison duty in Picardy, thereby releasing French troops for action whilst minimising the likelihood of English losses.

Philip's response to the humiliation of Cadiz and the apparent rallying of his enemies was to focus his energies against England. Peace feelers were extended to France in the hope of breaking up the revived Anglo-French entente and contacts were stepped up with Tyrone in Ireland, which was intended as the target of a fleet hurriedly assembled during August and September. However, the prolonged preparation of the fleet meant that it did not sail until mid-October, when autumnal gales usually made naval operations too risky. Philip consequently changed the fleet's instructions, directing it instead to seize Brest, to rebuild 'El León' and prepare for an invasion of

England in the following spring. With more than 100 ships, including 30 galleons, the fleet was in some ways a more effective naval force than the lumbering armed convoy of 1588. However, the objectives of the fleet were far more limited than those of the *Gran Armada* and the number of troop soldiers aboard was considerably smaller.[11]

The details and objectives of the new Spanish fleet remained elusive to Elizabeth's government, which only learned of the threat after most of the queen's warships had been laid up at Chatham for the winter. The news that Spain was launching a fleet in the 'close season' came as a terrible shock and sparked a full-scale invasion alarm. Although the privy council ordered the immediate recommissioning of the battle-fleet, westerly winds kept the queen's ships penned in the Medway and even prevented scout ships from putting to sea. As a result, the south-west of England was left without naval protection and naval planners were left blind as to Spanish intentions. The front line of England's defences therefore rested upon its ramshackle coastal fortifications and the trained bands of the maritime counties. This was precisely the situation which Elizabeth's government – with its emphasis upon naval defence and constant doubts about the reliability of county forces – had always sought to avoid. Throughout October and most of November, the council scrambled to deal with this sudden nightmare, issuing a stream of orders to reinforce coastal garrisons and ready the trained bands for action. As in 1588, a small committee of military experts was appointed to advise the council, but the leading role was accorded to Essex, who would command the realm's forces if the enemy landed. In fact, this expensive mobilisation was actually unnecessary because the same seasonal gales which kept the queen's ships in port also destroyed the Spanish fleet only four days after it left port. A quarter of its ships (mainly small troop-carriers) sank and 3000 men were lost. However, it was not until late November that certain news of the Spanish disaster reached England and the realm's defences could finally be stood down.[12]

The Azores Expedition and the Spanish 'Armada' of 1597

The Spanish fleet was crippled in October 1596, but not destroyed. The assembly and repair of the Spanish ships at Ferrol therefore set the scene for the preparation of a new 'Armada' in 1597. This, in turn, demanded that England launch a pre-emptive strike against Ferrol, in keeping with its strategy of forward naval defence – attacking the enemy in or near their own ports, while they still constituted a sitting target. This strategy had become an article of faith since its adoption in 1588 because it made defence easier to coordinate (and potentially cheaper) and appealed to the aggressive nature of military men, but it had never been implemented successfully. Events in 1597 would again demonstrate how difficult it was to execute with sixteenth-century sailing technology and infrastructure. The immediate consequence of the lingering Spanish threat, however, was the continued pre-eminence of the earl of Essex. Since the events of 1596 had shown Lord Admiral Howard was now too old for further service at sea, Essex was the only viable commander for the new strike against Spain. Although his real expertise lay in land warfare and the majority of his military followers were army officers, the new voyage gave him the opportunity to implement the ideas which he had developed in 1596 – but now with Elizabeth's grudging approval.

During his return home from Cadiz, Essex began sketching out a new strategy which combined his abortive plans for Cadiz with the failed 'double blockade' scheme of 1589–90. The result was the most ambitious and comprehensive military strategy of the Elizabethan era. By seizing an enemy port such as Cadiz or Lisbon, Essex argued, an English fleet could neutralise Spanish seapower and maintain a permanent blockade of Spanish ports, starving Philip of silver from the New World and grain and essential naval supplies from the Baltic. Like earlier proponents of maritime supremacy, he believed such a blockade would not only bring Spain to its knees, but also clear the way for England to usurp Spain's place as the dominant power in the East and West Indies, making Elizabeth 'Queen of the Seas' and able to exert economic pressure across Europe. For Essex, however, the linch-pin of this vision would not be a fleet, but a small, highly trained army, which could secure the fleet's forward operating base and protect it from whatever forces Philip could throw against it. In contrast to the lumbering army which sailed on the Portugal expedition or even the army which occupied Cadiz in 1596, this would be a extremely compact force – 3000 men – which would trust in quality rather than quantity. Essex's belief in the superiority of such a force was testimony both to the repeated poor performance of the Spanish militia (whom he dismissed as 'artificers and clownes who know nothing of the warres') and the growing confidence of English commanders in the quality of the troops which they could now commit to battle.[13]

Before Essex was confirmed as commander of the new expedition to Spain, he was entrusted with two other tasks for reforming England's war effort. In March 1597, he was appointed master of the ordnance office and given a mandate by the queen to sweep away its inefficiency and the corruption of its officers. This was an objective which he never achieved, thanks to the distractions of campaigning and politics and the expert stone-walling of long-time office-holders. In the light of the previous autumn's emergency and a new alarm that Spain might reinforce its hold on Calais by attacking Boulogne, Essex also sought to reform the trained bands. His plan was to generate a small army of 4000 'choice men' from the trained bands – in effect, élite trained bands – which could serve in offensive or defensive operations with minimal support from Low Countries veterans. Essex created the machinery for raising these troops by superimposing a new system of regimental districts upon the county system, with each district consisting of one or more counties and overseen by a 'superintendent'. In the usual pattern, the trained bands were restricted to home defence and local authorities responded to demands from the privy council for specific numbers of men to serve overseas by filling their quota with criminals and other undesirables. This practice may have encouraged 'good order' in the local community, but it produced poor soldiers who were prone to desertion. By contrast, Essex envisaged the superintendents working with lords lieutenant and JPs to select the best possible soldiers. While local authorities usually ignored the council's regular demands for better recruits, Essex's scheme depended upon securing local cooperation by drawing upon his own contacts and appointing superintendents who combined military experience with local ties – a more personal approach than the privy council and one which looked towards future cooperation. Once selected, the troops were grouped in companies of 150 and trained by the superintendent or his subordinate captains, who would also lead the men into action. How successful this new model militia might have become is hard to judge. Although mobilised for service on Essex's new expedition, the troops never actually saw combat. Whether because it was too expensive or because it was too intimately associated with Essex himself, the system was discontinued after 1597, curtailing an experiment which carried the logic behind the trained bands to its obvious conclusion and ending the further modernisation of England's militia.[14]

The importance which the Elizabethan government attached to destroying the Spanish fleet at Ferrol was demonstrated by its willingness to earmark the 4000 élite militia troops for the operation, reinforced by 1000 Low Countries veterans under Sir Francis Vere. The fleet included 15 of the queen's front-line warships, in addition to the captured *San Andres* and *San Mateo* and enough armed merchantmen to fill out three squadrons. A fourth squadron was provided by the Dutch. This was the best prepared Elizabethan expeditionary force – even better than that of 1596 – and Essex planned to use it to execute his grand design. Once the Spanish fleet at Ferrol had been neutralised, he would seize and garrison an enemy port, opening the way for the blockade which he had described the previous autumn.

However, despite his careful preparations, things soon fell apart. When the fleet sailed in July, storms quickly battered most of the fleet back home. In the six weeks which followed, logistical problems and disease forced Essex to release all of the 'choice' militia, reducing his army to Vere's veterans. This killed his hopes of seizing a port and offered only a marginal chance of success against the defences at Ferrol. The fleet sailed again in August, but more rough weather scattered the troop-ships and crippled the *San Andres* and *San Mateo* (which Essex had earmarked to escort fireships into Ferrol), ending all hope of attacking the enemy fleet in port. For a while, like Hawkins in 1590, Essex's fleet patrolled the Spanish coast, seeking to blockade Ferrol whilst hoping to intercept the incoming *flota*. As with Hawkins, the prospect of catching the *flota* in the Azores and securing sufficient plunder to appease the queen soon proved irresistible. This decision converted the expedition into the sort of 'idle wandering upon the sea' which Essex had condemned in 1596 and which cruelly exposed his inadequacies as a naval commander.

Confused sailing orders and growing bitterness between Essex's partisans and Sir Walter Ralegh resulted in the former demanding
Ralegh's court martial after he landed troops at Fayal without waiting
for Essex's arrival. Essex ultimately dismissed the charges, but they
reflected the recriminations which accompanied military failure. Sir
Francis Vere, who had previously been close to Essex, had already
begun to back away, furious that the earl had appointed his friend
Lord Mountjoy as the expedition's second-in-command. The frustrations of this 'Islands voyage' were compounded when the fleet failed
to intercept the *flota* by a hair's breadth, which epitomised Essex's
extraordinary run of ill fortune in 1597.[15]

Like Hawkins in 1590, Essex's dash for the Azores opened the way
for the Spanish fleet to leave Ferrol and head north. The Spanish
'Armada' of 1597 was bigger than that of 1596, but anxiety about
Essex's intentions and rough weather delayed its departure until late
in the season. After thoughts of an invasion of England were rejected
because it was impossible to raise the 30,000 troops considered necessary for the task, Philip ordered the fleet to attack Brest, reviving his
orders of 1596. However, the departure of Essex's fleet towards the
Azores prompted a late change, with Philip instructing his admiral to
sail for England and seize Falmouth as a base for operations against
the returning English fleet. Comprising 136 ships, 9000 troops and
4000 sailors, the new 'Armada' did not leave Ferrol until early
October. As the Spanish fleet neared the Channel and approached
Falmouth, the privy council was still ignorant of its arrival, believing
that Essex had bottled the enemy up in Spain. Essex had taken over
half the queen's major warships with him, while others had already
been berthed for the winter to save costs, leaving only the small
Channel squadron available for defence.

Reports that Spanish ships had been sighted in the Channel came
as a stunning blow. For the second successive autumn, the vulnerable
south-west was lacking any naval protection. Even the news that
Essex's fleet had arrived safely at Plymouth offered little comfort.
After three months at sea, his fleet was utterly exhausted and, just as
in 1588, contrary winds kept it penned in Plymouth Sound. Although
the trained bands near Falmouth had been freshly exercised and the
English veterans in Picardy had recently been recalled to Portsmouth,

it is likely the Spanish fleet would have succeeded in landing had it not been scattered, almost at the last minute, by a fierce storm. Even if the Spaniards had not been able to hold Falmouth, they might still have 'done a Cadiz' and humiliated Elizabeth's royal honour by destroying the town. Only timely gales saved England from acute military embarrassment.[16]

The War Reshaped, 1598

The expeditions of 1597 proved resounding and costly disappointments for both England and Spain. Although the Spanish and French armies were still slugging it out like two punch-drunk boxers, talk of peace now assumed real urgency. When Henri IV and Philip made peace by the Treaty of Vervins in April 1598 (although it was concealed until May), the Triple Alliance was shattered and Elizabeth was forced to consider emulating the French king. The debate about entering peace negotiations with Spain proved bitterly divisive in England. While Burghley urged the merits of peace and the heavy social and economic impact of war and four years of poor harvests, Essex utterly opposed all talk of negotiation, believing that Spain's 'ambitious and revengefull humours' made real peace impossible. He feared peace would merely result in England running down its defences, leaving it vulnerable to attack in the future. Rather than withdrawing from the war, he urged, Elizabeth should reinforce her endeavours by guaranteeing an annual military budget of £100,000–£250,000, to be controlled by a new 'counsell of warre'. This suggestion took Essex's desire to emulate Spanish practices to a new height and raised the prospect of the earl and his military followers dominating a body which might rival the privy council, which consisted overwhelmingly of civilians. Embittered by his failures in 1596 and 1597 and the recent defection of his French allies, Essex clearly hoped to regain the initiative against his domestic rivals by using this new council effectively to militarise English politics, locking Elizabeth into full-scale war against Spain and forcing both the queen and his rivals to accord him the deference owed to military men in time of war.[17]

Not surprisingly, this proposal found no favour with the queen, but Essex at least had the satisfaction of seeing talk of negotiations with Spain abandoned. This was not necessarily the earl's doing. Although Essex was the most strident opponent of renewing contacts with the enemy, Elizabeth herself remained deeply wary of Philip's intentions and many of her advisers felt the same. More importantly, the Dutch government's refusal to entertain any dealings with Spain gave Elizabeth little option but to continue the war. Once the main Spanish army withdrew from France, the Dutch would again become its chief target. Although the Dutch were now in a far stronger position than in 1585, this would revive the strategic concerns which had prompted England's entry into the war in the first place. Breaking with the Dutch would also imperil repayment of the enormous sums which Elizabeth had spent in the Low Countries. Instead of initiating peace talks with Spain, therefore, the immediate consequence of Vervins was a renegotiation of the Anglo-Dutch alliance. This was finally accomplished in August 1598, when the Dutch acknowledged a war debt of £800,000 and agreed to reimbursement of £30,000 a year. They also took over payment of Vere's field forces – which became a regiment of the Dutch army – and most of the English troops garrisoning the cautionary towns. These undertakings should have generated savings of £60,000 a year, but England continued to pay the garrison troops to maintain its hold on the cautionary towns, reducing the savings. Nevertheless, the annual cost of England's forces in the Low Countries during the last years of the reign fell as low as £25,000–30,000.[18]

The new treaty of 1598 represented an excellent deal for England, especially as the relative importance of English troops for Dutch defence continued to decline. When the queen had had to pay their wages, English units were kept under strength to save money – a mere 4300 were mustered in 1593 and 4700 foot and 225 horse in 1597. The regular withdrawal of English veterans for service elsewhere also hampered operations in the Low Countries and infuriated the Dutch. Thus, although Vere and his men played a prominent role in Prince Maurice's annihilation of a Spanish army at Turnhout in February 1597, when enemy troops were caught unprepared for action by Maurice's cavalry, the Azores expedition deprived Maurice of Vere's presence during his successful autumn campaign against the last Spanish garrisons north of the Rhine and Waal rivers.

The character of the war in the Low Countries changed after the Treaty of Vervins enabled Spain to concentrate its forces there again. During 1598 and 1599, the Spanish took the offensive and Maurice's outnumbered army was forced into operations aimed at delaying the enemy and minimising the loss of territory. In 1599, Dutch efforts to boost the size of their army resulted in fresh recruitment to bring Vere's English regiment up to full strength. Although already encumbered by levies for Ireland, Elizabeth's government permitted this because the queen did not bear the cost. Far larger numbers of French, Swiss and Dutch troops were also hired in 1599, reducing the numerical importance of English troops in the Low Countries. However, the long service of the English regiment and the accumulated experience of many of its officers and soldiers meant that it (like its Scottish equivalent) retained a significant qualitative importance in Maurice's army, as the events of 1600 would demonstrate.[19]

Although he had long been the chief advocate of the Dutch on the privy council (as he had been for Henri IV), Essex was not involved in the renegotiation of the Dutch alliance. Caught up in an increasingly bitter struggle with rivals at court and on the council, Essex made the mistake of venting his frustrations against Elizabeth herself in a meeting on 1 July. The result was a 'great quarrel' which kept him away from court for much of the summer and ensured that he lost out in the division of spoils which followed Burghley's death in August 1598. Essex's clash with the queen confirmed the decline in his fortunes since the failure of the Azores expedition and raised doubts about his behaviour among many of his supporters. However, Essex remained a talismanic figure in England and his opinions still carried weight. Despite his remorseless self-aggrandisement, there was also substance to many of his complaints about the failings of England's war effort. When he demanded the creation of a council of war and the appointment of 'an honest and sufficient treasurer for the warres', Essex not only sought to buttress his own position, but also emphasised that his reforms would stamp out the corruption which plagued military administration. His response to being labelled a warmonger by his opponents was therefore to revive the debate which had followed Cadiz and to insinuate that his critics were corrupt and war profiteers.

In part, this represented a criticism of the ailing Burghley, who had consistently failed to stem massive peculation by royal officials – to the tune of tens of thousands of pounds – and instead concealed the scandals. More generally, though, it reflected the soldier's traditional conceit that civilians were too corrupt to administer war and military men would do a better job. The root of the problem was not so much Burghley himself, who was relatively modest in his acceptance of bribes, but the sheer impossibility of exerting any sustained control over royal officials who viewed their offices as means of self-enrichment – itself the inevitable result of restricting royal wages to token amounts, to save money. The very parsimony of Elizabethan government itself encouraged a culture of corruption and resistance to administrative reform among royal office-holders (in the exchequer and ordnance office, for example) which severely undermined governmental efficiency. Such problems were endemic in early modern Europe, but presented special difficulties when the Elizabethan regime went to war in the 1580s. After years of peace, in which they had been able to use royal funds for private speculation, exchequer officials suddenly found themselves pressed for cash – with near-disastrous results, which Burghley had to hide from the queen. At one point, the lord treasurer apparently feared that these scandals might bring his own downfall. Other officials were burdened (and tempted) by the sheer novelty of handling the huge sums of money required by war. Sir Thomas Sherley, for example, who became paymaster for English troops on the Continent in 1587, went bankrupt in March 1597. During these ten years, £1.4 million passed through his hands. Months of investigation finally determined that Sherley had received £15,000 in bribes from the merchant William Beecher since 1589 and that Sherley owed the queen £23,000. Even larger sums went missing in Ireland, where Sir George Cary, Sherley's equivalent for the period 1599–1606, allegedly defrauded the crown of £150,000. An entrenched culture of corruption in the ordnance office also supposedly cost the crown almost £100,000 in the 1580s and 1590s. This figure is probably exaggerated, but the problems in the ordnance office remained so bad that the privy council was forced to order a formal inquiry in December 1600.[20]

The problem of military corruption was undoubtedly worsened by the queen's gender. Unlike Henry VIII, whose presence on campaign ensured that the forces accompanying him were properly supplied and problems were speedily rectified, Elizabeth was unable to observe the effects of administrative and financial malfeasance at first-hand. By necessity, she had to delegate military command to trusted male subordinates, who lacked the moral authority of a sovereign and were compromised by their need to retain the support of friends and followers. As Lord Mountjoy's secretary, Fynes Moryson, observed, the armies of the pope – another non-combatant monarch – were notorious for being 'more abused in their musters of soldiers then any other prince . . . but I will boldly say that Queene Elizabeth, of happy memory, fighting by her generalls, was incredibly abused in the musters of her army'.[21]

Although individual captains cost the crown a great deal of money by routinely pocketing the wages of non-existent soldiers, military men such as Essex saw a fundamental distinction between this sort of peculation, which provided an incentive for gentlemen to serve as officers and enabled them to live according to their social status while on campaign, and the windfalls which merchants and bureaucrats were able to secure for themselves without venturing near the front line. While the former was seen as integral to an officer's 'credit' – in the dual sense of spending power and personal honour – the latter seemed odious, especially when such profit-taking endangered soldiers' health or lives. The privy council's efforts to control military expenditure increased tensions over these issues in the 1590s. By trying to curtail the ability of captains to accumulate cash or booty and increasingly relying upon large-scale contractors for the provision of apparel, victuals and arms, the council's reforms threatened the autonomy of captains and ensured that shoddy shoes, defective swords or spoiled beer contributed to grumbling against those who stayed at home and made money at soldiers' expense. In this light, it is not surprising that Essex's conspicuous generosity to subordinate officers and famed commitment to martial honour brought him wide acclaim among military men and that some of them constituted 'a community of honour' who would stick with him until the very end.[22]

Essex also exerted a powerful attraction for captains because his lobbying for new military operations offered the best prospect of renewed employment, or advancement, for the scores of army officers who could not secure a permanent command in the Low Countries or Ireland. After campaigns such as the Cadiz expedition, Essex's London home literally swarmed with captains anxiously seeking news of the next venture. In contrast to the decades of peace, when England had lacked sufficient experienced officers, the realm now had a surplus of captains – a trend which was reinforced by the new military practices learned in the Low Countries, which required a greater number of officers to command smaller, but more numerous, company units.[23] Ironically, the events of 1598 ensured there would soon be plenty of employment for these officers – including Essex himself – in the one theatre of war which Essex had consistently belittled and treated as a distraction from the 'real' war against Spain: Ireland.

Although it had been intended to overawe Tyrone and his allies and to encourage them to make peace without the need for more expensive military operations, the transfer of Sir John Norris and his Brittany survivors to Ireland in 1595 failed to solve the military crisis which was looming in Ulster and Connacht. Norris's arrival also divided the English command in Ireland because his appointment was regarded as a threat by the lord deputy, Sir William Russell. Russell had taken Leicester's side in the bitter feuding among English officers in the Low Countries in 1586–87 and rival policies towards Tyrone now gave him fresh reason to clash with the prickly Norris. While Norris represented a policy of negotiation with Tyrone, Russell championed a hard-line military approach. When the latter failed comprehensively following Bagenal's defeat at Clontibret, the crown was forced to buy time by making a truce with Tyrone, but Russell ensured it was Norris, not himself, who had to deal with the enemy.

For the next two years, Russell and Norris sniped at each other and a series of truces spared Elizabeth the cost of full-scale war in Ireland while England was preoccupied with the threat of new Spanish 'Armadas'. However, Tyrone's less than secret overtures for Spanish intervention in Ireland meant these agreements were increasingly cynical exercises. When Norris and Tyrone met on horseback in the middle of a stream in January 1597 and failed to agree a new truce, even the pretence of peace was no longer possible. Elizabeth responded by replacing Russell with Lord Burgh and despatching 2500 fresh reinforcements, boosting her costs in Ireland to £12,000 a month. Burgh's appointment was a grievous blow to Norris, who had hoped for the deputyship himself and attributed his failure to the intervention of Essex. If so, this was the final blow in a feud which had rumbled on since 1590. Norris died, allegedly of exhaustion and despair, in September 1597.[24]

After years of service in the Low Countries, Burgh expected an easy victory by emulating Sir Henry Sidney's old strategy of launching coordinated attacks into Ulster from the south, while ships landed more troops in Tyrone's rear on Lough Foyle. He soon learned the Irish were formidable opponents and that the military balance in Ireland had changed radically since 1566. One prong of Burgh's plan dissolved when Sir Conyers Clifford's force of 1200 men was surrounded by O'Donnell in Connacht and forced to endure hours of skirmishing while they desperately sought to escape the trap. With their powder exhausted, Clifford's men were saved only by a providential rainstorm, which rendered the Irish guns useless and allowed the English to fight their way out with pikes. Burgh himself planted a fort on the Blackwater River, but then had to retreat to Newry. Finding sufficient troops for a landing at Lough Foyle proved impossible.

When Burgh died on 13 October, English plans for 1597 collapsed completely and the crown was forced to seek another truce. This ensured that Burgh's Blackwater Fort remained unsupported and vulnerable. When the truce expired in mid-1598, Tyrone immediately blockaded it, forcing the English to relieve it. The result was that Sir Henry Bagenal suffered the catastrophic defeat which he had so nearly experienced at Clontibret. Thanks to the recent arrival of 1500 raw recruits, Bagenal was able to march towards Blackwater Fort with almost 4000 foot and 300 cavalry, many of whom were actually Irish rather than English or Welsh – because they were cheaper to hire – and not all of them proved dependable. On 14 August 1598, Bagenal's force stumbled into what became known as the battle of Yellow

Ford. As at Clontibret, the English troops were ambushed while try-ing to march around Tyrone's army, which had again assumed a blocking position. Although Bagenal knew what to expect and tried to organise his troops accordingly, they were caught up in bogs and peppered with shot from the surrounding woods. By the time the vanguard had fought its way through enemy trenchwork and reached a river ford, Bagenal recognised the advance could not con-tinue, but turning the army around proved difficult. Bagenal's own death – shot through the head – added to the panic. Despite individ-ual acts of bravery, the army disintegrated and the retreat became a rout. More than 800 'English' troops were killed, while another 400 were wounded and 300 deserted to the enemy. It was the greatest English military disaster since the surrender of Newhaven in 1563, but its significance was even more dramatic. Before Yellow Ford, the chief threat to English rule in Ireland was Tyrone and O'Donnell's Ulster confederation. After this calamitous defeat, the Dublin admin-istration was revealed as a toothless tiger and challenges to English authority engulfed virtually the whole of Ireland. The regional threat had become a nationwide revolt and Elizabeth now faced the very real prospect of losing her only 'overseas' dominion.[25]

Essex in Ireland, 1599

The prospect of utter disaster in Ireland forced Elizabeth and her gov-ernment to treat the situation there with an urgency which had pre-viously been reserved for invasion threats to England itself. Indeed, the Irish crisis was regarded as the first step towards invasion, for contemporary opinion held that Ireland had replaced Scotland as England's 'postern gate' – 'he who would England win, must with Ireland begin'. Elizabeth's own determination not to bow to 'rebel subjects' also ensured the new priority accorded to Ireland. As queen, she had spent her whole reign resisting the demands of domineering males and asserting her own royal primacy. Her refusal to bargain seriously with Tyrone in the early-1590s had in many ways driven him into opposition and the prospect that she might now face mili-tary defeat at his hands was as unpalatable to her as the idea that she might preside over a diminution of the royal inheritance which she had received from her father. Being the daughter of Henry VIII was central to Elizabeth's self-identity – as symbolised by her famous red wig – and living up to her father's reputation required nothing less than a crushing victory in Ireland, whatever the cost. The Elizabethan regime therefore poured men, money and supplies into Ireland on a scale far greater than any other enterprise of the reign, stretching the realm to its very limits.

Although Essex had always despised war in Ireland (perhaps partly influenced by the misfortunes of his father), the huge scale of the army being prepared for the spring of 1599 meant that there would be precious little opportunity for military service anywhere else. Anxious to preserve his own status as the undisputed colossus of English military affairs, he criticised previous campaigns in Ireland and stubbornly rejected the idea that anyone else was suitable for such a command, even his friend Lord Mountjoy. Inevitably, this consistent belittling of others and boasting of his own capabilities meant he had to accept the command in Ireland himself or back down and let a new commander take the lead. Having built his career around soldiering, Essex could not bear to let this opportunity slip, despite his fears about being absent from court for so long and allowing his enemies to poison the queen's mind against him. The basis of his plan was therefore to secure a rapid victory and return to court in triumph, trading upon his success to sweep aside his rivals and reinforce his hold upon royal favour. For their part, Essex's factional enemies calculated that Elizabeth would never allow him to capitalise fully on his victory and that failure would finally bring him down. The stage was set for the great new campaign to be waged against a background of bitter and barely disguised political animosity.

Although it was barely larger than the vanguard of Henry VIII's army of 1544, Essex's army of 16,000 foot (including 2000 veterans from the Low Countries) and 1300 cavalry was vastly bigger and more expensive than any previous force fielded by the Elizabethan regime. Moreover, the council planned to send 2000 fresh reinforcements every three months. This represented a huge shift from earlier military endeavours, which aimed to send abroad only a few thousand soldiers. Creating and sustaining such a large army required administrative and logistical – not to mention financial – efforts on a completely different scale from what had gone before. Wages for officers and men alone amounted to almost £290,000 a year, quite apart from all the ancillary costs such as naval operations, transportation and munitions. The latter included orders for 4000 new calivers and muskets from 40 different gunmakers, as well as an increase in gunpowder production to 200 barrels (2000lb) a month and the reworking of a similar quantity of 'decayed' powder taken from existing stocks.

In contrast to the 1560s and 1570s, England now possessed a major arms industry, with a handful of large contractors each able to provide hundreds of weapons at a time by sub-contracting production to a mass of small craftsmen and workshops, mostly centred around London. In many ways, these workshops were the engine-room of England's war effort and their proliferation, together with the larger scale of government purchasing, sharply reduced the unit-cost of weapons by the late 1590s. Although the sea crossing from England to Ireland remained as troublesome as ever, the land and sea routes which brought men and *matériel* to Bristol and Chester for trans-shipment to Ireland also now constituted a well-worn 'Irish road', which merited comparison with the famous 'Spanish road' by which Spain moved troops and supplies to the Low Countries. Despite occasional hiccups and unavoidable problems with weather, the privy council and its agents across the realm were increasingly practised at ensuring the goods which were being produced in England actually reached Ireland in useful condition.[26]

Essex intended a short, sharp campaign to ensure his own speedy return to England. Adopting the now conventional strategy of a three-fold assault on Ulster, he planned to crush Tyrone by advancing northwards towards Armagh, while a subsidiary thrust entered from Connacht in the west and a fleet landed troops on Lough Foyle. However, it was soon clear that neither the resources at hand nor the state of the countryside would permit an immediate attack on Tyrone. Essex and his advisers consequently postponed the Ulster operation until June and instead launched a sweep through Leinster. Essex continued this expedition into Munster, capturing the supposedly impregnable Cahir Castle on 30 May and relieving a fort at Askeaton in early June. These operations safeguarded southern

Ireland from the rumoured threat of a Spanish landing, but consumed time, money and supplies. Worse, they left half the army tied up in southern garrisons. Essex exhibited considerable professionalism in his tactical operations, but his subordinates were less adept. While Essex was besieging Cahir Castle, 500 men under Sir Henry Harington were ambushed and routed by the O'Byrnes near Wicklow. Anxious to set an example, Essex hanged one officer, cashiered the rest and implemented the ancient Roman practice of decimation – executing every tenth man – for the rank-and-file.

By the time Essex returned to Dublin on 11 July, he was exhausted, sick and disillusioned by the tenacity of Irish resistance. He could only envisage victory by a long and costly war of attrition – precisely the sort of struggle which he wanted to avoid, given his earlier promises of rapid success and his growing belief that his opponents at home were poisoning the queen against him. Elizabeth needed little prompting to lash out in her letters to Essex. Already angry over the vast cost of his expedition, she was further enraged by his profligacy in bestowing knighthoods, demands for more men and supplies, and lack of action against Tyrone. In fact, Essex had concluded that he lacked the numbers to attack Tyrone, even before Sir Conyers Clifford suffered a bloody defeat in the Curlew Mountains on 5 August. Clifford's 2000 men had been earmarked for the advance into Ulster from Connacht, but they were ambushed on a relief mission. After exhausting their powder during prolonged skirmishing, they were overwhelmed by O'Donnell's troops and Clifford himself was killed – a fate which he had barely escaped in 1597.

Clifford's death, problems with shipping for the landing on Lough Foyle and the general shortage of troops for field operations quashed any hope of coordinated attacks on Ulster. Believing that he was being stabbed in the back by his enemies at home, Essex's thoughts increasingly focused on leaving Ireland and settling matters at court as quickly as possible. Secret overtures were made to Tyrone, and Essex himself even considered shipping his army to Wales and taking the field against his domestic enemies. Ultimately, such open treason proved too large a step to take. Despite his continuing protestations about the impossibility of confronting Tyrone's large army, Essex obeyed the queen's command to march north at the end of August.

Outnumbered and unable to outflank the enemy's prepared positions, he agreed to Tyrone's request for a parley on 7 September. Echoing Norris's meeting 18 months earlier, the two earls rode their horses into the middle of the River Lagan at the Bellaclynthe ford and talked privately for half an hour. Tyrone later told a Spanish priest that he almost convinced Essex to turn against Elizabeth, but Essex could not reconcile himself to becoming an ally of Spain. Although this may have been merely empty boasting on Tyrone's part, Essex's alienation from the Elizabethan court had now become so extreme that he was virtually a rogue general, willing to use force to free the queen from the clutches of rivals whom he considered to be 'evil counsellors'. Essex and Tyrone agreed a fresh truce, but it was soon apparent Elizabeth would not accept Essex's actions. Alarmed by the furious tone of her letters, he decided to return to court immediately, despite her recent order to the contrary. Trusting in speed rather than numbers, Essex rushed home with only a few companions on 24 September.[27]

Although distorted by his bitter hatred for his rivals, Essex's perception that events were moving against him in England had some foundation. While he was in Ireland, fresh feelers for peace talks were extended to Elizabeth by Archduke Albert, the new Spanish ruler of Flanders. Confusingly, Albert's overtures for negotiation came at the same time as Philip III of Spain proved himself to be even more hostile towards England than his father (who had died in September 1598). From Essex's perspective, the privy council's back-channel responses to Albert on behalf of the queen looked dangerously like treason. Equally disturbing was the invasion scare of July–August 1599, which arose from wild rumours that a new 'Armada' was about to set sail. Like 1588, a full naval call out was initiated and a large army began to muster around London. Low Countries veterans were recalled to reinforce the trained bands in Kent and contingents of soldiers raised by noblemen and royal servants gathered near London. After being caught out in 1596 and 1597, the privy council was determined to take no chances and pulled out all the stops, capitalising on everything that had been learned in earlier defensive mobilisations. In reality, this 'invisible Armada' was a Spanish fleet which sailed for the Canary Islands in pursuit of a Dutch fleet and the whole effort was an expensive false alarm. However, the episode reinforced Essex's belief about Spanish 'treachery' and raised dark thoughts about his rivals flexing their military muscles under the guise of an invasion scare. These suspicions underlined the extent to which the overt war against Tyrone and Spain was now being shadowed – at least in the minds of Essex and his diehard followers in Ireland – by the potential for a civil war against their enemies at home. In the event, Essex and his partisans never had an opportunity to take such a drastic step. Although Essex felt confident enough to burst into the queen's chamber before she was fully dressed on the morning of 28 September, he was soon placed under arrest. As he realised the full magnitude of his failure – and that his rivals would now monopolise power during the closing years of the reign – he underwent a physical and mental breakdown. Although he finally rose from his sickbed after New Year, Essex was never the same again.[28]

Ireland and the Low Countries, 1600–01

Essex's arrest confirmed Tyrone's belief that there was no possibility of accommodation with the Elizabethan regime and shattered the truce which he had agreed with Essex. By the time Lord Mountjoy arrived as the new lord deputy in February 1600, much of the limited stability which Essex had imposed during 1599 had been swept away again. With his power-base in Ulster seemingly untouchable, Tyrone stepped up his efforts in Munster. However, Mountjoy had learned from the fate of his friend and was prepared to fight the sort of prolonged attritional war which Essex had deliberately eschewed. Since Tyrone's Ulster confederation was too strong to be overwhelmed by direct attack, Mountjoy aimed to isolate and undermine his enemy, using whatever means were necessary to enforce surrender. English settlers such as the poet Edmund Spenser had long urged a final solution to the Irish problem: 'till Ireland be famished, it cannot be subdued'. Mountjoy and his subordinates would actually implement this policy of wholesale destruction, denying the Irish food to eat or even woods in which to hide. In a sense, this would be a war not just against Irish 'rebels', but against the land itself. The resort to such extreme measures underlined the military effectiveness of Tyrone and his allies, but the policy was only possible because England's naval and logistical capabilities allowed its army in Ireland to subsist almost entirely on supplies shipped across the Irish Sea. The London merchants John Jolles and William Cokayne, for example, delivered biscuit, beef, pork, butter, cheese and fish equivalent to 7.7 million daily rations for the army in Ireland between March 1600 and July 1602, while John Woods provided another 3.7 million portions. The contracts let to Jolles and Cokayne alone were worth £129,000. Although the quality sometimes brought complaints, the provision of such enormous quantities of food represented a triumph for the council's policy of military contracting and gave Mountjoy's army a decisive edge over the Irish, who depended upon the success of local harvests.[29]

After more than a decade of war, Elizabethan England was forced to commit an unprecedented quantity of money and resources to the conflict in Ireland. At £336,554, expenditure in 1599 alone almost matched what had been spent on Ireland over the preceding four years (£342,000). Operations in 1600–02 would add another £828,000 to the bill. A later estimate suggests the real cost of confronting Tyrone was even higher – £1,924,000 between mid-1594 and March 1603. Revenue-raising therefore became a matter of extreme urgency for the crown. Parliament was persuaded to authorise a new triple subsidy in 1597 and an unprecedented quadruple subsidy in 1601, the former raising £473,000 over three years and the latter £602,000. Subjects who refused to attend church were compelled to pay for cavalry for Ireland, financial 'gifts' were demanded from lawyers and royal servants, and large loans were sought from the City of London. The collection of customs was again leased out to merchant contractors and new duties were imposed to raise extra revenue. Many of these measures prompted dismay among the queen's subjects, especially the practice of granting courtiers or merchants monopoly rights for the sale or manufacture of products as diverse as soap, playing cards and white salt. In the 1560s, such patents had been justified in terms of economic development, but their proliferation in the 1590s generated income for the crown at the cost of widespread public indignation. Nevertheless, these expedients proved insufficient and Elizabeth was forced to authorise the largest sales of crown lands of the whole reign in 1599 and 1601, ultimately raising £400,000. In October 1600, many of the queen's old jewels, including 540 'very small diamons' and 'a small wyer cheyne with a jewell lyke a shippe set with diamons & a great raged pearle pendant', were also made available for commercial appraisal and sale. Yet the cost of subduing 'the land of ire' (as Sir Robert Cecil called it) demanded still more money and the privy council finally succumbed to the desperate mid-Tudor remedy of debasing the currency, albeit only in Ireland itself. Launched in 1601, the debasement was such a failure that it is not even clear it brought the crown any profit.[30]

The combination of debasement, asset sales, crushing taxes and large loans (albeit from domestic rather than foreign creditors) represented the same mix of measures which had been adopted in the 1540s and 1550s and underlined that the Tudor state was still trapped in the same financial strait-jacket. Despite 40 years of cutting and budgetary tinkering, the extraordinary demands of the war had finally brought English government back to where it had been at the start of Elizabeth's reign. Yet, unlike the mid-Tudor wars, the campaigns of Elizabeth's final years did not bring a decline in the nation's military effort, but an acceleration. Although the crown's finances were strained to breaking point and the realm was growing increasingly restive, the personal authority of Elizabeth – and the consequent ability of her privy council to mobilise the resources of her subjects – ensured that, for a few years at least, England's war effort could be sustained at levels which proved militarily decisive. This was a remarkable achievement and one of which Henry VIII and most of his contemporaries would never have believed a female ruler capable.

The crushing burden of such military expenditure meant that Mountjoy's army in 1600 was slightly smaller than Essex's and Elizabeth was anxious to cut its strength still further. Mountjoy insisted on 14,000 foot as the minimum viable force and ultimately secured a return to the force levels of 1599. With the war balanced so precariously, even Elizabeth's fear about the possible political consequences of heavy spending had to yield to military necessity. Mountjoy's arrival in February 1600 and news that the English would once again try to land troops on Lough Foyle forced Tyrone to abandon his efforts in Munster and return to Ulster. Nevertheless, he was taken by surprise when Mountjoy marched north to Newry in May with only 3500 men. Tyrone rushed to ambush the attackers and Mountjoy's force barely made it back to Dundalk. Yet Mountjoy's sally achieved its objective, for it drew Irish forces away from Lough Foyle and enabled Sir Henry Docwra to land 3000 troops there virtually unopposed on 14 May. Docwra quickly planted a fort at Derry and prepared for a siege, knowing that Tyrone and his confederates lacked the cannon necessary to attack fortifications. Despite the toughness of Irish troops and their famed accuracy with musket and caliver, the lack of siege guns meant they could never capitalise on their dominance of the countryside by capturing the towns. This fundamental shortcoming had saved England from losing its grip on Ireland entirely after Yellow Ford. It now underpinned Mountjoy's strategy of ringing Ulster with forts. By bottling up Tyrone and O'Donnell, these forts would isolate the fountainhead of the rebellion and prevent large-scale enemy reinforcements from the north interfering with Sir George Carew's pacification of Munster and Sir Arthur Savage's operations in Connacht.

In July and August, Mountjoy demonstrated his new scorched earth policy by devastating the harvest in Leix and Offaly. A few weeks later, when O'Donnell's siege of Derry was becoming intense and Docwra's men were dying from disease in large numbers, Mountjoy sought to relieve the pressure by marching into Ulster towards Armagh. This was a major gamble because autumn was setting in and he could only raise 3000 men. Tyrone blocked Mountjoy's advance at the notorious Moyry Pass on 25 September, using superior numbers, elaborate fieldworks and the wooded terrain to create an impassable barrier. Remarkably, Mountjoy decided to attack, and sustained the effort for a fortnight, despite constant downpours and resolute opposition. On 2 October, the English army spent three hours fighting its way through two lines of enemy trenchworks, only to be confronted by a third. Mountjoy ordered a retreat, forcing his men again to run the gauntlet of enemy sniping and skirmishers. Unlike Bagenal at Yellow Ford, however, Mountjoy controlled the withdrawal and averted disaster. Three days later, he sought to outflank the defences, but failed. Although Mountjoy hoped to try again, his army was exhausted and showing the effects of wearing sodden clothes for 20 days. On 9 October, he finally withdrew, only to learn five days later that Tyrone had abandoned the pass. Mountjoy swiftly returned to Moyry Pass and dismantled its defences, even felling the woods which provided cover for ambush.

The reasons behind Tyrone's withdrawal remain uncertain. He may have been forced to retreat by the excessive cost of sustaining his army so late in the season or by news that O'Donnell's ambitious cousin, Neill Garve O'Donnell, had defected to the crown, which rocked the Ulster confederation and underlined the political threat posed by Docwra's base at Derry. Whatever the reason, Mountjoy's belated clearing of Moyry Pass transformed a tactical defeat into a strategic victory, opening the way for English penetration into eastern Ulster and denting Tyrone's prestige badly enough to encourage defections by Irish lords unhappy with O'Neill domination. A similar unravelling of Irish solidarity began in Munster, where Irish resistance proved remarkably brittle when confronted by Sir George Carew's combination of using siege guns to destroy enemy strongholds and crafty diplomacy aimed at exploiting local rivalries.[31]

Although the operations in Ireland constituted the main English military effort in 1600 – and certainly the most expensive – English troops were also involved in a large and dangerous venture in the Low Countries. With the Spanish Army of Flanders paralysed by mutiny, Maurice's civilian paymasters in the States demanded that he take advantage by launching an offensive. Siege operations in March and April resulted in the capture of two enemy towns, but the major offensive was delayed until June. Against his better judgement, Maurice agreed to invade Flanders and relieve enemy pressure against Ostend by capturing Nieupoort and Dunkirk. A vast flotilla of small boats carried Maurice's army to the vicinity of Nieupoort, in preparation for a siege. However, the plan went horribly wrong when news arrived – contrary to all expectation – that Archduke Albert had gathered enough troops to take the field and was about to trap the Dutch army against the coast. Maurice's men now had to fight for their lives. About a quarter of the Dutch force present were English troops, who were organised in two regiments under Vere and his brother Horace. The rival armies faced each other across a beach, but the rising tide forced them up into the dunes and the cavalry moved even further inland. Each side numbered about 10,000 men. All the English troops were concentrated in the Dutch front line, where they took the full force of the enemy attack. The desperate struggle gradually drew in the two armies' second lines, but Maurice's cavalry finally scattered its opponents, whose retreat threw the large Spanish infantry formations into disorder.

This was the signal for a general Dutch advance and the Spanish army collapsed into chaos as the pike formations fell apart. After more than two hours of fighting, the battle became a rout. Spanish casualties approached 4000, while the Dutch army lost 1000 dead and another 700 badly wounded. The two English regiments suffered 800 casualties – a third of their strength. Nieupoort was hailed as the greatest set-piece battle of its day and was celebrated in English circles as definitive proof that their troops were now the equal of any in western Europe. Vere's own account in the 'Commentaries' which he wrote in his retirement almost implied that he and his soldiers won the battle by themselves. Nevertheless, Archduke Albert soon fielded fresh troops and Maurice was sufficiently shaken by the near-disaster to abandon all thought of besieging Nieupoort and sent his army home.[32]

England's war effort was also disturbed by events nearer home. Over the course of 1600, the earl of Essex's confinement was gradually eased, until finally he was permitted to live at Essex House in London without a council-appointed warder. Although Essex himself oscillated between anger and despair at his fate, a group of die-hard supporters anxiously plotted to see him restored to power and sweep his rivals away, while some hostile government officials sought to frame treason charges against Essex to destroy him completely. The opening of exploratory negotiations between English and Spanish representatives at Boulogne between May and July 1600 – despite the launching of the Flanders offensive – seemed to confirm the Essexians' belief that their domestic enemies were bent upon selling out to Spain, even though the envoys could not even agree basic matters of protocol, let alone matters of substance. Essex's collapse into bankruptcy at the end of October, after spending so much money on war, also threatened his servants with being arrested for debt. Essex House now became the focus of frantic plotting, but the earl's plans were still incomplete when the privy council moved against him. The prospect of arrest panicked Essex and his gathering of aristocrats and army officers into an ill-conceived insurrection on Sunday 8 February 1601, when he and 300 'swagringe companions' marched through London, appealing for assistance to save Essex from assassination and rescue Elizabeth from the clutches of their enemies. The calls brought stunned confusion and Essex was forced to flee home, where he soon surrendered.[33]

Essex was subsequently tried and beheaded, but his fall implicated a large part of the English aristocracy. His companions on 8 February had included three earls, three barons, the younger brothers of several noblemen and a swag of knights, most of whom he had dubbed during his various campaigns. Although this rump following was held together by a range of different motivations, concern for 'honour' and the belief that soldiers were not being properly rewarded for their service was perhaps the most important. Virtually all of Essex's companions had served in the war and resented their lack of recompense. In part, this reflected the political rivalry which had emerged in the mid-1590s, which made Essex's factional enemies unwilling to reward men too closely associated with the earl. However, the resentment which underpinned Essex's insurrection also reflected systemic problems within the Elizabethan regime. Even before the advent of war, Elizabeth had lacked the means to reward royal service in the grand manner of her father. As a woman whose personal authority depended upon man-management, she was also simply unwilling to reward men too easily or extravagantly. Both of these characteristics became even more pronounced during war-time.

The ancient tradition that military service was the chief – and most honourable – means for entry into the peerage, or promotion within it, had been powerfully reinforced by Henry VIII. During his reign, the English peerage had been almost completely remade and his creations had invariably reflected at least an element of military service. Elizabeth's war with Spain aroused similar expectations, but instead comprehensively dashed the hopes of a whole generation of aristocrats who aspired to new titles. Although she created four new barons in 1586, she made only two further wartime creations, promoting the lord admiral (Lord Howard of Effingham) to become earl of Nottingham in 1597 and elevating Lord Thomas Howard as Baron Howard of Walden in 1601. Despite talk of new peerages after the defeat of the *Gran Armada* in 1588 and furious lobbying by Essex for his friends in the mid-1590s, other suitors for titles were denied. The sons of noblemen who served as lords lieutenant also found Elizabeth increasingly unwilling to appoint them to their father's place. The disappointment of peers (and would-be peers) at the lack of recognition for military service was palpable by the late 1590s, especially among the younger aristocrats who gathered around Essex. In their view, the explanation for the queen's failure to recognise their service in the expected manner was the 'dishonourable' nature of Essex's rivals. In reality, the problem was Elizabeth herself and her fear of the financial and political consequences of bestowing new titles. Essex's insurrection briefly relieved this pressure by plunging his supporters into temporary disgrace, but the unfulfilled expectation of new peerages which flowed from the war would ultimately have to be met by her successor.[34]

The rebellion of Elizabeth's former favourite effectively destroyed her characteristic mode of queenship. Courtiers still praised the queen as if they sought her hand in marriage, but the practice of the realm's leading men treating an elderly woman as if she were a nubile teenager now seemed increasingly incongruous. The collapse of Essex's following also meant Elizabeth was entirely dependent upon the group of councillors and courtiers who had organised themselves against the earl. This gave the government added cohesion during her final years, but it was also a small and socially undistinguished group, especially in comparison with the range of men who had been councillors and courtiers in the 1570s and 1580s. Essex's challenge had drained the Elizabethan regime of much of its variety and vitality, and Elizabeth herself knew it.

Ostend and Kinsale

The cost of Maurice's failure to capture Nieupoort or Dunkirk in 1600 became apparent in June 1601, when Dutch plans for a new offensive were disrupted by Albert laying siege to Ostend. As the only port on the Flanders coast in Anglo-Dutch hands, Ostend was surrounded by enemy territory and had been the subject of repeated enemy attempts to take it by force or treachery. Until recently, it had been controlled by a succession of English governors and its garrison still included large numbers of English soldiers. Sir Francis Vere was immediately ordered to reinforce the garrison and fresh levies from England (which had been intended for the new Dutch offensive) were diverted to the town's defence. The last 2000 of these recruits were ordered to Ostend on 19 July – the same day that a staggered levy of 5000 men was announced for Ireland. If this were not enough, reports of a fresh Spanish 'Armada' also demanded the setting-out of an Anglo-Dutch squadron to intercept the enemy fleet. England now faced a war on multiple fronts in which all of the fronts were simultaneously active.[35]

While the siege of Ostend ground on, swallowing the men and resources of both sides, Mountjoy's war against Tyrone continued remorselessly in Ireland. Unlike earlier lord deputies, Mountjoy had campaigned over the winter of 1600–01, exploiting the reduced possibilities for ambush (thanks to the seasonal shedding of leaves) to turn a traditional period of inactivity into one of action. Mountjoy had an additional incentive for action because he was involved in Essex's plotting during 1600 and had to prove to the queen and council that he was both irreplaceable and loyal. By March 1601, Mountjoy's devastation of the O'Byrnes's lands had driven them into submission, while Carew's operations in Munster encouraged large-scale defections and resulted in the capture of James Fitzthomas Fitzgerald, the claimant to the earldom of Desmond, at the end of May.

During the summer, Mountjoy returned to Ulster and planted garrisons at Moyry Pass and Armagh, while Docwra's lodgement at Derry continued to prove a lightning rod for disaffection towards Tyrone and O'Donnell. Sir Arthur Chichester also exploited local rivalries to press inland into eastern Ulster from the port-base of Carrickfergus. Although far from beaten, Tyrone and his allies could now only hope for victory if they received aid from Spain, which could re-energise the opposition to England with troops and siege guns. Tyrone had urged Spanish intervention in Ireland for many years and had been repeatedly frustrated in his hopes, most cruelly in 1596 when Philip II belatedly diverted a fleet bound for Ireland towards Brest, with disastrous consequences. Tyrone's hopes were finally realised in 1601, partly because Philip III calculated that Elizabeth's government would be distracted by the fall of Essex. Although under-strength and late in setting out, an initial force of 1700 Spanish troops under Don Juan del Aguila landed at Kinsale on 22 September. Within a week, Aguila's force increased to 3400 men. Thanks to Sir Robert Cecil's belief that this was another false alarm and the consequent slow pace of English naval preparations, the Spanish fleet was able to land its troops in Munster before the English warships intended to stop it had even left port.[36]

If English uncertainty about their enemy's intentions and concern to avoid unnecessary expenditure had allowed the Spanish to land in Ireland, the latter found it difficult to exploit their success. Carew's success in Munster deprived the Spanish of substantial local support, while the privy council's frenetic reaction to news of the landing put England's war effort into overdrive. The first 2000 of the new levies announced in July were speedily loaded aboard warships and despatched to Ireland, while another 2000 recruits were ordered to leave by 20 October. On 6 October the final 1000 men of the July levies were ordered to Lough Foyle and 2000 more recruits were demanded for Kinsale. This flood of troops was accompanied by a torrent of supplies to feed, arm and clothe them. Siege guns were shipped in from both England and Dublin. With the ships that landed them unable to remain in Irish waters, Aguila's troops were swiftly blockaded by English warships and surrounded by a steadily growing number of English troops on land – 6900 foot and 600 horse by 27 October. By contrast, Spanish efforts to reinforce Aguila failed miserably. A mere 80 men reached Kinsale in December, while a few hundred were scattered elsewhere in Ireland. Thanks to English control of the seas and the effectiveness of England's 'Irish road', Aguila would require full-scale Irish assistance to escape the trap which Kinsale had become.[37]

Tyrone had always insisted that Spanish troops should land in Munster because the province contained numerous excellent ports which offered easy access to Spain. However, news that Aguila had landed in virtually the southernmost part of Munster came as an unwelcome surprise, especially as English pressure in the north had become increasingly threatening. When Tyrone and O'Donnell broke out of Ulster in November and led their armies south, they left their heartlands vulnerable and gambled heavily on the victory which they hoped would follow union with Aguila's army. Mountjoy learned of Tyrone's slow approach and tried to overwhelm Kinsale before the Irish could arrive, but an assault on 1 December proved a costly failure. Foul weather also transformed what had become a desperate campaign. Fierce storms prevented resupply by sea for six whole weeks and Tyrone's approach ended contact by land. As the winter sent in, Mountjoy's troops shivered in their sodden trenches and their horses lost condition. The English army numbered more than 11,500 in mid-November, but 40 men a day died from exposure and the total plummeted towards 6000 effectives in December. Sir George Carew later claimed that 6000 of the queen's men died during this winter ordeal. The casualties were so heavy that the privy council subsequently ordered the conscription of 500 men from the London trained bands to provide stiffening for the new wave of replacements sent in January 1602. Such men had hitherto been reserved almost exclusively for home defence, but their commitment to Ireland was a sign both of the insatiable demand for fresh troops and of the government's anxiety about the toughness of the campaign.[38]

When the rains finally let up, Tyrone and O'Donnell advanced towards Kinsale, planning to break through the English siegeworks to meet Aguila on the night of 23–24 December. Tyrone had wanted to starve the English out, but O'Donnell allegedly demanded an assault as a matter of honour. Although tradition has it that the Irish plan was betrayed to the English for a bottle of whisky, it seems more likely that Mountjoy was alerted by letters taken from captured Irish messengers. Mountjoy left 4000 men under Carew to watch the Spanish in Kinsale and went to intercept Tyrone and O'Donnell with barely 2000 men, including his whole force of 500 cavalry. The Irish numbered perhaps 6000, divided into three large bodies of men loosely modelled on Spanish *tercios*.

When Tyrone found Mountjoy's troops blocking his advance in the early dawn of 24 December, he retreated almost a mile and formed up his army on firm open ground. Mountjoy followed, his leading horse and foot gradually beating back Irish skirmishers to cross a bog which lay in front of the Irish lines. Overjoyed at the prospect of tackling the Irish on open ground, the first English horsemen across the bog charged at the nearest mass of Irish footmen, but were fended off. Once the whole English force was across the bog, the entire cavalry force charged at the Irish horsemen, whose light arms and armour could not resist their heavier English opponents. As at Nieupoort, the retreating Irish cavalry threw their own infantry into confusion and the English cavalry were able to get amongst the enemy pikemen and shot, who fled in terror. The panic soon spread to the other two Irish formations, which had been spaced too far apart to support each other. Each, in turn, was shattered and routed. The Irish army included 200 Spanish soldiers who had been unable to join up with Aguila at Kinsale. Burdened by heavier armour than the Irish footmen, they could not join the general flight and most were killed before the remainder surrendered. By the end, perhaps 1000 of the Irish were killed – and the slaughter would have been even worse if the English cavalry horses had been in better condition. English losses numbered barely a handful.

The victory was testimony to Mountjoy's boldness (or perhaps desperation) and the inexperience of Irish troops in open battle. It was also a reminder of the power of heavy cavalry, which English commanders had always sought to maintain, despite the exorbitant costs involved. In 1596, Essex had been so eager for mounted power on the expedition to Cadiz that he paid for a company of 'lancers' out of his own pocket. Although pistols and swords had largely replaced lances, armoured horsemen retained a special appeal for English aristocrats, who never really shared the willingness of Spanish aristocrats to 'trail a pike' as an infantryman and still regularly jousted before the queen like knights of old. As Sir Francis Vere told one of his ambitious young subordinates: 'if you ever wish to be a soldier, get up on horseback'.[39]

Although it is doubtful they could have broken through Carew's trenches, the Spanish in Kinsale failed to react until they heard the firing which celebrated the return of Mountjoy's victorious troops to camp. The significance of events finally dawned on them when they saw the colours taken from the Spanish troops who had accompanied Tyrone's army. Aguila now knew there would be no junction with Tyrone and O'Donnell. Instead, he feared England would ship over more men and supplies until his troops were finally overwhelmed. Surrender negotiations began and an agreement was finally signed on 2 January 1602. Aguila and his men were allowed to return home, but Spain's intervention in Ireland was at an end. Although the human and material cost to England had been frightful, Spain had been humiliated and the last hope for Tyrone and his confederates had been defeated. Tyrone himself returned to Ulster with barely a fraction of the men who had left in November, while O'Donnell left Ireland for Spain, never to return.

During the weeks when the desperate wintery struggle at Kinsale was approaching its climax, things seemed equally grim for the defenders of Ostend. By mid-December (the eve of Christmas according to the calendar used on the Continent), Sir Francis Vere believed that too few men remained to man Ostend's defences against the imminent Spanish onslaught. Vere demanded a cease-fire, ostensibly to discuss terms for surrender. However, his real intention was 'to amuse the enemy with a parle and so to wynn tyme' for the arrival of reinforcements. On the third day, the expected reinforcements arrived. Albert immediately terminated the cease-fire, furious at this dishonourable deception. The assault finally came on the evening of 28 December, by which time the defenders had been boosted by 2000 extra men. These reinforcements proved crucial because they enabled Vere to funnel the enemy attack into an area of low-lying ground, which he promptly flooded once the tide had risen sufficiently. When the sluices were opened, almost 1000 Spanish troops were killed and the assault was quickly abandoned. The consequence was stalemate, with both sides forced to live in water-logged trenches and endure heavy losses from exposure, disease and the steady exchange of gunfire. Nevertheless, the English crown sought to make a profit from this hell-hole. Thanks to Dutch payments and the transfer of recruitment costs to the counties, the privy council calculated it could gain £4000 for every thousand fresh recruits sent to the Low Countries.[40]

Shuffling Towards Peace, 1602–04

By 1602, Philip III's attempts to strike a decisive blow against England in revenge for his father's failures had proven equally unsuccessful. Although he still hoped to invade England, the grandiose plans of Philip and his hawkish advisers were increasingly out of step with Spain's resources, especially as northern Europe was only one of the theatres of war in which Spanish forces were fighting. The landing of troops at Kinsale, for example, came only weeks after the disastrous failure of a major expedition to capture Algiers in North Africa. The peace with France was also proving distinctly uneasy, with French attacks on Savoy in 1600–01 reducing the 'Spanish road' to the Low Countries to a precarious thread and forcing Spain to reinforce its position in northern Italy against further French aggression. Although large quantities of silver still flowed across the Atlantic, Philip's military commitments swallowed all this money, and more. By 1601, the Spanish government was so desperate for cash it considered confiscating all the silver held in Spain. When this scheme failed, it was forced into a massive debasement of its copper currency in 1602. Like England in the 1550s, Spain also suffered from appalling epidemics. In Castile, the political and military heartland of Spain's dominions, 500,000 people died between 1596 and 1602 – almost 10 per cent of the population – and the recruitment of troops became exceptionally difficult. The average number of recruits in a foot company, which had been 256 in the 1570s and 161 in the 1580s, fell to a mere 77 men in 1596–1602.[41]

While Spain flailed about in its attempts to regain the military initiative, England's strategy for 1602 focused on Ostend, Ireland and naval defence. Aiding the Dutch defence of Ostend ensured a large measure of safety for England because the siege absorbed most of Spain's resources in Flanders and made it impossible for Albert to support any new Armada. When Philip III sought to build up resources in Flanders for an attack on England, Albert repeatedly commandeered them for his own use. After investing so much of his prestige in assailing Ostend, he could not afford to discontinue the effort or allow it to fail. This was recognised in England, where Cecil argued the necessity of defending the town: 'if we can still engage and waste that army which is the garland of Spain before that place, [Philip III] will be at little ease to think of other enterprises'. By the spring of 1603, more than 7000 Dutch troops and 18,000 Spanish had died there. Despite the terrible human cost involved, defending Ostend offered a means of tying up Spain's best troops and bleeding them into military anaemia. In both its nature and purpose, the siege of Ostend thus explicitly foreshadowed the appalling struggle for Verdun in World War I, and assumed a similar political and psychological importance.[42]

Although the enemy threat from Flanders was bottled up at Ostend, the privy council still feared the possibility of a new Armada from Spain, aimed either at delivering fresh troops to aid Tyrone in Ireland or establishing a bridgehead in England which might allow Philip III to dictate the selection of Elizabeth's successor. By 1602, Elizabeth was in her sixty-ninth year and the unanswered question of who would succeed her was becoming more pressing every day. The council consequently sought to implement its now standard naval strategy of forward defence. This caused heartburn in Ireland, where Mountjoy complained that very few of the queen's ships would be available to support his army, but the council persisted, arguing that England lacked sufficient ships to cover all the harbours of Ireland. Nevertheless, mounting a prolonged blockade of the Spanish coast was a challenging task, even with Dutch support. The latter had been promised in May 1601, in return for English support in the Flanders offensive, but both ventures had been thwarted by Albert's attack on Ostend. The shared blockade was now revived for 1602, with the council planning for 12 Dutch ships to support a similar number of English ships (under Sir Richard Leveson) in patrolling the Iberian coastline. Although it would push the limits of habitability aboard crowded warships to the limit, supply ships would be despatched in June to keep the fleet on station until autumn.

Such plans soon proved too ambitious. When the Dutch failed to arrive by early spring, Leveson set sail with a reduced force. On 31 March, he intercepted the incoming *flota* off the Spanish coast, but his squadron was too weak to tackle the enemy warships escorting the merchantmen home. The sole occasion when English ships actually intercepted a treasure fleet – after so many years of trying – therefore resulted in total failure. Given the extreme pressure on the queen's finances, this misfortune caused great anguish to the privy council, who blamed the Dutch. Leveson had more success in early June, when he learned a great carrack was sheltering off the Portuguese town of Cezimbra. Although the *Sao Valentin* was guarded by harbour defences and 11 galleys, the English attacked, finally routing the galleys and forcing the carrack's surrender. Exhaustion and concern to ensure the carrack's safe arrival in England soon encouraged Leveson to head homewards. Strong winds blew the squadron back to Plymouth, where it found its supply ships still trapped in the harbour. Leveson's unexpected return sparked alarm in London, since it left the approaches to Ireland unprotected when intelligence reported that Spain was preparing a fresh landing there. Nevertheless, it was only at the end of August that part of Leveson's force could get back to sea, now under the command of Sir William Monson. Monson soon discovered that Spanish plans for sending another army to Ireland had collapsed, but he achieved little else before his battered ships straggled home in November.[43]

Although the capture of the *Sao Valentin* paid for most of the year's voyaging, the blockade had again proved unsustainable and coordination with the Dutch had failed entirely. This sort of operation was difficult enough for the Royal Navy of Nelson's day, but it strained sixteenth-century ships and logistics to breaking-point. Although sound in concept, forward defence at sea proved consistently fallible in execution and the minor panic of August 1602 represented an almost annual occurrence during the years after 1595, when the realm's naval screen repeatedly failed. Fortunately, the lumbering Spanish naval infrastructure was poorly adapted to take advantage of these slips, thanks to competition with the army for resources and the inordinate time which it took to get fleets to sea. England's royal dockyards were far more efficient and – as the repeated invasion scares showed – its naval officials were generally more adept at swift action and improvisation. The events of 1602 also conclusively proved the superiority of galleons over galleys. This had long been a matter of serious concern, especially as galley-borne landings now seemed the only means by which Spain might attack England itself. In 1601–02, the council even sought to counter this threat by building

four galleys for the queen's fleet. The victory at Cezimbra represented a signal triumph over galleys, but English and Dutch ships
achieved an even greater success in September, when six galleys
bound for Sluis were intercepted off the Downs. Only two escaped
destruction (both badly damaged) and over 3000 enemy soldiers and
galley slaves were killed.[44]

Further bad news for Spain came from the Caribbean, where
English and Dutch privateers continued to inflict costly losses on the
Spanish crown and its subjects. Almost every year, English privateers
scored some new demoralising triumph over Spain. In 1598, for
example, the earl of Cumberland achieved what Drake and Hawkins
had failed to do by storming San Juan in Puerto Rico. In February
1602, William Parker of Plymouth surprised the Spanish fort at Porto
Bello in Panama, captured two frigates in the harbour and pillaged
the town with a force of only a few score men. The general intensity
of English attacks and illegal trading in the Caribbean also increased
after the end of 1598, when Spanish diplomacy finally succeeded in
disrupting England's cloth trade with northern Europe. This hurt
English merchants, but encouraged more of them into privateering.
The accumulation of experience and capital by English 'adventurers'
also encouraged more ambitious ventures. By 1600, merchants and
seamen based in London were confident enough of their ability to
contest Portugal's trade monopoly in Asia to form the East India
Company and launch its first voyage to the East. Nevertheless,
English privateers were increasingly outnumbered by Dutchmen,
who swarmed around the coast of Spain and its colonial outposts
after Philip III imposed a ban on Dutch trade in early 1599. This ban
removed a major bone of contention between England and the
Dutch – since English merchants, unlike their Dutch equivalents, had
been banned from trading with Spain since 1585 – and spurred
greater official and unofficial Dutch involvement in the maritime
war against Spain, which helped to ease the burden on Elizabeth's
overstretched finances.[45]

The last and most important element of England's war effort was
the war in Ireland. Although overtures for peace had been made to
Tyrone after the battle of Kinsale and he could no longer pay his
'bonnaghts' by February 1602, an end to the war remained elusive.

Mountjoy and Carew were desperate to return home, but Elizabeth remained adamantly opposed to dealing with Tyrone and vetoed further contact. As a result, the war continued and the crown was forced to increase its forces in Ireland, despite the crippling cost. On 26 August 1602, Mountjoy's army totalled 1375 horse and 16,100 foot, in addition to 200 Irish horse and 1700 Irish foot who received half-pay. Such expenditure could not be sustained for long, as the privy council recognised when it debated the future course of the war in May 1602. The lord treasurer, Lord Buckhurst, urged peace with Spain as soon as possible – 'before we be to farre spent'. However, Cecil, the lord admiral and Sir William Knollys were far more sceptical about the possibilities of dealing with Spain, perhaps recalling that the last overture from Albert had coincided with the landing at Kinsale – an unfortunate echo of 1588 which prompted Elizabeth to dismiss the envoy out-of-hand. More importantly, they believed peace with Spain was impossible while the unrest continued in Ireland.

Since England's security still depended upon the Low Countries remaining free from occupation by Spanish or French armies, the queen would have to continue providing secret military aid to the Dutch, who refused to make peace with Spain. This would inevitably provoke retaliation in kind by the Spanish, who 'have & will ayd the rebels in Ireland', which would undermine the chief attractions of making peace in the first place – especially as everyone agreed that 'it was the Irish warres [which] had impoverished England, & not the warres of Spaine or Low Countreys'. The privy council therefore realised there must be peace in Ireland before there could be any serious negotiation with Spain. Unfortunately, this meant the path towards peace remained blocked until they could convince Elizabeth to overcome her aversion to dealing with Tyrone. This proved extremely difficult because she was determined to show him no mercy. Some contemporaries believed she was so inflexible because of a deep-seated grief about the fate of the earl of Essex, as if she feared the hypocrisy of approving the very act for which she had destroyed Essex's career at the end of 1599, with all that had followed in 1600–01.[46]

In the end, it was not until early 1603 that Elizabeth overcame her misgivings. Even then, she had to be 'in a manner forced by the council' to grant a pardon to Tyrone. The final treaty, which was signed at Mellifont in March, was remarkably favourable to Tyrone, who was required to submit to Elizabeth and renounce his title of O'Neill, but was guaranteed most of the lands and titles which he had claimed before the rebellion. Many English officials in Ireland and loyalist Irish were disgusted that Tyrone had been treated so well, but Mountjoy (like the privy council) was eager for a quick settlement. The treaty acknowledged England's military victory in Ireland, but the survivors would now have to struggle to win the peace.[47]

By the time the treaty had been finalised at Mellifont and Tyrone had accompanied Mountjoy back to Dublin, Elizabeth was dead. She died at Richmond Palace in the early hours of 24 March 1603. Elizabeth's wars would now be ended by a peace negotiated in the name of her successor, James I. James immediately ordered the suspension of a new levy of troops for Ostend and declared a cease-fire in the war at sea. Although English troops in the Low Countries continued to fight in the Dutch army, hostilities between England and Spain were effectively ended after Elizabeth's death. Even the erosion of key fortifications at Ostend by the sea and consequent Dutch pleas for urgent military aid failed to move James. Serious peace-making with Spain took many months and required much hard bargaining. Real negotiation about the location and nature of peace talks only began in December and the peace conference itself was delayed until May 1604. Nevertheless, the general trend of the discussions was in England's favour. By the time peace was sealed in August 1604, Spain had been forced to concede the holding of the conference in London, permit England to retain control of the cautionary towns (although the garrisons were not to aid the Dutch war effort), and abandon its long-cherished ambition of securing toleration for Catholics in England. By contrast, English travellers and seamen visiting Spain would no longer be subject to the Inquisition. Deadlock over English demands for the right to trade in the East and West Indies, which Spain adamantly opposed, resulted in the Treaty of London avoiding all mention of the matter. England regarded this as tacit approval of its claim, but in reality Spain simply recognised that it would have to defend its trade monopolies by force, as it had tried to do in the 1560s. Both sides pledged to refrain from aiding the other's rebels. This clause helped to muzzle Tyrone in Ireland, while its application to the Low Countries resulted in James allowing both the States and the archduke to recruit English volunteers for their armies. The number of English and Welshmen who actually volunteered for the arch-duke's army came as a nasty surprise to the council, who had expect-ed few takers. However, war had been a central feature of English life for a whole generation and service in the Spanish army seemed appealing to those who sought adventure and employment, espe-cially given the rapid wind-down of England's own forces after March 1603.[48]

As the deadlock over trade with the Indies showed, the peace of 1604 did not solve all the problems which had pushed England and Spain towards war in 1585. Although the Treaty of London contained vague pledges to encourage peace between Spain and the Dutch, the war in the Low Countries continued, although now with English troops on both sides. Supporters of the Dutch cause in England were alarmed that the treaty gave James no formal means of protecting the Dutch. This made the treaty unpopular in many quarters, especially as its signing virtually coincided with the ominous news that Ostend had finally surrendered, after a siege lasting three years and three months. However, the Dutch state ultimately proved strong enough to survive and prosper, despite some awkward moments when it faced the full weight of Spain's army in 1605–06. The Treaty of London represented the best alternative for England to a ruinous continuation of the war, which could not be sustained much longer by either side. While its terms did not suit the hawks in England (or, for that matter, in Spain), the peace probably reflected the sort of compromise which Elizabeth would have sought. It was certainly far more favourable to England than pessimists would have imagined when the realm first plunged into open war with Europe's greatest power in 1585, supported only by the Dutch, who then seemed more of a liability than an ally. Although the human and material cost had been very high, Elizabeth's wars had finally delivered a successful and honourable conclusion.

7   The Reformation of War

Elizabeth's wars are an object lesson in the difficult balance which all governments must strike when they go to war between the pursuit of military effectiveness, financial constraints and the need to maintain domestic political stability. This balancing act was made especially difficult for Elizabeth by the disastrous effects of Henry VIII's two-front war against France and Scotland in the 1540s and the revival of hostilities during the reigns of Edward VI and Mary I. The cumulative impact of these wars on England's military capacity and on the financial – and, ultimately, political – power of the English crown meant that Elizabeth's whole reign was spent in the shadow of the mid-Tudor struggles. The 'imperial' crown which Henry VIII had so loftily celebrated in the 1530s was likened to 'a bone thrown between two dogs' by the time Elizabeth became queen in 1558.

The psychological scarring caused by the mid-Tudor period was evident in the consistent Elizabethan concern, shared by privy councillors and country gentlemen alike, to avoid repeating the problems of those years. This basic attitude underpinned the frequent attempts to force Elizabeth into marriage to secure the royal succession (and the development of what Patrick Collinson has christened 'monarchical republicanism' when she failed to do so), the determination of Protestants not to allow a revival of Catholicism, and the widespread anxiety to prevent a return of the frightening 'stirs' of 1549. Until the 1590s, Elizabeth's government retained a collective memory of the military and financial traumas of the 1540s and 1550s, based upon direct personal experience. When Burghley contemplated the financial implications of standing alone against Spain in the Low Countries, he feared Elizabeth would be forced to defend the cautionary towns on her own, which would involve 'greater charges . . . than ij [i.e. two] Boloignes'. Burghley was therefore more willing to consider peace with Spain in 1587 because he recalled the ruinous consequences of Henry VIII's Continental adventure 40 years earlier. Similarly, memories of Calais troubled Lord Hunsdon, the absentee governor of Berwick. By the late 1580s, Berwick had become a military backwater and a place of refuge for bankrupts, who joined the garrison to win legal protection from their creditors, secure in the belief that they would never be called upon for serious combat. This practice – which boosted the income of Berwick's captains – deeply worried Hunsdon, who feared 'the town will become Callis, which I will not suffer.' For Hunsdon, as for Elizabeth, who tried to force Henri IV into granting her control of Calais in 1596, the memory of England's humiliation in 1558 still smouldered even decades later.[1]

A more graphic measure of the extent to which the wars of the 1540s and 1550s constrained English government during the remainder of the century is the relative spending power of Elizabeth and her immediate predecessors. As Table 7.1 shows, Henry VIII's average annual revenue for the three-year period 1543–46 was approximately £747,000, while Elizabeth's revenues peaked at an average of £667,000 during the first three years of her reign and only approached £600,000 again during the final crisis in Ireland (Column A). However, like all the figures cited in earlier chapters, these are *nominal* figures and do not reflect the impact of inflation. Many scholars have put a great deal of effort into trying to reconstruct economic data from the sixteenth century to measure the nature and impact of inflation during this period. None of these measures has proved entirely satisfactory and, given the difficulties of gathering suitable data and modelling its impact across the realm, no set of figures will ever be perfect. However, the best available measure is a composite index constructed by P. K. O'Brien and P. A. Hunt for their large-scale study of English government finances. This index combines estimates for the annual impact of inflation on craftsmen's wages and a range of agricultural and industrial products, baselined on the period 1451–75. Although the weighting between its three components is somewhat arbitrary, this price deflator is more sensitive and sophisticated than the widely used Phelps-Brown and Hopkins model. The index numbers for the O'Brien and Hunt deflator show how dramatically inflation affected Elizabethan finances, revealing a general trend which more than halved the real value of money between the 1540s and the 1590s (Column C). The index also highlights the sudden impact of price rises in the early 1550s, with the 1549–52 triennial average jumping 30 per cent over that for 1546–49. The only comparable spike during the remainder of the century occurred during the harvest failures of the mid-1590s, when the average index for 1591–94 jumped 28 per cent in 1594–97. Given the magnitude of these sudden spikes, it is not surprising that Edward VI's reign witnessed alarming social and political instability. Conversely, the ability of the Elizabethan government to prevent a recurrence of the Edwardian tumults during the spike of the mid-1590s underlines the value of decisive leadership and urgent countermeasures.

1596

risings

Applying the O'Brien and Hunt deflator to their own figures for crown revenues in the sixteenth century demonstrates how severely strait-jacketed were Elizabeth's finances (Column B). While Henry's war of 1544–46 was waged on revenues worth approximately £515,000 in 1451–75 values, the peak of her Irish war had to be fought on revenues which averaged a mere £170,000–190,000 in constant-value money. Even Elizabeth's highest average annual revenues, which occurred in the opening years of her reign, were really only equivalent to £294,000. The same pattern of the falling real value of Elizabeth's income can be seen in a separate set of figures produced by F. C. Dietz for exchequer receipts (Columns D, E). Unlike the figures for crown revenues – which include gross revenues gathered by local receivers (even though some of this money was diverted to local charges upon the crown) and monies generated in a particular year, even if they were received much later – exchequer receipts simply reflect the income accounted for at the exchequer during a specific financial year (which ran October–September). Until the final years of the reign, the figures for exchequer receipts are considerably lower than O'Brien and Hunt's figures for crown revenues. The change in 1597, when exchequer receipts begin to match and even exceed the figures for crown revenues, reflects difficulties with the figures themselves (Dietz prints two different sets of receipts figures for 1597–1603), which should be treated with caution. Nevertheless, the figures for revenues and receipts both confirm the sharp erosion of the real value of Elizabeth's income.[2]

Table 7.1   English crown revenues and the impact of inflation,
1540–1603

	A	B	C	D	E
Oct. 1540–Sept. 1543	385	294	1.31	–	–
Oct. 1543–Sept. 1546	747	515	1.45	–	–
Oct. 1546–Sept. 1549	471	298	1.58	–	–
Oct. 1549–Sept. 1552	446	217	2.06	–	–
Oct. 1552–Sept. 1555	227	106	2.15	–	–
Oct. 1555–Sept. 1558	324	147	2.20	–	–
Oct. 1558–Sept. 1561	667	294	2.27	360	159
Oct. 1561–Sept. 1564	362	151	2.39	292	122
Oct. 1564–Sept. 1567	257	110	2.33	179	77
Oct. 1567–Sept. 1570	245	103	2.38	177	74
Oct. 1570–Sept. 1573	317	123	2.58	228	88
Oct. 1573–Sept. 1576	274	105	2.61	198	76
Oct. 1576–Sept. 1579	331	124	2.66	243	91
Oct. 1579–Sept. 1582	391	141	2.78	217	78
Oct. 1582–Sept. 1585	344	125	2.76	220	80
Oct. 1585–Sept. 1588	433	147	2.95	292	99
Oct. 1588–Sept. 1591	538	174	3.09	341	110
Oct. 1591–Sept. 1594	468	157	2.98	374	126
Oct. 1594–Sept. 1597	519	137	3.80	423	111
Oct. 1597–Sept. 1600	580	170	3.41	577	169
Oct. 1600–Sept. 1603	591	187	3.16	607	192

A. English crown revenues (nominal values)
B. Deflated crown revenues (using O'Brien and Hunt index)
C. O'Brien and Hunt composite index of inflation (1451–75 = 1.0)
D. Exchequer receipts (nominal values)
E. Deflated exchequer receipts (using O'Brien and Hunt index)

The figures in columns A, B, D, E represent annual averages for the three-year periods stated and are expressed in thousands of pounds sterling. Totals have been rounded to the nearest thousand pounds. There are no reliable figures for crown revenues in 1561 and 1574. There are multiple totals for exchequer receipts for 1597–1603 and the figures used here are derived from the series which normally gives the highest totals for these years.

Sources: www.le.ac.uk/hi/bon/ESFDB/obrien; F. C. Dietz, *The exchequer in Elizabeth's reign* (Smith College Studies in History, vol. 8, no. 2 Northampton, M., 1923), 80–90; P. K. O'Brien and P. A. Hunt, 'The rise of the fiscal state in England, 1485–1815', *Historical Research*, 66 (1993), 129–76.

The military impact of these trends can be seen most directly in the English crown's expenditure on war. Table 7.2 shows a range of figures estimating the cost of specific Tudor military campaigns, in both nominal and constant-value terms. Although none of these figures can be considered precise, they clearly show that, in real terms, Elizabeth's expenditure on war was remarkably modest. Even her most expensive years – the Armada year of 1588 and 1601, when Ireland alone consumed £415,000 – represent barely a third of the real value of Henry's spending in 1544. Combining the costs for Ireland, the Low Countries, France and the navy suggests a rough total of £5.3 million for military expenditure by the English crown between 1585 and 1603, which should be rounded up to at least £6 million to cover other costs, such as the ordnance office. Using the O'Brien and Hunt deflator on each of the component figures suggests that Elizabeth's war cost £1.8 million, in real terms, whereas Henry's wars between 1542 and 1547 cost almost £1.5 million in constant values. However, while Henry's wars were fought over a period of five years (of which only the period 1544–46 involved really intensive combat), Elizabeth's war was waged over 18 years. Elizabeth's war may have been 20 per cent more expensive than her father's, in real terms, but this burden was spread over a period at least three times as long.

The figures cited for Elizabeth's royal income and military expenditure demonstrate that she had to wage war on a distinctly limited budget, especially in comparison with her father in the 1540s. Nevertheless, she succeeded in doing so for 18 years and finally forced Tyrone into submission and prepared the way for an honourable peace with Spain. How was this possible? One explanation is that Elizabeth's regime fought a very different kind of war from Henry's invasion of France in 1544 or Somerset's invasion of Scotland in 1547. Instead of launching a single massive effort to achieve a specific objective such as the capture of Boulogne or carving out a new English Pale in southern Scotland, Elizabethan military operations before 1599 were notable mainly for their limited and defensive nature. Much to the dismay of aggressive military men like Drake and Essex, Elizabeth restricted her military and financial commitments as much as possible and left the boldest operations (such as the Portugal

Limited budget of the wars.

Table 7.2 Selected military expenditure of the English crown,
1544–1603

	Theatre	£ Nominal	£ Deflated
1544	France and Scotland	650,000	422,000
1544–75	France and Scotland	1,300,000	890,000
1542–74	France and Scotland	2,100,000	1,483,000
1547–52	Scotland and Ireland	1,500,000	790,000
1559–60	Scotland	178,000	77,000
1560–07	Ireland: Shane O'Neill	100,000	42,373
1562–63	France: Newhaven	245,000	98,000
1579–83	Ireland: Desmond rebellion	300,000	109,000
1587–88	Total exchequer issues	400,000	143,400
1585–1603	Low Countries	1,420,000	440,000
1585–1603	navy	1,450,000	453,000
1585–94	Ireland	250,000	84,000
1589–95, 97	France	297,000	77,750
1594–1603	Ireland	1,924,000	558,000
1594–1603	Ireland and Low Countries	2,458,470	712,600
1601	Ireland	415,000	125,800

Deflated totals calculated using O'Brien and Hunt deflator.

Sources: PRO, SP 10/15/11; ibid., SP 12/287/59; Dietz, *EPF, 1558–1640*, 431–2, 440–1; *HMCS*, 15: 1–2; Parker, 'Dreadnought', 289.

expedition of 1589) largely to the purses of private 'adventurers'. Inevitably, these semi-private expeditions involved maritime or amphibious operations, where the possibilities of making a large profit seemed most enticing and the costs were far lower than prolonged campaigns involving a substantial army. Even 'official' naval expeditions such as those to Cadiz and the Azores involved a healthy leavening of private investment. Moreover, these operations won the queen's approval only because she saw them as essential defensive measures and the cheapest means of spiking Spanish naval power. Elizabeth's ability to limit military commitments was challenged in the early 1590s by England's commitment to a 'common cause' with

Hanner relies a lot of this

Henri IV, which repeatedly forced her to send troops to France despite her own deep misgivings. Even so, she never provided as many men or as much money as her commanders in France urged and regularly dismissed fresh demands from Henri. However, Elizabeth's efforts to economise and retain control of events proved unsustainable after the defeat at Yellow Ford. From the end of 1598 until early 1603, she had no choice but to commit large quantities of men, money and resources to avert disaster in Ireland.

Elizabeth's policy of trying to limit her military commitments was dictated by financial, personal and strategic imperatives. Elizabeth plainly could not afford the sort of lavish expeditions mounted in the 1540s and she was acutely aware of the economic, social and political dangers of spending beyond her means. Where Henry and Somerset had fixed their eyes on martial glory, she focused on the exorbitant costs involved. As a woman, she was also expected to demonstrate qualities associated with peace rather than conquest, which was seen as a masculine aspiration. Elizabeth herself clearly believed that the 'glory of war' was not worth a candle. At best, war was a costly and dangerous gamble which might bring fleeting renown and would certainly encourage dangerous expectations of reward and political influence on the part of successful soldiers, as occurred with Essex in the 1590s. At worst, it threatened the sort of disaster which her sister Mary had experienced at Calais or even an invasion, as nearly happened in 1588. War for 'glory' therefore had little appeal for Elizabeth. As a sovereign whose fundamental objective was to preserve the territories and authority she had inherited – whether against the chauvinist presumptions of her male courtiers or the armed aggression of foreign enemies – her natural inclinations were essentially conservative and defensive, and this was reflected in her approach to war.

Strategic considerations reinforced Elizabeth's natural caution and desire to set limits. Henry VIII had been willing to gamble on a massive strike against Boulogne because he counted upon France being distracted by war with Charles V and because England had traditionally been able to practise a 'raiding' strategy against France. After a season campaigning on the Continent, English troops would return home for the winter, trusting in the protection afforded by the walls of Calais and the waters of the Channel. However, Henry's campaign showed this strategy no longer worked because the same weak defences which enabled him to capture Boulogne within a single season also required him to sustain a heavy year-round commitment of men and money to defend the town against French efforts to recapture it. Since England's military and financial system was geared towards occasional periods of intense effort over the summer, followed by months or years of inactivity, this sustained effort strained the realm to breaking-point. Elizabeth possessed neither Boulogne nor Calais, which meant that England itself became the potential front line. Worse, the religious divisions which hardened in the 1550s and 1560s raised the prospect of disaffected English Catholics aiding foreign invaders, as the northern rebels sought to do in 1569. In these circumstances, Elizabeth's government understandably became preoccupied with the problem of home defence. This encouraged greater emphasis on the navy, but it also resulted in most of the realm's best potential soldiers being reserved strictly for home defence when the trained bands were created. This completely reversed the military priorities of earlier reigns, when the best troops had accompanied the king overseas. Under Elizabeth, foreign campaigns had to be fought using only men and resources which were regarded as surplus to the requirements of national defence, which severely limited the possibilities for aggressive action.

Elizabeth's concern to limit cost and risk meant that she sought to avoid war for as long as possible and placed great reliance upon 'deniable' alternatives to open conflict. Once the war with Spain began, she was prepared to authorise aggressive action at sea because it was relatively cheap and offered the prospect of simultaneously restocking her treasury and denying money to Spain. On land, however, she stood upon the strategic defensive. Leicester's instructions in 1585 pointedly required him 'rather to make a defensive then an offensyve warr and not in any sort to hazard a battaile without great advantage'. To the dismay of her more bellicose subjects, Elizabeth never sought to defeat Spain or even to drive its forces out of the Low Countries. Her objective was merely to force a compromise peace which would remove the Spanish army from the region, whilst ensuring that Spain retained sufficient influence there to avoid creating a power vacuum which might invite French occupation. Even if the destruction of Spanish power had been financially and militarily feasible, Elizabeth viewed such a policy as entirely self-defeating. Without a strong Spain to occupy the attentions of France, England would simply exchange one hostile Continental power for another, even more dangerous enemy, and at terrible cost.[3]

With rare exceptions, Elizabeth permitted major commitments of troops only in regions which posed a direct threat to England itself – the Low Countries, northern France and Brittany – and only for as long as the threat persisted. These areas represented England's outer approaches and their capture by Spain would make the realm's naval and coastal defence extremely uncertain. Sending troops to aid the Dutch and Henri IV pre-empted this danger and also ensured that English troops could rely upon local allies and fortifications. This enabled Elizabeth to limit her military commitments by counting upon her Continental allies to carry most of the burden of the land war. The force-multiplying effect of modern defences also permitted relatively small numbers of English troops to have a significant military and political impact by garrisoning local towns. As repeated examples showed, even a few hundred soldiers constituted a very formidable obstacle when protected by *trace italienne* fortifications. Unfortunately, the same logic also applied to enemy garrisons, which meant that offensive operations required large numbers of troops and a steady flow of supplies and reinforcements – precisely the sort of burdensome commitment which Elizabeth wanted to avoid. Even in Ireland, which was one of her own dominions, she was only prepared to launch half-hearted offensive operations until the collapse of English military power there finally left her no choice. The step-change in England's war effort which occurred at the end of 1598 can therefore be seen as a shift from waging 'defensive . . . warr' on land to the far more demanding requirements of offensive operations. Although Ireland lacked the *trace italienne* defences found on the Continent, this proved an arduous task because the bogs made the movement of siege guns difficult and the Irish were highly skilled at using the terrain to create improvised defences. Moreover, unlike on the Continent, England had to provide all the manpower for the war in Ireland without allied support.

The rhythms of Elizabeth's wars can be seen in the numbers of men recruited for service abroad. The most widely cited overview of royal levies is a table by C. G. Cruickshank, who calcuated that 105,810 English and Welsh soldiers were levied for foreign service between 1585 and 1602, fully a third of them (35,219) being recruited in the period 1598–1602. However, early modern statistics are a notoriously difficult source and Cruickshank's figures erroneously include 3300 men raised in 1602 who were actually paid by the States General and exclude 2000 men sent to Picardy in 1596. His total for the Portugal expedition (listed as 6000 men in 1588) is also well short of the approximately 13,400 soldiers who set sail in April 1589. As part of his forthcoming study of English and Welsh soldiers who served in the French and Dutch armies, David Trim has therefore recalculated Cruickshank's figures and produced some slightly different totals (see Table 7.3). However, even Trim's improved figures reflect some of the difficulties of constructing reliable totals. His total of 6100 men levied in 1588 includes only 100 Shropshire men sent to Ireland, 4500 levied for the Portugal expedition and 1500 new recruits who were sent to the Low Countries to release veteran troops for Portugal. This means that Trim's 1588 total will need to be increased by another 8900 men to take full account of the Portugal expedition, boosting the 1585–1602 total to 117,525. This would also bring recruitment in 1588 to approximately 15,000 – the highest figure for the whole reign. Although this peak is slightly artificial because some of the recruitment for the Portugal expedition clearly spilled over into the opening months of 1589, this new total underlines the extraordinary demand for manpower which the realm was forced to meet in the immediate aftermath of the Armada campaign.[4]

These revised figures give a grand total of 117,525 being recruited by the crown between 1585 and 1602 – an average of 6529 men per year across the full 18 years or 6426 men a year for 1585–97 and 6796 a year for 1598–1602. Even at its most intense – in late 1588 and early 1589 – Elizabethan recruitment is far removed from the 32,000 troops who accompanied Henry VIII to France in 1544. Yet the latter effort completely drained the realm's 'quasi-feudal' forces and Henry's government was barely able to sustain the war until 1546, even with massive numbers of foreign mercenaries and conscripting the county militia for service overseas.

Table 7.3   Royal recruitment of troops for service abroad,
1585–1602

	Cruickshank	Trim
1585	7500	7500
1586	4870	4870
1587	4800	4800
1588	6000	6100 (15,000, with addition of 8900)
1589	4850	4950
1590	4250	4250
1591	8425	8425
1592	2490	2520
1593	3025	3025
1594	4800	5900
1595	1806	1781
1596	8940	11,237
1597	8835	9285
1598	9164	9564
1599	5250	2760
1600	4885	7833
1601	12,620	9790
1602	3300	4035
Total	105,810	108,625 (+8900 extra for 1588) = 117,525

Sources: Cruickshank, *EA*, 290; D. J. B. Trim, '"Fighting Jacob's warres": the employment of English and Welsh mercenaries in the European Wars of Religion: France and
the Netherlands, 1562–1610' (unpub. PhD thesis, University of London, 2002),
Appendix 10, Table 14.

By contrast, Elizabeth's government was able to raise 15,000 men
in the wake of the exhausting Armada campaign of 1588, 11,000 men
in 1596 during the depths of the worst run of bad harvests of the
whole century, and further drafts of more than 9000 men in 1597,
1598 and 1601. These surges were possible because the privy council
and county authorities had become practised at levying smaller
numbers of men on a regular basis and were able to step up their
efforts when faced by military crises, often on multiple fronts. The

means by which the Elizabethan regime raised men was also more flexible. As the Boulogne campaign showed, Henry's 'quasi-feudal' army was effectively a one-shot weapon which was difficult to sustain in the field for long and could not easily be replenished. It created an impressive expeditionary force, but was less effective for fighting a prolonged war than the old practice of issuing recruitment contracts ('indentures'), which had worked well during the Hundred Years War. Elizabeth's government made some use of indentures – Norris and Drake, for example, were given commissions to press men for the Portugal expedition of 1589 – but raised most troops for overseas service simply by directing the lord lieutenant of a county to order the levying of a specific number of recruits from among the local adult males who were not exempt by reason of belonging to the county's trained bands, the clergy or being servants of the crown or nobility. This left the choice of individual men to local discretion and ensured that local officials tended to select men whose absence would have the least impact upon their own community. On the other hand, many of those drafted were vagrants or criminals, which removed potential local trouble-makers but made for poor soldiers.[5]

Although the numbers of soldiers officially recruited for overseas service demonstrate the intensity of the war effort, they do not provide a comprehensive measure of the full extent to which the manpower of Elizabethan England was mobilised for war. At one level, these totals are too high because they contain a mixture of nominal and actual figures – in other words, they mix together some figures which reflect the actual number of men who were sent overseas and other figures which include a fictional 10 per cent of men, whose inclusion in the payroll was intended merely to allow extra money for discretionary payments by the captains. These non-existent soldiers were known as 'dead pays' and meant that a company of 150 was only expected to have 135 soldiers when it was at full-strength (i.e. it included 15 'dead pays'). Reducing the total for levies by about 7 per cent to allow for a high proportion of 'dead pays' would reduce the estimated number of soldiers who actually left the realm to about 110,000. However, these levies were by no means the only men who were actively involved in the war. Even a very incomplete tally of the number of sailors who served in naval operations between 1585 and

1602 reaches 50,000 men (an average of almost 3000 a year). Many men also volunteered for the war. Perhaps 5000 (roughly 300 a year) served as supernumerary soldiers on the expeditions commanded by Leicester, Essex, Norris and Mountjoy. Large numbers of English and Welsh troops also fought in the Dutch and French armies. David Trim has calculated that almost 70,000 soldiers fought with these foreign armies during Elizabeth's reign, 43,000 of them between 1585 and 1602 (an average of 2388 a year over the 18-year period). Although not strictly members of a military organisation, privateers also played an active role in the war. An average of 150 vessels with 25 crew would suggest 3750 men putting to sea each year. Taken together, these figures imply a total of about 275,000 men involved in military operations (or quasi-military, in the case of privateers) outside the realm between 1585 and 1602, an average of about 16,000 a year. This excludes the impact of war on members of the trained bands – 92,000 men in 1588 – who underwent regular training and many of whom turned out for the invasion scares of 1588 and the later 1590s. The figures also exclude the 16,000 men who constituted the remnants of the 'quasi-feudal' army – servants and tenants of the aristocracy, royal servants and the clergy – who were mobilised in 1588 and 1599. These additions would boost the total military participation to approximately 385,000. Although this figure involves some double-counting (for example, a small number of men from the trained bands also served overseas), this should be more than balanced by the need to include additional men, such as the permanent garrisons in Ireland and Berwick. The important point about these figures is not their precision, which can only be approximate, but the impression which they give of the impact of war on Elizabeth's realm during the second half of her reign. The best estimates are that the population of England and Wales was approximately 3.8 million in 1586 and 4.1 million in 1601. In this light, the demands of war on Elizabethan society were very substantial, especially as a large part of the population was permanently occupied with the labour-intensive agriculture which was necessary for the production of food and the raw materials needed for manufacturing.[6]

The impact of these national figures was by no means evenly distributed across the realm. The border counties in the north of

England provided no levies for overseas service between 1585 and 1602 because they traditionally had a special role in defending against any threat from Scotland. Wales, Cheshire and Lancashire, by contrast, levied relatively few men for the Low Countries or France, but faced repeated and onerous demands for soldiers to fight in Ireland. This meant they were consistently forced to raise men and money even in the years before 1585 and found the accelerating demand for resources to fight in Ireland after 1594 especially difficult. According to the local authorities of Carmarthenshire, repeated levies for Ireland had substantially denuded that county of men and arms even by 1588. The problems in Carmarthenshire were accentuated by the pervasive local influence of the earls of Essex, which resulted in many local men joining the first earl's campaigns in Ulster in the early 1570s and ensured that many of the county's men were exempt from serving the county in the 1580s and 1590s because they formed part of the second earl's large contingent of 'quasi-feudal' troops. A similar local aristocratic connection explains why so many East Anglians died at Leith in 1560. Thanks to the appointment of the duke of Norfolk as Lord Grey's superior in the north, large numbers of men from Norfolk and Suffolk were recruited to join Grey's army in Scotland. England's southern counties traditionally focused on threats from across the Channel and consequently shipped off large numbers of men to fight in the Low Countries and France. However, the desperate need for troops and the growing exhaustion of the western counties meant that even Kent – England's front line against Spanish forces in Flanders – was forced to raise contingents for Ireland by the mid-1590s. The crown's need was especially acute in the case of cavalry, which was both expensive and in chronically short supply. This resulted in the potentially disastrous expedient of shipping 51 horsemen and their mounts to Ireland from Kent between 1598 and 1602 (more than from any other county), even though English cavalry power would have been critical if the Spanish had succeeded in landing there.[7]

The burden on the communities of England and Wales was further compounded by the second general explanation for Elizabeth's ability to sustain war for 18 years: the wholesale transfer of military expenditure from the crown to the realm's towns and counties. This was necessary because of the crown's limited financial resources and its spiralling military commitments, despite the government's best efforts to contain expenditure. J. S. Nolan has calculated that the English crown was forced to pay wages for 286,000 'man-years' for the army alone between 1585 and 1602, at an average of almost 16,000 a year. This meant Elizabeth had to pay a notional 16,000 soldiers each year for 18 years. Nolan's figures bear little relationship to the real numbers of soldiers who actually served overseas because they contain 10 per cent worth of supernumerary payments ('dead pays') and, more importantly, because units were almost always substantially under-strength. Sir John Norris's army in Brittany, for example, nominally totalled 4000 men, but actually numbered 1668 soldiers in December 1592 and perhaps only 800 in July 1593. Nevertheless, Nolan's figures are significant because of their financial implications. Assuming that every soldier in royal pay was a footman (and ignoring the higher costs associated with cavalry and officers), Nolan's figures imply a *minimum* average wage bill for the army alone of £177,000 a year. This equates to £3,186,000 over 18 years, which seems consistent with the estimated cost of individual campaigns cited above. In practice, the crown minimised its cash payments by allowing its troops only weekly 'lendings' for protracted periods. This delayed the problem of meeting 'full pay', but did not resolve it. Moreover, the calculations based upon Nolan's figures make no allowance for other large army costs such as victuals, clothing, transport costs, arms and munitions – let alone the huge expense of running the navy. In this light, it seems understandable, even inevitable, that Elizabeth's government would seek to transfer as many financial commitments as possible to local authorities.[8]

The shifting of military costs to towns and counties became a major issue in 1588, when county authorities were suddenly required to meet the cost of expanding their trained bands and coastal communities were presented with demands for fully equipped ships to supplement the queen's fleet. These charges continued after 1588. Setting out four large ships for the Cadiz expedition in 1596, for example, cost the Cinque Ports of Kent and Sussex £3500, while the brief mobilisation of 4000 men from the Kent trained bands during the invasion scare of August 1599 cost the county £1000. The small inland county of Cambridgeshire paid out £3600 simply to meet the costs of levying 991 soldiers for service overseas between 1591 and 1602, of which the crown repaid only £315. Training the 700 men of the county's trained bands was a heavy additional cost. In the City of London, parliamentary taxation averaged £6533 per annum between 1585 and 1603, but local charges averaged no less than £5207 per annum during this period. As noted in Chapter 5, the burden of local military expenditure and the consequent imposition of frequent local imposts, calculated according to subsidy assessments, encouraged massive tax avoidance by the gentry. This had the double effect of reducing the crown's tax revenues and shifting more of the war's costs to the less wealthy members of society, who were unable to manipulate the assessment system to their own advantage in the manner of the élite.[9]

In many parts of the realm, the cumulative effect of local imposts for the war effort (not to mention for incidental costs, such as repairs to bridges which had been damaged by heavy wagons carrying military supplies) gradually encouraged an inability, or an unwillingness, to comply fully with new requests from the privy council. Demands for ports to provide ships for naval service in the 1590s often produced fewer and smaller vessels than needed, while new levies of men for Ireland regularly drew reprimands from the council to the county authorities about the quality and equipment of the recruits. This sluggishness typifies the sort of 'contribution fatigue' which affects any society after years of sustained warfare. However, the friction generated by the needs of England's escalating war effort in the late 1590s also reflected the privy council's declining effectiveness as an interface between central and local government. This was, in turn, a result of the council's shrinking size and 'quality' (i.e. level of noble representation). In contrast with the late 1580s, few counties had a privy councillor as their lord lieutenant by the late 1590s. Indeed, a growing number of counties had no lieutenant at all, with the latter's administrative duties being discharged by 'muster commissioners', who lacked the lieutenant's social and political weight. These phenomena must be attributed to the queen herself. Whether because she did not want to disturb the political balance between Essex and his rivals or because her advancing age made change seem unpalatable, Elizabeth became increasingly unwilling to appoint new councillors and lieutenants to replace those who died.

The trends affecting the privy council and lieutenancies are significant because the transfer of military costs from central to local government was accompanied by greater efforts on the part of the privy council to dictate the actions of local authorities. In addition to demanding new levies of men or materiel for the war overseas, the council set targets for the size and equipment holdings of county trained bands, demanded the appointment of professional muster-masters to drill them and even specified who the muster-master should be, but required the counties to bear all the costs. This caused considerable anger in some quarters, especially as the salaries of muster-masters were substantial (£80 a year in Hampshire) and these veteran officers were often seen as intruders into county affairs. In Chester, the Mr Stapleton who was hired to oversee the trained bands allegedly showed himself 'rather seeming to ruel the whole incorporation than to obey the same' and the city tried to dismiss him. Elsewhere, local gentlemen sometimes offered uncongenial muster-masters bribes to resign or refused to cooperate with them, forcing the lord lieutenant or even the privy council to intervene.[10]

As a result of such exceptional incidents, and the publication of excellent modern case studies of turbulent counties like Kent and Norfolk (where conciliar demands sometimes provoked sustained haggling over war costs), many scholars have tended to imply that late-Elizabethan government was riven by tensions and that widespread resistance to the council's demands helped to make the war effort chronically inefficient. Such generalisations over-dramatise the problems and miss the point that the Elizabethan war effort actually stood up to the strain of the Irish crisis of 1598–1603 surprisingly well. The frequent complaints and problems show the system was certainly under considerable strain, but they do not signify imminent crisis. E. J. Bourgeois's work on Cambridgeshire, which was a politically harmonious county (and, not coincidentally, where the lord lieutenant was a member of the privy council), shows a remarkably effective and efficient interaction between local and central government. In Cambridgeshire, there were almost no difficulties over local imposts and conciliar demands for men and money were consistently met on time and in the numbers required. This reflected precisely the sort of smooth cooperation which enabled the Elizabethan regime to flood the area around Kinsale with troops and supplies during the autumn of 1601 and sustain them there (despite enemy efforts and the worst winter weather) until victory was won. When it really counted, Elizabethan government was able to do what was necessary for military success.[11]

The Elizabethan Military Achievement

Although most modern scholarship emphasises the limitations of the Elizabethan war effort and the financial and political strains which it placed upon the realm, the military achievements of Elizabeth's regime warrant greater recognition than they have hitherto received. Despite the chronic military weakness which proved so alarming in the 1560s, Elizabeth's government was able to wage a prolonged war against the might of Spain from 1585 until 1603–04. England suffered very few significant defeats in this war and won some notable victories. According to Elizabeth's own limited war aims, which aspired to compromise with Spain and the maintenance of the international balance of power rather than outright victory, the war was an undoubted success. However, some of the queen's subjects hankered after more expansive and 'glorious' objectives. By the time peace was finally agreed, there was a widespread conviction that – as Sir Walter Ralegh later claimed – England should have 'beaten that great empire in pieces, and made their kings kings of figs and oranges'. Such boasting reflected wildly optimistic estimates of English strength and Spanish weakness, but the military confidence of late Elizabethan England – on land and sea – represented a major cultural shift away from the (well-justified) anxiety about war which characterised the 1560s and 1570s.

The final years of Elizabeth's reign also saw English military supremacy established across the whole of Ireland for the first time. This required enormous effort, but the very skill and tenacity of Irish resistance underlines the significance of the achievement. Despite the earl of Essex's complaint that it was a 'miserable beggerly . . . war' in comparison to the fighting on the Continent, Ireland saw Elizabeth's armies reach their peak in size and effectiveness. Even in Continental terms, the forces commanded by Essex and Mountjoy represented sizeable armies and the campaigns there were no less complex or tough than the wars of the Low Countries or France. Indeed, the core of both the English and Irish armies were veterans of the Continental wars.

Underlying these military successes in Ireland and against Spain were significant changes in the way England waged war. Henry VIII possessed a large fleet of warships which carried relatively few heavy cannon and a very impressive array of siege guns, which he used to try to overwhelm Boulogne. Elizabeth retained a healthy siege train, but she concentrated a far greater number of heavy cannon aboard her warships. From the early 1570s, the queen's battlefleet was built (or rebuilt) as 'all big-gun' warships – what Geoffrey Parker has termed the original '*Dreadnought* revolution'. This enabled Elizabeth's ships to neutralise the huge manpower advantage of Spain's *Gran Armada* in 1588 and inflict heavy damage on the Spanish fleet once the latter's defensive formation was disrupted. English naval gunnery also proved decisive at Cadiz in 1587 and 1596 and at Cezimbra and off the Downs in 1602. If Sir Richard Grenville had not been so rash in the Azores in 1591, Elizabeth's navy might have gone through the entire war with Spain without losing a single ship to enemy action. Ironically, Grenville's *Revenge* was lost fighting the sort of hand-to-hand combat for which Henry VIII's fleet had been designed and which Elizabeth's sailors had deliberately avoided in 1588.

The Elizabethan government's commitment to naval power was expressed in its consistently high expenditure on the royal fleet during the 1570s and 1580s, despite competing pressures on the queen's purse. No other contemporary European state spent so heavily on its navy during peacetime.[12] As a result, England possessed both superior ships and an experienced naval logistics system when war broke out in 1585. This proved critical during invasion scares like those in 1588 and 1599, as well as in Ireland. Regular naval patrols prevented Tyrone and his allies from importing siege guns from overseas, which left them dependent upon intervention by Spain to overcome English control of the towns. Spain twice succeeded in landing troops in Ireland – at Smerwick in 1579 and Kinsale in 1601 – but English naval superiority ensured that it could not reinforce or resupply these troops, dooming them to surrender unless they could be rescued by the Irish. This enabled English troops to fight and win decisive battles, aided by seaborne supplies and naval firepower. The foundation stone of English military success in Ireland – and, indeed, elsewhere – therefore lay in the ability to exploit synergies between land and sea forces.

Although the earl of Hertford landed troops at Leith in 1544 and an attempt was made to attack Brest in 1558, the geographical scale of Elizabethan naval and amphibious operations reflected a extraordinary leap from what had gone before. As N. A. M. Rodger has observed, probably no English captain could navigate his way to the Caribbean in 1558 and only one could do so in 1568.[13] Nevertheless, England's chief offensive action in 1585 was to launch a substantial fleet against the West Indies, giving the war against Spain a transatlantic character from the outset. Major 'official' expeditions were launched against Spain and Portugal in 1585, 1587, 1589–91, 1596–97 and 1602 and against Spanish targets in the Caribbean in 1585–86 and 1595–96. In 1602, the privy council even sought to sustain a small fleet off the Spanish coast for eight months on end.

Like so many of these ambitious naval plans, the practical results in 1602 failed to meet the council's hopes. Time and again, naval strategies such as forward defence and the 'silver blockade' proved to be at the very limits of what was technically and logistically possible in the sixteenth century. Although Francis Drake showed that Englishmen could sail around the world in 1580 and the armed merchant ships of privateers haunted the waters off Spain and the Caribbean every spring and summer in the 1590s, coordinating and sustaining oceanic operations by whole fleets of warships was far more demanding. At heart, most Elizabethan naval strategy reflected the privateering origins of the men who created it and won acceptance from the queen because it offered the prospect of both financial and military benefit. However, the large crews and limited storage space aboard the queen's 'all big-gun' warships made them poorly suited to long-range, privateer-style patrolling, especially when they also carried large numbers of troops for amphibious landings. Dogged determination and sheer sailing skill almost made these schemes work, but Elizabethan England's best chance of naval success may have been the strategy formulated in 1596 by the earl of Essex (significantly, a soldier rather than a former privateer) for basing a blockading fleet in a Spanish port which had been captured and garrisoned by English troops. Essex's plan was certainly risky and never implemented, but he may have been correct in arguing that it required a nearby port – and hence an army garrison – to ensure Elizabethan warships had sufficient endurance to mount a prolonged blockade of the Spanish and Portuguese coast.

Although naval developments have gained most of the attention (and plaudits) of modern scholars, the reformation of Elizabethan land forces was more significant at the time and required considerably greater effort. While the queen owned a fleet of purpose-built warships and could count upon support from a growing number of armed privately owned vessels, there was, properly speaking, no 'Elizabethan army'. A few hundred men were employed by the crown as permanent garrisons in Ireland, at Berwick and various fortifications along England's south coast, but expeditionary forces had to be raised from scratch and the county militias were poorly equipped, virtually untrained and intensely parochial. Beginning in the 1570s, Elizabeth's government made strenuous efforts to recast the county militias into a genuine national militia – the trained bands – which was armed and exercised according to national standards. Given local sensitivities about cost and the prestige of rival county families, 'nationalising' the militia was an undertaking of immense difficulty. Nevertheless, this monumental task was essentially complete by the 1590s. In late-Elizabethan Cambridgeshire, the trained bands were exercised regularly and totalled 700 men, 360 of them armed with calivers and muskets and 340 armed with pikes and a few remaining bills. The county also had a reserve of 300 untrained men, all armed with guns and pikes or bills, and 100 pioneers. During the invasion scare of August 1599, Cambridgeshire was able to have 500 trained infantry and 50 cavalry on the road to London within a week of the privy council's first warning and only two days after the council amended its orders to require immediate mobilisation. The county authorities also promptly levied £620 to cover the cost of the deployment.[14]

The reformation of the militia to make it more capable of resisting a French or Spanish invasion required the abandonment of the long-bow as a battlefield weapon (although, like other bows, it remained useful for shooting fire arrows). It also demanded a new class of professional military expert, the muster-master, who brought experience and skills gained in Continental warfare to the English counties. The modernisation of the militia therefore depended upon the availabilty of a substantial number of veteran officers. Experienced officers were also critical whenever the government assembled troops for service overseas, especially as the men who joined expeditionary forces were not members of the trained bands, but raw recruits. At the start of Elizabeth's reign, England had a large number of veterans of the wars of the 1540s and 1550s, but their ranks thinned out in the 1560s and 1570s. Although some officers found employment in Ireland, the key to building a new cadre of officers were the companies of English and Welsh 'volunteers' who fought in France and the Low Countries. These men learned painful lessons in the Continental wars, but the survivors gathered experience that was unattainable at home. Without former 'volunteer' officers such as Sir John Norris and Sir Roger Williams, and the veteran soldiers who followed them, the army which Leicester took to the Low Countries in 1585 would probably have been little more effective than Grey's army in Scotland in 1560. Although Leicester's expedition generated fierce rivalries among his officers – in part, between Norris's former 'volunteer' officers and new arrivals who had strong ties with the earl – the campaigns in the Low Countries blooded a large number of new officers. This enabled the privy council to insist on professional muster-masters for the trained bands in the late 1580s and ensured that England could absorb the heavy casualties of Norris's Portugal expedition in 1589. By the mid-1590s, the realm probably had a surplus of experienced officers. As a result, even though political considerations and the need for rapid expansion meant that the armies which Essex and Mountjoy took to Ireland contained significant numbers of untried captains, the accumulated experience of the many veteran officers gave these armies a solid core of tested leadership.

The Low Countries were also crucial to solving the problem of establishing a steady supply of experienced common soldiers. This was a fundamental weakness of Elizabeth's armies in the 1560s, thanks to her unwillingness to hire foreign mercenaries and the loss of the crown's ability to divert veteran troops from the garrison at Calais. These had formed the chief means of providing a core of 'old soldiers' for the armies of Henry VIII and Edward VI. The initial Elizabethan solution to this problem was to call upon the 'volunteers', starting with the 'perfect harguebushiers' who returned home from the Low Countries in 1573 for employment in Ireland. However, this approach produced only a few hundred men who were not easily replaced. The definitive solution came with Elizabeth's commitment in 1585 to maintain substantial garrisons in the Low Countries, which enabled these forces to become a new and larger version of the old Calais garrison. From the late 1580s, thousands of English 'old soldiers' from the Low Countries were withdrawn to provide a cutting edge for expeditionary forces which were raised to fight in France, Ireland or the Atlantic. These veterans were normally replaced in the Low Countries by fresh recruits from home, creating a system comparable to the Spanish practice of seasoning new soldiers in the *presidios* of Italy before marching them north to join the Army of Flanders. The circulation of trained and untrained soldiers through the Low Countries also had the enormous advantage of exposing English troops to the new tactical system developed by the Dutch in the 1590s. Thanks to this experience, Dutch-style drill and compact companies and regiments rapidly became the norm for English armies.

The proliferation of experienced officers and the ability to muster substantial numbers of 'old soldiers' made Elizabethan armies increasingly confident of their ability to match the forces of Spain. However, English troops were hampered by poor systems for pay and supplies. To be fair, similar problems bedevilled the armies of every nation in early modern Europe, including Spain. The Spanish Army of Flanders, for example, was repeatedly immobilised by mutinies over pay. Nevertheless, supply problems were especially troublesome for England because it could usually deploy fewer men and resources than its enemies, which made wastage all the more critical.

When Elizabeth committed troops to the Low Countries in 1585, Leicester's force effectively had to establish its basic administrative processes upon arrival because it had been so long since the previous official English expedition to the Continent and because of the complications caused by cooperation with the Dutch. England was therefore required to improvise an army for war on the Continent at the very time when Spain found itself compelled to improvise a fleet for naval operations in the Atlantic – a comparison which highlights the contrasting challenges faced by the two sides. The lessons learned in the Low Countries benefited subsequent expeditionary forces, but the peculiarities of each theatre of war (the difficulties of dealing with Henri IV in Normandy, for example, or the adverse pattern of winds and tides in Brittany) meant that every operation posed new problems and the troops employed in the early stages of a campaign usually suffered badly. Nevertheless, it was ultimately England's ability to sustain large numbers of troops in Ireland which proved the key to victory there at the end of the reign. English ships and massive quantities of rations enabled Mountjoy to surround Ulster with garrisons and employ scorched-earth tactics against the Irish. When Spanish troops finally arrived at Kinsale, the hard-won efficiency of England's 'Irish road' permitted Mountjoy to launch a major siege of the port and gave him sufficient flexibility (albeit barely) to win the decisive battle against Tyrone's relief force.

An Elizabethan 'Military Revolution'?

Elizabeth's wars were distinctly international in character and the changes in military practices which occurred during her reign were largely driven by the need to raise the performance of English forces to match international 'best practice'. On land, this entailed creating armies which could confront those of Spain. At sea, English efforts concentrated on maximising the benefits of naval firepower, in which the realm established a significant lead over the rest of Europe by the 1570s. Elizabethan England therefore embraced many of the practices which have been described as characteristics of the 'military revolution' of early modern Europe.

The idea that warfare underwent 'revolutionary' changes in the sixteenth century because of the proliferation of gunpowder weapons is an old one, but it gained new currency in the 1950s and was further refined and popularised by Geoffrey Parker in the 1970s and 1980s. In Parker's controversial, but profoundly influential, formulation of the 'military revolution', the spread of cannon-resistant fortifications during the course of the sixteenth century slowed the pace of war and required European states to raise greater numbers of soldiers, which made war vastly more expensive and demanded higher taxes and more elaborate government bureaucracy. States whose rulers had sufficient wealth or credit were able to field – and, more importantly, sustain – large armies because the adoption of guns and pikes removed traditional restrictions on army size. These weapons could be mass-produced and new recruits could be trained to use them relatively quickly, whereas knights and archers needed years of training to be effective, which severely limited the numbers available and made it difficult to replace those who died. At sea, the development of cannon-armed sailing ships effectively created mobile fortresses and enabled European firepower to be deployed in the New World and beyond.[15]

In Parker's estimation, with the exception of naval developments, Tudor England was a notable laggard in adapting to the military and political implications of the 'military revolution'. He argues the process of transformation was patchy and incomplete by Elizabeth's death. This judgement is based upon a far more critical view of Elizabethan military history than has been advanced in this book and partly reflects the excessively negative assessment of Tudor soldiers which characterises most previous writing on the subject. It also pays insufficient attention to the creation of the trained bands or the significance of the Low Countries garrisons. Nevertheless, this emphasis on the tardiness of English military modernisation is also reflected in the rival interpretation of David Eltis, who seeks to challenge key aspects of Parker's thesis. Eltis argues for a modified version of the 'military revolution' which is largely confined to the sixteenth century (unlike Parker's more sprawling chronology) and based upon the deadly penetrative power of firearms against armour, which gave a decisive advantage to defenders over attackers. Like Parker's *trace italienne* fortifications, this made sieges slower and more costly, and required larger armies. Exploiting the benefits of firearms, and minimising their weaknesses, also demanded the writing and dissemination of a whole new range of works on military theory, which Eltis sees as one of the hallmarks of his 'revolution' (as it is of Parker's model). In England, these publications were rare before the 1570s, but thereafter there was a flood of books such as William Bourne's *Inventions or devises very necessary for all generalles and captaines* (1578), Thomas Styward's *The pathwaie to martiall discipline* (1581) and Robert Barret's *The theorike and practike of moderne warres* (1598). These new books reflected both the impact of the experience of English volunteers in the Low Countries wars and the enormous commercial opportunity for offering 'how to' guides for inexperienced gentlemen officers following the inauguration of the trained bands in the 1570s. In the light of these developments, Eltis claims that Tudor England experienced 'revolutionary' changes in military practice and culture only in the last third of the sixteenth century.[16]

Although he devotes far greater attention to military developments in England than Parker, Eltis can be criticised for ignoring important practices which pre-date his rather arbitrary starting-point of 1500. If Parker's span of the late 1400s to 1800 seems cumbersome, Eltis's concentration on the sixteenth century seems excessively narrow. Eltis also exaggerates the revolutionary impact of guns and pikes on the battlefield. As Gervase Phillips has argued, guns and pikes were not treated as exotic new weapons, but as more effective replacements for bows and halberds, respectively, and were initially accommodated within the existing tactical systems which had been created for bows and halberds. The emergence of 'pike and shot' warfare was therefore an evolutionary process rather than a revolutionary one. Indeed, in the English case, the final transition from bows to firearms was probably delayed by the inability of short-ranged arquebuses and calivers to replicate the long-range harrassing fire that could be delivered against an enemy by longbows. Although the later introduction of the musket pushed the range of accurate lethal gunfire out to 100 yards, some military experts continued to extol the merits of the longbow well after it effectively disappeared from English armies around 1590. Phillips also argues that Eltis's emphasis on English military modernisation in the latter half of Elizabeth's reign ignores the tactical sophistication of the armies of

Henry VIII and the duke of Somerset in the late 1540s. During the campaigns against Scotland, these armies made extensive use of guns and pikes, operated under the cover of cannon-armed warships, and constructed the first *trace italienne* fortifications in the British Isles – all prime characteristics of Parker's 'military revolution'. Despite his emphasis on evolutionary developments at the tactical level, Phillips therefore seeks to ascribe profound significance to the war-fighting practices of Somerset's war, in particular. According to Phillips, 1547–50 constituted 'those crucial three years in British military history'.[17]

The arguments advanced in the previous chapters of this book suggest the none of these perspectives can be endorsed without qualification. Phillips is correct to underline the military effectiveness of England's armies deployed against Scotland in the late 1540s, which reflected the lessons which had been learned from the war against France around Boulogne. Yet this level of military efficiency proved politically and financially unsustainable, and contributed to Somerset's own downfall. Under Elizabeth, who could not draw upon a pool of professional soldiers from the garrisons at Calais and declined to employ foreign mercenaries, English armies proved critically lacking in experience and skill, and could not match the performance of the late 1540s. From the 1570s, therefore, Elizabeth's government had to sponsor a military revival based as far as possible upon the realm's native resources. Instead of France, it was now the Low Countries which became 'the schoole of war' for English soldiers. It is this second wave of military modernisation which Eltis sees as evidence of England's belated participation in Europe's 'military revolution', overlooking the efflorescence of the late 1540s. This second burst of modernisation, beginning about 1570, was clearly far more significant than the short-lived mastery of 1547–50. Thanks to the creation of the trained bands and the proliferation of books and treatises on war, the new adaptations to contemporary warfare and knowledge of 'military science' were disseminated to an unprecedented degree. Nevertheless, it remains difficult to argue that even this latter burst of modernisation amounted to a 'revolution'. If the term 'military revolution' means anything, it must imply rapid, profound and lasting changes in the way states waged war. The military improvements of Elizabeth's reign clearly do not meet these criteria.

Despite Eltis's assertions that a 'military revolution' was substantially and irreversibly underway by the latter years of Elizabeth's reign, Geoffrey Parker's doubts about the extent and permanence of Elizabethan responses to modern warfare seem nearer the mark.

In general, Elizabethan England adapted itself to the onerous demands of war by making the minimum changes necessary to achieve the desired result – the sort of largely *ad hoc* approach which Ralegh lamented as doing 'all by halves'. Elizabeth herself regarded this as sensibly limiting the impact of war upon her kingdom. Although the queen's warships were rebuilt according to a revolutionary new 'all big-gun' design and the county militias were transformed into 'trained bands', no permanent new army administrative structures evolved to institutionalise the benefits of wartime experience and the government's financial situation at the end of the reign was eerily similar to that of the reign's opening years. Once the fighting ceased, the army in Ireland was run down, the newly developed industries which had supplied arms and rations for military contracts turned to making new products and even the navy was allowed to slump into stagnation and disrepair. The swift evaporation of English military power under James I underlines how much the achievements of Elizabeth's reign were driven by sheer political willpower on the part of the queen and her privy council, and supported by a sense of common enterprise on the part of her subjects.

While defeat traditionally acts as a spur to military innovation, success in war often encourages complacency or, if circumstances permit, substantial demobilisation. James I was able to embrace the latter course. Although the trained bands were retained and many of the libraries of country gentlemen still held the military treatises and manuals which had poured from the printing presses during the 1580s and 1590s, the realm's level of military preparedness became distinctly half-hearted, especially during the first decade after Elizabeth's death. Given the cost and intensity of the war effort under Elizabeth, this decline was inevitable and perhaps necessary. Nevertheless, it caused acute difficulties when England again found itself at war in the mid-1620s.[18]

Under Charles I, the realm suffered a succession of humiliating defeats against both France and Spain which showed that most of the hard-won military experience of Elizabeth's reign had been lost. The comparison was all the more painful because one of the defeats was at Cadiz, the scene of famous victories in 1587 and 1596, and the commanders included Sir Robert Cecil's nephew and Essex's son. News of the disaster prompted the witticism that 'there were now no more Drakes in England, all were hens'. Numerous tracts about the Elizabethan wars and the 'heroes' who had fought them made the same general point. Almost a generation after the queen's death, the military achievements of her reign assumed a nostalgiac glow which obscured failures like the Portugal expedition of 1589 and highlighted the problems of Charles's war. The contrast seemed so powerful that praise for the Elizabethan era became a (barely) veiled means of criticising Charles's government.[19]

In the 1620s, Charles actually faced a similar problem to Elizabeth's regime in the 1560s, when the cost of war seemed unbearable and the queen's inexperienced soldiers proved far less capable than the armies of her father and the duke of Somerset. Like its Elizabethan predecessor, Charles's government responded to its military problems by embracing a foreign policy which avoided war, by trying to reform the militia (revising orders for the trained bands to create a so-called 'perfect' militia) and by investing heavily in the navy. Thanks to the king's political ineptitude, all of these actions stirred up fresh political discontent. Nevertheless, the similarity between Charles's position and Elizabeth's 60 years earlier underlines the difficulties caused by England's lack of permanent military structures to capture and retain the fruits of war-fighting experience. Elizabeth was undoubtedly lucky that her first brush with war brought victory, albeit an awkward one. Charles was less fortunate and paid a high political price for the failings of his military forces in the 1620s, and did so again in 1638–40. Ironically, England would not finally begin to develop lasting military and financial structures for land war until the Civil War of the 1640s, when Charles himself became their victim. Despite the military advances evident in Elizabeth's wars, it would ultimately require a political revolution to anchor the 'military revolution' in early modern England.[20]

Abbreviations

APC	*Acts of the privy council of England*, new series, ed. J. R. Dasent, E. G. Atkinson, et al. (46 vols, London, 1890–1964)
Apologie	[Robert Devereux, second earl of Essex], *An apologie of the earle of Essex* (London, 1603)
BIHR	*Bulletin of the Institute of Historical Research*
BL	British Library
Carew MSS	*Calendar of the Carew MSS preserved in the archiepiscopal library at Lambeth*, ed. J. S. Brewer and W. Bullen (6 vols, London, 1867–73)
CSPD, EVI	*Calendar of state papers, domestic series, of the reign of Edward VI, 1547–1553*, revised edn, ed. C. S. Knighton (London, 1992)
CSPD, Mary	*Calendar of state papers, domestic series, of the reign of Mary I, 1553–1558*, revised edn, ed. C. S. Knighton (London, 1998)
CSPI	*Calendar of state papers relating to Ireland, of the reign of Elizabeth*, ed. H. C. Hamilton et al. (11 vols, London, 1860–1912; revised series, 2000–)
CSPSp	*Calendar of letters and state papers, relating to English affairs, preserved principally in the archives of Simancas: Elizabeth*, ed. M. A. S. Hume (4 vols, London, 1896–99)
DNB	*Dictionary of National Biography*, ed. L. Stephen and S. Lee, London, 1885–1900 (22 vols, 1908–9 edn).
EcHR	*Economic History Review*
EHR	*English Historical Review*
FSL	Folger Shakespeare Library, Washington DC
HJ	*Historical Journal*

HMC	Historical Manuscripts Commission
HR	*Historical Research* (formerly *BIHR*)
IHR	*Irish Historical Review*
JMH	*Journal of Modern History*
JSAHR	*Journal of the Society for Army Historical Research*
L&A	*List and analysis of state papers, foreign series, Elizabeth I*, ed. R. B. Wernham (7 vols, London, 1964–2000)
LP	*Letters and papers, foreign and domestic, of the reign of Henry VIII, 1509–1547*, ed. J. S. Brewer et al. (21 vols, London, 1862–1910)
LPL	Lambeth Palace Library
MM	*Mariner's Mirror*
P&P	*Past & Present*
PRO	Public Record Office
SHR	*Scottish Historical Review*
Stow, *Annales*	John Stow, *The annales of England . . . untill this present yeere, 1601* (London, 1601)

Notes

Introduction

1. 'On a marriage between Prince Henry and a daughter of Savoy', in W. Oldys and T. Birch (eds), *The works of Sir Walter Ralegh* (8 vols, 1829), 8: 246.
2. P. E. J. Hammer, *The polarisation of Elizabethan politics: the political career of Robert Devereux, 2nd earl of Essex, 1585–1597* (Cambridge, 1999), 242–6, 260, 320, 330–3; G. Ungerer (ed.), *A Spaniard in Elizabethan England: the correspondence of Antonio Perez's exile* (2 vols, London, 1974–6), 1: 329, 354, 367, 401–2; 2: 365–6.
3. FSL, V.b.214, fol. 109v.
4. Sir John Hayward, *Annals of the first four years of the reign of Elizabeth*, ed. J. Bruce, Camden Society, 1st series, 7 (1840), 96.
5. M. Christy, 'Queen Elizabeth's visit to Tilbury in 1588', *English Historical Review*, 34 (1919), 43–61; J. M. Green, '"I my self": Queen Elizabeth I's oration at Tilbury camp', *Sixteenth Century Journal*, 28 (1997), 421–45; S. Frye, 'The myth of Elizabeth of Tilbury', *Sixteenth Century Journal*, 23 (1992), 95–114.
6. See Table 7.1, p. 239.
7. See, for example, E. L. Rasor, *The Spanish Armada of 1588: historiography and annotated bibliography* (Westport, CT, 1993), and A. Lambert, *The foundations of naval history : John Knox Laughton, the Royal Navy and the historical profession* (London, 1998).
8. C. Oman, *A history of the art of war in the sixteenth century* (1937, London, 1987 edn), 388 (quote); C. G. Cruickshank, *Elizabeth's army* (2nd edn, Oxford, 1966); J. S. Nolan, 'The militarization of the Elizabethan state', *Journal of Military History*, 58 (1994), 391 (quote).
9. R. B. Wernham, *Before the Armada: the growth of English foreign policy, 1485–1588* (London, 1966); idem, *After the Armada: Elizabethan England and the struggle for western Europe, 1588–1595* (Oxford, 1984); idem, *The return of the Armadas: the last years of the Elizabethan war against Spain, 1595–1603* (Oxford, 1994). These works are cited hereafter as *BTA*, *ATA* and *RTA*, respectively. For notable 'amphibian' studies, see R. B. Wernham (ed.), *The expedition of Sir John Norris and Sir Francis Drake to Spain and Portugal, 1589* (Navy Records Society, 127, 1988), and B. Lenman, *England's colonial*

wars, 1550–1688 (Harlow, 2001). For misconceptions about land and sea war, see R. B. Wernham, 'Elizabethan war aims and strategy', in S. T. Bindoff et al. (eds), *Elizabethan government and society* (London, 1961), 367; *idem, ATA*, vi–vii, 563ff.

1   The Glory of War:
operations and developments, 1544–1558

1. *LP,* 19 (i), nos 271–6; G. J. Millar, *Tudor mercenaries and auxiliaries, 1485–1547* (Charlottesville, VA, 1980), 46–7.

2. J. J. Scarisbrick, *Henry VIII* (London, 1968), 426–7; D. Potter, 'Foreign policy', in D. MacCulloch (ed.), *The reign of Henry VIII: politics, policy and piety* (Basingstoke, 1995), 107; E. A. Bonner, 'The genesis of Henry VIII's "Rough Wooing" of the Scots', *Northern History,* 33 (1997), 42ff.; C. P. Hotle, *Thorns and thistles: diplomacy between Henry VIII and James V* (Lanham, MD, 1996), 164ff.; N. MacDougall, *An antidote to the English: the auld alliance, 1295–1560* (East Linton, 2001).

3. S. Gunn, 'The French wars of Henry VIII', in J. Black (ed.), *The origins of war in early modern Europe* (Edinburgh, 1987), 28–51; A. Curry, *The battle of Agincourt: sources and interpretations* (Woodbridge, 2000), 195ff.

4. Potter, 'Foreign policy', 119–23; G. Redworth, *In defence of the Church Catholic: the life of Stephen Gardiner* (Oxford, 1990), 130–55, 181–2.

5. P. Cunich, 'Revolution and crisis in English state finance, 1534–47', in M. Ormrod, M. Bonney and R. Bonney (eds), *Crises, revolutions and self-sustained growth: essays in European fiscal history, 1130–1830* (Stamford, 1999), 135–7; F. C. Dietz, *English public finance, 1485–1558* (2nd edn, London, 1964), 152 (hereafter *EPF, 1485–1558*); J. R. Hale, 'The defence of the realm, 1485–1558', in H. M. Colvin (ed.), *The history of the King's Works, vol. 4* (London, 1982), 367–83; N. Longmate, *Defending the island from Caesar to the Armada* (London, 1989, 2001 edn), 378–88; W. J. Tighe, 'The Gentlemen Pensioners in Elizabethan politics and government' (unpub. PhD thesis, University of Cambridge, 1983), 14–35; G. A. Raikes, *The history of the Honourable Artillery Company, vol. 1* (London, 1878), 17.

6. *LP,* 18 (i), no. 144; Millar, 71–3; Stow, *Annales,* 984–5.

7. G. Phillips, *The Anglo-Scots wars, 1513–1550* (Woodbridge, 1999), 148, 150–3; M. Merriman, *The Rough Wooings: Mary Queen of Scots, 1542–1551* (East Linton, 2000), 77–82, 111ff. (hereafter cited as *RW*).

8. C. S. L. Davies, 'Provisions for armies, 1509–50: a study in the effectiveness of early Tudor government', *EcHR,* 2nd series, 17 (1964–5), 236; Phillips, *Wars,* 161–2, 167–8; D. Loades, *The Tudor navy: an administrative, political and military history* (Aldershot, 1992), 127 (hereafter *TN*); 'The late expedition in Scotland ... 1544', in A. F. Pollard (ed.), *Tudor tracts, 1532–1588* (New York, 1964 edn), 40 (quote), 45–6; Merriman, *RW,* 145–9.

9. *LP*, 18 (ii), no. 526 (quote); ibid., 19 (i), no. 730 (p. 449) (quote); S. J. Gunn, 'The duke of Suffolk's march on Paris in 1523', *EHR*, 101 (1986), 596–634; M. B. Davies (ed.), 'Suffolk's expedition to Montdidier, 1523', *Bulletin of the Faculty of Arts, Fouad I University*, 7 (1944), 33–43; C. G. Cruickshank, *The English occupation of Tournai, 1513–1519* (Oxford, 1971).

10. M. B. Davies (ed.), 'The "enterprises" of Paris and Boulogne', *Bulletin of the Faculty of Arts, Fouad I University*, 11 (1949), 71.

11. *LP*, 19 (i), no. 903; Davies, 'Paris and Boulogne', 58 (quote); Millar, 104–9.

12. Davies, 'Paris and Boulogne', 86–7, 89–93 (quote: 91); Millar, 114, 121–3; Blaise de Monluc, *The Valois-Habsburg wars and the French Wars of Religion*, ed. I. Roy (London, 1971), 119–27.

13. C. S. L. Davies, 'Henry VIII and Henry V: the wars in France' in J. L. Watts (ed.), *The end of Middle Ages?* (Stroud, 1998), 248; Davies, 'Paris and Boulogne', 55 (quote).

14. Phillips, *Wars*, 169–71; *LP*, 20 (i), nos 958, 1078; Millar, 133–6, 146–9.

15. M. Rule, *The Mary Rose: the excavation and raising of Henry VIII's flagship* (2nd edn, London, 1983), 26–7, 149ff. N. A. M. Rodger, *The safeguard of the seas: a naval history of Britain, vol. 1, 660–1649* (London, 1997), 210 defines 'heavy cannon' as demi-culverins and larger guns.

16. Loades, *TN*, 131; *idem, John Dudley, duke of Northumberland, 1504–1553* (Oxford, 1996), 69.

17. Rule, 36–8; Loades, *TN*, 130–5; M. B. Davies (ed.), 'Boulogne and Calais from 1545 to 1550', *Bulletin of the Faculty of Arts, Fouad I University*, 12 (1950), 19–20; Rodger, *Safeguard*, 182–3; Loades, *Dudley*, 70–2.

18. Davies, 'Boulogne and Calais', 21–2, 31 (quotes).

19. Phillips, *Wars*, 171–5; Merriman, *RW*, 160–1.

20. L. R. Shelby, *John Rogers: Tudor military engineer* (Oxford, 1967), 67–8, 94ff.; W. A. Sessions, *Henry Howard, the poet earl of Surrey: a life* (Oxford, 1999), 319ff.; Scarisbrick, 462–4; Merriman, *RW*, 195–201, 206–7, 219–20; E. Bonner, 'The recovery of St Andrew's Castle in 1547: French naval policy and diplomacy in the British Isles', *EHR*, 111 (1996), 578–98.

21. Davies, 'Provisions', 244–5, 247

22. *LP*, 20 (ii), no. 453.

23. *LP*, 20 (ii), no. 368; D. Stewart, 'Sickness and mortality rates of the English army in the sixteenth century', *Journal of the Royal Army Medical Corps*, 91 (1948), 34; Shelby, 92–3.

24. Millar, 138; Davies, 'Paris and Boulogne', 94 (quote).

25. J. J. Goring, 'The military obligations of the English people, 1511–1558' (unpub. PhD thesis, University of London, 1955), *passim*. For examples of the urgent levying of militia men for France in September and October 1544, see I. W. Archer, 'Gazeteer of military levies from the City of London, 1509–1603', nos 11–12, (http: //senior.keble.ox.ac.uk/ fellows/extrapages/iarcher/levies.htm).

26. *Pace* Goring, 'Military obligations', 279–80.

27. Davies, 'Paris and Boulogne', 63 (quote); Eltis, 11–13; Monluc, 129 (quote); N. Barr, *Flodden, 1513* (Stroud, 2001), 48, 100–01; G. Phillips, 'In the shadow of Flodden: technology and Scottish military effectiveness, 1513–1550', *SHR*, 77 (1998), 172–3. Cf. *idem*, 'The army of Henry VIII: a reassessment', *JSAHR*, 75 (1997), 13–15, 17–21.

28. D. Potter, 'The international mercenary market in the sixteenth century: Anglo-French competition in Germany, 1543–50', *EHR*, 111 (1996), 24–58; Millar, 139–42, 171–2. Cf. C. Cruickshank, *Henry VIII and the invasion of France* (Stroud, 1990 edn), 91.

29. *LP*, 18 (i), no. 272 (2), (3); Cunich, 136–7; Dietz, *EPF, 1485–1558*, 152–3. For the problems of selling the lead: W. C. Richardson, 'Some financial expedients of Henry VIII', *EcHR*, 2nd series, 7 (1954), 37–47; *CSPD, EVI*, no. 721 (SP 10/15, no. 11); Rodger, *Safeguard*, 189; Shelby, 54; *CSPD, EVI*, no. 721 (SP 10/15, no. 11).

30. R. B. Outhwaite, 'The trials of foreign borrowing: the English crown and the Antwerp money market in the mid-sixteenth century', *EcHR*, 2nd series, 19 (1966), 290; W. C. Richardson, *Stephen Vaughan, financial agent of Henry VIII* (Baton Rouge, LA, 1953), 77, 99; R. Hoyle, 'War and public finance', in MacCulloch (ed.), *Reign of Henry VIII*, 91ff.; *idem*, 'Taxation and the mid-Tudor crisis', *EcHR*, 2nd series, 51 (1998), 649–75.

31. C. E. Challis, *The Tudor coinage* (Manchester, 1978), 84ff.; *LP*, 20 (ii), no. 729 (quote).

32. Hoyle, 'War and finance', 95–6; D. M. Palliser, *The age of Elizabeth: England under the later Tudors, 1547–1603* (2nd edn, London, 1992), ch. 5; J. R. Wordie, 'Deflationary factors in the Tudor price rise', *P&P*, no. 154 (1997), 32–70; C. Muldrew, '"Hard food for Midas": cash and its social value in early modern England', *P&P*, no. 170 (2001), 78–120.

33. E. Shagan, 'Protector Somerset and the 1549 rebellions: new sources and perspectives', *EHR*, 114 (1999), 49; M. L. Bush, *The government policy of Protector Somerset* (London, 1975), 9–10; F. J. Baumgartner, *Henry II: king of France, 1547–1559* (Durham, NC, and London, 1988), 142.

34. Bush, 13ff; Phillips, *Wars*, 178–81; Merriman, *RW*, 232ff., 265–91; M. Merriman, 'The fortresses in Scotland, 1547–50', in Colvin (ed.), 694–726; *idem*, 'The forts of Eyemouth: anvils of British Union?', *SHR*, 67 (1988), 145–6.

35. W. Patten, 'The expedition into Scotland of the most worthy prince Edward, duke of Somerset', in Pollard (ed.), 124–5 (quote); Phillips, *Wars*, 178–200; D. H. Caldwell, 'The battle of Pinkie', in N. MacDougall (ed.), *Scotland and war, AD 79–1918* (Edinburgh, 1991), 61–94; P. de M. G. Egerton (ed.), *A commentary of the services and charges of William Lord Grey of Wilton, KG, by his son Arthur Lord Grey of Wilton, KG*, Camden Society, 1st series, 40 (1847), 15 (quote).

36. Merriman, 'Eyemouth', 147; Phillips, *Wars*, 206; Bush, 33–5.

37. Loades, *TN*, 145; Rodger, *Safeguard*, 186; Phillips, *Wars*, 220–1; Merriman, *RW*, 306–8.

38. Egerton, *Grey*, 16–17; Phillips, *Wars*, 224–49; Merriman, *RW*, 317–19.

39. Challis, 95ff.; D. E. Hoak, *The king's council in the reign of Edward VI* (Cambridge, 1976), 186; Palliser, 163.

40. Bush, 40ff.; J. Goring, 'Social change and military decline in mid-Tudor England', *History*, 60 (1975), 185–8, 195; D. MacCulloch, *Tudor Church militant: Edward VI and the Protestant Reformation* (London, 1999), *passim*.

41. B. L. Beer, *Rebellion and riot: popular disorder in england during the reign of Edward VI* (Kent State University Press, OH, 1982), 123–4; J. Cornwall, *Revolt of the peasantry, 1549* (London, 1977), 173.

42. Beer, 69, 149.

43. Beer, 78–81, 125–39 (quote: 130); Cornwall, 176–226; Loades, *Dudley*, 126–8.

44. *CSPD, EVI*, no. 416 (SP 10/9, no. 46).

45. D. L. Potter (ed.), 'Documents concerning the negotiation of the Anglo-French treaty of March 1550', *Camden Miscellany 28* (1984), 58–180; Merriman, *RW*, 346–8; Loades, *Dudley*, 165–6; D. Starkey (ed.), *The inventory of Henry VIII: the transcript* (London, 1998), 99–101; R. B. Wernham, *Before the Armada: the growth of English foreign policy, 1485–1588* (London, 1966), 194ff. (hereafter *BTA*); *CSPD, EVI*, no. 721 (SP 10/15, no. 11); B. L. Beer and S. M. Jack (eds), 'The letters of William, Lord Paget of Beaudesert, 1547–1563', *Camden Miscellany 25* (1974), 31 (quote). For Ireland, see chapter 2 in this volume.

46. A. Dyer, 'The English sweating sickness of 1551: an epidemic anatomized', *Medical History*, 41 (1997), 362–84.

47. Challis, 105–9; Dietz, *EPF, 1485–1558*, 194–5.

48. Hale in Colvin, (ed.), 399; Loades, *TN*, 154–6; Hoak, *King's council*, 198–201 (quote: 199); J. G. Nichols (ed.), *The diary of Henry Machyn, citizen and merchant-taylor of London, from AD 1550 to AD 1563*, Camden Society, 1st series, 42 (1848), 12–13, 18–20 (quote: 18); Stow, *Annales*, 1024–6; Loades, *Dudley*, 230–71; D. MacCulloch (ed.), 'The *Vita brevis Angliae Reginae Mariae* of Robert Wingfield of Brantham', *Camden Miscellany 28* (1984), 188ff., 244ff.

49. D. Loades, *The reign of Mary Tudor* (2nd edn, London, 1991), 129ff., 232ff.; C. Coleman, 'Artifice or accident? The reorganization of the exchequer of receipt, *c.*1554–1572', in C. Coleman and D. Starkey (eds), *Revolution reassessed: revisions in the history of Tudor administration and government* (Oxford, 1986), 163ff.; E. A. Wrigley and R. S. Schofield, *The population history of England, 1541–1871* (London, 1981), 333; Palliser, 62.

50. J. Proctor, 'The history of Wyat's rebellion', in Pollard (ed.), 199–257; MacCulloch, '*Vita brevis*', 279–84; D. Loades, *Two Tudor conspiracies* (Cambridge, 1965), 12–127; S. Adams, 'A puritan crusade? The composition of the earl of Leicester's expedition to the Netherlands, 1585–86', in

idem, Leicester and the Court: essays on Elizabethan politics (Manchester, 2002), 178–9; E. H. Harbison, *Rival ambassadors at the court of Queen Mary* (Princeton, NJ, 1940); Loades, *Conspiracies*, 128–217; D. Starkey, *Elizabeth: apprenticeship* (London, 2000), 191ff.

51. Loades, *TN*, 81ff., 159–61, 166–8; J. Glete, *Navies and nations: warships, navies and state building in Europe and America, 1500–1860* (2 vols, Stockholm, 1993), 1: 130–1, 2: 558; T. Glasgow, 'The navy in Philip and Mary's war, 1557–1558', *MM*, 53 (1967), 322–3; C. S. L. Davies, 'The administration of the Royal Navy under Henry VIII: the origins of the Navy Board', *EHR*, 80 (1965), 268–88; Rodger, *Safeguard*, 223ff.; *CSPD, Mary*, no. 536 (SP 11/10, no. 1); T. Glasgow, 'Maturing of naval administration', *MM*, 56 (1970), 7–8; M. Oppenheim, *A history of the administration of the Royal Navy and of merchant shipping in relation to the Navy from 1509 to 1660* (1896, London, 1988 edn), 111–13.

52. Loades, *Reign of Mary*, 304–9.

53. C. S. L. Davies, 'England and the French war', in J. Loach and R. Tittler (eds), *The mid-Tudor polity, c.1540–1560* (London, 1980), 165–6; Adams, 'Puritan crusade?', 182; Loades, *Reign of Mary*, 312–14; Merriman, 'Eyemouth', 152–3.

54. G. Ferrers, 'The winning of Calais by the French, January 1558 AD', in Pollard (ed.), 294 (quote); Davies, 'French war', 168–78; Loades, *Reign of Mary*, 316–19; D. Potter, 'The duc de Guise and the fall of Calais, 1557–1558', *EHR*, 98 (1983), 486–93; J. Sumption, *Trial by battle: the Hundred Years War: I* (London, 1990), 535–83; Egerton, *Grey*, 33 (quote); T. Churchyard, 'Thomas Churchyard, the poet['s] share in, and eye witness account of, the siege of Guisnes, 11th–22nd January, 1558 AD', in Pollard (ed.), 330.

55. Nichols, *Machyn*, 163 (quote); Starkey, *Inventory*, 117–27

56. *CSPD, Mary*, nos 699–700, 703, 706, 708–9 (SP 11/12, nos 22, 25, 26, 30, 33–4).

57. Philip and Mary 4 and 5, cc. 2–3; A. Hassell Smith, 'Militia rates and militia statutes, 1558–1663', in P. Clark et al. (eds), *The English commonwealth, 1547–1640* (Leicester, 1979), 93–110; L. Boynton, *The Elizabethan militia, 1558–1638* (London, 1967), 9–11 (hereafter *EM*); C. G. Cruickshank, *Elizabeth's army* (2nd edn, Oxford, 1966), 17, 130–1 (hereafter *EA*); Loades, *Reign of Mary*, 329–30.

58. Loades, *Reign of Mary*, 320–1, 347–8; Dyer, 380.

59. Glasgow, 'Philip and Mary's war', 336–7.

2   The Burden of War: operations and developments, 1558–c.1572

1. *CSPF*, 2: 3.

2. Wernham, *BTA*, 245–6; N. M. Sutherland, 'The origins of Queen Elizabeth's relations with the Huguenots, 1559–62', in *idem, Princes,*

politics and religion, 1547–1589 (London, 1984), 73–4; M. R. Thorp, 'Catholic conspiracy in early Elizabethan foreign policy', *Sixteenth Century Journal*, 15 (1984), 431–48; W. T. MacCaffrey, 'The Newhaven expedition, 1562–1563', *HJ*, 40 (1997), 1–3.

3.   J. W. Burgon, *The life and times of Sir Thomas Gresham* (2 vols, London, 1839), 1: 320 (quote), 478–9; R. W. Stewart, *The English ordnance office, 1585–1625* (Woodbridge, 1995), 105; Loades, *Reign of Mary*, 356–7; F. C. Dietz, *English public finance, 1558–1641* (New York, 1932), 16–17 (hereafter *EPF, 1558–1641*).

4.   Colvin (ed.), 400, 644ff.

5.   *The state papers and letters of Sir Ralph Sadler*, ed. A. Clifford (3 vols, London, 1809), 1: 438–9 (quote); ibid., 2: 72, 89–90, 108, 111 (quote), 173, 179–80; *CSPF*, 2: 578; Merriman, 'Eyemouth', 154–5; W. T. MacCaffrey, *The shaping of the Elizabethan regime: Elizabethan politics, 1558–1572* (Princeton, 1968), 71–9; S. Alford, *The early Elizabethan polity: William Cecil and the British succession crisis, 1558–1569* (Cambridge, 1998), 64–70; Loades, *TN*, 210–11.

6.   C. Read, *Mr Secretary Cecil and Queen Elizabeth* (London, 1955), 142 (quote); J. E. A. Dawson, 'William Cecil and the British dimension of early Elizabethan foreign policy', *History*, 74 (1989), 196–216; T. Wright, *Queen Elizabeth and her times* (2 vols, London, 1838), 1: 24–5; Wernham, *BTA*, 255; Alford, 74–5; N. M. Sutherland, 'Queen Elizabeth and the conspiracy of Amboise, March 1560', in idem, *Princes, politics and religion*, 97–112; G. Parker, *The grand strategy of Philip II* (New Haven, CT, 1998), 152–3.

7.   Egerton, *Grey*, 37; Cruickshank, *EA*, 216.

8.   Sir John Hayward, *Annals of the first four years of the reign of Elizabeth*, ed. J. Bruce, Camden Society, 1st series, 7 (1840), 58–60, 63–7 (quotes: 63, 64); S. Haynes, *A collection of state papers . . . 1542 to 1570* (London, 1740), 304–5 (quote: 304); *CSPF*, 3: 25–8; Cruickshank, *EA*, 224–31; Wernham, *BTA*, 257; Read, *Cecil*, ch. 8.

9.   Challis, 115–28, 261–3.

10. Read, *Cecil*, 248–9; *CSPF*, 3: 185 (quote).

11. Hayward, *Annals*, 100; D. J. B. Trim, 'The "foundation-stone of the British army"?: the Normandy campaign of 1562', *JSAHR*, 77 (1999), 71–87; MacCaffrey, 'Newhaven', 6–12; Wernham, *BTA*, 264–5.

12. Trim, 'Normandy', 86; K. B. Neuschel, *Word of honor: interpreting noble culture in sixteenth-century France* (Ithaca, NY, 1989), ix–x; R. J. Knecht, *The French civil wars* (Harlow, 2000), 99–117; MacCaffrey, 'Newhaven', 14–17; *CSPF*, 6: 431–2; T. Glasgow, 'The navy in the Le Havre expedition, 1562–1564', *MM*, 54 (1968), 291–2; *CSPF*, 6: 480–1.

13. Stow, *Annales*, 1112; Dietz, *EPF, 1558–1641*, 12.

14. Cruickshank, *EA*, 6ff., 27; M. C. Fissel, *English warfare, 1511–1642* (London, 2001), 84ff. (hereafter *EW*); Adams, 'Puritan crusade?'.

15. Dietz, *EPF*, 1558–1641, 9–12, 16–24; R. B. Outhwaite, 'Royal borrowing in the reign of Elizabeth I: the aftermath of Antwerp', *EHR*, 86 (1971), 260; R. W. Hoyle (ed.), *The estates of the English crown, 1558–1640* (Cambridge, 1992), 16; Loades, *Reign of Mary*, 354–5, 357;.

16. Glasgow, 'Maturing', 12–13, 17–18; Dietz, *EPF, 1558–1641*, 35–6, 413–14, 425–6, 430; A. Sheehan, 'Irish revenues and English subventions, 1559–1622', *Proceedings of the Irish Academy*, 90, C: 2 (1990), 47; H. M. Wallace, 'Berwick in the reign of Queen Elizabeth', *EHR*, 46 (1931), 80.

17. D. J. B. Trim, 'Protestant refugees in Elizabethan England and confessional conflict in France and the Netherlands, 1562–c.1610', in R. Vigne and C. Littleton (eds), *From citizens to strangers* (Brighton, 2001), 68–79; idem, 'The "secret war" of Elizabeth I: England and the Huguenots during the early Wars of Religion, 1562–1577', *Proceedings of the Huguenot Society*, 27 (1999), 189–99.

18. Rodger, *Safeguard*, 198–200; Wernham, *BTA*, 281–2.

19. C. Brady, 'The captains' games: army and society in Elizabethan Ireland', in T. Bartlett and K. Jeffrey (eds), *A military history of Ireland* (Cambridge, 1996), 148; Challis, 251–2, 257–8; Sheehan, 'Irish revenues and English subventions', 49–50.

20. Brady, 'Captains' games', 145–6; S. G. Ellis, 'The collapse of the Gaelic world, 1450–1650', *IHS*, 31 (1999), 458–9; G. Phillips, 'Irish *ceatharnaigh* in English service, 1544–1550, and the development of "Gaelic warfare"', *JSAHR*, 78 (2000), 163–72; G. A. Hayes-McCoy, *Scots mercenary forces in Ireland (1565–1603)* (Dublin, 1937); idem, *Irish battles* (London, 1969; New York, 1997 reprint), 48–66; C. Falls, *Elizabeth's Irish wars* (London, 1950), 67–85 (hereafter *EIW*); Alford, 75–6, 87, 141.

21. S. G. Ellis, 'The Tudors and the origins of the modern Irish states: a standing army', in Bartlett and Jeffrey (eds), 120–30; D. Potter, 'French intrigue in Ireland during the reign of Henri II, 1547–1559', *International History Review*, 5 (1983), 159–76; Bush, 133–4; S. G. Ellis, *Ireland in the age of the Tudors, 1447–1603* (2nd edn, London, 1998), 265ff.; D. G. White, 'The reign of Edward VI in Ireland: some political, social and economic aspects', *IHS*, 14 (1965), 197–211; N. P. Canny, *The Elizabethan conquest of Ireland: a pattern established, 1565–76* (Hassocks, Sussex, 1976), 35–44; C. Brady, *The chief governors: the rise and fall of reform government in Tudor Ireland, 1536–1588* (Cambridge, 1994), 94–6, 260–4; D. Edwards, 'Beyond reform: martial law and the Tudor conquest of Ireland', *History Ireland*, 5 (1997), 16–22.

22. Ellis, *Tudor Ireland*, 275–8, 290–1; Falls, 86–99; Hayes-McCoy, *Irish battles*, 68–85; idem, *Scots mercenary forces*, 77–109.

23. D. Edwards, 'The Butler revolt of 1569', *IHS*, 28 (1993), 228–55; Ellis, *Tudor Ireland*, 295–8, 301; Falls, 100–12; Canny, *Elizabethan conquest*, 101–2, 121–2, 142–8.

24. H. Morgan, 'The colonial venture of Sir Thomas Smith in Ulster, 1571–1575', *HJ*, 28 (1985), 261–78; Canny, *Elizabethan conquest*, 85–8, 128–9;

CSPI, 1571–1575 (revised edn, 2000), no. 1574; Ellis, *Tudor Ireland*, 302–4; Canny, *Elizabethan conquest*, 88–92, 120–1; J. S. Nolan, *Sir John Norreys and the Elizabethan military world* (Exeter, 1997), 18–31.

25. K. R. Andrews, *Trade, plunder and settlement: maritime enterprise and the genesis of the British Empire, 1480–1630* (Cambridge, 1984), 6–9; G. D. Ramsay, *The City of London in international politics at the accession of Elizabeth Tudor* (Manchester, 1975), 195ff.

26. Palliser, 303ff.; E. W. Bovill, 'Queen Elizabeth's gunpowder', *MM*, 33 (1947), 179–86; B. S. Hall, *Weapons and warfare in Renaissance Europe* (Baltimore, MD, 1997), 74–9; Read, *Cecil*, 271–4; T. E. Hartley (ed.), *Proceedings in the parliaments of Elizabeth I* (3 vols, Leicester, 1981–95), 1: 103–7.

27. H. R. Schubert, *History of the British iron and steel industry from c.450 BC to AD 1775* (London, 1957), 170ff., 246–55; B. G. Awty, 'Parson Levett and English cannon founding', *Sussex Archaeological Collections*, 127 (1989), 133–45; J. J. Goring, 'Wealden ironmasters in the age of Elizabeth', in E. W. Ives, et al. (eds), *Wealth and power in Tudor England* (London, 1978), 204–27; Rodger, *Safeguard*, 213–14.

28. M. J. G. Stanford, 'The Raleghs take to the sea', *MM*, 48 (1962), 18–35. See also G. Connell-Smith, *Fore-runners of Drake* (London, 1954).

29. H. Kelsey, *Sir Francis Drake: the queen's pirate* (New Haven, CT, 1998), 11–39; J. Cummins, *Francis Drake* (London, 1995), 1–3, 19–29.

30. C. Read, 'Queen Elizabeth's seizure of the duke of Alva's pay-ships', *JMH*, 5 (1933), 443–64; G. D. Ramsay, *The queen's merchants and the revolt of the Netherlands* (Manchester, 1986), 90ff.

31. MacCaffrey, *Shaping*, ch. 13; M. E. James, 'The concept of order and the Northern Rising of 1569', *P&P* no. 60 (1973), 49–83; A. Fletcher and D. MacCulloch, *Tudor rebellions* (4th edn, London, 1997), 94–110; Stow, *Annales*, 1125–6.

32. R. Pollitt, 'The defeat of the Northern Rebellion and the shaping of Anglo-Scottish relations', *SHR*, 64 (1985), 1–21; G. McD. Fraser, *The steel bonnets: the story of the Anglo-Scottish border reivers* (London, 1971, 1995 edn), 298–310; I. B. Cowan, 'The Marian civil war, 1567–73', in MacDougall (ed.), *Scotland and war*, 95–112; Stow, *Annales*, 1126–9, 1143–5; Fissel, *EW*, 135–6.

33. F. Edwards, *The marvellous chance: Thomas Howard, fourth duke of Norfolk, and the Ridolphi Plot, 1570–1572* (London, 1968); J. A. Williamson, *Hawkins of Plymouth* (2nd edn, London, 1969), 177–88; Parker, *Grand strategy*, 159–63.

34. Andrews, *Trade*, 127–34; Kelsey, 43–67; Cummins, 33–64.

35. Andrews, *Trade*, 138–41, 183ff.

36. N. M. Sutherland, 'The foreign policy of Queen Elizabeth, the Sea Beggars and the capture of Brille, 1572', in *idem*, *Princes, politics and religion*, 183–206; J. B. Black, 'Queen Elizabeth, the Sea Beggars and the

capture of Brille, 1572', *EHR*, 46 (1931), 30–47; G. Parker, *The Dutch Revolt* (London, 1977), 118–40; Wernham, *BTA*, 314–23; C. Read, *Lord Burghley and Queen Elizabeth* (London, 1960), 66–79; J. X. Evans (ed.), *The works of Sir Roger Williams* (Oxford, 1972), 224.

37.   Read, *Burghley*, 86–7, 89ff; Wernham, *BTA*, 324–6.
38.   W. S. Maltby, *Alba: a biography of Fernando Alvarez de Toledo, third duke of Alba, 1507–1582* (Berkeley, CA, 1983), 238–61; Parker, *Dutch Revolt*, 148; idem, *The Army of Flanders and the Spanish Road, 1567–1659* (Cambridge, 1972), 232–5; idem, *Grand strategy*, 126ff; idem, 'The etiquette of atrocity: the laws of war in early modern Europe', in idem, *Empire, war and faith in early modern Europe* (London, 2002), 155–7; Wernham, *BTA*, 327ff; Read, 'Pay-ships', 462–4.
39.   D. Caldecott-Baird (ed.), *The expedition in Holland, 1572–1574* (London, 1976), 90–6 (quote: 94); Evans, 109–21 (quote: 120).
40.   Evans, 125–30, 148 (quote); Caldecott-Baird, 133–8; Hall, *Weapons*, 176–9.

3   The Spectre of War:
operations and developments, c.1572–1585

1.   T. Glasgow, 'List of ships in the Royal Navy from 1539 to 1588 . . .', *MM*, 56 (1970), 299–307; G. Parker, 'The *Dreadnought* revolution of Tudor England', *MM*, 82 (1996), 269–300; P. Earle, *The last fight of the Revenge* (London, 1992), 38ff.
2.   Earle, 18, 44; FSL, MS J.a.1, fol. 165r.
3.   Earle, 17, 41–2; N. A. M. Rodger, 'Guns and sails in the first phase of English colonisation, 1500–1650', in N. Canny (ed.), *The Oxford history of the British Empire. Vol. I: the origins of Empire* (Oxford, 1998), 87; J. S. Corbett (ed.), *Papers relating to the navy during Spanish War, 1585–1587* (Navy Records Society, 11, 1898), 263, 271; FSL, MS J.a.1, fols 162r, 163v.
4.   Rodger, *Safeguard*, 219.
5.   Hartley, *Parliaments of Elizabeth I*, 1: 141.
6.   Figures calculated from Parker, 'Dreadnought', 289; S. Adams, 'New light on the "reformation" of John Hawkins: the Ellesmere naval survey of January 1584', *EHR*, 105 (1990), 96–111; Loades, *TN*, 184–5.
7.   R. Pollitt, 'Contingency planning and the defeat of the Spanish Armada', in D. M. Masterson (ed.), *Naval history: the sixth symposium of the US Naval Academy* (Wilmington, DE, 1987), 70–81; Rodger, *Safeguard*, 327–9.
8.   Read, *Cecil*, 438 (quote); Boynton, *EM*, 60–1, 70ff.
9.   Stow, *Annales*, 1136; PRO, SP 12/91/26, 30; Boynton, *EM*, 91ff.; J. Youings, 'Bowmen, billmen and hackbutters: the Elizabethan militia in the south west', in R. Higham (ed.), *Security and defence in south-west England before 1800* (Exeter Studies in History, 19, 1987), 52.

10. Boynton, *EM*, 93–4; PRO, SP 12/173/99.

11. University College, London, Ogden MS 7/41, fol. 18v, Cecil to Sir Christopher Hatton, [2–3 Sept.] 1591.

12. Parker, *Army*, 12–13; N. Canny, *Making Ireland British, 1580–1650* (Oxford, 2001), 69 (quote); *CSPD, Mary*, nos 728, 772–3, 775–7, 784; J. G. Nichols (ed.), *The chronicle of Calais in the reigns of Henry VII and Henry VIII to the year 1540* (Camden Society, 1st series, 35, 1846); Davies, 'Paris and Boulogne', esp. 40–5; S. Adams, 'The English military clientele, 1542–1618', in C. Giry-Deloison and R. Mettam (eds), *Patronages et clientélismes, 1550–1750 (France, Angleterre, Espagne, Italie)* (Lille and London, 1995), 217–27; D. Grummitt, 'The defence of Calais and the development of gunpowder weaponry in England in the late fifteenth century', *War in History*, 7 (2000), 253–72; [R.] Holinshed, *Chronicles of England, Scotland and Ireland* (6 vols, London, 1807–8 edn), 4: 217, 237.

13. Parker, *Dutch Revolt*, 156–98.

14. Wernham, *BTA*, 330–1, 326, 332–5; Dietz, *EPF, 1558–1641*, 38–9; M. P. Holt, *The duke of Anjou and the politique struggle during the Wars of Religion* (Cambridge, 1986), 21–7, 104, 107–10, 116–25; S. Doran, *Monarchy and matrimony: the courtships of Elizabeth I* (London, 1996), esp. ch. 7; W. T. MacCaffrey, *Queen Elizabeth and the making of policy, 1572–1588* (Princeton, NJ, 1981), esp. 243–66; B. Worden, *The sound of virtue: Philip Sidney's Arcadia and Elizabethan politics* (New Haven, CT, 1996), *passim*.

15. MacCaffrey, *Elizabeth and policy*, 147–8, 150, 253, 325–6, 409ff.; Parker, *Grand strategy*, 4–5 (quote), 164–7 (quote: 167); M. L. Carrafiello, 'English Catholicism and the Jesuit mission of 1580–1581', *HJ*, 37 (1994), 761–74.

16. MacCaffrey, *Elizabeth and policy*, 411ff.; H. G. Stafford, *James VI of Scotland and the throne of England* (New York, 1940).

17. Falls, 128–9; R. Bagwell, *Ireland under the Tudors* (3 vols, London, 1885–90), 3: 28–9; Holinshed, *Chronicles*, 6: 416 (quote).

18. Falls, 142, 147, 149 (quote); T. Glasgow, 'The Elizabethan navy in Ireland (1558–1603)', *Irish Sword*, 7 (1965–6), 298; Edwards, 'Beyond reform', 20 (quote); Falls, 149; Dietz, *EPF, 1558–1641*, 431–2.

19. Kelsey, 75–219; Cummins, 72–123; K. R. Andrews, *Drake's voyages: a reassessment of their place in Elizabethan maritime expansion* (London, 1967), 58–80; Rodger, *Safeguard*, 244–5; http://www.le.ac.uk/hi/bon/ESFDB/obrien/engd004.txt.

20. Stow, *Annales*, 1165; S. Adams, 'The *Gran Armada*: 1988 and after', *History*, 76 (1991), 245–6; G. K. McBride, 'Elizabethan foreign policy in microcosm: the Portuguese pretender, 1580–89', *Albion*, 5 (1973), 197; Parker, *Grand strategy*, 166–7, 170–1

21. MacCaffrey, *Elizabeth and policy*, 277, 279; Holt, 166–9, 195–8.

22. MacCaffrey, *Elizabeth and policy*, 303ff.

23. G. Gates, *The defence of the militarie profession* (London, 1579), 58–61; E. van Meteren, *A true discourse historicall of the succeeding governours in the*

Netherlands (London, 1602), 31–2; *CSPF*, 13: 48–9, 114–16, 178, 210; *CSPF*, 18: 202, 210, 238–9, 240–2, 246–7, 255; Nolan, *Norreys*, 50–64; D. J. B. Trim, 'Ideology, greed and social discontent in early modern Europe: mercenaries and mutinies in the rebellious Netherlands, 1568–1609', in J. Hathaway (ed.), *Rebellion, repression, reinvention: mutiny in comparative contexts* (Westport, CT, 2001), 50.

24. *CSPF*, 19: 254.

25. *CSPF*, 18: 622; ibid., 19: 95–9; *HMCS*, 3: 67–70; BL, Harleian MS 168, fol. 105r (quote); W. Camden, *The history of the most renowned and victorious princess Elizabeth, late queen of England* (4th edn, London, 1688), 319–20 (quote).

26. Dietz, *EPF*, 1558–1641, 44, 317–24; P. Croft, 'English commerce with Spain and the Armada war, 1558–1603', in M. J. Rodriguez-Salgado and S. Adams (eds), *England, Spain and the Gran Armada, 1585–1604* (Edinburgh, 1991), 236–63; Read, *Burghley*, 308 (quote). Cf. *HMCS*, 3: 69.

27. PRO, SP 12/173/4 (quote); C. Read, *Mr Secretary Walsingham and the policy of Queen Elizabeth* (3 vols, Oxford, 1925), 2: 374ff., 398–9; L. Hicks, *An Elizabethan problem* (London, 1964), 23–4, 235–8.

28. Read, *Walsingham*, 2: 381–90; Parker, *Grand strategy*, 169.

29. PRO, SP 12/173/5 (quote); P. Collinson, 'The monarchical republic of Queen Elizabeth I', in idem, *Elizabethan essays* (London, 1994), 31–57.

30. M. F. Keeler (ed.), *Sir Francis Drake's West Indian voyage, 1585–1586* (Hakluyt Society, 2nd series, 148, 1981 for 1975), 9–14; S. Adams, 'The outbreak of the Elizabethan naval war against the Spanish empire: the embargo of May 1585 and Sir Francis Drake's West Indies voyage', in Rodriguez-Salgado and Adams (eds), 50ff.; Andrews, *Trade*, 200ff.

31. Adams, 'Outbreak', 45–8; Parker, *Grand strategy*, 173–5.

32. *CSPF*, 19: 646–7, 708; F. G. Oosterhoff, *Leicester and the Netherlands, 1586–1587* (Utrecht, 1988), 42–7; Nolan, *Norreys*, 86; *CSPF*, 20: 701–2.

4 The Perils of War:
operations and developments, 1585–1588

1. *CSPF*, 20: 25, 48; Keeler, 26, 78–88, 108–9, 180–3, 218–23.

2. Parker, *Grand strategy*, 134–45, 147–77; M. J. Rodriguez-Salgado, 'The Anglo-Spanish war: the final episode in the "Wars of the Roses"?', in Rodriguez-Salgado and Adams (eds), 3–7; Parker, *Dutch Revolt*, 187–8; I. A. A. Thompson, 'The Spanish Armada: naval warfare between the Mediterranean and the Atlantic', in Rodriguez-Salgado and Adams (eds), 70–94.

3. *CSPF*, 20: 84–5, 219 (quotes); Nolan, *Norreys*, 90–1.

4. *CSPF*, 20: 278 (quotes); Adams, 'Puritan crusade?', esp. 184–6.

5. J. E. Neale, 'Elizabeth and the Netherlands, 1586–7', in idem, *Essays in*

Elizabethan history (London, 1958), 170–201; Cruickshank, *EA*, 78–9, 137–9, 145ff., 161–3.

6. J. Bruce (ed.), *Correspondence of Robert Dudley, earl of Leycester, during his government of the Low Countries*, Camden Society, 1st series, 27 (1844), 12 (quote), 105–10, 197.

7. J. L. Motley, *History of the United Netherlands from the death of William the Silent to the Twelve Years' Truce, 1609* (4 vols, New York, 1900 edn), 2: 10–13; Nolan, *Norreys*, 92–3.

8. Bruce, *Leycester*, 338–9 (quote); P. E. J. Hammer, *The polarisation of Elizabethan politics: the political career of Robert Devereux, 2nd earl of Essex, 1585–1597* (Cambridge, 1999), 50 (quote); CSPF, 21(2): 173–4; CSPF, 21(2): 150–3.

9. Motley, 2: 47–55; van Meteren, 87–9; Parker, *Army*, 11; F. Barker, 'Sir Philip Sidney and the forgotten war of 1586', *History Today*, 36 (Nov. 1986), 46; Stow, *Annales*, 1236–7; Hammer, *Polarisation*, 51–2, 53.

10. Bruce, *Leycester*, 428; CSPF, 21(2): 186–7.

11. Bruce, *Leycester*, 173.

12. Keeler, 99, 111, 235–6 (quotes); I. A. Wright (ed.), *Further English voyages to Spanish America, 1583–1594* (Hakluyt Society, 2nd series, 99, 1951 for 1949), li (quote).

13. Bruce, *Leycester*, 173 (quote); Keeler, 99, 111, 235–6 and *passim*; Wright xxxiv–lxiii, li (quote); Andrews, *Drake's voyages*, 96–109; Kelsey, 240–79; Cummins, 135–60; J. McDermott, *Martin Frobisher: Elizabethan privateer* (New Haven, CT, 2001), 297–323.

14. CSPSp, 3: 644, 651, 656, 667, 669, 670–2, 674; CSPF, 21(2): 233.

15. CSPF, 21(2): 265; Neale, 'Elizabeth and the Netherlands', 172, 174–7, 186–90; Wernham, *BTA*, 377–8.

16. S. Adams, 'Stanley, York and Elizabeth's Catholics', *History Today*, 37 (July 1987), 46–50; A. J. Loomie, *The Spanish Elizabethans* (New York, 1963), 129ff.; P. E. J. Hammer, 'A Welshman abroad: Captain Peter Wynn of Jamestown', *Parergon*, new series, 16 (1998), 63ff.

17. CSPF, 21(2): xxv–viii, 143–4; MacCaffrey, *Elizabeth and policy*, 391ff.; Motley, 1: 490ff; Oosterhoff, 51–2, 139–74.

18. Van Meteren, 95–102; Evans, 43, 45–51; Neale, 'Elizabeth and the Netherlands', 174, 178–80; Oosterhoff, 176–86.

19. Corbett, *Papers*, 148.

20. Corbett, *Papers*, 189, 200–6; Kelsey, 287–306; Cummins, 163–78.

21. Parker, *Grand strategy*, 157, 181 (quote).

22. Rodriguez-Salgado, 'Anglo-Spanish war', in Rodriguez-Salgado and Adams (eds), 7–8; Parker, *Grand strategy*, 179–88; Read, *Walsingham*, 3: 1–70.

23. J. Calvar, 'The *Nueva coleccion documental de las hostilidades entre Espana e Inglaterra (1568–1604)*', in P. Gallagher and D. W. Cruickshank (eds), *God's obvious design* (London, 1990), 188–9; Parker, *Grand strategy*, 194–9;

C. Martin and G. Parker, *The Spanish Armada* (2nd edn, Manchester, 1999), 114–22.

24. Parker, *Grand strategy*, 209–28; Glasgow, 'List', 306; Colvin (ed.), 403–6; Boynton, *EM*, 127–32; A. J. Loomie, 'The Armadas and the Catholics of England', *Catholic Historical Review*, 59 (1973), 389–91; G. F. Nuttall, 'The English martyrs, 1535–1680: a statistical review', *Journal of Ecclesiastical History*, 22 (1971), 193.

25. G. S. Thomson, *Lords lieutenants in the sixteenth century* (London, 1923).

26. BL, Harleian MS 168, fols 110r–14r, 166r–72v.

27. J. N. McGurk, 'Armada preparations in Kent and arrangements made after the defeat (1587–1589)', *Archaeologia Cantiana*, 85 (1970), 77–8; PRO, SP 12/212/62 (quote).

28. B. Pearce, 'Elizabethan food policy and the armed forces', *EcHR*, 1st series, 12 (1942), 39–46; J. D. Gould, 'The crisis in the export trade, 1586–1587', *EHR*, 71 (1956), 212–22; J. D. Jones, 'The Hampshire beacon plot of 1586', *Proceedings of the Hampshire Field Club and Archaeological Society*, 25 (1969 for 1968), 105–18; Palliser, 222; Loades, *Tudor navy*, 205–6 (quote).

29. Coleman, 195; http://www.le.ac.uk/hi/bon/ESFDB/obrien/engd004.txt; J. K. Laughton (ed.), *State papers relating to the defeat of the Spanish Armada, anno 1588* (2 vols, Navy Records Society, 1–2, 2nd edn, 1895), 1: 144–5; Read, *Burghley*, 424–5.

30. MacCaffrey, *Elizabeth and policy*, 394–9; Parker, *Grand strategy*, 200–1, 212–13; Calvar, 189.

31. Boynton, *EM*, 159–63; M. J. Braddick, '"Uppon this instant extraordinarie occasion": military mobilization in Yorkshire before and after the Armada', *Huntington Library Quarterly*, 61 (2000), 442; Laughton,1: 321 (quote).

32. PRO, SP 12/209/40; Laughton, 1: 159, 167–9, 179–80, 186–90, 200, 202–3; Rodger, *Safeguard*, 261–2.

33. P. Pierson, *Commander of the Armada: the seventh duke of Medina Sidonia* (New Haven, 1989), 108–30; S. Daultrey, 'The weather of north-west Europe during the summer and autumn of 1588', in Gallagher and Cruickshank (eds), 113–41; *CSPSp*, 4: 245–50.

34. Pierson, 126, 133–9; Laughton, 2: 324–31; W. L. Clowes, *The Royal Navy: a history from the earliest times to 1900*, vol. 1 (1897, reprint 1996), 588–97; Martin and Parker, 72–4, 147ff.

35. Parker, *Grand strategy*, 229–50; S. Adams, 'The battle that never was: the Downs and the Armada campaign', in Rodriguez-Salgado and Adams (eds), 173–96; Pierson, 113–16, 128–61; Martin and Parker, 148–73; Adams, 'Gran Armada', 247–8; J. C. A. Schokkenbroek, 'The role of the Dutch fleet in the conflict of 1588', in Gallagher and Cruickshank (eds), 101–11; Daultrey, figs 9–34.

36. Pierson, 156–70; Martin and Parker, 173–242 (quote: 179); Clowes,

575–85; D. Higueras and M. P. San Pio, 'Irish wrecks of the Great Armada: the testimony of survivors', in Gallagher and Cruickshank (eds), 143–61.

37. PRO, SP 12/212/66 (quote); Laughton, 2: 6–7, 39, 96–7, 110; Martin and Parker, 237; Rodger, *Safeguard*, 316; Read, *Walsingham*, 3: 324.

38. R. B. Wernham, *After the Armada: Elizabethan England and the struggle for western Europe, 1588–1595* (Oxford, 1984), 15 (hereafter *ATA*); Dietz, *EPF, 1558–1641*, 440–1; Coleman, 197; Stow, *Annales*, 1259.

5   The Depths of War:
operations and developments, 1589–1595

1. Wernham, 'War aims', 357–8; J. Gouws (ed.), *The prose works of Fulke Greville, Lord Brooke* (Oxford, 1986), 53 (quote).

2. R. B. Wernham (ed.), *The expedition of Sir John Norris and Sir Francis Drake to Spain and Portugal, 1589* (Navy Records Society, 127, 1988), 8–10.

3. Wernham, *Expedition*, xx–xxxiii, 250; Nolan, *Norreys*, 128, 135.

4. Wernham, *Expedition*, xlii–iv, xlix, 82–8, 102–3, 185, 187, 190, 220–1, 222, 225, 257ff., 266–7 (quote), 275–6, 280; Nolan, *Norreys*, 142–54.

5. Wernham, *Expedition*, xxxii, lvii–lxii, lxiv–v, 237, 346–50; Nolan, *Norreys*, 153.

6. Wernham, *Expedition*, xxxvi–vii; *CSPSp*, 4: 417–548; D. S. Katz, *The Jews in the history of England, 1485–1850* (Oxford, 1994), 69ff.

7. Hammer, *Polarisation*, 74–5, 82ff., 88, 231; *Apologie*, sig. A3v (quote); Wernham,. *Expedition*, 190, 266.

8. *L&A*, 1, no. 641; Earle, 83ff.; Rodger, *Safeguard*, 179; D. Goodman, *Spanish naval power, 1589–1665* (Cambridge, 1997), 9; Pierson, 194; Glete, 1: 149.

9. PRO, SP 12/218/31–2 (quote); Loades, *TN*, 279; B. Dietz, 'The royal bounty and English merchant shipping in the sixteenth and seventeenth centuries', *MM*, 77 (1991), 7, 15–17.

10. Wernham, *ATA*, 236–8, 241–5; R. T. Spence, *The privateering earl: George Clifford, 3rd earl of Cumberland* (Stroud, 1995), 84–91; McDermott, 377–84; H. A. Lloyd, 'Sir John Hawkins' instructions, 1590', *BIHR*, 44 (1971), 125–8; Wright, lxxi–lxxxvi; Earle, 58–9, 64–6; Williamson, *Hawkins*, 319–23.

11. Wernham, *ATA*, 338–43; Earle, 49–54, 97–161.

12. Earle, 114–16, 123–4, 162–70.

13. PRO C 115/100, no. 7364 (quote).

14. K. R. Andrews, *Elizabethan privateering* (Cambridge, 1964), 4–5, 32–4, 124–8 (hereafter *EP*); Wright, lxxvi–ix; Earle, 67–9; Spence, 84–90.

15. G. V. Scammell, 'The sinews of war: manning and provisioning English fighting ships, c.1550–1650', *MM*, 73 (1987), 351–62 (quote: 352); Corbett, *Papers*, 287–8; Rodger, *Safeguard*, 314ff.

16. Spence, 91–2, 101–12; C. L. Kingsford, 'The taking of the Madre de Dios, anno 1592', in *Naval miscellany, Vol. 2* (Navy Records Society, 40, 1912), 85–121; E. W. Bovill, 'The *Madre de Dios*', MM, 54 (1968), 129–52; C. R. Boxer, 'The taking of the *Madre de Deus*, 1592', MM, 67 (1981), 82–4; Wernham, *ATA*, 250–61; McDermott, 372–5, 384–5, 388, 392–406.

17. APC, 15: 68; CSPF, 21(4): 168–9; PRO, SP 12/218/51; Dietz, *EPF, 1558–1641*, 62; Cruickshank, *EA*, 143–4; HMC, *Report on the manuscripts of the earl of Ancaster* (London, 1907), 473–7.

18. CSPF, 22: 166–70, 188–9, 202–6, 218–19, 279, 284, 308, 322–3; Cruickshank, *EA*, 169–71.

19. Trim, 'Ideology, greed and social discontent', 47–59; Wernham, *Expedition*, 238, 255; CSPF, 22: 308. Cf. G. Parker, 'Mutiny and discontent in the Spanish Army of Flanders, 1572–1607', in *idem, Spain and the Netherlands, 1559–1659* (London, 1979), 106–21; *idem, Army*, 185–206.

20. CSPF, 21(4): 10; HMC, *Ancaster*, 186–214; Wernham, *ATA*, 37–47, 82–3; Motley, 2: 537–44.

21. *L&A*, 1, nos 78, 87; *DNB*, sub 'Vere, Sir Francis'

22. *L&A*, 1, nos 58–61, 78, 87; Wernham, *ATA*, 208, 302–4, 347–8, 397–9, 422–3; W. Dillingham (ed.), *The commentaries of Sir Francis Vere* (London, 1657), 1–24; M. van der Hoeven (ed.), *Exercise of arms: warfare in the Netherlands, 1568–1648* (Leiden, 1997), ix.

23. HMC, *A calendar of the manuscripts of the Most Hon. the marquis of Salisbury* (24 vols, London, 1883–1976), 5: 284, 286 (quote); ibid., 8: 356 (quote); J. Israel, *The Dutch Republic: its rise, greatness and fall, 1477–1806* (Oxford, 1995), 267–71; J. A. de Moor, 'Experience and experiment: some reflections upon the military developments in 16th and 17th century Western Europe', in van der Hoeven (ed.), 25–7; H. L. Zwitzer, 'The Eighty Years' War', in ibid., 35–9; J. P. Puype, 'Victory at Nieuwpoort, 2 July 1600', in ibid., 76–87; O. van Nimwegen, 'Maurits van Nassau and siege warfare (1590–1597)', in ibid., 113–31; B. H. Nickle, 'The military reforms of Prince Maurice of Nassau' (unpub. PhD thesis, University of Delaware, 1975), *passim*.

24. Dietz, *EPF, 1558–1641*, 63–4; Hoyle, *Estates*, 16.

25. Wernham, *ATA*, 150–80; Cruickshank, *EA*, 236–51; *L&A*, 1, nos 531 (quote), 543, 554; *HMCA*, 301–2, 305 (quote).

26. Wernham, *ATA*, 268ff; Nolan, 172–90; E. S. Tenace, 'The Spanish intervention in Brittany and the failure of Philip II's bid for European hegemony, 1589–1598', (unpub. PhD thesis, University of Illinois, 1997), esp. pp. 130ff., 209ff.; van Meteren, 119–33.

27. H. A. Lloyd, *The Rouen campaign, 1590–1592* (Oxford, 1973), *passim*; Wernham, *ATA*, 286–381; Hammer, *Polarisation*, esp. 93ff.; UCL, Ogden MS 7/41, fols 2–35.

28. Tenace, 230, 250; J. G. Nichols (ed.), 'Journal of the siege of Rouen, 1591, by Sir Thomas Coningsby', *Camden Miscellany*, 1 (1847), 27; Hammer, *Polarisation*, 115, 222–5, 231; H. Leonard, 'Knights and knighthood in

Tudor England' (unpub. PhD thesis, University of London, 1970), esp. 116ff.

29. Nolan, *Norreys*, 191ff.; Tenace, 195ff.; Wernham, *ATA*, 401ff.
30. BL, Cotton MS Caligula E IX (i), fol. 182v.
31. J. S. Nolan, 'English operations around Brest, 1594', *MM*, 81 (1995), 259–74; *idem, Norreys*, 204–17; Tenace, 324ff.; Wernham, *ATA*, 499ff., 521ff., 539ff.; McDermott, 407–23; van Meteren, 134–43.
32. *Apologie*, sig. E1v.
33. P. E. J. Hammer, 'The crucible of war: English foreign policy, 1589–1603', in S. Doran and G. Richardson (eds), *Tudor foreign policy* (Basingstoke and New York, 2003).
34. G. A. Hayes-McCoy, 'The army of Ulster, 1593–1601', *Irish Sword*, 1 (1949–53), 105–17; *idem, Irish battles*, 87–105; C. Falls, 'The growth of Irish military strength in the second half of the sixteenth century', *Irish Sword*, 2 (1954–6), 103–8; *idem, Elizabeth's Irish wars*, 187–8; D. O'Carroll, 'Change and continuity in weapons and tactics, 1594–1691', in P. Lenihan (ed.), *Conquest and resistance: war in seventeenth-century Ireland* (Leiden, 2001), 222ff.; H. Morgan, *Tyrone's rebellion* (Woodbridge, 1993), *passim*.
35. R. Schofield, 'Taxation and the political limits of the Tudor state', in C. Cross et al. (eds), *Law and government under the Tudors* (Cambridge, 1988), esp. 232–5, 238ff.; J. E. Neale, *Elizabeth I and her parliaments, 1584–1601* (London, 1957), 298–312, 411–22; H. Miller, 'Subsidy assessments of the peerage in the sixteenth century', *BIHR*, 28 (1955), 22–3; I. W. Archer, 'The burden of taxation in sixteenth-century London', *HJ*, 44 (2001), 608–9.
36. PRO, SP 12/212/62 (quote); Archer, 'Burden', 608; Hassell Smith, 'Militia rates', 97–8.
37. J. Sharpe, 'Social strain and social dislocation, 1585–1603', in J. Guy (ed.), *The reign of Elizabeth I: court and culture in the last decade* (Cambridge, 1995), 192–211; P. Thomas, 'Military mayhem in Elizabethan Chester: the privy council's response to vagrant soldiers', *JSAHR*, 76 (1998), 226–47; J. McGurk, *The Elizabethan conquest of Ireland* (Manchester, 1997), 137–64; Stow, *Annales*, 1264(i); PRO, C 115/100, no. 7362 (quote); Nolan, *Norreys*, 155–6; *CSPSp*, 4: 558–9; L. Boynton, 'The Tudor provost-marshal', *EHR*, 77 (1962), 437–55; R. B. Manning, *Village revolts* (Oxford, 1988), 157–86.
38. Stow, *Annales*, 1279–81; Manning, 180, 208–10, 221–9; J. Walter, 'A "rising of the people"? The Oxfordshire Rising of 1596', *P&P*, no. 107 (1985), 90–143; Palliser, 57–8.
39. Fissell, *EW*, 91–4; Hammer, *Polarisation*, 352–6, 374.
40. Hammer, *Polarisation*, 187–9; Tenace, 381–3; R. B. Wernham, *The return of the Armadas: the last years of the Elizabethan war against Spain, 1595–1603* (Oxford, 1994), 32 (hereafter *RTA*); K. R. Andrews, *The last voyage of Drake & Hawkins* (Hakluyt Society, 2nd series, 142, 1972), esp. 12–19 (hereafter *LV*).

6   The Limits of War:
operations and developments, 1596–1604

1. Tenace, 381–2; Andrews, *EP*, 209–12; *idem, LV*, 12–18, 33 (quote).
2. Andrews, *LV*, esp. 86 (quote), 92–3, 96–8, 106–7, 118–21; Kelsey, 379–91; Williamson, 332–42.
3. PRO, SP 12/256/10; Hammer, *Polarisation*, 227–8.
4. Stow, *Annales*, 1281–2; Archer, 'Gazeteer', no. 85.
5. PRO, SP 12/257/3–39; Hammer, *Polarisation*, 249, 362, 367–8; Wernham, *RTA*, 62ff.
6. FSL, V.b.214, fol. 60v (quote); PRO, SP 12/259/12 (quote); LPL, MS 657, fol. 140r (quote); Hammer, *Polarisation*, 249–51, 366–8.
7. BL, Lansdowne MS 243, fols 4r–v, 16r–17r; PRO, SP 78/25, fol. 366r (quote); S and E. Usherwood, *The counter-Armada, 1596: the journall of the 'Mary Rose'* (London, 1983), 20; Wernham, *RTA*, 57, 83; Parker, *Army*, 40–1.
8. P. E. J. Hammer, 'New light on the Cadiz expedition of 1596', *HR*, 70 (1997), esp. 188–91, 195–6 (quote: 195); Parker, 'Dreadnought', 274–7; R. C. Bald, *John Donne* (Oxford, 1970), 82–3; J. S. Corbett, *The successors of Drake* (London, 1900), chs 3–4; Pierson, 195–213; Dillingham, *Vere*, 27–45.
9. Hammer, *Polarisation*, 251–2; Usherwood, 146–9, 156–8; Wernham, *RTA*, 116–17.
10. Hammer, *Polarisation*, 252–5, 371–5 (quote: 373); *idem*, 'Myth-making: politics, propaganda and the capture of Cadiz in 1596', *HJ*, 40 (1997), 621–42; Wernham, *RTA*, 118–23.
11. Tenace, 395–402; Wernham, *RTA*, 69–81; W. Graham, *The Spanish Armadas* (London, 1972), 217–24. Wernham's emphasis upon this and subsequent Spanish fleets as 'Armadas' exaggerates their similarities with the *Gran Armada* of 1588.
12. Wernham, *RTA*, 132–40; Hammer, *Polarisation*, 377–8.
13. L. W. Henry, 'The earl of Essex as strategist and military organizer (1596–7)', *EHR*, 68 (1953), 364–70; BL, Add. MS 74287, fol. 8r (quote).
14. Stewart, *Ordnance*, ch. 3; R. Ashley, 'War in the ordnance office: the Essex connection and Sir John Davis', *HR*, 67 (1994), 337–45; Hammer, *Polarisation*, 279–80, 376–7, 379–80; Henry, 'Strategist', 373–8; Corbett, 161–3; Boynton, 196.
15. Wernham, *RTA*, 143–83; Henry, 'Strategist', 378–90; BL, Add. MS 74287, fol. 13v (quote); Corbett, 152–211; Dillingham, *Vere*, 45–67.
16. Tenace, 414–25; Corbett, 212–25; Graham, 232–42; Boynton, 196–7.
17. Wernham, *RTA*, 210ff.; *Apologie*, sig. B4v, D3v (quotes). Cf. I. A. A. Thompson, *War and government in Habsburg Spain, 1560–1620* (London, 1976), 38ff.
18. Wernham, *RTA*, 233ff.; J. C. Grayson, 'From protectorate to partnership: Anglo-Dutch relations, 1598–1625' (unpub. PhD thesis, University of London, 1978), 23–34; W. T. MacCaffrey, *Elizabeth I: war and politics*,

1588–1603 (Princeton, NJ, 1992), 209–19 (hereafter MacCaffrey, *EWP*); Dietz, *EPF, 1558–1641*, 455–6.

19. Dietz, *EPF, 1558–1641*, 454; Motley, 3: 422–34; Puype, 71–2; Nickle, 25ff., 189–90, 196–8; Dillingham, *Vere*, 72–80.

20. *Apologie*, sig. D3v (quote); Hammer, *Polarisation*, 354; J. Guy, *Tudor England* (Oxford, 1988), 393–5; Folger Shakespeare Library, Washington DC., MS V.a.460, fol. 58r; Coleman, 'Artifice or accident?', 195–7; Dietz, *EPF, 1558–1641*, 453; McGurk, *Conquest*, 38; Cecil MS 250/72 (printed in *HMCS*, 10: 399); Stewart, *Ordnance*, 44, 46, 50; *APC*, 30: 817–18.

21. Cruickshank, *Invasion*, 84; C. Levin, *The heart and stomach of a king: Elizabeth I and the politics of sex and power* (Philadelphia, PA, 1994), 140 (quote).

22. M. James, 'At a crossroads of the political culture: the Essex Revolt, 1601', in *idem, Society, politics and culture* (Cambridge, 1986), esp. 424ff.

23. Eg. BL, Lansdowne MS 1218, fols 114r–40v.

24. Morgan, *Tyrone's rebellion*, esp. 186–7, 193ff.; Nolan, *Norreys*, 219–39; McGurk, *Conquest*, 39–40, 67–9; J. J. Silke, *Kinsale: the Spanish intervention in Ireland at the end of the Elizabethan wars* (Dublin, 2000 edn), 28–31.

25. Falls, 200ff.; Hayes-McCoy, *Irish battles*, 106–31; *CSPI*, 7: 227–8, 234–8; *Carew MSS*, 3: 280–1.

26. *CSPI*, 7: 482–3; 8: 13, 91–5; R. W. Stewart, 'The "Irish road": military supply and arms for Elizabeth's army during the O'Neill Rebellion in Ireland, 1595–1601', in M. C. Fissel (ed.), *War and government in Britain, 1598–1650* (Manchester, 1991), 16–37; *idem, Ordnance*, 87, 96ff.; J. S. Wheeler, 'The logistics of conquest', in Lenihan (ed.), 178–88.

27. *CSPI*, 8: 36–42, 144–7; *Carew MSS*, 3: 301–25; *CSPSp*, 4: 685; Falls, 230–41; L. W. Henry, 'The earl of Essex and Ireland, 1599', *BIHR*, 32 (1959), 1–23; Wernham, *RTA*, 299–318; B. Lenman, *England's colonial wars, 1550–1688* (Harlow, 2001), 132–5.

28. Hammer, 'Crucible'; BL, Harleian MS 168, fols 131v–56r; Wernham, *RTA*, 264–71; Graham, 253–4; Corbett, 253–90.

29. Fynes Moryson, *An itinerary containing his ten yeeres' travell* (4 vols, Glasgow, 1907–8 edn), 2: 279–80; F. M. Jones, *Mountjoy* (Dublin, 1958), 54ff., 77 (quote); Canny, *Making Ireland British*, 1–58; Wheeler, 184–6; J. McGurk, 'Terrain and conquest, 1600–1603', in Lenihan (ed.), 92–3.

30. Dietz, *Eliz.*, 102–4; *HMCS*, 10: 345, 15: 1–2; Neale, *Parliaments*, 376–93; Hoyle, 16; Challis, 268–74; Cecil MS 82/2, 6 (quotes).

31. Moryson, 2: 304–7; *CSPI*, 10: 20–3, 27–31; Jones, *Mountjoy*, 71–84; Hayes-McCoy, *Battles*, 132–43; Falls, *Wars*, 253–73, 282ff.

32. Puype, 87–111; Nickle, 30–8; Motley, 4: 1–54; Dillingham, 81–117.

33. MacCaffrey, *EWP*, 225ff.; FSL, G.b.4, no. 70.

34. H. Miller, *Henry VIII and the English nobility* (Oxford, 1986); PRO, SP 12/222/21; L. L. Peck, 'Peers, patronage and the politics of history', in Guy (ed.), 88–98.

35. E. Belleroche, 'The siege of Ostend or the new Troy, 1601–1604', *Proceedings of the Huguenot Society of London*, 3 (1888–91), 427ff.; Dillingham, 118ff.; Wernham, *RTA*, 374–5; APC, 22: 69ff.

36. Moryson, 2: 370–1, 399, 450–1; Jones, *Mountjoy*, 91–2, 103–115; Falls, *Wars*, 276–80, 287–9; McGurk, 'Terrain', 95ff.; Silke, 92–110; P. C. Allen, *Philip III and the pax Hispanica, 1598–1621* (New Haven, CT, 2000), 59–60; Corbett, 318–22.

37. Moryson, 3: 14; Wernham, *RTA*, 378; Hayes-McCoy, *Battles*, 154; Stewart, 'Road', 30–1; Allen, 76.

38. [M. K. Walsh], '*Destruction by peace*': *Hugh O'Neill after Kinsale* (Monaghan, 1986), 190; F. M. Jones, 'The destination of Don Juan del Aguila in 1601', *Irish Sword*, 2 (1954–6), 29–32; Moryson, 3: 28, 35–6, 39–40, 65–6, 72, 74–6; Jones, *Mountjoy*, 59, 132–3; Silke, 92–111, 128; *Carew MSS*, 4: 305; W. H. and H. C. Overall (eds), *Analytical index to the series of records known as the Remembrancia, preserved among the archives of the City of London, A.D. 1579–1664* (London, 1878), 245; Archer, 'Gazeteer', no. 114.

39. Moryson, 3: 74–96; *CSPI*, 11: 209–11, 220, 238–42, 267–9, 272–3; *Carew MSS*, 4: 191–4; Hayes-McCoy, *Battles*, 152–70; Silke, 123–52; Falls, 292–318; A. Young, *Tudor and Jacobean tournaments* (London, 1987), *passim*; BL, Royal MS 18 C XXIII, p. 46 (quote). Cf. Evans, 28–35.

40. Belleroche, 442–63, 495–502 (quote: 497); Dillingham, 143–61, 165–77; Allen, 65–9, 79–80; Dietz, *EPF*, 1558–1641, 95–6.

41. Allen, 61ff., 91; G. Parker, 'The Treaty of Lyon (1601) and the Spanish Road', in *idem*, *Empire*, 127–42; Thompson, *War*, 105–6.

42. Allen, 62–3, 69, 84–5; *HMCS*, 12: 86 (quote); Fissell, *EW*, 184–8.

43. Corbett, 355–82; Loades, *TN*, 268–9; N. E. McLure (ed.), *The letters of John Chamberlain* (2 vols, American Philosophical Society, Memoirs, 12, 1939), 1: 116; Wernham, *RTA*, 392–400; Grayling, 43.

44. E. Grimeston, *The generall historie of Spaine* (London, 1612), 1320–3; Loades, *TN*, 279; T. Glasgow, 'Oared vessels in the Elizabethan navy', *MM*, 52 (1966), 372; Allen, 91–2; Corbett, 386–94; Motley, 4: 114–16.

45. K. R. Andrews, 'Caribbean rivalry and the Anglo-Spanish peace of 1604', *History*, 59 (1974), 2–4; Spence, 157–75; Andrews, *EP*, 178–9; Appleby, 68ff.

46. *Carew MSS*, 4: 212–14; *CSPI*, 11: 476–7; H. S. Scott (ed.), 'The journal of Sir Roger Wilbraham', *Camden Miscellany*, 10 (1902), 49–50 (quotes); Allen, 75.

47. T. Birch, *Memoirs of the reign of Queen Elizabeth* (2 vols, London, 1754), 2: 506 (quote); N. P. Canny, 'The Treaty of Mellifont and the re-organisation of Ulster, 1603', *Irish Sword*, 9 (1969–70), 249–62; Walsh, 27ff.

48. Grimeston, 1326–31; Allen, 108–40; A. J. Loomie, 'Toleration and diplomacy: the religious issue in Anglo-Spanish relations, 1603–1605', *Transactions of the American Philosophical Society*, n.s., 53, part vi (1963), 5–51. Grayling, 48–70; Andrews, 'Caribbean', 10–17; Parker, *Army*, 52.

7   The Reformation of War

1. Collinson, 'Monarchical republic'; PRO, SP 12/201/15 (quote); ibid., WO 55/1939, fol. 91v (quote). In 1599, Hunsdon's successor as governor, Lord Willoughby, also expressed this fear that Berwick might become another Calais: Cecil MS 59/10.

2. Dr Ian Archer has produced similar results using data and price indices which relate specifically to London: according to his figures, the crown's exactions on the City of London in the 1590s, in real terms, were only one-third of the level achieved by Henry VIII in the 1540s ('Burden', 624).

3. Wernham, 'War aims', esp. 341–7.

4. Dr Trim also draws upon the work of J. McGurk in breaking down and cross-checking Cruickshank's figures. The addition of 8900 men to the total for 1588 is derived from Trim's figure of only 4500 men being levied directly for the Portugal expedition and the estimate of 13,400 soldiers who sailed in April 1589 (see Chapter 5). Note that the estimate of 13,400 is actually a considerable *under*estimate of the numbers of soldiers who initially gathered to join the expedition. Troop numbers peaked at about 18,000, but declined in the period before the fleet finally sailed. The new estimate of 15,000 for men raised in 1588 is complicated by the fact that the Portugal force contained many volunteers and some recruits were raised by indenture, rather than by the normal process of local levies. In addition, as noted in the text, a fair proportion of these men must have been raised in early 1589 rather than 1588. Nevertheless, the estimate of 15,000 reflects the fearsome demand for manpower at the end of 1588 and is clearly distinct from the new military burdens imposed by France and the Low Countries, which are reflected in the figures cited for 1589.

5. Cruickshank, *EA*, 17–40; M. Prestwich, *Armies and warfare in the Middle Ages: the English experience* (New Haven, CT, 1996), 88ff.

6. Estimates for sailors on naval expeditions are as follows: 2300 (Drake's West Indies voyage of 1585–86), 2650 (Cadiz expedition of 1587), 16,000 (total fleet to oppose the *Gran Armada* of 1588), 4000 (Portugal expedition of 1589), 2420 (Lord Thomas Howard's fleet of 1591), 1500 (Drake and Hawkins' expedition, 1595–96), 6800 (Cadiz expedition of 1596), 5000 (queen's ships in Azores expedition of 1597), 5000 (queen's ships in fleet to oppose 'Invisible Armada' of 1599), 1800 (Leveson's squadron, 1602): 47,470 total. These figures also include soldiers where the latter have not been included in the figures for royal levies (e.g. the troops who joined Drake's West Indies voyage in 1585–86). Trim's figures for volunteers serving abroad are given in 'Jacob's warres', Appendix 2, Tables 6, 7. The figures for privateers and supernumerary

volunteers are ball-park estimates. For population, see Wrigley and Schofield, 528.

7.   Cruickshank, *EA*, 290–1; H. A. Lloyd, *The gentry of southwest Wales, 1540–1640* (Cardiff, 1968), 118ff.; Hammer, *Polarisation*, 73; McGurk, *Conquest*, 65, 81ff., 108ff.; Fissel, *EW*, 52,103.

8.   Nolan, 'Militarization', 418; *idem, Norreys*, 199–200; Wernham, *ATA*, 204. Calculations based upon daily pay for a footman of 8d for 12 months, each of four weeks (i.e. a 28-day month, as used by Elizabethan planners).

9.   P. Clark, *English provincial society from the Reformation to the Revolution: religion, politics and society in Kent, 1500–1640* (Hassocks, Sussex, 1977), 224, 227; E. J. Bourgeois II (ed.), *A Cambridgeshire lieutenancy letterbook, 1595–1605* (Cambridgeshire Records Society, 12, 1997), 41–2; Archer, 'Burden', 624. Clark's estimate (p. 225) that Kent's military expenditure between 1585 and 1603 exceeded £10,000 seems a considerable underestimate.

10. Boynton, *EM*, 179–81; C. F. Patterson, *Urban patronage in early modern England* (Stanford, CA, 1999), 181–2.

11. E. J. Bourgeois II, 'Meeting the demands of war: late-Elizabethan militia management in Cambridgeshire', *The Local Historian*, 26 (1996), 130–41; *idem, Letterbook*, 8–41.

12. Parker, 'Dreadnought', 284–6.

13. Rodger, *Safeguard*, 244.

14. Bourgeois, *Letterbook*, 35–41, 148–9, 153–4, 157–61.

15. G. Parker, 'The 'military revolution, 1560–1660': a myth?', *Journal of Modern History*, 48 (1976), 195–214; *idem, The military revolution: military innovation and the rise of the West, 1500–1800* (Cambridge, 1988, 2nd edn 1996). Parker's thesis builds upon M. Roberts, 'The military revolution, 1560–1660' (orig. pub. 1956), which is reprinted with various critiques of Parker in C. J. Rogers (ed.), *The military revolution debate* (Boulder, CO, 1995). See also J. Black, *A military revolution? Military change and European society, 1550–1800* (Basingstoke, 1991); *idem, European warfare, 1660–1815* (London, 1994), esp. ch. 1; A. Ayton and J. L. Price, 'The military revolution from a medieval perspective', in *idem* (eds), *The medieval military revolution* (London, 1995), 1–22; Eltis, esp. ch. 2; Hall, *Weapons and warfare*; T. F. Arnold, 'War in sixteenth-century Europe: revolution and renaissance', in J. Black (ed.), *European warfare, 1453–1815* (Basingstoke, 1999), 23–44.

16. Parker, *Military revolution*, esp. 32–3, Eltis, esp. ch. 5. See also H. J. Webb, *Elizabethan military science: the books and the practice* (Madison, WI, 1965); and M. J. D. Cockle, *A bibliography of military books up to 1642* (London, 1900, 2nd edn, 1957).

17. Phillips, *Wars*, 6, 13, 17–18, 39, 256–7 (quote: 256). For the role of the longbow in English military practice, see Hall, *Weapons and warfare*,

ch. 1. Although muskets could inflict terrible wounds on unprotected flesh at longer range, they exhibited very poor accuracy and limited piercing power beyond 100 metres (108 yards). High-quality armour, as worn by wealthy officers, was probably 'proof' against gunshots down to much shorter range (ibid., ch. 5).

18. Boynton, *EM*, ch. 7.
19. Hammer, 'Myth-making', 642 (quote); Fissel, *EW*, ch. 11.
20. M. C. Fissel, *The Bishops' Wars: Charles I's campaigns against Scotland, 1638–1640* (Cambridge, 1994); J. S. Wheeler, *The making of a world power: war and the military revolution in seventeenth-century England* (Stroud, 1999).

Select Bibliography of Modern Sources

Adams, S., 'A puritan crusade? The composition of the earl of Leicester's expedition to the Netherlands, 1585–86', in *idem, Leicester and the court: essays on Elizabethan politics* (Manchester, 2002), 176–95.

—— 'The English military clientele, 1542–1618', in C. Giry-Deloison and R. Mettam (eds), *Patronages et clientélismes, 1550–1750 (France, Angleterre, Espagne, Italie)* (Lille and London, 1995), 217–27.

—— 'The battle that never was: the Downs and the Armada campaign', in Rodriguez-Salgado and Adams (eds), 173–96.

—— 'The outbreak of the Elizabethan naval war against the Spanish empire: the embargo of May 1585 and Sir Francis Drake's West Indies voyage', in Rodriguez-Salgado and Adams (eds), 45–69.

—— 'The *Gran Armada*: 1988 and after', *History*, 76 (1991), 238–49.

—— 'New light on the "reformation" of John Hawkins: the Ellesmere naval survey of January 1584', *EHR*, 105 (1990), 96–111.

Allen, P. C., *Philip III and the pax Hispanica, 1598–1621* (New Haven, CT, 2000).

Andrews, K. R., *Trade, plunder and settlement: maritime enterprise and the genesis of the British Empire, 1480–1630* (Cambridge, 1984).

—— 'Caribbean rivalry and the Anglo-Spanish peace of 1604', *History*, 59 (1974), 1–17.

—— *The last voyage of Drake & Hawkins* (Hakluyt Society, 2nd series, 142, 1972).

—— *Drake's voyages: a re-assessment of their place in Elizabethan maritime expansion* (London, 1967).

—— *Elizabethan privateering* (Cambridge, 1964).

Archbold, W. A. J., 'A diary of the expedition of 1544', *EHR*, 16 (1901), 503–7.

Archer, I. W., 'Gazeteer of military levies from the City of London, 1509–1603', at website: http: //senior.keble.ox.ac.uk/fellows/extrapages/iarcher/levies.htm

—— 'The burden of taxation on sixteenth-century London', *HJ*, 44 (2001), 599–627.

Ashley, R., 'War in the ordnance office: the Essex connection and Sir John Davis', *HR*, 67 (1994), 337–45

Awty, B. G., 'Parson Levett and English cannon founding', *Sussex Archaeological Collections*, 127 (1989), 133–45.

Bagwell, R., *Ireland under the Tudors* (3 vols, London, 1885–90).

Barr, N., *Flodden, 1513* (Stroud, 2001).

Bartlett, T., and Jeffrey, K., (eds), *A military history of Ireland* (Cambridge, 1996).

Beer, B. L., *Rebellion and riot: popular disorder in England during the reign of Edward VI* (Kent State University Press, 1982).

Belleroche, E.,'The siege of Ostend or the new Troy, 1601–1604', *Proceedings of the Huguenot Society of London*, 3 (1888–91), 427–539.

Black, J. B., 'Queen Elizabeth, the Sea Beggars and the capture of Brille, 1572', *EHR*, 46 (1931), 30–47.

Bonner, E. A., 'The genesis of Henry VIII's "Rough Wooing" of the Scots', *Northern History*, 33 (1997), 36–53.

Bourgeois, E. J., 'Meeting the demands of war: late-Elizabethan militia management in Cambridgeshire', *The Local Historian*, 26 (1996), 130–41.

Bovill, E. W.,'The *Madre de Dios*', *MM*, 54 (1968), 129–52.

—— 'Queen Elizabeth's gunpowder', *MM*, 33 (1947), 179–86.

Boxer, C. R.,'The taking of the *Madre de Deus*, 1592', *MM*, 67 (1981), 82–4.

Boynton, L., *The Elizabethan militia, 1558–1638* (London, 1967).

—— 'The Tudor provost-marshal', *EHR*, 77 (1962), 437–55.

Braddick, M. J.,'"Uppon this instant extraordinarie occasion": military mobilization in Yorkshire before and after the Armada', *Huntington Library Quarterly*, 61 (2000), 429–55.

Brady, C., 'The captains' games: army and society in Elizabethan Ireland', in Bartlett and Jeffrey (eds), 136–59.

—— *The chief governors: the rise and fall of reform government in Tudor Ireland, 1536–1588* (Cambridge, 1994).

Bruce, J. (ed.), *Correspondence of Robert Dudley, earl of Leycester, during his government of the Low Countries*, Camden Society, 1st series, 27 (1844).

Burgon, J. W., *The life and times of Sir Thomas Gresham* (2 vols, London, 1839).

Bush, M. L., *The government policy of Protector Somerset* (London, 1975).

Calvar, J.,'The *Nueva coleccion documental de las hostilidades entre Espana e Inglaterra (1568–1604)*', in Gallagher and Cruickshank (eds), 187–94.

Caldecott-Baird, D. (ed.), *The expedition in Holland, 1572–1574* (London, 1976).

Caldwell, D. H., 'The battle of Pinkie', in MacDougall (ed.), 61–94.

Canny, N. (ed.), *The Oxford history of the British empire. Vol. I: the origins of empire* (Oxford, 1998).

Canny, N. P., *The Elizabethan conquest of Ireland: a pattern established, 1565–76* (Hassocks, Sussex, 1976).

—— 'The Treaty of Mellifont and the reorganisation of Ulster, 1603', *Irish Sword*, 9 (1969–70), 249–62.

Challis, C. E., *The Tudor coinage* (Manchester, 1978).

——— 'The debasement of the coinage, 1542–1551', *EcHR*, 2nd series, 20 (1967), 441–66.

Christy, M., 'Queen Elizabeth's visit to Tilbury in 1588', *EHR*, 34 (1919), 43–61.

Clowes, W. L., *The Royal Navy: a history from the earliest times to 1900*, vol. 1 (1897, reprint 1996).

Coleman, C., 'Artifice or accident? The reorganization of the exchequer of receipt, c.1554–1572', in C. Coleman and D. Starkey (eds), *Revolution reassessed: revisions in the history of Tudor administration and government* (Oxford, 1986), 163–98.

Collinson, P., 'The monarchical republic of Queen Elizabeth I', in *idem*, *Elizabethan essays* (London, 1994), 31–57.

Colvin, H. M. (ed.), *The history of the King's Works, vol. 4*, (London, 1982).

Connell-Smith, G., *Fore-runners of Drake* (London, 1954).

Corbett, J. S., *The successors of Drake* (London, 1900).

——— (ed.), *Papers relating to the navy during Spanish War, 1585–1587* (Navy Records Society, 11, 1898).

Cornwall, J., *Revolt of the peasantry, 1549* (London, 1977).

Croft, P., 'English commerce with Spain and the Armada war, 1558–1603', in Rodriguez-Salgado and Adams (eds), 236–63.

——— 'English mariners trading with Spain and Portugal, 1558–1625', *MM*, 69 (1983), 251–66.

Cruickshank, C., *Henry VIII and the invasion of France* (Stroud, 1990 edn).

Cruickshank, C. G., *Elizabeth's army* (2nd edn, Oxford, 1966).

Cummins, J., *Francis Drake* (London, 1995).

Cunich, P., 'Revolution and crisis in English state finance, 1534–47', in M. Ormrod, M. Bonney and R. Bonney (eds), *Crises, revolutions and self-sustained growth: essays in European fiscal history, 1130–1830* (Stamford, 1999), 110–37.

Daultrey, S.,'The weather of north-west Europe during the summer and autumn of 1588', in Gallagher and Cruickshank (eds), 113–41.

Davies, C. S. L., 'Henry VIII and Henry V: the wars in France', in J. L. Watts (ed.), *The end of Middle Ages?* (Stroud, 1998), 235–62.

——— 'Tournai and the English crown, 1513–1519', *HJ*, 41 (1998), 1–26.

——— 'England and the French war', in J. Loach and R. Tittler (eds), *The mid-Tudor polity, c.1540–1560* (London, 1980), 159–85.

——— 'The administration of the Royal Navy under Henry VIII: the origins of the Navy Board', *EHR*, 80 (1965), 268–88.

——— 'Provisions for armies, 1509–50: a study in the effectiveness of early Tudor government', *EcHR*, 2nd series, 17 (1964–5), 234–48.

Davies, M. B. (ed.), 'Boulogne and Calais from 1545 to 1550', *Bulletin of the Faculty of Arts, Fouad I University*, 12 (1950), 1–90.

——— (ed.), 'The "enterprises" of Paris and Boulogne', *Bulletin of the Faculty of Arts, Fouad I University*, 11 (1949), 37–95.

——— (ed.), 'Suffolk's expedition to Montdidier, 1523', *Bulletin of the Faculty of Arts, Fouad I University*, 7 (1944), 33–43.

Dawson, J. E. A., 'William Cecil and the British dimension of early Elizabethan foreign policy', *History*, 74 (1989), 196–216.

De Moor, J. A.,'Experience and experiment: some reflections upon the military developments in 16th and 17th century western Europe', in van der Hoeven (ed.), 17–32.

Dietz, B.,'The royal bounty and English merchant shipping in the sixteenth and seventeenth centuries', MM, 77 (1991), 5–20.

Dietz, F. C., *English public finance, 1485–1558* (2nd edn, London, 1964).

—— *English public finance, 1558–1641* (New York, 1932).

—— *The exchequer in Elizabeth's reign* (Smith College Studies in History, vol. 8, no. 2, Northampton, MA, 1923).

Dyer, A., 'The English sweating sickness of 1551: an epidemic anatomized', *Medical History*, 41 (1997), 362–84.

Earle, P., *The last fight of the Revenge* (London, 1992).

Edwards, D., 'Beyond reform: martial law and the Tudor conquest of Ireland', *History Ireland*, 5 (1997), 16–22.

—— 'The Butler revolt of 1569', *IHS*, 28 (1993), 228–55.

Egerton, P. de M. G. (ed.), *A commentary of the services and charges of William Lord Grey of Wilton, KG, by his son Arthur Lord Grey of Wilton, KG*, Camden Society, 1st series, 40 (1847).

Ellis, S. G., *Ireland in the age of the Tudors, 1447–1603* (2nd edn, London, 1998).

—— 'The Tudors and the origins of the modern Irish states: a standing army', in Bartlett and Jeffrey (eds), 116–35.

Eltis, D., *The military revolution in sixteenth-century Europe* (London, 1998).

Evans, J. X., (ed.), *The works of Sir Roger Williams* (Oxford, 1972).

Falls, C.,'The growth of Irish military strength in the second half of the sixteenth century', *Irish Sword*, 2 (1954–6), 103–8.

—— *Elizabeth's Irish wars* (London, 1950),

Fissel, M. C., *English warfare, 1511–1642* (London, 2001).

Fletcher, A., and MacCulloch, D., *Tudor rebellions* (4th edn, London, 1997).

Fraser, G. McD., *The steel bonnets: the story of the Anglo-Scottish border reivers* (London, 1971, 1995 edn).

Gallagher, P., and Cruickshank, D. W. (eds), *God's obvious design: papers for the Spanish Armada Symposium, Sligo, 1988* (London, 1990).

Glasgow, T., 'List of ships in the Royal Navy from 1539 to 1588', MM, 56 (1970), 299–307.

—— 'Maturing of naval administration', MM, 56 (1970), 3–26.

—— 'The navy in the first Elizabethan undeclared war, 1559–1560', MM, 54 (1968), 23–37.

—— 'The navy in the Le Havre expedition, 1562–1564', MM, 54 (1968), 281–96.

—— 'The navy in Philip and Mary's war, 1557–1558', MM, 53 (1967), 321–42.

—— 'Oared vessels in the Elizabethan navy', MM, 52 (1966), 371–7.

—— 'The Elizabethan navy in Ireland (1558–1603)', *Irish Sword*, 7 (1965–6), 291–307.

Glete, J., *Navies and nations: warships, navies and state building in Europe and America, 1500–1860* (2 vols, Stockholm, 1993).

Goring, J., 'Social change and military decline in mid-Tudor England', *History*, 60 (1975), 185–97.

Goring, J. J., 'Wealden ironmasters in the age of Elizabeth', in E. W. Ives, R. J. Knecht and J. J. Scarisbrick (eds), *Wealth and power in Tudor England* (London, 1978), 204–27.

—— 'The military obligations of the English people, 1511–1558' (unpub. PhD thesis, University of London, 1955).

Graham, W., *The Spanish Armadas* (London, 1972).

Grayson, J. C., 'From protectorate to partnership: Anglo-Dutch relations, 1598–1625' (unpub. PhD thesis, University of London, 1978).

Green, J. M., '"I my self": Queen Elizabeth I's oration at Tilbury camp', *Sixteenth Century Journal*, 28 (1997), 421–45.

Grummitt, D.,'The defence of Calais and the development of gunpowder weaponry in England in the late fifteenth century', *War in History*, 7 (2000), 253–72.

Gunn, S. J., 'The duke of Suffolk's march on Paris in 1523', *EHR*, 101 (1986), 596–634.

Gunn, S., 'The French wars of Henry VIII', in J. Black (ed.), *The origins of war in early modern Europe* (Edinburgh, 1987), 28–51.

Guy, J. (ed.), *The reign of Elizabeth I: court and culture in the last decade* (Cambridge, 1995).

—— *Tudor England* (Oxford, 1988).

Hale, J. R., 'The defence of the realm, 1485–1558', in Colvin (ed.), 367–83.

Hall, B. S., *Weapons and warfare in Renaissance Europe* (Baltimore, MD, 1997).

Hammer, P. E. J., *The polarisation of Elizabethan politics: the political career of Robert Devereux, 2nd earl of Essex, 1585–1597* (Cambridge, 1999).

—— 'A Welshman abroad: Captain Peter Wynn of Jamestown', *Parergon*, new series, 16 (1998), 59–92.

—— 'Myth-making: politics, propaganda and the capture of Cadiz in 1596', *HJ*, 40 (1997), 621–42.

—— 'New light on the Cadiz expedition of 1596', *HR*, 70 (1997), 182–202.

Hassell Smith, A., 'Militia rates and militia statutes, 1558–1663', in P. Clark et al. (eds), *The English commonwealth, 1547–1640* (Leicester, 1979), 93–110.

Hayes-McCoy, G. A., *Irish battles: a military history of Ireland* (London, 1969, repr. New York, 1997).

—— *Irish battles* (London, 1969; New York, 1997 reprint).

—— 'The army of Ulster, 1593–1601', *Irish Sword*, 1 (1949–53), 105–17.

—— *Scots mercenary forces in Ireland (1565–1603)* (Dublin, 1937).

Henry, L. W.,'The earl of Essex and Ireland, 1599', *BIHR*, 32 (1959), 1–23.

—— 'The earl of Essex as strategist and military organizer (1596–7)', *EHR*, 68 (1953), 363–93.

Hoak, D. E., *The king's council in the reign of Edward VI* (Cambridge, 1976).

Hoyle, R., 'War and public finance', in MacCulloch (ed.), 75–99.

Hoyle, R. W., 'Taxation and the mid-Tudor crisis', *EcHR*, 2nd series, 51 (1998), 649–75.

—— (ed.), *The estates of the English crown, 1558–1640* (Cambridge, 1992).

James, M., *Society, politics and culture in early modern England* (Cambridge, 1986).

Jones, F. M., *Mountjoy* (Dublin, 1958).

—— 'The destination of Don Juan del Aguila in 1601', *Irish Sword*, 2 (1954–6), 29–32.

Jones, J. D., 'The Hampshire beacon plot of 1586', *Proceedings of the Hampshire Field Club and Archaeological Society*, 25 (1969 for 1968), 105–18.

Keeler, M. F. (ed.), *Sir Francis Drake's West Indian voyage, 1585–1586* (Hakluyt Society, 2nd series, 148, 1981 for 1975).

Kelsey, H., *Sir Francis Drake: the queen's pirate* (New Haven, CT, 1998).

Kingsford, C. L., 'The taking of the *Madre de Dios*, anno 1592', in *Naval miscellany, vol. 2* (Navy Records Society, 40, 1912), 85–121.

Knecht, R. J., *The French civil wars* (Harlow, 2000).

Laughton, J. K., (ed.), *State papers relating to the defeat of the Spanish Armada, anno 1588* (2 vols, Navy Records Society, 1–2, 2nd edn, 1895).

Lenihan, P. (ed.), *Conquest and resistance: war in seventeenth-century Ireland* (Leiden, 2001).

Lenman, B., *England's colonial wars, 1550–1688* (Harlow, 2001).

Leonard, H., 'Knights and knighthood in Tudor England' (unpub. PhD thesis, University of London, 1970).

Leslie, J. H., 'The siege and capture of Boulogne – 1544', *JSAHR*, 1 (1922), 188–99.

Lloyd, H. A., *The Rouen campaign, 1590–1592* (Oxford, 1973).

—— 'Sir John Hawkins' instructions, 1590', *BIHR*, 44 (1971), 125–8.

Loades, D., *John Dudley, duke of Northumberland, 1504–1553* (Oxford, 1996).

—— *The Tudor navy: an administrative, political and military history* (Aldershot, 1992).

—— *The reign of Mary Tudor* (2nd edn, London, 1991).

Longmate, N., *Defending the island from Caesar to the Armada* (London, 1989, 2001 edn).

Loomie, A. J., 'The Armadas and the Catholics of England', *Catholic Historical Review*, 59 (1973), 385–403.

—— *The Spanish Elizabethans* (New York, 1963).

MacCaffrey, W. T., 'The Newhaven expedition, 1562–1563', *HJ*, 40 (1997), 1–21.

—— *Elizabeth I: war and politics, 1588–1603* (Princeton, NJ, 1992).

—— *Queen Elizabeth and the making of policy, 1572–1588* (Princeton, NJ, 1981).

—— *The shaping of the Elizabethan regime: Elizabethan politics, 1558–1572* (Princeton, NJ, 1968).

MacCulloch, D., *Tudor Church militant: Edward VI and the Protestant Reformation* (London, 1999).

—— (ed.), *The reign of Henry VIII: politics, policy and piety* (Basingstoke, 1995).

MacDougall, N., *An antidote to the English: the auld alliance, 1295–1560* (East Linton, 2001).

—— (ed.), *Scotland and war, AD 78–1918* (Edinburgh, 1991).

Maltby, W. S., *Alba: a biography of Fernando Alvarez de Toledo, third duke of Alba, 1507–1582* (Berkeley, CA, 1983).

Manning, R. B.,*Village revolts* (Oxford, 1988).

Mayhew, G. J., 'Rye and the defence of the Narrow Seas: a 16th-century town at war', *Sussex Archaeological Collections*, 122 (1984), 107–26.

McBride, G. K., 'Elizabethan foreign policy in microcosm: the Portuguese pretender, 1580–89', *Albion*, 5 (1973), 193–210.

McDermott, J., *Martin Frobisher: Elizabethan privateer* (New Haven, CT, 2001).

McLure, N. E. (ed.), *The letters of John Chamberlain* (2 vols, American Philosophical Society, Memoirs, 12, 1939).

McGurk, J., 'Terrain and conquest, 1600–1603', in Lenihan (ed.), 87–114.

—— *The Elizabethan conquest of Ireland* (Manchester, 1997).

McGurk, J. J. N., 'Casualties and welfare measures for the sick and wounded of the Nine Year War in Ireland, 1593–1602', *JSAHR*, 68 (1990), 22–35 and 188–204 (two parts).

McGurk, J. N., 'Armada preparations in Kent and arrangements made after the defeat (1587–1589)', *Archaeologia Cantiana*, 85 (1970), 71–93.

Merriman, M., *The Rough Wooings: Mary Queen of Scots, 1542–1551* (East Linton, 2000).

—— 'The forts of Eyemouth: anvils of British Union?', *SHR*, 67 (1988), 142–55.

—— 'The fortresses in Scotland, 1547–50' in Colvin (ed.), 694–726.

Millar, G. J., *Tudor mercenaries and auxiliaries, 1485–1547* (Charlottesville, VA, 1980).

Miller, H., *Henry VIII and the English nobility* (Oxford, 1986).

—— 'Subsidy assessments of the peerage in the sixteenth century', *BIHR*, 28 (1955), 15–34.

Monluc, Blaise de, *The Valois-Habsburg wars and the French Wars of Religion*, ed. I. Roy (London, 1971).

Morgan, H., *Tyrone's rebellion* (Woodbridge, 1993).

—— 'The colonial venture of Sir Thomas Smith in Ulster, 1571–1575', *HJ*, 28 (1985), 261–78.

Moryson, Fynes, *An itinerary containing his ten yeeres' travell* (4 vols, Glasgow, 1907–8 edn).

Motley, J. L., *History of the United Netherlands from the death of William the Silent to the Twelve Years' Truce, 1609* (4 vols, New York, 1900 edn).

Neale, J. E., 'Elizabeth and the Netherlands, 1586–7', in *idem, Essays in Elizabethan history* (London, 1958), 170–201.

Nichols, J. G. (ed.), *The diary of Henry Machyn, citizen and merchant-taylor of London, from AD 1550 to AD 1563*, Camden Society, 1st series, 42 (1848).

—— (ed.), 'Journal of the siege of Rouen, 1591, by Sir Thomas Coningsby', *Camden Miscellany* 1 (1847).

—— (ed.), *The chronicle of Calais in the reigns of Henry VII and Henry VIII to the year 1540* (Camden Society, 1st series, 35, 1846).

Nickle, B. H., 'The military reforms of Prince Maurice of Nassau' (unpub. PhD thesis, University of Delaware, 1975).

Nolan, J. S., *Sir John Norreys and the Elizabethan military world* (Exeter, 1997).

—— 'English operations around Brest, 1594', MM, 81 (1995), 259–74.

—— 'The militarization of the Elizabethan state', *Journal of Military History*, 58 (1994), 391–420.

O'Brien, P. K., and Hunt, P. A., 'The rise of a fiscal state in England, 1485–1815', *Historical Research*, 66 (1993), 129–76.

O'Carroll, D., 'Change and continuity in weapons and tactics, 1594–1691', in Lenihan (ed.), 211–55.

Oman, C., *A history of the art of war in the sixteenth century* (London, 1937).

Oosterhoff, F. G., *Leicester and the Netherlands, 1586–1587* (Utrecht, 1988).

Oppenheim, M., *A history of the administration of the Royal Navy and of merchant shipping in relation to the Navy from 1509 to 1660* (1896, London, 1988 edn).

Outhwaite, R. B., 'Royal borrowing in the reign of Elizabeth I: the aftermath of Antwerp', *EHR*, 86 (1971), 251–63.

—— 'The trials of foreign borrowing: the English crown and the Antwerp money market in the mid-sixteenth century', *EcHR*, 2nd series, 19 (1966), 289–305.

Palliser, D. M., *The age of Elizabeth: England under the later Tudors, 1547–1603* (2nd edn, London, 1992).

Parker, G., *Empire, war and faith in early modern Europe* (London, 2002).

—— *The grand strategy of Philip II* (New Haven, CT, 1998).

—— 'The *Dreadnought* revolution of Tudor England', MM, 82 (1996), 269–300.

—— *The military revolution: military innovation and the rise of the West, 1500–1800* (Cambridge, 1988, 2nd edn 1996).

—— 'Mutiny and discontent in the Spanish Army of Flanders, 1572–1607', in idem, *Spain and the Netherlands, 1559–1659* (London, 1979), 106–21.

—— *The Dutch revolt* (London, 1977).

—— *The Army of Flanders and the Spanish Road, 1567–1659* (Cambridge, 1972).

Pearce, B., 'Elizabethan food policy and the armed forces', *EcHR*, 1st series, 12 (1942), 39–46.

Phillips, G., 'Irish *ceatharnaigh* in English service, 1544–1550, and the development of "Gaelic warfare"', *JSAHR*, 78 (2000), 163–72.

—— *The Anglo-Scots wars, 1513–1550* (Woodbridge, 1999).

—— 'In the shadow of Flodden: technology and Scottish military effectiveness, 1513–1550', *SHR*, 77 (1998), 162–82.

—— 'The army of Henry VIII: a reassessment', *JSAHR*, 75 (1997), 8–22.

Pierson, P., *Commander of the Armada: the seventh duke of Medina Sidonia* (New Haven, CT, 1989).

Pollard, A. F. (ed.), *Tudor tracts, 1532–1588* (New York, 1964 edn).

Pollitt, R.,'Contingency planning and the defeat of the Spanish Armada', in D. M. Masterson (ed.), *Naval history: the sixth symposium of the US Naval Academy* (Wilmington, DE, 1987), 70–81.

—— 'The defeat of the Northern Rebellion and the shaping of Anglo-Scottish relations', *SHR*, 64 (1985), 1–21.

Potter, D., 'The international mercenary market in the sixteenth century: Anglo-French competition in Germany, 1543–50', *EHR*, 111 (1996), 24–58.

—— 'Foreign policy', in MacCulloch (ed.), *Reign*, 101–33.

—— 'French intrigue in Ireland during the reign of Henri II, 1547–1559', *International History Review*, 5 (1983), 159–76.

—— 'The duc de Guise and the fall of Calais, 1557–1558', *EHR*, 98 (1983), 486–93.

Puype, J. P., 'Victory at Nieuwpoort, 2 July 1600', in van der Hoeven (ed.), 69–112.

Ramsay, G. D., *The queen's merchants and the revolt of the Netherlands* (Manchester, 1986).

—— *The City of London in international politics at the accession of Elizabeth Tudor* (Manchester, 1975).

Read, C., *Lord Burghley and Queen Elizabeth* (London, 1960).

—— *Mr Secretary Cecil and Queen Elizabeth* (London, 1955).

—— 'Queen Elizabeth's seizure of the duke of Alva's pay-ships', *JMH*, 5 (1933), 443–64.

—— *Mr Secretary Walsingham and the policy of Queen Elizabeth* (3 vols, Oxford, 1925).

Richardson, W. C., 'Some financial expedients of Henry VIII', *EcHR*, 2nd series, 7 (1954), 37–47.

—— *Stephen Vaughan, financial agent of Henry VIII* (Baton Rouge, LA, 1953).

Rodger, N. A. M., 'Guns and sails in the first phase of English colonisation, 1500–1650', in N. Canny (ed.), 79–98

—— *The safeguard of the sea: a naval history of Britain. Vol. 1, 660–1649* (London, 1997).

Rodriguez-Salgado, M. J., and Adams, S. (eds), *England, Spain and the Gran Armada, 1585–1604: essays from the Anglo-Spanish conferences, London and Madrid, 1988* (Edinburgh, 1991).

Rodriguez-Salgado, M. J., 'The Anglo-Spanish war: the final episode in the "Wars of the Roses"?', in Rodriguez-Salgado and Adams (eds), 1–44.

Rule, M., *The Mary Rose: the excavation and raising of Henry VIII's flagship* (2nd edn, London, 1983).

Scammell, G. V., 'The sinews of war: manning and provisioning English fighting ships, c.1550–1650', *MM*, 73 (1987), 351–67.

Scarisbrick, J. J., *Henry VIII* (London, 1968).

Schofield, R., 'Taxation and the political limits of the Tudor state', in C. Cross, David Loades and J. J. Scarisbrick (eds), *Law and government under the Tudors* (Cambridge, 1988), 227–55.

Schubert, H. R., *History of the British iron and steel industry from c.450 BC to AD 1775* (London, 1957).

Schokkenbroek, J. C. A., 'The role of the Dutch fleet in the conflict of 1588', in Gallagher and Cruickshank (eds), 101–12.

Sharpe, J., 'Social strain and social dislocation, 1585–1603', in Guy (ed.), 192–211.

Sheehan, A., 'Irish revenues and English subventions, 1559–1622', *Proceedings of the Irish Academy*, 90, C: 2 (1990), 2–65.

Shelby, L. R., *John Rogers: Tudor military engineer* (Oxford, 1967).

Silke, J. J., *Kinsale: the Spanish intervention in Ireland at the end of the Elizabethan wars* (Dublin, 2000 edn).

Spence, R. T., *The privateering earl: George Clifford, 3rd earl of Cumberland* (Stroud, 1995).

Stanford, M. J. G., 'The Raleghs take to the sea', MM, 48 (1962), 18–35.

Starkey , D. (ed.), *The inventory of Henry VIII: the transcript* (London, 1998).

Stewart, D., 'Sickness and mortality rates of the English army in the sixteenth century', *Journal of the Royal Army Medical Corps*, 91 (1948), 23–35.

Stewart, R. W., *The English ordnance office, 1585–1625* (Woodbridge, 1995).

—— 'The "Irish road": military supply and arms for Elizabeth's army during the O'Neill Rebellion in Ireland, 1595–1601', in M. C. Fissel (ed.), *War and government in Britain, 1598–1650* (Manchester, 1991), 16–37.

Sutherland, N. M., *Princes, politics and religion, 1547–1589* (London, 1984).

Tenace, E. S., 'The Spanish intervention in Brittany and the failure of Philip II's bid for European hegemony, 1589–1598' (unpub. PhD thesis, University of Illinois, 1997).

Thomas, P., 'Military mayhem in Elizabethan Chester: the privy council's response to vagrant soldiers', JSAHR, 76 (1998), 226–47.

Thompson, I. A. A.,'The Spanish Armada: naval warfare between the Mediterranean and the Atlantic', in Rodriguez-Salgado and Adams (eds), 70–94.

—— *War and government in Habsburg Spain, 1560–1620* (London, 1976).

Thomson, G. S., *Lords lieutenants in the sixteenth century* (London, 1923).

Thorp, M. R., 'Catholic conspiracy in early Elizabethan foreign policy', *Sixteenth Century Journal*, 15 (1984), 431–48.

Tighe, W. J., 'The Gentlemen Pensioners in Elizabethan politics and government' (unpub. PhD thesis, University of Cambridge, 1983).

Trim, D. J. B., 'Ideology, greed and social discontent in early modern Europe: mercenaries and mutinies in the rebellious Netherlands, 1568–1609', in J. Hathaway (ed.), *Rebellion, repression, reinvention: mutiny in comparative contexts* (Westport, CT, 2001), 49–59.

—— 'Protestant refugees in Elizabethan England and confessional conflict in France and the Netherlands, 1562–c.1610', in R. Vigne and C. Littleton (eds), *From citizens to strangers* (Brighton, 2001), 68–79.

—— '*Fin de siècle*: the English soldier's experience at the end of the sixteenth century', *Military and Naval History Journal*, 10 (1999), 1–13.

—— 'The "foundation-stone of the British army"?: the Normandy campaign of 1562', *JSAHR*, 77 (1999), 71–87.

—— 'The "secret war" of Elizabeth I: England and the Huguenots during the early Wars of Religion, 1562–1577', *Proceedings of the Huguenot Society*, 27 (1999), 189–99.

Usherwood, S., and Usherwood, E., *The counter-Armada, 1596: the journall of the 'Mary Rose'* (London, 1983).

Van der Hoeven, M. (ed.), *Exercise of arms: warfare in the Netherlands, 1568–1648* (Leiden, 1997).

Van Nimwegen, O., 'Maurits van Nassau and siege warfare (1590–1597)', in van der Hoeven (ed.), 113–32.

Wallace, H. M., 'Berwick in the reign of Queen Elizabeth', *EHR*, 46 (1931), 79–88.

[Walsh, M. K.], *'Destruction by peace': Hugh O'Neill after Kinsale* (Monaghan, 1986).

Walter, J., 'A "rising of the people"? The Oxfordshire Rising of 1596', *P&P*, no. 107 (1985), 90–143.

Webb, H. J., *Elizabethan military science: the books and the practice* (Madison, WI, 1965).

Wernham, R. B., *The return of the Armadas: the last years of the Elizabethan war against Spain, 1595–1603* (Oxford, 1994).

—— (ed.), *The expedition of Sir John Norris and Sir Francis Drake to Spain and Portugal, 1589* (Navy Records Society, 127, 1988).

—— *After the Armada: Elizabethan England and the struggle for western Europe, 1588–1595* (Oxford, 1984).

—— *Before the Armada: the growth of English foreign policy, 1485–1588* (London, 1966).

—— 'Elizabethan war aims and strategy', in S. T. Bindoff, J. Hurstfield and C. H. Williams (eds), *Elizabethan government and society* (London, 1961), 340–68.

Wheeler, J. S., 'The logistics of conquest' in Lenihan (ed.), 177–209.

—— *The making of a world power: war and the military revolution in seventeenth-century England* (Stroud, 1999).

White, D. G., 'The reign of Edward VI in Ireland: some political, social and economic aspects', *IHS*, 14 (1965), 197–211.

Williamson, J. A., *Hawkins of Plymouth* (2nd edn, London, 1969).

Wright, I. A. (ed.), *Further English voyages to Spanish America, 1583–1594* (Hakluyt Society, 2nd series, 99, 1951 for 1949).

Wrigley, E. A. and Schofield, R. S., *The population history of England, 1541–1871* (London, 1981).

Youings, J., 'Bowmen, billmen and hackbutters: the Elizabethan militia in the south west', in R. Higham (ed.), *Security and defence in south-west England before 1800* (Exeter Studies in History, 19, 1987), 51–68.

Zwitzer, H. L., 'The Eighty Years' War', in van der Hoeven (ed.), 33–56.

Maps

Map 1   England and Wales
Source: Adapted from P. W. Hasler (ed.), *The History of Parliament: The House of Commons, 1558–1603* (3 vols, London, 1981), vol. 1, endpapers.

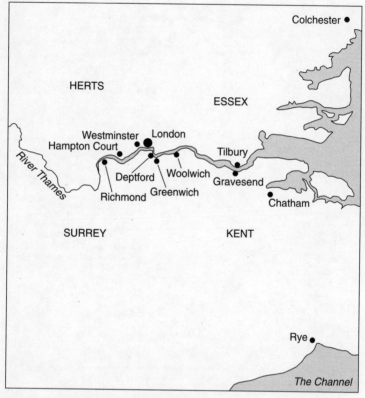

Map 2   London and its Environs
Source: Adapted from J. D. Campbell and Clinton Lewis (eds), *Atlas of the World* (Oxford, 1951).

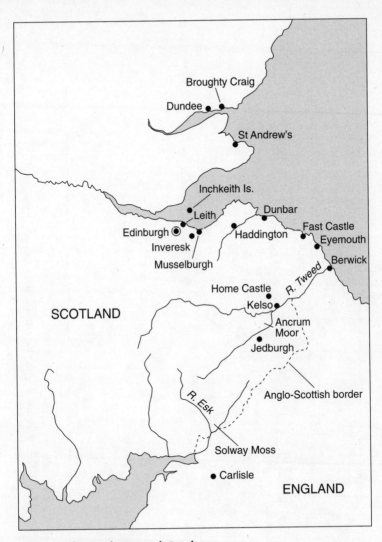

Map 3   The Anglo-Scottish Borders
Source: Adapted from M. L. Bush, *The Government Policy of Protector Somerset* (London, 1975).

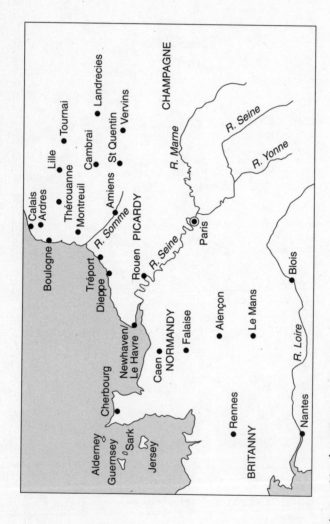

Map 4   Northern France
Source: Adapted from R. B. Wernham, *After the Armada* (Oxford, 1984), map 3.

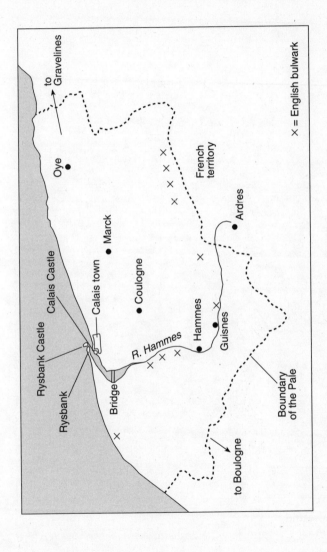

Map 5   The Pale of Calais

Source: Adapted from H. M. Colvin (ed.), *The History of the King's Works*, vol. 4 (London, 1982), fig. 4.

× = English bulwark

Map 6   Ireland
Source: Adapted from R. B. Wernham, *After the Armada* (Oxford, 1984), map 7.

Map 7   The Low Countries
Source: Adapted from P. Geyl, *The Revolt of the Netherlands* (New York, 1958), p. 22.

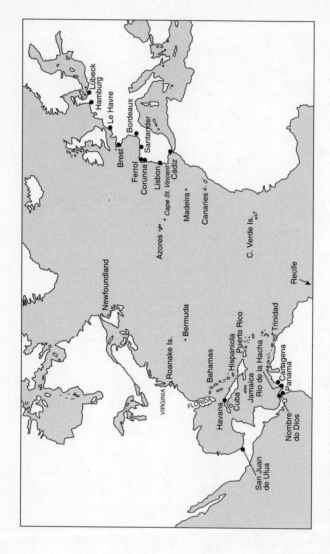

Map 8 The North Atlantic and Caribbean
Source: Adapted from R. B. Wernham, *After the Armada* (Oxford, 1984), map 4.

Map 9 Spain, Portugal and Western France
Source: Adapted from R. B. Wernham, *After the Armada* (Oxford, 1984), map 2.

Index

Essex's 194, 200–01, 202, 204, 256
'forward defence' 147–8, 188–9, 200, 203–4, 230–1
Henry VIII's 10, 17, 25–6, 242–3
Ireland 74–5, 210, 213, 216–17, 224
responses to 'deep war' 175–6, 177, 181, 182
Somerset's 'garrisons policy' 34–5, 37, 73
Spanish 'enterprise of England' 137ff., 166, 177, 181, 198–9, 215, 229–30
see also 'deniability', Elizabeth, war aims of; *and* 'Rough Wooing'
Styward, Thomas 261
Suffolk 144, 249
Suffolk, Charles Brandon, duke of (d. 1545) 18, 19, 23
Sussex 117, 250
Sussex, Thomas Radcliffe, 3rd earl of (d. 1583) 83, 87

taxation 13, 32, 33, 46, 67–8, 95–6, 185–6, 217, 218, 251
Ter Goes 90–1
Thérouanne 17
Throckmorton, Francis (d. 1584) 117
Tilbury 4
Tournai 17
Tower of London 42, 51, 187, 188
trade, England's foreign 44, 78, 79–80, 85, 88, 90, 116, 119, 138, 155, 167, 169, 232, 234
trained bands 99ff., 141–3, 146–7, 199, 201–2, 215, 226, 243, 248, 250, 251, 252, 256–7, 261, 262, 263
treaties:
  Blois (1572) 87, 89, 105
  Boulogne (1550) 42
  Camp (1546) 25, 55
  Cateau–Cambrésis (1559) 55, 58
  Crépy (1544) 18, 29, 46

  Edinburgh (1560) 61–2
  Greenwich (1543) 15
  Hampton Court (1562) 64
  London (1598) 205
  London (1604) 234–5
  Mellifont (1603) 234
  Nonsuch (1585) 120, 172
  Norham (1551) 42
  Triple Alliance (1596) 194, 198
  Vervins (1598) 204, 205, 206
Tréport 23, 26
Triple Alliance: *see* treaties
Turks, Ottoman 89, 122
Turnhout 205
Tyrone, Hugh O'Neill, 2nd earl of (d. 1616) 184–5, 198, 209–35, 254, 259

Ulster 74, 76ff., 86, 92, 156, 184, 209, 211, 213, 214, 215, 216, 219, 220, 224, 226, 249
Utrecht 105, 121, 127
Utrecht, Union of 105

Vassy 63
Vaughan, Stephen 32
Verdun 230
Vere, Sir Francis (d. 1609) 172ff., 195, 196, 197, 202, 203, 205, 206, 220–1, 224, 227, 228
Vere, Horace (d. 1635) 220
victuals 24, 26
Vigo 159
Virginia 118
'volunteers', English and Welsh 58, 63, 64, 69, 88, 89, 89ff., 102, 104, 111, 113ff., 120, 121, 125, 132, 180, 193, 195, 248, 257, 258, 261, 262
see also mercenaries

Wales 90, 91, 133, 166, 214, 249
Walsingham, Sir Francis (d. 1590) 87, 102, 114, 116, 117, 118, 129, 134, 139

war and honour 5–6, 9ff., 20, 24–5,
    34, 91, 158–9, 165–6, 174, 180,
    196, 198, 207, 208, 222–3, 228,
    242
war, declarations of 14, 49, 121, 183
warships, design of 21–2, 93ff., 160,
    161, 162, 231–2, 254, 263
Warwick, Ambrose Dudley, earl of
    (d. 1590) 65, 66, 68, 83
Warwick, John Dudley, earl of
    (d. 1553): *see* Northumberland,
    duke of
Watts, John 167
Wentworth, Thomas Wentworth,
    2nd Lord (d. 1584) 50
West Indies: *see* Caribbean
Westminster 187
Westmorland, Charles Neville, 6th
    earl of (d. 1601) 82, 83
Wexford 75
Wicklow 214
Wight, Isle of 23, 150, 151, 166
Williams, Sir John, later Lord

William of Thame (d. 1559) 41
Williams, Sir Roger (d. 1558) 90, 91,
    92, 129, 135, 142, 161, 177, 178,
    180, 195, 257
Willoughby, Peregrine Bertie, 13th
    Lord (d. 1601) 128, 129, 157,
    171–2, 173, 176–7, 198
Wingfield, Jacques 71
Winter, Sir William (d. 1589) 58,
    60
Woods, John 217
Wriothesley, Sir Thomas, later 1st
    earl of Southampton (d. 1550)
    26, 33

Yarmouth 97
Yellow Ford 210–11, 219
York, Rowland (d. 1588) 133, 140
Yorkshire 48, 49

Zealand 90, 104, 105
Zuniga, Don Juan de (d. 1586) 137
Zutphen 128–30, 133, 161, 173

Look at general military &
foreign situation —

Lee — "Illustrates" aspects
            illumines
of the

Study of Lee's actions &
letters throws a spotlig
on the general situation
Illustrating in practical
terms events &
aspects dealt with
in "generalities"

1559-61 ① 'ly

Massive restocking of Armaments
by Gresham. look at 'State of the Stores'
1561 Lee corselets SPENT
② had already been reflected in 1558
campaigns - short of 'furniture'
③
Hunsdon - 'absentee Governor of Berwick'
had a phobia about Calais

Armada - 4 armies ready
Huntingdon - north
BUT because of France - parsimony -
musters left very late - (or 'harvest'?)
doubts if they could have all been
called in time - WAS IT AWARENESS
OF HARVEST? LATER IN NORTH??

Carrion - carting in Sussex -
Law Order - would a company have led
overnight?
PUT Lee operates in an age of
transition in warfare — reflected
in calivers etc.

Tourncoli - UTTY — transiti